Other Works by Henry James
Published by Grove Press

Literary Reviews and Essays

by Henry James

on AMERICAN, ENGLISH, and FRENCH LITERATURE

Edited by
ALBERT MORDELL

GROVE PRESS, INC.   NEW YORK

First Black Cat Edition 1979
First Printing 1979
ISBN: 0-394-17098-9
Grove Press ISBN: 0-8021-4271-0
Library of Congress Catalog Card Number: 58-8375

LIBRARY OF CONGRESS CATALOGING IN PUBLICATION DATA

James, Henry, 1843–1916.
    Literary reviews and essays on American, English, and French literature.

    (A Black cat book)
    1. French literature — 19th century — History and criticism — Addresses, essays, lectures.   2. American literature — 19th century — History and criticism — Addresses, essays, lectures.   3. English literature — 19th century — History and criticism — Addresses, essays, lectures.   4. Books — Reviews.   I. Mordell, Albert, 1885–   II. Title.
[PN761.J27 1979]   809'.034   79-9213   ISBN 0-394-17098-9

Manufactured in the United States of America

Distributed by Random House, Inc., New York

GROVE PRESS, INC., 196 West Houston Street, New York, N.Y. 10014

TABLE OF CONTENTS

INTRODUCTION

I

The present volume of literary essays and book reviews by Henry James comprises more than sixty items, hitherto never collected before, either by the author himself or anyone else, and covers the first twenty years of his literary life. They set forth the critical principles he then entertained and by which he was guided when he wrote the series of tales and novels between *The Passionate Pilgrim and Other Tales* and *The Portrait of a Lady*. He soon wrote his celebrated essay "The Art of Fiction" and began his so-called middle period with the publication of *The Bostonians*. The first period was closed with the issue of a uniform edition of his fiction in twelve volumes. By these essays we are offered a tangible means of evaluating this fiction. They are of importance, however, in themselves as setting forth his philosophy of literary criticism in this period. They relate to the time when he was under some influences exercised by novelists like Hawthorne, Turgenev, George Sand, and George Eliot, and by critics such as Edmond Schérer, Matthew Arnold, and Sainte-Beuve.

The plan of this collection has been to have two sections, one devoted to James's articles on French literature, and the other to American and English. If the first section includes the French translation of *Virgin Soil*, it is because Turgenev supervised the translation. If the second section includes Carlyle's translation of *Wilhelm Meister*, it is because that work has been virtually naturalized in English literature. Herein are included all those other articles on books and authors upon which James had already written or subsequently wrote, which had been collected by himself or by others. He wrote more than once on some authors, on Sainte-Beuve, Schérer, George Sand, Hugo, Flaubert, Edmond de Goncourt, Mérimée, Daudet, Turgenev, Howells, Parkman, Louisa M. Alcott, George Eliot, and Matthew

Arnold. The gathering of the uncollected essays on these authors therefore completes James's writings about them. In fact it will be noticed that there are several articles about the same authors in the present volume.

This collection was begun and largely completed about forty years ago[1] at the time when the present writer suggested to a publisher that he reprint James's novelette *Gabrielle de Bergerac*,[2] and through the same publisher brought out a volume of hitherto uncollected[3] tales, by Henry James. Through another publisher, he also issued two[4] volumes of tales that had never been gathered together in America but in England only.

One need not apologize for collecting articles by Henry James. This has not been done by James himself nor by others. As a matter of fact, he approved of posthumous collections of authors who were worthwhile. When the process was formed of gathering the posthumous writings of Théophile Gautier in France, James in the article on them herein reprinted, wrote that his admirers would be pleased to hear that a well-earned honor was bestowed on his literary remains and that an immense number of short stories, criticisms, feuilletons, sketches, and notices scattered throughout the newspapers and magazines had been gathered into volumes under sympathetic and intelligent editorial supervision. "We ourselves rejoice greatly," James wrote, "in this undertaking, for we confess to a peculiar, and in its nature almost inexpressible, kindness for the author of the *Voyage en Espagne* and *Émaux et Camées*." Should this not be justification for the same kind of service for James's own uncollected writings, especially since some of his admirers consider him a greater writer than Gautier? Whether the present editor has exercised intelligent editorial revision must be left to the judgment of his readers. One thing cannot be denied and that is that his attitude has been sympathetic.

Later in life James referred only on a few occasions to his early reviews, and to the very first one[5] disparagingly. He wrote that Charles Eliot Norton, the acting editor of the *North American Review* accepted an article of his,—a piece of good fortune that gave him an "ineffable" thrill. James also atoned for the fact that in writing for the *Nation* he perpetrated some savage and devastating articles for which he blamed the editor, Edwin L. Godkin.[6] He later came to believe only in sympathetic literary criticism. He shows, however, in his letters that he could in private speak very disparagingly of some writers. Some of his early reviews were in the old *Blackwood's Edinburgh Magazine* tomahawk-wielding manner.

Finally we have a more lengthy account by James of his connection with the *Nation*.[7] He contributed to a symposium in that periodical when it celebrated the fiftieth anniversary of its inauguration. His sub-title was "Recollections of the Fairies that Attended its Birth." Indeed, the fairies had taken care of him for Norton was again his benefactor and spoke to Godkin about him when he was founding the *Nation*. Godkin went to Boston and visited James and asked him "to contribute." Of course he was happy about it as well he might be, for the *Nation* was to have the leading writers and scholars of America among its contributors with whom the young man of 22 was to share space in the weekly. James contributed an article to the first number. Like all the reviews in the *Nation*, it was anonymous. His reviews were never corrected, disapproved, postponed, or omitted, though there were misprints.

He continued writing reviews even when in Europe and they appeared for about twelve years. His brother William who went to Europe for his health, thought he recognized some of these reviews, one of a novel by George Sand, another of W. Morris's new poem, and still another, of *The Spanish Gypsy*, as he was reading several issues of the *Nation* that were sent to him, and he wrote to his brother his suspicion as to their authorship.[8] James does not in printing his brother's letter acknowledge this. We know now that William guessed right; two of the pieces, those on George Eliot's *Spanish Gypsy* and the notice of George Sand's novel *Mademoiselle Merquem* are herein reprinted.

About half of the articles in this collection are concerned with French writers or books. James spent two years of his boyhood in Paris and acquired a knowledge of the language. He made numerous other visits to France in later years. While still a youth in America he came under the influence of John

La Farge who made him acquainted with the work of Mérimée and Balzac, and he read the *Revue de deux Mondes*. Thus he was enabled to air his learning and give advice to a novelist Harriet E. Prescott (later Spofford[9]) who was eight years older than he, and advise her in his second review to read Mérimée and *Eugénie Grandet*.[10] As will be noticed a number of books by French authors were reviewed from their originals, before English translations appeared. And it will also be noticed that even before Lafcadio Hearn, James was severe upon faithless translations by hack writers and he castigated a few translators who garbled the originals, but he praised those who did well. The fact of the matter is that he was intensely absorbed in translations, and the very first literary work he did was to make some translations from Mérimée and Alfred de Musset,[11] but these never acquired the dignity of print. In his reviews of French authors from the original he occasionally introduced translations of his own of some passage or other, and he also made some brief translations here and there in the *Nation*.[12]

James subsequently met some of the French writers about whom he wrote and whose books he reviewed, and he probably hoped that in the case of those whom he noticed adversely they never found out. He became acquainted with Flaubert, Daudet, Edmond de Goncourt, Zola, and Taine. His real thrill was in meeting Turgenev, which was in 1876. But Turgenev knew of a favorable article James had written about him for it had been sent to him. He met Taine much later and in view of the fact that James had written five articles about his works, their meeting has an unusual interest. It brought James a surprise for since he had found his style intellectual and logical, he did not think that personally Taine would have so much geniality as he found in him. He was especially pleased with Taine's tribute to Turgenev. Undoubtedly in this case Taine must have known that James had reviewed some of his work.

A sidelight on James's method as a critic and description of a celebrity whom he met later appears in connection with one of the last reviews he wrote for the *Nation*[13] of a two volume selection of essays by Abraham Hayward, the translator in prose of the first part of *Faust*, which some have called the best ever made. I have not included this review in the present volume as it chiefly repeats some of the anecdotes he found in the book. Several years later James met the aged man then past eighty at a gathering and sought to engage him in conversation. James noted that the anecdotes Hayward recounted consisted of mere facts. He himself like Dickens detested facts. To James the fact was a point of departure, and he stated that his own partiality was for outlook, imagination, ideas. None such came.[14] Hayward the man bore out James's conception of Hayward the essayist.

I have reprinted three articles on literary matters from the New York *Tribune* for which James wrote from Paris chiefly in 1876. Most of his articles there dealt with French politics, art, the theatre, and social life. Though James regarded the letters "poor stuff" as he later confided to his Notebooks, yet he considered them too good for the *Tribune,* and he added that of course they did not succeed. He however reprinted a few of the sketches himself.

James made the connection with the *Tribune* through John Hay who interceded in his behalf with the owner White-law Reid. But a half a year or so later James found that he considered the paper vulgar and repulsive. In August he received a letter from Reid asking him to write in a more popular vein. James refused to do so; he had virtually received a dismissal and severed his connection.

This experience with the paper had a profound effect upon the life and art of James. Nearly twenty years later, he records that he ought to write a story suggested by past memories of his own frustrated ambition when Reid asked him to make his letters to the paper baser and more paltry. James says that he told Reid that his letters were the worst that he could do. He realized that his letters were not wanted and he launched this final barb against Reid. He was now thinking of writing a small tragedy of literary life. He later returned in his Notebooks to "the old story of his letters to the Tribune." He would show a similar case or one identical with his adventure with the *Tribune.* The story *"The Next Time"* was immediately written and published. It was for James an apology for his whole career in writing novels which the public did not relish. He was Ralph Limbert of the tale. He said, however, later in his preface to the story when it appeared in the revised edition of his works, that it was in essence a story about the public, but he did not mention the *Tribune* in his preface. When James wrote the story his popularity was almost at its lowest. This accounted no doubt for the sensitiveness, nay pain, he displays.

II

Certainly one of the reasons for James's unpopularity is that he was an intellectual and particularly interested in developing an idea. He never started on a story unless he had an idea to promulgate. Yet he was not a propagandist. He shows in all his critical writings that he is looking for the ideas at the base of an author's writings. He "leavens" all writings with thought, even if this was to prove unprofitable, as he once wrote to his brother William.

One wonders why so many able critics have quoted with approval, nay awe, T. S. Eliot's remarks that James's "intelligence was so fine that no idea could violate it," that his critical genius comes out "in his mastery over and baffling escape from ideas"—such escape being in Eliot's opinion the final test of superior intelligence. And all this notwithstanding Eliot's view that James was not a successful literary critic and that his criticism of books was feeble. A fear that England and America might be infected with ideas (of course only liberal ideas) and a regret that France should be the home of ideas is natural to conservative minds and worshippers of tradition, but one notices that they have an idea—that we should not welcome ideas although they venture their own idea to this effect, and are prolific in ideas in defense of movements they favor. Some of Eliot's admirers have sought in devious ways to show that he meant something else. The remark originally appeared in 1918,[15] but Eliot never reprinted the essay containing it in his *Selected Essays*. However, he did give permission to Edmund Wilson and F. W. Dupee to reprint it in collections they made.

James wrote in his well-known essay "The Art of Fiction"[16] that the deepest quality for a work of art will always be the quality of the mind of the producer, that his novel will partake of the substance of beauty and truth in proportion as the intelligence is fine, and that no good novel will ever proceed from a superficial mind. He had not changed his opinion of nearly twenty years before when speaking of George Eliot's novels;[17] he had referred to her ripest reflection, called her a serious thinker, and spoke of her play of lively and vigorous thought, while at the same time he pointed out her limitations in contrast with the more open mind of George Sand. As Richard Blackmuir put it in his preface to the collection of James's Prefaces, art to James was nothing without intelligence.

It would be a mistake not to emphasize James's stress upon the value of ideas, his receptibility to them, nay his quest for them. He said in his first essay on Turgenev[18] that what counted in a great writer was how he felt about life, what in the last analysis was his philosophy of life. He believed that the most interesting thing a great writer offered was some expression of a total view of the world he was observing. James always regarded the subject matter of art important, even though he came to lay stress on form and structure more than ever. He held that a reviewer must be interested in underlying principles and must be a philosopher.

Lafcadio Hearn once classed James as "pure and talented a writer of realistic fiction as the English century has produced."[19]

James, except on rare occasions was not friendly to the romantic novel. True, he preferred a good one like *Treasure Island* to what he considered a bad realistic novel, like Edmond de Goncourt's *Chérie* (because in this case it failed in tracing the moral consciousness of a child)—a novel that was a favorite of Maupassant. I think Edel was relying too much upon his memory when he said that Stevenson, who had entered into the controversy between Walter Besant and James on the matter of realism, in his essay "A Humble Remonstrance" "essentially agreed" with James. On the contrary he differed essentially. James had said that no art can successfully compete with life; he held that it does its best. Stevenson on the other hand held that it was not even in the province of art to compete with life. He stated the romantic position against James who defended the novel of character. Stevenson stands up for that of adventure. James says that the whole life of man is the subject of novels; Stevenson says it is not, adding that he must "differ by the whole width of heaven from Mr. James" in holding that the novelist selects subjects from the inexhaustible magazine. Stevenson then divides the novel into three classes, the adventure novel, the character novel, and the dramatic novel, which deals with passion. James is not concerned with adventure or passion, Stevenson truly says, and adds that to much of what he has said James would demur and somewhat impatiently acquiesce. Stevenson states that his own preference was for the novel of adventure: "Danger is the matter with which this class of novels deals; fear, the passion with which it and the characters are portrayed only so far as they realize the sense of danger and provoke the sympathy of fear." Such novels, he maintains, represent a wish fulfillment of the boy.

James in his Preface to *The American* must have had unconscious memories of this passage and its phraseology when he wrote that the panting pursuit of a certain kind of danger is the pursuit of life itself. He held that a definition of romance is weak and inadequate when it reduces itself to the idea of the facing of danger, the acceptance of great risks for the fascination, the very love, of their uncertainty, the joy of success if possible, and of battle in any case. Here he was adapting Stevenson's own language to criticize him.

Robert Le Clair heads one of his chapters in *Young Henry James* "The Birth of a Realist," putting the date in the early seventies and quoting James's Preface to *The American* to the effect that the real represents things we may know sooner or later, while the romantic stands for things we can never directly know. This conception of James as a realist has in recent years been modified, and Dr. Robert E. Spiller in his bibliographical essay on Henry James approvingly and properly sustains the view of R. P. Falk expressed in an article in the *Development of American Literary Criticism* that James did not accept realism because he was too much concerned with the personal in literature to be interested in a term which was socialistic in its implications and that he became the reconciler of the ideal and real.

Sidney E. Lind says that James in his story "The Private Life," where Clare Vawdrey is Robert Browning, was writing disguised autobiography and "transposed to the background of the story general and specific aspects of his own life and these are presented in sufficient detail to be recognized. 'The Private Life' illustrates how he projects his autobiography into a day dream."[20]

The next matter of interest is to what extent James was subjective, personal, and impressionistic in his literary criticism, as he was, as generally conceded, in much of his fiction. Nevertheless, it has been held by some like Miss Cornelia Pulsifer Kelley, who in her *The Early Development of Henry James* deals largely with literary influences upon James, that he was objective in his novels and tales in spite of the fact that he put Minnie Temple into his *Portrait of a Lady*. This theory of objectivity is defended on the ground that an incident related to him by someone or a suggestion thrown out by another became the starting point of a novel. Yes, but once he started, he drew on his own experiences and his past emotional life. It is now realized that *The Ambassadors* was not only motivated by the remark about which he heard, that Howells regretted he had really not squeezed out of life all that he might, but by the fact that, as he told Hugh Walpole, he himself had not embraced certain opportunities he had in youth which he now regretted, as F. W. Dupee records in his *Henry James*, (1956), p. 187. He spoke in his biographies, of the starved romance of his life as Dupee further relates (*ibid*). Indeed Strether had in him more of James than of Howells, who had at least married.

We should also not ignore the possible personal element in James's literary criticism. As a matter of fact, and I am speaking chiefly of his criticism in the first twenty years of his literary life, he was an impressionist and largely a writer of causeries. He preferred the critical writings of the French to those of the English because these were more often causeries. As early as 1868 he said that the day of dogmatic criticism was over, and that the critic was simply a reader who like others prints his impressions and does not pretend that he tells the whole truth. His impressionism was noted by reviewers of his first book of literary criticism, *French Poets and Novelists,* and even of the later *Partial Portraits* the *Nation* said that the personal elements of the author were at the basis of the volume.[21] Other critics also called attention to the fact that too many personal impressions prevailed, that he often recounted anecdotes, and that he passed no final judgment on authors.

The subjectivity of Henry James as a critic may be shown by his adverse reference to anything in a book that he believed vulgar. The words "vulgar" and "vulgarity" appear so frequently in his writings that they testify to a strong personal aversion to vulgarity. Though there are matters relating to sex in his later novels covertly touched on, he deprecated accounts wherein it figured too blatantly, as was noticed in many instances and in later life in his articles on Matilda Serao and Gabriel D'Annunzio. He regarded as vulgar, scenes of violence, descriptions of low life, accounts of poverty, portrayals of ignorant characters, but when he found a great novelist like Dickens depicting what was really vulgar, he fell back upon the defense for him that he was only showing the odd and droll. Graham Greene suspected vulgarity in James himself because he turned to the writing of plays to make money. And Justice Holmes regarded James's "drooling" on the social relations of important Americans with the Old World "a trifle underbred."

Yet there is nothing vulgar in the ordinary sense in his own books. Someone has said that they might have been improved had there been some vulgarity in them. As a matter of fact his marked hostility to the vulgar contradicts his theory of the novel, which was to express all of life and all experiences wholly as they manifest themselves. He used his distaste for vulgarity as a measuring rod in his literary criticism for disapproval of a book. Fortunately it did not always interfere with his judgment. Though he censured books in which sexual freedom was shown, he admired the French novelists who indulged in it; but he was not partial to romance in which there were introduced adventure and scenes of danger. He admired the

work of Stevenson, however, and in spite of their controversy on the subject became a close friend and wrote two articles
about him. While he considers scenes of violence vulgar, he
wrote an introduction for a collection of Kipling's early tales
(though he could not abide the later Kipling who wrote about
machines); and in spite of his disparagement of propaganda
and condemnation of a journalistic style, he was an admirer
of H. G. Wells (who pained him later in his satire about him).

No doubt it is annoying to find James harping on the same
note that art should not deal with the vulgar. Yet he could not
help but know that Balzac was vulgar, that the scenes by Shakespeare in the Boar's Head Tavern were vulgar, that some of the
characters as well as stories in Chaucer's *Canterbury Tales* were
vulgar. Falstaff, Micawber, Natty Bumpo were vulgar persons. We
like to read about vulgar scenes and even rejoice in the portrayal
of vulgar personages in literature; we do not have to haunt such
scenes or mingle with such characters in real life; as a matter
of fact we do not and even shun doing so. Falstaffs are found
in taverns, throughout the country and Boar's Head taverns are
among them; Micawbers live in the slums; yet one is not obliged
to concern oneself with the real article, but the taking in of such
scenes and characters into works of art under the hand of a
master gives them a new lease on life, a permanent literary one.
We admire Wordsworth's account of the leech-gatherer on the
moor, and his beggar and pedlars; we revel among George
Borrow's gypsies; we keep company with Cooper's, Marryat's,
and Conrad's sailors and with Melville's whalers, although we
might not go around the corner to see them.

Some of our modern writers, however, have produced great
art just because they have depicted the very lowest of the low.
If you remove from the world's literature all that is vulgar
in James's conception, you would do away with a very large
part of it.

The charge of snobbery, however, is not valid against James
and has largely been discounted by his admirers. He had the
right to tell stories about cultured people and persons who were
comfortable financially and in the social swim, about the refined rather than the crude. After all, learned authors can best

write about such people, and the élite prefer to read about those like themselves. We should really be grateful to James for dealing with persons he knew best, and with whom he mingled, because he could write about them so well. He had the right to write about artists and writers and people who were to take trips to Europe and sojourn there. Reading about them does not make for worse reading than about poor Southern whites and cowboys on the one hand, and gangsters and gamblers on the other. After all, the love affairs of the rich and learned have the same vicissitudes as those of the lower classes.

Curiously enough, Upton Sinclair—James, if he had read *The Jungle,* probably would not have liked it, for he could not abide accounts of the smell of blood in a slaughterhouse or take an interest in impoverished immigrants—wrote quite a favorable article on James in a book, *Mammonart,*[22] wherein he advances theories of art utterly repugnant to James. Sinclair says that in his youth he had read James's forty volumes and wrote an article about him which he could not get published. He regarded him with reverence and even later regarded him with affection because of the remembered reverence. He considers *The Ambassadors* as the world's great international novel and remembered it so well after twenty years that the characters and stories were as vivid as ever in his mind. I pass over Sinclair's strictures about James's later style, his preoccupation with rich people and indifference to the search for a remedy to wipe out poverty. Sinclair takes the position that is usually taken today that when James left America his aesthetic sensibilities became less puritanical and more cosmopolitan. As he says, two civilizations meet in *The Ambassadors* and in the clash between them we see the heart of both revealed.

Arnold Bennett gave up reading *The Ambassadors* and said that the book was not quite worth the trouble of reading it. The *Journal of Arnold Bennett* (p. 206). F. R. Lewis in *The Great Tradition* (pp. 155-156) said the novel was not only a bad one but exhibited an even more interesting disease than senility.

James's criticism reveals his personality no less than his tales. When a novelist or poet gives a lecture or writes an article about his craft, even if he does not mention his own novels or poems, he is unconsciously referring to them and approving them. Both James and Stevenson did this. Wordsworth and Whitman wrote magnificent criticisms on poetry but these implied that their own poetry was the right kind and the only kind.

James attributed his mental processes, his ideas, his theories to the writers he praised, whether critics or novelists. When 22 years old he told Thomas Sergeant Perry that he sought a career as a writer, that he wanted to be the American Sainte-Beuve. He referred incidentally to three reviews of his, two of which are herein reprinted, of Feuillet's *Camors* and Sainte-Beuve's *Portraits.* He also wrote to his brother that he would like to be a Sainte-Beuve and to acquire something of his intelligence. He soon found support for his own intelligence by projecting himself upon Sainte-Beuve and unconsciously ascribing his own ideas to him, thus really unknowingly, nay naively, confirming himself in his own views. This was the same process in his treatment of Arnold, and when James differed with or criticised an author he virtually said that that author did not have James's own mental processes; James could not project himself upon him.

Projection is more or less a feature in all literary criticism and accounts for differences of judgment. We foist our own views upon our favorite author. We make Shakespeare a Catholic, a Protestant, a Freethinker, a feudalist, a democrat, in accordance with our views—to give prestige to them. The greatest poets have been projectionists; Dante attributed to the pagan Virgil his own theological views.

The process of projection is worth taking into consideration. Psychoanalysts, in treating patients, realize that they have a tendency to what is known as projection. Dr. Ernest Jones describes it as an ascription to the outer world of mental processes that are not recognized to be of personal origin.[23] It is, however, often indulged in by perfectly normal people to bolster their confidence, to support their own attitudes, to confirm them in their ideas and support them in their views. It may be a development of the habit of the child who looks up to its father for confirmation of the conceptions that it itself entertains, and of course it never for one moment doubts that its father's approval is not correct.

Biographers often choose as subjects the lives of people with whom they believe they find some intellectual, psychological and moral affinity, unconscious that they often attribute some of their own characteristics to the subjects of their biographies. They ascribe to others, the outer world, their own mental processes. A marked instance of this was shown by Ernest Renan when he wrote his *Life of Jesus* to whom he attributes his own virtues unconsciously, as he has set them forth later in his own autobiography. Carlyle's essay on Burns is a complete self-revelation of Carlyle, for he finds in his fellow Scotsman parallels to his most cherished views, though Burns never entertained them. Another instance of projection is the manner in which James Russell Lowell as a critic treated Lessing with whom he identified himself. And Swinburne thought that he was almost Shelley incarnate.

James, being an impressionistic and a suggestive literary critic, also projected himself upon other critics whom he admired besides Sainte-Beuve and Matthew Arnold, Edmond Schérer, for instance. He found, rightly or wrongly, that they held the same views on literature that he held. He felt supported by them and became certain through them that his various views were right. He praised novelists who used the same methods as he himself, like Turgenev, for example. He believed he learned his methods from Turgenev. He had been employing them as a matter of fact before the latter revealed to him his own.

The application of the principle of projection to James's literary criticism opens up the path as to other procedures which could connect it with processes that have been largely unconscious with him. As is well known, several of his tales have been analysed by critics who showed how unconscious fantasies pervaded them, the most notable one being "The Turn of the Screw." Such an interpretation was begun cautiously by Edna Kenton without the use of Freudian terminology and carried one more step by Edmund Wilson.[24] True, some critics have disagreed with Wilson, but I think they are wrong.

Leon Edel contributed to the psychoanalytical interpretation of many of James's ghostly tales by holding that the supernatural features therein were the result of unconscious fantasies.[25]

Clifton Fadiman has also applied Freudian methods in analyzing some of the short stories of Henry James.

The Appendix contains a psychoanalytical interpretation of my own about one of James's tales, "Mme. de Mauves."

III

James has become a classic, and there is no question that he deserves the title Master which has been bestowed upon him; his early literary criticism should not be therefore overlooked. It is important not only in itself but in relation to his later criticism and to his entire fictional output; in the same sense as Poe's literary articles in the *Southern Literary Messenger,* which have been collected, are to his poems, tales and later literary essays.

Much has been written about the so-called James revival. In a sense he had never been neglected by the critics. Two books were published about him in his lifetime and two shortly after his death. Numerous reviews and articles appeared in periodicals during his literary life; more praised than condemned him. Even before the revival in the forties, renewed interest had been taken in him. There can be no objection to the term, but it reflected chiefly a changed and more reverential attitude toward him. His later work was rescued from virtual obloquy and set above his earlier. There had however always been some who saw the merits in the later novels. Anthologies of his tales have since been produced, selections of his critical essays have been reprinted, new editions of some of his novels have appeared, and certainly more people have been reading him than before. He is now even in paper-backs. Up to the time of this revival, however, concentration was chiefly on one or two of his tales and novels. The present writer recalls that during the first and second decades of this century first editions of James's novels were on the shelves of Leary's book store at fifty cents a copy, year after year with no purchasers, and he availed himself of the opportunity to obtain some. James was sensitive about the fact that he was not widely read. Shortly before he achieved some measure of popularity with the publication of *Daisy Miller* and after that of *The American* he wrote to James Osgood, his publisher, when asking among others for some copies of the latter novel that he hoped it was going as well as such a book at present could be expected to.[26]

James has become a favorite in the academic world; theses and essays have multiplied about him; his sources and images have been receiving attention; the revisions of his later style have been set beside his earlier; he has been put down as an expositor of the American tradition by some, while by others he has been deemed an English writer, a view that justly no longer has many adherents; he has been accepted as the mouthpiece of various literary cults who have found in his utterances, rightly or wrongly, justification for their own cherished doctrines.

All in all, James scholarship has been magnificent and has produced articles and books that in themselves are literature of a high order; he surely has been fortunate in his posthumous fame. Yet, notwithstanding what has been called a revival—for which several scholars have accounted various reasons—he was never dead. He is the same James in 1957 as he was in 1916. He was really never dead—any more than Whitman, Melville or Mark Twain, who have also experienced revivals. His many works of a high quality not only in fiction, but in criticism and books of travel always had readers. In the number of novels he exceeded that of Hawthorne, Melville or Mark Twain, each of whom is supposed to have written the greatest American novel; they produced only a few additional novels along with their masterpieces. James, whether his novels reached as high a plane as theirs or not, wrote probably a dozen novels of a high order, and many distinguished novelettes and tales.

Many people, however, still believe in connection with his later involved style, that the adverse criticism and analysis by his brother William, were not far from the truth.

James's merits were recognized even before Howells accepted his tale, "Poor Richard" for the *Atlantic Monthly,* for the *Nation* in its monthly notices of the new magazines had praised "My Friend Bingham" and commented favorably on the other few stories he had written. Noticing this tale it said that it "showed skill in analysis of character and a liking for dwelling upon the shades of feeling . . .[27]

But unknown to James another laudatory opinion was being passed in a private letter, when the first instalment of "Poor Richard" appeared, from the pen of one of the well-known woman writers of the day, Gail Hamilton (Mary A. Dodge). It did not appear in print till her letters were published in 1901.

She was ten years older than James. She had been corresponding with the Elder James, and writing to a friend, Judge French (Henry F., father of the sculptor Daniel C. French), she said that the young Henry had a way of surprising you that is highly amusing and was one of the most promising writers, and that his stories were studies. She as a woman was in a position to call attention to his treatment of women in the few stories she had read, "His women, if they are wicked or foolish, have their own way of being so. They are not the old block-women handed down by tradition, with only the change of waterfalls and rats, or whatever is the last new style, I don't know." This undated letter was written probably early in June 1867.[28]

I should like to quote a later tribute to James because like Gail Hamilton's and Upton Sinclair's given above it is never as far as I know quoted or mentioned in James bibliographies. I refer to one by Lafcadio Hearn. He had mentioned James in his letters and some of his editorials written in the eighties when employed on New Orleans newspapers.

Hearn in his lectures to his Japanese students in the late nineties said: "In my opinion, Henry James is by far the greatest living American writer . . . He has lived in England during a greater part of his life; and has written much more wonderful things there than he could have written in America. He is, indeed, the only writer of English novels possessing the same kind of psychological art as distinguishes the great modern novelists of France—such as Daudet and Bourget. And he is capable of astonishing variety of work."[29] These words written before the great novels of the fourth period, contain the view of James that has evolved after much spilling of ink, that James profited by going to England.

It is singular that James never wrote about the great Danish critic, Georg Brandes, who also like him was a disciple of Sainte-Beuve. And yet James was a great admirer of Ibsen whose merits Brandes had done much in expounding, and whose *John Gabriel Borkman* James praised highly when it was first translated.[30] Besides, Brandes was the author of a very notable essay on James's favorite, Flaubert. When Brandes was in this country in 1914 he often put to reporters and men who came to interview him the question whether they had ever read James's *The American*. The answer was invariably "no"— and he commented to the present writer who had the good fortune to meet him, "Why, the Americans don't know their own literature."

The last book James published in his life-time was a volume of literary criticism, *Notes on Novelists with Some Other Notes*. He regarded the calling of literary critic very high. His first ambition had been to be a literary critic and it may be questioned whether secretly he did not cherish a hope that he had established a reputation as one of the leading critics of the age. He had once been held by Brander Matthews, on the appearance of *Poets and Novelists,* to be only slightly below the leading critics of America and England at the time, James Russell Lowell and Matthew Arnold, respectively. Let us quote his words sixty years ago in a second essay on Lowell (reprinted by Edel from *Library of World's Best Literature* edited by Charles Dudley Warner, 1897) about literary criticism:

"So far from being a chamber surrendering itself from the threshold to the ignorant young of either sex, criticism is positively and miraculously *not* the simplest and most immediate, but the most postponed and complicated of the arts, the last qualified for and arrived at, the one requiring behind it most maturity, most power to understand and compare."

To some extent features of literary criticism entered into his fiction, and his imaginative novelist's mind characterized his literary criticism.

Philadelphia, August 1957   ALBERT MORDELL

ESSAYS ON FRENCH LITERATURE

THE REMINISCENCES OF ERNEST RENAN

There has always been an element of the magical in the style of M. Ernest Renan—an art of saying things in a way to make them beautiful. At the present moment he is the first writer in France; no one has in an equal degree the secret of fairness of expression. His style is fair in both the senses in which we use the word—in that of being temperate and just, and in that of being without a flaw; and these Reminiscences of his younger years,[1] lately collected from the Revue des Deux Mondes, are perhaps the most complete revelation of it. His problem here was unusually difficult, and his success has been proportionately brilliant. He proposed to talk uninterruptedly about himself, and yet he proposed—or rather he was naturally disposed—to remain a model of delicacy. M. Renan is the great apostle of the delicate; he upholds this waning fashion on every occasion. His mission is to say delicate things, to plead the cause of intellectual good manners, and he is wonderfully competent to discharge it. No one to-day says such things so well, though in our own language Mr. Matthew Arnold often approaches him. Among his own countrymen, Sainte-Beuve cultivated the same art, and there was nothing too delicate for Sainte-Beuve to attempt to say. But he spoke less simply—his delicacy was always a greater complexity. M. Renan, on the other hand, delivers himself of those truths which he has arrived at through the fineness of his perception and the purity of his taste with a candid confidence, an absence of personal precautions, which leave the image as perfect and as naked as an old Greek statue. It is needless to say that there is nothing crude in M. Renan; but the soft serenity with which, in the presence of a mocking world, he leaves his usual plea for the ideal to any fate that may await it is an example

1. *Souvenirs d'Enfance et de Jeunesse.* Par Ernest Renan, Membre de l'Institut, etc. Paris: Calmann Lévy. 1883. (*Atlantic Monthly*, August 1883.)

(A translation from the French by C. Y. Pitman, revised by Madame Renan, was published in the same year under the title *Recollections of My Youth*, in both London and New York.)

of how extremes may sometimes meet. It is not enough to say of him that he has the courage of his opinions; for that, after all, is a comparatively frequent virtue. He has the resignation; he has the indifference; he has, above all, the good humor. He combines qualities the most diverse, and, lighted up as he is by the interesting confessions of the volume before us, he presents himself as an extraordinary figure. He makes the remark that in his opinion less importance will be attached to talent as the world goes on; what we shall care for will be simply truth. This declaration is singular in many ways, among others in this: that it appears to overlook the fact that one of the great uses of talent will always be to discover truth and present it; and that, being an eminently personal thing, and therefore susceptible of great variety, it can hardly fail to be included in the estimate that the world will continue to make of persons. M. Renan makes light of his own talent—he can well afford to; if he appears to be quite conscious of the degree in which it exists, he minimizes as much as possible the merit that attaches to it. This is a part of that constant play of taste which animates his style, governs his judgments, colors all his thought; for nothing can be in better taste, of course, than to temper the violence with which you happen to strike people. To make your estimate of your own gifts as low as may seem probable is a form of high consideration for others; it corresponds perfectly with that canon of good manners which requires us to take up a moderate space at table. At the feast of existence we may not jostle our neighbors, and to be considerate is for M. Renan an indefeasible necessity. He informs us of this himself; it is true that we had long ago guessed it. He places the fact before us, however, in a relation to other facts, which makes it doubly interesting; he gives us the history of his modesty, his erudition, his amiability, his temperance of appetite, his indifference to gain. The reader will easily perceive the value that must attach to such explanations on the part of a man of M. Renan's intelligence. He finds himself in constant agreement with the author, who does nothing but interpret with extraordinary tact the latent impressions of his critic.

M. Renan carries to such a high point the art of pleasing that we enter without a protest into the pleasantness of the account he gives of himself. He is incapable of evil, learned, happy, cheerful, witty, devoted to the ideal, indifferent to every vulgar aim. He demonstrates all this with such grace, such discretion and good humor, that the operation, exempt from vulgar vanity, from motives of self-interest, M. Renan being at that point of literary eminence where a writer has nothing more to gain, seems to go on in the pure ether of the abstract, among the causes of things and above all questions of relative success. Speaking of his ancestors in Brittany, whom he traces back to the fifth century, simple tillers of the earth and fishers of the sea, he says, with great felicity, "There they led for thirteen hundred years a life of obscurity, saving up their thoughts and sensations into an accumulated capital, which has fallen at last to me. I feel that I think for them and that they live in me. . . . My incapacity to be bad, or even to appear so, comes to me from them." Many men would hesitate to speak so freely of their incapacity to be bad; others, still more of their incapacity to appear so. But M. Renan has polished to such clearness the plate of glass through which he allows us to look at him that we are quite unable to charge him with deceiving us. If we fail to see in him so much good as that, it is simply that our vision is more dim, our intelligence less fine. "I have a strong taste for the people, for the poor. I have been able, alone in my age, to understand Jesus and Francis of Assisi." There is a great serenity in that, and though, detached from the text, it may startle us a little, it will not seem to the reader who meets it in its place to be a boastful note. M. Renan does not indeed mean to say that he has been the only Christian of his time; he means he is not acquainted with any description of the character of Jesus containing as much historic truth as the Life he published in 1864. The passage is curious, however, as showing the lengths to which a man of high delicacy may go when he undertakes to be perfectly frank. That, indeed, is the interest of the whole volume. Many of its pages are rare and precious, in that they offer us together certain qualities that are almost never combined. The aristocratic intellect is not prone to confess itself, to take other minds into its confidence. M. Renan believes in a caste of intellectual nobles, and of course does not himself belong to any inferior order. Yet in these volumes he has alighted from his gilded coach, as it were; he has come down into the streets and walked about with the multitude. He has, in a word, waived the question of privacy—a great question for such a man as M. Renan to waive. When the impersonal becomes personal the change is great, and it is interesting to see that sooner or later it must become so. Naturally, for us English readers, the difference of race renders such a fact more difficult to appreciate; for we have a traditional theory that when it comes to making confidences a Frenchman is capable of almost anything. He is certainly more gracefully egotistic than people of other stock, though he may have more real reserve than his style would indicate. His modesty is individual, his style is generic; he writes in a language which makes everything definite, including confessions and other forms of self-reference. The truth is that he talks better than other people, and that the genius of talk carries him far. There is nothing into which it carries people more naturally than egotism. M. Renan's volume is a prolonged *causerie*, and he has both the privileges and the success of the talker.

There are many things in his composition and many things in his writing; more than we have any hope of describing in their order. "I was not a priest in profession; I was a priest in mind. All my defects are owing to that: they are the defects of the priest." The basis of M. Renan's character and his work is the qualities that led him to study for the priesthood, and the experience of a youth passed in Catholic seminaries. "Le pli était pris—the bent was taken," as he says; in spite of changes, renunciations, a rupture with these early aspirations as complete as it was painful, he has remained indefinably, ineffaceably, clerical. The higher education of a Catholic priest is an education of subtleties, and subtlety is the note, as we say to-day, of M. Renan's view of things. But he is a profane philosopher as well as a product of the seminary, and he is in the bargain a Parisian and a man of letters; so that the groundwork has embroidered itself with many patterns. When we add to this the high scholarship, the artistic feeling, the urbanity, the amenity of temper, that quality of ripeness and completeness, the air of being permeated by civilization, which our author owes to his great experience of human knowledge, to his eminent position in literature and science, to his association with innumerable accomplished and distinguished minds—when we piece these things together we feel that the portrait he has, both by intention and by implication, painted of himself has not wanted an inspiring model. The episode which M. Renan has had mainly to relate in these pages is of course the interruption of his clerical career. He has made the history so suggestive, so interesting, and given such a charm to his narrative, that we have little hesitation in saying that these chapters will rank among the most brilliant he has produced. We are almost ashamed to express ourselves in this manner, for, as we have said, M. Renan makes very light of literary glory, and cares little for this kind of commendation. Indeed, when we turn to the page in which he gives us the measure of his indifference to successful form we feel almost tempted to blot out what we have written. "I do not share the error of the literary judgments of our time . . . I tried to care for literature for a while only to gratify M. Sainte-Beuve, who had a great deal of influence over me. Since his death I care no longer. I see very well that talent has a value only because the world is childish. If it had a strong enough head it would content itself with truth . . . I have never sought to make use of this inferior quality [literary skill], which has injured me more as a *savant* than it has helped me for itself. I have never in the least rested on it . . . I have always been the least literary of men." The reader may be tempted to ask himself whether these remarks are but a refinement of coquetry; whether a faculty of expression so perfect as M. Renan's was ever a simple accident. He will do well, however, to decide that the writer is sincere, for he speaks from the point of view of a seeker of scientific truth. M. Renan is deeply versed in the achievements of German science: he knows what has been done by scholars who have not sacrificed to the graces, and in the presence of these great examples he would fain persuade himself that he has not, at least consentingly, been guilty of that weakness. In spite of this he will continue to pass for one of the most characteristic children of the race that is preëminent in the art of statement. It is a proof of the richness of his genius that we may derive so much entertainment from those parts of it which he regards as least essential. We do not pretend in this place to

ESSAYS ON FRENCH LITERATURE: RENAN

speak, with critical or other intention, of the various admirable
works which have presented M. Renan to the world as one of the
most acute explorers of the mysteries of early Christian history;
we take for granted the fact that they have been largely appreciated, and that the writer, as he stands before us here, has the benefit of all the authority which a great task executed in a great manner can confer. But we venture to say that, fascinating, touching,
as his style, to whatever applied, never ceases to be, none of the
great subjects he has treated has taken a more charming light
from the process than these evocations of his own laborious past.

And we say this with a perfect consciousness that the volume
before us is after all, in a certain sense, but an elaborate *jeu
d'esprit*. M. Renan is a philosopher, but he is a sportive philosopher; he is full of soft irony, of ingenious fancy, of poetic sympathies, of transcendent tastes. He speaks more than once of his
natural gayety, and of that quality in members of the Breton
race which leads them to move freely in the moral world and to
divert themselves with ideas, with sentiments. Half of the ideas,
the feelings, that M. Renan expresses in these pages (and they
spring from under his pen with wonderful facility) are put forward with a smile which seems a constant admission that he
knows that everything that one may say has eventually to be
qualified. The qualification may be in one's tact, one's discretion,
one's civility, one's desire not to be dogmatic; in other considerations, too numerous for us to mention. M. Renan has a horror of
dogmatism; he thinks that one should always leave that to one's
opponent, as it is an instrument with which he ends by cutting
himself. He has a high conception of generosity, and though his
mind contains several very positive convictions, he is of the opinion that there is always a certain grossness in insistence. Two
or three curious passages throw light upon this disposition. "Not
having amused myself when I was young, and yet having in my
character a great deal of irony and gayety, I have been obliged,
at the age at which one sees the vanity of everything, to become
extremely indulgent to foibles with which I had never had to reproach myself: so that various persons, who perhaps have not
behaved so well as I, have sometimes found themselves scandalized
at my complaisance. In political matters, above all, people of

a Puritan turn cannot imagine what I am about; it is the order of things in which I like myself best, and yet ever so many persons think my laxity in this respect extreme. I cannot get it out of my head that it is perhaps, after all, the libertine who is right and who practices the true philosophy of life. From this source have sprung in me certain surprises. Sainte-Beuve, Théophile Gautier, pleased me a little too much. Their affectation of immorality prevented me from seeing how little their philosophy hung together (*le dècousu de leur philosophie*)." There is a certain stiffly literal sense in which, of course, these lines are not to be taken; but they are a charming specimen of what one may call delicacy of confession. The great thing is to have been able to afford to write them; on that condition they are delightfully human and charged with the soft irony of which I have spoken —the element to which M. Renan alludes in a passage that occurs shortly after the one I have quoted, and in which he mentions that, "save the small number of persons with whom I recognize an intellectual fraternity, I say to every one what I suppose must give him pleasure." He says that he expresses himself freely only with people "whom I know to be liberated from any opinion, and to be able to take the stand-points of a kindly universal irony." "For the rest," he remarks, "I have sometimes, in my conversation and my correspondence, *d'étranges défaillances* . . . My inanity with people I meet in society exceeds all belief. . . . Devoted on a kind of system to an exaggerated politeness, the politeness of the priest, I try to find out what my interlocutor would like me to say to him. . . . This is the result of a supposition that few men are sufficiently detached from their own ideas not to be wounded if you say something different from what they think." We should not omit to explain that what we have just quoted applies only to M. Renan's conversation and letters. "In my published writings I have been of an absolute sincerity. Not only have I not said anything that I do not think, but, a much more rare and more difficult thing, I have said all that I think." It will be seen that M. Renan tells us a good deal about himself.

His Reminiscences are ushered in by a preface which is one of the happiest pieces of writing that has ever proceeded from his pen, and in which he delivers himself of his opinion on that very striking spectacle, the democratization of the world. He is preëminently a man of general views. Few men have more of them at their command; few men face the occasion for speech with greater serenity, or avail themselves of it with more grace. His prefaces have always been important and eloquent; readers of the first collection of his critical essays, published upwards of thirty years ago, will not have forgotten the enchanting pages that introduced it. We feel a real obligation to quote the opening lines of the preface before us; from the point of view of style they give the key of the rest of the volume. We must add that it is not easy to transport their exquisite rhythm into another tongue. "Among the legends most diffused in Brittany is that of a so-called town of Is, which at an unknown period must have been engulfed by the sea. They show you, in sundry places on the coast, the site of this fabled city, and the fishermen tell you strange stories about it. They assure you that on days of storm the tip of the spires of its churches may be seen in the hollows of the waves; that on days of calm you may hear the sound of its bells come up from the deeps, intoning the hymn of the day. It seems to me often that I have in the bottom of my heart a city of Is, which still rings bells that persist in gathering to sacred rites the faithful who no longer hear. At times I stop to lend an ear to these trembling vibrations, which appear to me to come from infinite depths, like the voices of another world. On the limits of old age, above all, I have taken pleasure in collecting together such echoes of an Atlantis that has passed away." It may have been that M. Renan wrote these harmonious lines with the same ignorance of what he was about that characterized M. Jourdain; in this case he is only to be congratulated the more. The city of Is represents his early education, his early faith, a state of mind that was peopled with spires and bells, but has long since sunk deep into the sea of time. He explains in some degree the manner in which he has retraced this history, choosing to speak of certain things and to pass in silence over others, and then proceeds, by those transitions through which no one glides so gracefully as he, to sundry charming considerations upon the present state of mankind and the apparent future of our society. We call his reflections charming, because M. Renan's view of life always strikes us as a work of art, and we naturally apply to it the epithets which we should use in speaking of any delightful achievement. As a votary of the ideal, a person who takes little interest in the practical, a distinguished member of that beneficent *noblesse* of intellect of which we have spoken, it would be natural that M. Renan should tend to conservative opinions; and he expresses such opinions, in various later pages, with exquisite humor and point: "In other terms, our great democratic machines exclude the polite man. I have long since given up using the omnibus; the conductors ended by taking me for a passenger of no intentions ... I was made for a society founded upon respect, in which one is saluted, classified, placed, according to his costume, and has not to protect himself ... The habit that I found in the East of walking only preceded by a forerunner suited me not ill; for one's modesty receives a lift from the apparatus of force. It is well to have under one's orders a man armed with a scourge which one prevents him from using. I should not be sorry to have the right of life and death, so that I might never put it into practice; and I should be very glad to own a few slaves, in order to be extremely mild with them and make them adore me." There is a certain dandyism of sensibility, if we may be allowed the expression, in that; but the author's perfect good-humor carries it off, as it always carries off the higher flights of his fastidiousness, making them seem simply a formal, a sort of cheerfully hopeless, protest in the name of the ideal. M. Renan is always ready to make the practical concession, and he shows that it is a great thing to have a fine taste, which tells us when to yield as well as when to resist, and points out, moreover, the beauty of passing things by. "One should never write save about what one likes. Forgetfulness and silence are the punishment that we inflict on what we find ugly or common in the walk that we take through life." This discretion helps M. Renan to feel that, though the immense material progress of this century is not favorable to good manners, it is a great mistake to put ourselves in opposition to what our age may be doing. "It does it without us, and probably it is right. The world moves toward a sort of Americanism, which wounds our refined ideas, but which, once the crisis of the present hour is passed, may very well be no worse than the old *régime* for the only thing that matters; that is, the emancipation and the progress of the human mind." And M. Renan develops the idea that, in spite of all that the votaries of disinterested speculation my find wanting in a society exclusively democratic and industrial, and however much they may miss the advantages of belonging to a protected class, their security is greater, on the whole, in the new order of things. "Perhaps some day the general vulgarity will be a condition of the happiness of the elect. The American vulgarity [*sic*] would not burn Giordano Bruno, would not persecute Galileo . . . People of taste live in America, on the condition of not being too exacting." So he terminates with the declaration that the best thing one can do is to accept one's age, if for no other reason than that it is after all a part of the past that one looks back to with regret. "All the centuries of a nation are the leaves of the same book." And in regard to this intelligent resignation, which fortifies itself with curiosity, M. Renan says several excellent things: "There will always be an advantage in having lighted on this planet as late as possible . . . One must never regret that one sees a little better." M. Renan's preface is a proof that he possesses the good spirits which he notes as an ingredient of his character. He is a *raffiné*, and a raffiné with an extraordinary gift of putting his finger on sensitive spots; with a reasoned ideal of the millennium. But a raffiné without bitterness is a very harmless person.

The first chapters of this volume are not the most vivid, though they contain a very interesting picture of the author's birthplace, the little dead town of Tréguier, a gray cluster of convents and churches on the coast of Catholic Brittany. Tréguier was intensely conventual, and the young Renan was, as a matter of course, predestined to the church. "This strange set of circumstances has given me for historic studies those qualities that I may possess. The essence of criticism is to be able to understand states very different from those in which we live. I have seen the primitive world. In Brittany, before 1830, the most distant past was still alive." The specimens which M. Renan gives of this primitive world are less happily sketched than the general picture; the coloring is rather pale; some of the anecdotes—that of the little Noémi, that of the Bonhomme Système—are perhaps slightly wanting in point. He remarks somewhere, in regard to the opposition, about which so much used to be said, between the classic and the romantic, that, though he fully admits the latter he admits it only as subject—not in the least as a possible form. To his mind there is only one form, which is the classic. And in another place he speaks of Flaubert, the novelist—"ce pauvre Flaubert"—as being quite unable to conceive of anything abstract. Putting these things together, we see a certain reason why M. Renan's personal portraits (with the exception of the picture of himself) should be wanting in reality. They are too general, too white; the author, wonderfully at home in the abstract, has rather neglected the concrete. "Ce pauvre Flaubert" would be revenged for M. Renan's allusion, if it were possible to him to read the episode of the Flax-Grinder—revenged (an exquisite revenge for an artist) by simply finding it flat. It is when he comes to dip into his own spiritual history that M. Renan shows himself a masterly narrator. In that region of abstractions, where the most tangible thing was the palpitating conscience, he moves with the firmest step. The chapters on the two seminaries in which he spent the first years of his residence in Paris, Saint Nicholas du Chardonnet and Saint Sulpice, are full of the most acute notation of moral and intellectual conditions. The little Breton seminarist moved too fast, and, to speak briefly, very soon transcended his instructors. He had a passion for science, and his great aptitude for philology promptly defined itself. He traces with singular art the process by which, young, simple, devout, dedicated to the church from his infancy, the object of maternal and pastoral hopes, he found himself confronted with the fact that he could no longer be a Catholic. He also points out well that it was the rigidity of the Catholic system that made continuance impossible, it being all of one piece, so that dissent as to one point involved rejection of the whole. "It is not my fault if my masters had taught me logic, and by their pitiless argumentations had converted my mind into a steel blade. I took seriously what I had learned— the scholastic philosophy, the rules of the syllogism, theology, Hebrew. I was a good scholar; I can never be damned for that." M. Renan holds, moreover, that little was wasted of his elaborate religious education.

"I left their hands [those of the priests] with a moral sentiment so prepared for every test that Parisian levity could afterwards put a surface on this jewel without hurting it. I was so effectually made up for the good, for the true, that it would have been impossible for me to follow any career not directed to the things of the soul. My masters rendered me so unfit for all temporal work that I was stamped with an irrevocable mark for the spiritual life . . . I persist in believing that existence is the most frivolous thing in the world, if one does not conceive it as a great and continual duty." This moral richness, these spiritual aspirations, of M. Renan's, of which we might quote many other examples, pervade all his utterances, even when they are interfused with susceptibilities which strike us at times as those of a dilettante; with refinements of idealism which suggest to us occasionally that they correspond to no possible reality, and even that the natural corrective for this would be that reality, in some of the forms which we children of less analytic race are obliged to make our peace with it, would impose itself a little more absolutely upon our critic. To what extent M. Renan's nature has been reduplicated, as it were, by his intellectual curiosity may be gathered from his belief, recorded in these pages, that he would have gone much further in the exploration of the universe if he had not taken his inspiration from the historical sciences. "Physiology and the natural sciences would have carried me along; and I may certainly say it, the extreme ardor which these vital sciences excited in my mind makes me believe that if I had cultivated them in a consecutive manner I should have arrived at several of the results of Darwin, of which I had had glimpses . . . I was drawn [instead] toward the historical sciences—little conjectural sciences which are pulled down as often as they are set up, and which will be neglected a hundred years hence." We know not what M. Renan may have missed, and we know not what may be the ultimate fate of historical conjecture and of the hapless literary art, in both of which he so brilliantly excels; but what such a volume as these mingled, but on the whole delightful, Reminiscences represents in the way of attainment, suggestion and sympathy is a sum not easily to be calculated. With his extraordinarily composite nature, his much-embracing culture, he is a most discriminating critic of life. Even his affectations are illuminating, for they are either exaggerations of generosity or ingenuities of resignation.

RENAN'S DIALOGUES AND
PHILOSOPHIC FRAGMENTS*

M. Ernest Renan has just published a new volume, which will not fail to find its way speedily into the hands of all lovers of good writing. A new volume by Renan is an intellectual feast; if he is not the first of French writers, I don't know who may claim the title. In these "Dialogues et Fragments Philosophiques," indeed, it is the dialogues alone that are new; they occupy but half of the volume, the rest of which is composed of reprinted pieces. The dialogues are a sort of *jeu d'esprit*, but a *jeu d'esprit* of a very superior kind—the re-creation of a man of elevated genius. They are prefaced by a few pages breathing a very devoted patriotism, and proving that the author's exorbitant intellectual reveries have not relaxed his sense of the plain duties of citizenship. To win back that esteem which he appears willing to concede that they have in some degree forfeited, he exhorts his fellow-countrymen above all things to work. Let each, he says, surpass himself in his own particular profession, "so that the world may still cry of us, 'These Frenchmen are still the sons of their fathers; eighty years ago Condorcet, in the midst of the Reign of Terror, waiting for death in his hiding-place in the Rue Servandoni, wrote his Sketch of the Progress of the Human Mind.'" M. Renan imagines a group of friends, who assemble in a quiet corner of a park of Versailles, to exchange reflections upon the "ensemble de l'Univers." The subject is extensive, and it may well take half a dozen talkers to cover the ground. Three persons, however, take

***

* *New York Daily Tribune*, Saturday, June 17, 1876. "Letter from Henry James, Jr." (Dated Paris, May 27).

the lead, each one of whom unfolds his particular view of the Cosmos. These three views are classed by M. Renan under the respective heads of "Certainties," "Probabilities," and "Reveries." He disclaims them all as a representation of his own opinions, and says that he has simply entertained himself with imagining what might be urged and argued in each direction. It is probable, however, that if his convictions and feelings are not identical with those of either of his interlocutors, they have a great deal in common with the whole mass of the discussion, and that Philalethes, Theophrastus, and Theoctistes are but names for certain moods of M. Renan's mind. If so, one can only congratulate him upon the extraordinary ingenuity and fertility of his intellect and the entertaining company of his thoughts. These pages are full of good things admirably said, of brilliant and exquisite suggestions, and of happy contributions to human wisdom. Their fault is the fault which for some time has been increasing in M. Renan's writing—a sort of intellectual foppishness, a love of paradox and of distinction for distinction's sake. His great merit has always been his natural distinction, but now, in this same distinction, in the affectation of views which are nothing if not exquisite, views sifted and filtered through an infinite intellectual experience, there is something rather self-conscious and artificial. The reader cannot help wishing that M. Renan might be brought into more immediate contact with general life itself—general life as distinguished from that horizon of pure learning which surrounds the *cabinet de travail* of a Parisian scholar—suspecting that, if this could happen, some of his fine-spun doubts and perplexities would find a very natural solution, and some of his fallacies die a very natural death.

Philalethes, the exponent of M. Renan's "Certainties," is not so certain about some things as his friends might have expected; but his skepticism is narrowed down to a point just fine enough to be graceful. "In fact," he says, "if I had been a priest, I should never have been willing to accept a fee for my mass; I should have been afraid of doing as the shopkeeper who delivers for money an empty bag. Just so I should have had a scruple about drawing a profit from my religious beliefs. I should have been afraid of seeming to distribute false notes and to prevent poor people, by putting them off with dubious hopes, from claiming their portion in this world. These things are substantial enough for us to talk about them, to live by them, to think of them always; but they are not certain enough to enable us to be sure that in pretending to teach them we are not mistaken as to the quality of the goods delivered." Theophrastus, who discourses on "Probabilities," takes, on the whole, a cheerful view of the future—it must be confessed with considerable abatements. He agrees probably in a great measure with Theoctistes, who remarks, "I have never said that the future was cheerful. Who knows whether the truth is not sad?" Theophrastus thinks that the maturity of the world is to arrive by the expansion of science —on condition, indeed, that the mechanical theory of heat succeeds within five or six hundred years in inventing a substitute for coal. If it fails—and the failure is quite probable—"humanity will enter into a sort of mediocrity from which she will hardly have the means to emerge." It must be added that Theophrastus is prepared to see art and beauty (as we have hitherto understood it) disappear; "the day will perhaps come (we already see its dawn) when a great artist, a virtuous man, will be antiquated, almost useless things."

The speculations of Theoctistes, however, are much the most curious. He imagines a development of science so infinite and immeasurable that it will extend our relations beyond the limits of the planet on which we dwell, and he deems the function of this perfected machine to be above all the production of great men. The great men may be so selected and sifted and improved that human perfection may at last concentrate itself in one extremely superior being, who will hold all the universe in cheerful and grateful subordination. This is what Theoctistes calls "God being realized." With these sentiments it is not surprising that he should not expect that God will be realized by a democracy. He gets into deeper water than he can always buffet, but his style is the perfection of expression. I must quote a few lines more. "For myself, I relish the universe through that sort of general sentiment to which we owe it that we are sad in a sad city, gay in a gay city. I enjoy thus the pleasures of those given up to pleasure, the debauchery of the debauchee, the worldliness of the worldling, the holiness of the virtuous man, the meditations of the *savant*, the austerity of the ascetic. By a sort of sweet sympathy I imagine to myself that I am their consciousness. The discoveries of the *savant* are my property; the triumphs of the ambitious are my festival. I should be sorry that anything should be missing in this world; for I have the consciousness of all that it contains. My only displeasure is that the age has fallen so low that it no longer knows how to enjoy. Then I take refuge in the past—in the sixteenth century, in the seventeenth, in antiquity; everything that has been beautiful, amiable, noble, just, makes a sort of paradise for me. With this I defy misfortune to touch me; I carry with me the charming garden of the variety of my thoughts." This paragraph seems to me magnificent; one would like to have written it. The charm of M. Renan's style is hard to define; it is ethereal as a perfume. It is a style above all things urbane, and, with its exquisite form, is suggestive of moral graces, amenity, delicacy, generosity. Now that Sainte-Beuve is dead, it strikes me as the most perfect vehicle of expression actually in operation in France. The only style to be compared to it is that of Mme. Sand; but for pure quality even this must yield the palm. Mme. Sand's style is, after all (with all respect), a woman's style.

TAINE'S ITALY*

A few years since M. Taine, appointed to a professorial chair in the School of Fine Arts in Paris, made a journey to Italy to put himself in the humor for his office. The result, in the course of time, in addition to his lectures, was two large volumes of notes, letters, and journals. The first of these, "Rome and Naples," has just been translated for the American public. Whether it will be largely read in this country we are unable to

---

* *Italy: Rome and Naples.* From the French of H. Taine. By John Durand. (New York: Leypoldt & Holt. 1868).

(The second volume of *Italy* referred to in the text, *Florence and Venice,* was also translated into English by J. Durand.) (*The Nation,* May 7, 1868).

say; but it is certain that M. Taine deserves well of English readers. He is the author of a really valuable history of English literature, and he has taken the trouble to arrive at a more intimate knowledge of the English mind than members of one race often care to possess of the idiosyncrasies of another. Add to this that he is one of the most powerful writers of the day—to our own taste, indeed, the most powerful; the writer of all others who throws over the reader's faculties, for the time, the most irresistible spell, and against whose influence, consequently, the mental reaction is most violent and salutary—and you have an idea of his just claim on your attention. M. Taine's manner and style are extremely individual, and it is somewhat odd that being, as he is, a great stickler, in literary and historical problems, for the credit of national and local influences, he should personally be a signal example of their possible futility. He is scarcely a Frenchman. Not that he is anything else; but he is before all things the brilliant, dogmatic, sombre, and (from a reader's point of view) extremely heartless offspring of his own resolute will. His style, literally translated (and Mr. Durand is very literal), makes very natural English. It has an energy, an impetus, a splendor to which no words of ours can do justice. It is not delicate, courteous, and persuasive like that of several of the most eminent French writers of the day—notably MM. Sainte-Beuve, Renan, and Cousin—it is vehement, impetuous, uncompromising, arrogant—insolent, if you will. The affirmative movement of M. Taine's mind is always a ringing hammer-blow. Every proposition is fastened down with a tenpenny nail. Finally, of course, this is very fatiguing; your head aches with the metallic resonance of the process. It is the climax of dogmatism. There was something ironical in M. Taine's being appointed professor; he was professor from the first, by natural right. His whole tone is didactic; every sentence comes *ex cathedra*. But with the essential energy and originality of his mind he invests the character with a new dignity, and reconciles it to the temperament of a man still young and audacious.

He has, intellectually, nothing of professorial dryness or prudery. Of all writers he is the most broadly picturesque. He throws into his language a wealth of color and a fulness of sound

which would set up in trade a hundred minor poets and story-
tellers. The secret of the power which he exerts on the mind, or
on many minds, at least, we take to be the union of this vast current of imagery, of descriptive vigor and splendor, and of sensuous susceptibility with great logical precision and large erudition. He describes a figure, a costume, a building, a picture, not
only with all the richness of his imagination, but with the authority and *prestige* of his knowledge. The pictorial element in his
style, its color and rythm, is not the substance of his thought, as
in so many charming second-class writers, but its mere vestment
and gait. Nevertheless, we admit that, to our perception, in spite
of his learning, his logic, and his merits as a metaphysician, or
rather an anti-metaphysician (whatever they may be), he remains
pre-eminently an artist, a *writer*. If we had doubted of the truth
of this judgment, we should have been convinced by that singular
work, recently published, "Notes sur Paris: Opinions de M.
Thomas Graindorge." Of feeling in the work there is none; of
ideas there are very few; but of images, pictures, description,
style, a most overwhelming superabundance. The same relation
between the two elements of his genius appears in the "History
of English Literature." In his appreciation of certain writers,
the faculty of perception, apprehension, without being absent,
is quite lost to sight in the energy of the act of portraiture.
There are a series of pages on Shakespeare which, although
full of controvertible propositions and precipitate formulas,
form to our mind a supremely valuable tribute to his genius,
inasmuch as of all attempts to appreciate and measure it they
are the most energetic, unreserved, and eloquent. They form
a direct homage to the immensity of the theme; they are almost
as vast as silence; they are, in short, on the Shakespearian scale.
The nurse of *Juliet* is not assuredly distinguished on the immortal page by a more animated and furious loquacity than M. Taine
exhibits on her behalf. But an example is more conclusive than
our own logic, and we find one to our hand in a striking passage
in the second volume (Florence and Venice) of the "Voyage en
Italie." This passage is interesting as showing, as it seems to us,
the thoroughly unreligious cast of the author's mind (for we
know few writers who appear to find it more natural to speak of

a religion—no matter which—from a distant external standpoint), and then its gravity, melancholy, and hopelessness, and then, finally, its supreme delight in the literary form. It begins, if we are not mistaken, in a moral key, and ends in an artistic one. It is tragical, but it is perfect, consciously perfect. We translate, premising that the author is speaking of the impression produced by certain primitive frescoes in various Italian churches, buried under the work of later painters, and restored to light by the excavation, as one may call it, of the subsequent applications of color:

"You raise your eyes then and find before you the four edifices of old Pisa, lonely on a square where the grass grows, with the dead paleness of their marbles outlined against the blue divine. What a mass of ruins; what a cemetery is history! How many human palpitations, of which there remains no trace but a form imprinted on a block of stone! What a careless smile is that of the peaceful sky; and what a cruel beauty dwells in that luminous dome, stretched over the decease of successive generations like a canopy at a common burial! We have read these ideas in books, and with the pride of youth we have treated them as mere talk; but when a man has gone over half of his career, and, retiring within himself, he counts up all the ambitions he has strangled, all the hopes he has plucked up, all the dead things he carries in his heart; the magnificence and the hardness of nature appear to him at once, and the heavy sob of his inward obsequies suggests to him a deeper lamentation—that of the great human tragedy which unfolds itself from age to age to lay low so many strugglers in a single tomb. He stops, feeling upon his own head, as upon that of others, the hand of the fateful powers, and comprehends his condition. This humanity, of which he is a member, has its image in the 'Niobe' of Florence. Around her, her daughters and her sons, all her loved ones, fall unceasingly beneath the bolts of invisible archers. One of them is prostrate on his back, his bosom tremulous with a piercing wound; another, still living, lifts her useless hands toward the celestial murderers; the youngest hides her head in the robe of her mother. She, meanwhile, cold and still, erects herself hopeless, and, with her eyes raised to heaven, gazes with wonder and horror upon the dazzling, deathly nimbus, the outstretched arms, the inevitable arrows, and the implacable serenity of the gods."

M. Taine may certainly be said to belong to the materialist school of thinkers. He is no sentimentalist; in the way of sentiment he rarely treats us to anything lighter than the passage just quoted. To his perception man is extremely interesting as an object of study, but he is without sanctity or mystery of any sort. He takes a positive satisfaction in reminding the reader of the purely objective and finite character of his organization, and he uses for this purpose a special vocabulary. "La tragédie, la comédie humaine," "la colonie humaine," "la plante humaine," "la machine humaine," these expressions continually recur. M. Taine, in effect, studies man as a plant or as a machine. You obtain an intimate knowledge of the plant by a study of the soil and climate in which it grows, and of the machine by taking it apart and inspecting its component pieces. M. Taine applies this process to the human mind, to history, art, and literature, with the most fruitful results. The question remains, indeed, with each reader as to whether, as the author claims, the description covers all the facts; as to whether his famous theory of *la race, le milieu, le moment* is an adequate explanation of the various complications of any human organism—his own (the reader's) in particular. But he will be willing, at least, to admit that the theory makes incomparable observers, and that in choosing a travelling companion he cannot do better than take him from the school of M. Taine. For, in fact, you can do your own moralizing and sentimentalizing; you can draw your own inferences and arrange your own creed; what you wish in a companion, a guide, is to help you accumulate *data,* to call your attention to facts. The present writer observes everything, and selects and describes the best.

M. Taine rapidly traversed Italy, and began his journey at Naples upward. The early portion of his book is pervaded by that strong feeling of joy natural to an ardent dogmatist at the prospect of an unexplored field. He describes the city of Naples with singular vividness; its radiant, transparent, natural loveliness, the latent tokens of its pure Greek origin, the traces of the Spanish dominion, the splendor and squalor, the sensuality in manners and art and religion. Nothing grand, nothing Gothic (even remotely, as in Northern Italy), nothing impressive and mysterious. Parisian light and gorgeousness, and careless joyousness and superstition, form the substance of his impressions. Having described a church bedizened with a wilderness of florid ornament in the artificial Italian style of the seventeenth century, he opens a vista to thought at the close of the chapter by touching with eloquent brevity upon a passionate and sombre Spanish painting: "The breath of the great period still stirs the machine; it is Euripides, if it is no longer Sophocles. Some of the pieces are splendid; among others, 'A Descent from the Cross,' of Ribera. The sun struck upon the head of Christ through the half-drawn curtain of red silk. The darksome background seemed the more mournful beside this sudden radiance of luminous flash, and the dolorous Spanish coloring; the expression, here mystical, there violent, of the passionate figures in the shadow gave to the scene the aspect of a vision, such as used to people the monastic, chivalrous brain of a Calderon or a Lope." These few lines are assuredly picturesque writing; but it seems to us that they serve to illustrate the difference between the picturesque as practiced by a writer with his facts in hand, and one who has nothing but fancies. At Naples, however, M. Taine found but few paintings, and these were to be his principal concern. *En revanche,* he gives us, *apropos* of the Greek and Roman relics of the neighborhood, some admirable pages on "Homeric Life and the City of Antiquity." It is not until he reaches Rome, Florence, and Venice that he really plunges into his subject. Here we are unable to follow him. We can only recommend him to the attentive perusal of all persons interested in the history of art, and gratified by the spectacle of an indefatigable critical *verve.* M. Taine is guilty, doubtless, of many errors of judgment; but we strongly suspect that the great masters—Michael Angelo, Raphael, Leonardo, and Titian—have never been more correctly, as well as more ardently, estimated. Several of the great painters of the second rank—notably, Veronese and Tintoretto—are celebrated with a splendor of coloring and a breadth of design which recall the aspect of their own inmortal works. Finally, we cannot help laying down our conviction that M. Taine's two volumes form a truly great production; great not in a moral sense, and very possibly not in a philosophical, but appreciably great as a contribution to literature and history. One feels at moments as if, before this writer, there had been no critics, no travellers, observers, or aesthetic inquisitors. This is, of course, a mistake, and we shall like no genuine critic the less (we personally, on the contrary, from the character of our sympathies, feel that we shall like him the more) for giving M. Taine his liberal dues. It is inexpressibly gratifying,—fortifying, one may say—to see a writer, *armé en guerre*, fling himself into his subject with such energy, such fury. It is an admirable intellectual feat. M. Taine is a representative of pure intellect, and he exhibits the necessarily partial character of all purely intellectual estimates. But there are days when we resort instinctively to an intellectual standpoint. On such days our author is excellent reading.

TAINE'S NOTES ON ENGLAND*

Now that by the issue of an English version of his "English Literature" M. Taine has been made one of the topics of the day, this volume of "Notes on England" may expect a double welcome. Offering, as it does, a glimpse of the documents and materials on which the "History" rests, it is a valuable complementary sequel to that work. These notes were taken, the author informs us in a short preface, during two visits, in 1861 and 1862; they have been revised and modified from the impressions of a visit last year, and, as they stand, they present an extremely copious and comprehensive record of personal experience.

The reader's foremost impression will be that the author is a singularly vigilant and methodical observer. His note-book

* *Notes sur l'Angleterre*. Par H. Taine, Paris. Hachette. 1872.

(This work was translated by W. F. Rae and published with his Introductory chapter in 1874, in New York by Henry Holt & Co. Taine refers to Fraser Rae's "very kindly" preface. *Life and Letters of H. Taine* Part III, p. 89.) (*The Nation*, January 25, 1872).

is never out of his hand, and facts, facts, is his constant demand. His work fairly bristles with them; his constant effort is to resolve his impression into a positive and definite statement. "I continue," he somewhere says, "to jot down conversations; nothing seems to me so pleasant as an evening passed in this way, with one or two interlocutors who are sincere, obliging, and unprejudiced, who have seen life and the world; national conceit does not interfere; you talk to learn, not to contend or shine. You venture to give the little characteristic fact, the precise, telling detail; each offers, as briefly as he can, the best of his experience . . . My mind has never fed so largely nor so well; I remained catechizing and listening till one o'clock in the morning." And again: "When I feel an inference beginning to take shape in my mind, I carry it to two or three English friends who have travelled; I submit it to their judgment; we reason about it; it comes out of the discussion corrected or developed, and the next day I write it down as it stands." As to the value of some of M. Taine's inferences there will be various opinions, but his manner is the right manner, and his temper is excellent.

He begins with the *dehors*—the outside look of things; and by the energy and vivacity of his pictorial faculty reminds us afresh of what we have formerly suspected—that descriptive and not philosophical writing is his strong point. He visits docks and workhouses and churches; he goes to the Derby, walks the streets, and lounges indefatigably in the parks; questions, converses, gazes, crowds item upon item. The climate seems to him detestable; he returns to it again and again with undiminished hostility, and exhausts his vocabulary in the attempt to express its abominations. We think that he exaggerates its influence as a factor in English character; but correctness here is a matter of degree. One thing certainly may be said; that if national temper is the product of external influences to the extent contended for by M. Taine, a larger sense of external beauty than he recognizes would have been apportioned to the English; for their climate, if not the most cheerful, is surely the most picturesque and, so to speak, the most pictorial in Europe. For a single "effect" in landscape and interior scenery produced in France or Italy at a given moment by the play of light and shade, there are a hundred in England. There is a hiatus here, as at various other points in M. Taine's reasoning. The moist, darksome, shifting, marine atmosphere which in his theory helps so largely to account for the idiosyncrasies of the Flemish and Dutch painters—their lowness of tone, their patient science and finish—has produced under English conditions the gaudiest school of art in Europe—a school in which color is nothing if not "telling," and in which, as a general thing, science and finish are conspicuously absent. In fact, we imagine foreign observers are apt to lapse into an easy fallacy as regards the English climate. There is, in the first place, the peculiar atmospheric medium of London, Liverpool, and Manchester—a monstrous and indefinable compound of fog and coal smoke and the myriad fine exhalations of serried hundreds of thousands of human creatures, half of them the most squalid in the world; then there is, in the second place, the English climate proper—the climate of villages and lanes and parks, of the whole vast world of English ruralism, and this, to the eye of sense (putting aside the eye of sentiment), fairly swarms with aesthetic suggestions. On the whole, M. Taine finds little beauty in the outward aspect of English life. He is overwhelmed, like most foreigners, with the massiveness and hugeness and multitudinousness of the material civilization, and he is struck, like Hawthorne, with a certain broad analogy between the English and the Romans of the Empire. The same vast and multifarious needs, gratified on the same huge scale—in the one case by conquest, in the other by industry; the same immense development of practical and material resources. The Crystal Palace at Sydenham, with its gigantic aggregation of specimens and trophies and pastimes, vividly recalls the traditional image of the baths and circuses and museums of the antique sovereign people. The want of taste is the salient fact: if it strikes an American, it must doubly offend a Frenchman; and it finds its most powerful expression in the costume of the women. "Their excessive overdress suggests the *lorette* or the *parvenue;* one is amazed to see reputable young women decked out in such a fashion. At Hyde Park, on Sunday, among the ladies and the young girls of the wealthy middle-class, the intemperance of dress is shocking; bonnets like piled-up tufts of rhododendrons, or

53

else of snowy whiteness and extraordinary smallness, with bundles
of red flowers and enormous ribbons; dresses of shiny violet silk,
with dazzling reflections, or of stiff tulle on a roundabout cage
of petticoats bristling with embroidery; immense shawls of black
lace falling to the heels, gloves of spotless white or of vivid purple;
chains of gold, belts of gold, with buckles of gold; hair falling in a
shining mass upon the back . . . Their heads are stiff on their
necks, like those of beadles in a church-march; their hair is
either plastered flat or excessively undone." And on top of all
this, no grace of movement. To the beauty of Englishwomen the
author in various other places does ample justice, and of their
moral graces, their steadfastness, their devotion, their precious
domestic virtues, he seems to have formed a most flattering opinion. But as to their social faculty he makes the following happy
discrimination:

"According to C., an Englishwoman is incapable of presiding in a drawing-room (*tenir un salon*) as skillfully as a
Frenchwoman; he knows but two or three women in this
country who could. The Englishwoman lacks the tact, the
promptitude, the pliancy, to enable her to accommodate
herself to people and things, to vary her greeting, to catch
a hint, slip in a compliment, make each guest the object of
a particular welcome. She is only affable; she has nothing
but kindness and calmness. For myself, I ask nothing more,
and I imagine nothing better. But it is plain that a woman
of the world, a woman who desires to make her house a
favored and valued place of reunion for distinguished people
of all kinds, has need of a talent more complex and more
delicate. C. vastly admires the ease with which, with us, a
young wife learns the world. A month after her marriage,
she knows how to do the honors of her home to all comers;
and, in the same way, a little *bourgeoise* takes her place at
the desk in the shop the day after her wedding, catches the
trick of the trade, talks, smiles, keeps customers. I saw the
contrast at Dieppe, in a restaurant. The husband, a Frenchman, always *empressé* and smiling, circulated among the
tables with all kinds of civilities, and seemed to be waiting
on people for his pleasure; the wife, an Englishwoman, stiff

and serious, said in icy tones to people as they rose from the table, '*Havé-vo payé, mosieur?*' "

For certain elderly gentlewomen of England he professes an especial relish. Here is a passage which at once expresses it, and indicates his admirable faculty for presenting his impressions as pictures:

"Two of these aged ladies have remained in my mind as a fine Dutch picture. It was in the country, in a lofty parlor, upholstered in white and pearl-gray; the high light was softened by the evening shadows. The broad middle window jutted out upon a series of flower-beds, showing masses of verdure through its brilliant panes. On a chair, near the light, a young girl—fair, intelligent, and cold—sat reading a little religious treatise. In the middle, two old ladies, before a tea table, entertained their guest. Faces with large features, serene, decided, even imperious; in this single point they differed from the Flemish portraits. For dress, gowns of black silk, in large folds, lace at the throat and at the wrists, rich gauze caps, with streamers, white embroideries at the bosom, as in the figures of Mierevelt; the combination of severity and opulence which is displeasing in the adornments of the younger woman harmonized with their age and their gravity. Around them, the signs of ample fortune, unquestioned position, a well-balanced mind, a healthy soul, a worthy life."

Upon education there is a very interesting chapter, especially in its remarks on the public schools and on Oxford. English children seem to him essentially different from French—the grand distinction being that, as regards boys especially, there is no definite line of division, as in France, between the moral life of the child and that of the grown man. "School and society are on a level, without intermediate wall or moat: one prepares for the other and leads into it, and the boy enters life not from a forcing-house and special atmosphere . . . The French collegian is *ennuyé*, embittered, over-refined, precocious—too precocious; he is kept in a cage, and his imagination ferments." The relation between English parents and children puzzles him, as it does most foreigners. The apparently reckless multiplication of offspring, the necessity not only of sons but of daughters shifting for themselves, the want of sentimental confidence between mothers and sons, are all at variance with French tradition. As to French habits under this last head, he mentions some facts which the unregenerate Anglo-Saxon mind hardly knows whether to pronounce very nice or (as Charles Lamb says) very nasty. He closes his account of Oxford with a reflection which admits us vividly into a certain bitter and, as it were, tragical phase of an intelligent Frenchman's consciousness—words which suggest afresh what so frequently occurs to students of French literature, that the rays of the sun of "glory" must, after all, be rather chilling ones:

"I visit [at Oxford] two or three of the professors' residences; some recalling old French *hôtels,* others modern and delightful, all with gardens and flowers, outlooks noble or graceful. In the very oldest, beneath the portraits of former occupants, are gathered all the elements of modern comfort. I compare them to those of our *savants*—denlike lodgings in some third story, in a great city, or to the gloomy quarters of the Sorbonne, and I think of the meagre, colorless aspect of our Collége de France. Poor French! poor, indeed, living here and there as we can! We are of yesterday; we have been ruined from father to son by Louis XIV., XV., by the Revolution, by the Empire. We had pulled down, and had to make over all things anew. Here the generation that follows never breaks with the generation that precedes; institutions are reformed by superposition, and the present, resting on the past, continues it."

Both the interest of M. Taine's work and the rigor of his method reach their climax in his chapter on "The English Mind." He has collected here a number of suggestive facts—such facts as a society rarely disengages by any spontaneous attempt at self-analysis, and for which it is generally indebted to the fresher vision of an alien. His main impression is that the characteristic English mind is indifferent and even hostile to ideas, and finds its almost exclusive pabulum in facts. The inside of an English head is like one of Murray's guide-books, crammed with facts,

figures, statistics, maps, bits of historical information, useful
moral admonitions; it lacks *vues d'ensemble*, spontaneity of
thought, the general harmonizing action of a sense of style and
form. Society furnishes the young Englishman when he enters it
with ready-made moulds (*cadres*) of thought; the religion is reasonable, the constitution excellent; the great lines of belief are
distinctly traced. The author says elsewhere, we remember, that
the Englishman who begins life finds on all things ready-made
answers; the young Frenchman nothing but ready-made doubts.
To theories, inferences, conclusions, to the more or less irresponsible play of conjecture, opinion, and invention, the Englishman
turns the cold shoulder. His power of conclusion strikes the
author as strangely unproportioned to his rate of information.
M. Taine cites as an example a letter in Carlyle's "Life of Sterling," written by Sterling from the West Indies to his mother
immediately after a fierce tornado had ravaged his estate and
almost destroyed his house. The writer is an author, a poet, a man
of fancy, but he confines himself to a naked statement of facts;
he accumulates details, he draws a diagram, he suggests Gulliver
and Robinson Crusoe. The point with M. Taine is that he makes
no phrases, no attempt to embroider, generalize, or round off
his picture. And this love of facts is the more striking, as it includes the taste for moral as well as material facts. M. Taine mentions two letters shown him by an English lady, from two young
friends recently married, each considering herself the happiest
woman in the world. One of these ladies gives an exhaustive account of her material circumstances—of her husband's appearance,
manners, temper, of their house, their neighbors, their expenditure, their whole external economy. The other traces, in equal
detail, the moral history of her courtship and honeymoon, and
reveals a singular aptitude for psychological observation. The
clearness, directness, and simplicity of each letter is the same;
each is a string of special facts, without a hint of general reflection or conception.

M. Taine touches further upon the comparative paucity in
English speech of abstract words and general terms. Nothing is
more natural in French than such a formula as *le vrai, le beau et
le bien;* nothing is less a matter of course in English than to

allude to the True, the Beautiful, and the Good. M. Taine, we suppose, pretends here to be dealing only with those straws which show how the wind blows, so that we may suggest a case even more in point—the common currency in French speech of the term *la femme,* as compared with its English analogue. For twenty times that this agreeable entity figures in an average French conversation, it puts in but the shadow of an appearance in an English one. M. Taine's theory may be infinitely fortified by special examples, and Americans, as a general thing, if they are not sensibly more furnished with the conceptive turn of mind, as we may roughly term it, than the English, are sufficiently less oppressed by that indefinable social proscription which, in England, weighs upon the jauntily-theorizing tendency, to feel a certain kindly fellowship with our author in his effort to establish his distinction. There is that in the walk and conversation of the average self-respecting Briton which denotes the belief that it is a sign of inferior, or at best of foreign, breeding to indulge, in the glow of conversational confidence, the occasional impulse to extemporize a picturesque formula, or to harmonize fact with fact by the plastic solvent of an "idea." This idiosyncrasy, definitely stated, however, belongs to that class of allegations which immediately evokes as large a body of contradictory as of confirmatory testimony; and to our minds a juster, or at least a simpler, expression of the prime intellectual difference between the English and French is to be found in their unequal apportionment of the sense of form and shape. The French possess that lively aesthetic conscience which, on the whole, is such a simplifier. Upon this point our author also touches: "In our magazines an article, even on science or on political economy, should have an exordium, a peroration, an architecture; there occur few in the *Revue des Deux Mondes* which are not preceded by a sort of porch of general ideas." That quality of the English mind on which M. Taine most insists—its imaginative force— might seem in some degree to undermine this charge of the want of intellectual agility; but in English imaginations it is the moral leaven that works most strongly; their home is the realm of psychology, and their fondest exercise not the elaboration of theories, but the exposition of the facts of human character, the mysteries and secrets of conscience and the innumerable incidents of life. The English genius for psychological observation has no correlative in France. Its vast range is indicated, in M. Taine's opinion, by that delicate scrutiny of the childish mind effected by so many English-writing novelists—Dickens, George Eliot, the author of the "Wide, Wide World." We may say, on the other hand, however, that the enquiry has perhaps been pushed at one end to its undue curtailment at the other. If there are no David Copperfields nor Tom Tullivers in French literature, there are no Madame Bovarys, Jacques, no Mauprats in English.

It is in fiction and in painting that this characteristic comes out most strongly; and upon the English school of art M. Taine has several very interesting pages. The absence of form, of the sense of design and of beauty, and the rich suggestiveness on the moral and sentimental line, seem to him here equally conspicuous. He professes a deep though restricted relish for Wilkie and Mulready, Landseer and Leslie:

"It is impossible to be more expressive, to expend more effort to address the mind through the senses, to illustrate an idea or a truth, to collect into a surface of twelve square inches a closer group of psychological observations. What patient and penetrating critics! What connoisseurs of man! . . . I find here and there masterpieces of this kind—that of Johnston, for example—'Lord and Lady Russell receiving the Sacrament.' Lord Russell is about to ascend the scaffold; his wife looks at him full in the face to learn if he is reconciled with God. This intense gaze of the wife and Christian is admirable; she is satisfied now of her husband's salvation. What a pity that it should have been painted instead of being written!"

The reader who remembers the work in question (at Kensington) will agree that it is a singularly characteristic mixture of sentimental delicacy and pictorial ineffectiveness. We refer him to the author's remarks on the further idiosyncrasies of English art and on Mr. Ruskin's theories. They will yield some of the elements of that critical corrective without which Ruskin is so erratic, and with which he is so profitable, a monitor. The art in which the English have best succeeded is that of poetry; the deep impressibility of the moral *ego* feeds the sources of their verse with unequalled generosity:

> "No poetry equals theirs, speaks so strongly and distinctly to the soul, moves it more to the depths, carries in its diction a heavier burden of meaning, reflects better the shocks and the strivings of our inward being, grasps the mind more potently and effectively, and draws from the innermost chords of personality sounds so magnificent and so searching."

The reader will be surprised after this handsome compliment to find M. Taine citing "Aurora Leigh" with infinite admiration as a representative English poem. This choice is a capital example of that want of *initiation* which his history so constantly betrays, of his insensibility to the color and mystery, as we may say, of English diction, and of his consequent failure to apprehend the native code of æsthetics and do justice to a whole great province of the English mind. This province he has hardly visited; he might have gathered there on the outskirts many a Tennysonian, a Wordsworthian, or even a Byronic lyric, telling more in its twenty lines of the real genius of English verse than Mrs. Browning in her twenty thousand. Mrs. Browning, however, was certainly a poet of English temper, and we have no desire to cut the ground from under the feet of genuine admiration.

M. Taine, reviewing his impressions, briefly concludes that the English are better off than the French in three main points: the stability and liberality of their political system; the morality and healthy tone of their religion; the extent of their acquired wealth, and their greater ease in acquiring and producing. Against these advantages he places in France: the better climate; the more equal distribution of property; and the *vie de famille et de société*. You have in France the immense advantage that—

> "In talk, you can say anything—go to the end of your story or your theory. Fiction, criticism, art, philosophy, and general curiosity are not shackled, as on the other side of the Channel, by religion, morality, and the official proprieties. . . . These differences make the English stronger, the French happier."

A very obvious remark is that if, just now, the French can manage to be happy, we can but wonder and admire. But, in fact, French optimism has been pretty rudely tested through the whole course of French history. The "spirit of conversation" apparently holds its own. May it still stand firm and continue to produce talents as vigorous, as living, as national as that of M. Taine!

TAINE'S ENGLISH LITERATURE

We hesitate to express perfect satisfaction at the appearance of an English version of M. Taine's massive essay.* On the one hand, the performance is no more than a proper compliment to a highly complimentary work; but, on the other, it involves so effective a violation of the spirit of that work and so rude a displacement of its stand-point, as to interfere with a just comprehension of it. M. Taine himself, however, stands sponsor in a short Preface, and the liberal reception of the two volumes seems to indicate that English readers are not sensible of having unduly lost by the transfer. The English version may fairly demand success on its own merits, being careful, exact, and spirited. It errs, we think, on the side of a too literal exactness, through which it frequently ceases to be idiomatic. "He tore from his vitals, . . ." for instance, "the idea which he had conceived," would render M. Taine's figure better than "he tore from his *entrails*." And it is surely in strong contradiction to the author's portrait of Lord Macaulay to translate his allusion to the great historian's *physionomie animée et pensante* by "an animated and pensive face." No one, we fancy, not even M. Taine, ever accused Lord Macaulay of being pensive.

M. Taine's work is a history of our literature only in a partial sense of the term. "Just as astronomy," he says, "is at bottom a problem in mechanics, and physiology a problem in chemistry,

---

* *History of English Literature.* By H. A. Taine. Translated by H. Van Laun. New York: Holt and Williams. 1871. (*Atlantic Monthly,* April 1872).

so history at bottom is a problem in psychology." His aim has been "to establish the psychology of a people." A happier title for his work, therefore, save for its amplitude, would be, "A Comparative Survey of the English Mind in the leading Works of its Literature." It is a picture of the English intellect, with literary examples and allusions in evidence, and not a record of works nor an accumulation of facts. To philological or biographical research it makes no claim. In this direction it is altogether incomplete. Various important works are unmentioned, common tradition as to facts is implicitly accepted, and dates, references, and minor detail conspicuous by their absence. The work is wholly critical and pictorial, and involves no larger information than the perusal of a vast body of common documents. Its purpose is to discover in the strongest features of the strongest works the temper of the race and time; which involves a considerable neglect not only of works, but of features. But what is mainly to the point with the English reader (as it is of course excessively obvious in the English version) is that M. Taine writes from an avowedly foreign stand-point. The unit of comparison is throughout assumed to be the French mind. The author's undertaking strikes us, therefore, constantly as an *excursion*. It is not as if he and our English tongue were old friends, as if through a taste early formed and long indulged he had gradually been won to the pious project of paying his debt and embodying his impressions; but as if rather, on reaching his intellectual majority and coming into a handsome property of doctrine and dogma, he had cast about him for a field to conquer, a likely subject for experiment, and, measuring the vast capacity of our English record of expression, he had made a deliberate and immediate choice. We may fancy him declaring, too, that he would do the thing handsomely; devote five or six years to it, and spend five or six months in the country. He has performed his task with a vigor proportionate to this sturdy resolve; but in the nature of the case his treatment of the subject lacks that indefinable quality of spiritual initiation which is the tardy consummate fruit of a wasteful, purposeless, passionate sympathy. His opinions are prompted, not by a sentiment, but by a design. He remains an interpreter of the English mind to the mind of another race; and only re-

motely, therefore,—only by allowance and assistance,—an interpreter of the English mind to itself. A greater fault than any of
his special errors of judgment is a certain reduced, contracted,
and limited air in the whole field. He has made his subject as
definite as his method.

M. Taine is fairly well known by this time as a man with a
method, the apostle of a theory,—the theory that "vice and virtue
are products, like vitriol and sugar," and that art, literature, and
conduct are the result of forces which differ from those of the
physical world only in being less easily ascertainable. His three
main factors—they have lately been reiterated to satiety—are the
race, the medium, and the time. Between them they shape the
phenomena of history. We have not the purpose of discussing this
doctrine; it opens up a dispute as ancient as history itself,—the
quarrel between the minds which cling to the supernatural and
the minds which dismiss it. M. Taine's originality is not in his
holding of these principles, but in his lively disposition to apply
them, or, rather, in the very temper and terms in which he applies
them. No real observer but perceives that a group of works is
more or less the product of a "situation," and that as he himself
is forever conscious of the attrition of infinite waves of circumstance, so the cause to which, by genius as by "fate," he contributes, is a larger deposit in a more general current. Observers
differ, first, as to whether there are elements in the deposit which
cannot be found in the current; second, as to the variety and
complexity of the elements: maintaining, on the one side, that
fairly to enumerate them and establish their mutual relations
the vision of science is as yet too dim; and, on the other, that
a complete analysis is at last decently possible, and with it a
complete explanation. M. Taine is an observer of the latter
class; in his own sole person indeed he almost includes it. He
pays in his Preface a handsome tribute to the great service rendered by Sainte-Beuve to the new criticism. Now Sainte-Beuve
is, to our sense, the better apostle of the two. In purpose the least
doctrinal of critics, it was by his very horror of dogmas, moulds,
and formulas, that he so effectively contributed to the science of
literary interpretation. The truly devout patience with which
he kept his final conclusion in abeyance until after an exhaus-

tive survey of the facts, after perpetual returns and ever-deferred farewells to them, is his living testimony to the importance of the facts. Just as he could never reconcile himself to saying his last word on book or author, so he never pretended to have devised a method which should be a key to truth. The truth for M. Taine lies stored up, as one may say, in great lumps and blocks, to be released and detached by a few lively hammer-blows; while for Sainte-Beuve it was a diffused and imponderable essence, as vague as the carbon in the air which nourishes vegetation, and, like it, to be disengaged by patient chemistry. His only method was fairly to dissolve his attention in the sea of circumstance surrounding the object of his study, and we cannot but think his frank provisional empiricism more truly scientific than M. Taine's premature philosophy. In fact, M. Taine plays fast and loose with his theory, and is mainly successful in so far as he is inconsequent to it. There is a constantly visible hiatus between his formula and his application of it. It serves as his badge and motto, but his best strokes are prompted by the independent personal impression. The larger conditions of his subject loom vaguely in the background, like a richly figured tapestry of good regulation pattern, gleaming here and there in the author's fitful glance, and serving a picturesque purpose decidedly more than a scientific one. This is especially noticeable in the early chapters of the present work, where the changes are rung to excess upon a note of rather slender strain,—the common "Gothic" properties of history and fiction,—Norse blood, gloomy climate, ferocious manners, considered as shaping forces. The same remark applies, we imagine, to the author's volumes on Italy, where a thin soil of historical evidence is often made to produce some most luxuriant flowers of deduction. The historical position is vague, light, and often insecure, and the author's passage from the general conditions to the particular case is apt to be a flying leap of fancy, which, though admirable writing, is rather imperfect science.

We of course lack space to discuss his work in its parts. His portrayal of authors and works is always an attempt to fix the leading or motive faculty, and through his neglect of familiar details and his amplification of the intellectual essence which is the object of his search, his figures often seem out of drawing to English eyes. He distorts the outline, confounds the light and shade, and alters the coloring. His judgments are sometimes very happy and sometimes very erroneous. He proposes some very wise amendments to critical tradition; in other cases he enforces the common verdict with admirable point and vigor. For Spenser, for instance, we doubt whether the case has ever been stated with a more sympathetic and penetrating eloquence. His errors and misjudgments arise partly from his being so thoroughly a stranger to what we may call the intellectual climate of our literature, and partly from his passionate desire to simplify his conception and reduce it to the limits, not merely of the distinctly knowable, but of the symmetrically and neatly presentable. The leading trait of his mind, and its great defect, is an inordinate haste to conclude, combined with a passion for a sort of largely pictorial and splendidly comprehensive expression. A glance at the list of his works will show how actively he has kept terms with each of these tendencies. He is, to our sense, far from being a man of perceptions; the bent of his genius seems to be to generate ideas and images on two distinct lines. For ourselves, on the whole, we prefer his images. These are immensely rich and vivid, and on this side the author is a great artist. His constant effort is to reconcile and harmonize these groups, and make them illumine and vivify each other. Where he succeeds his success is admirable, and the reader feels that he has rarely seen a truth so completely presented. Where he fails the violence of his diction only serves to emphasize the inadequacy of his conception. M. Taine's great strength is to be found close to his eminent fallibility as a critic,— in his magnificent power of eloquent and vivid statement and presentation. His style is admirable; we know of none that is at once more splendid and more definite, that has at once more structure and more color. Just as his natural preference is evidently for energy and vehemence in talent, his own movement is toward a sort of monstrous cumulative violence of expression; to clinch, to strike, to hit hard, to hit again, till the idea rings and resounds, to force color *à l'outrance* and make proportion massive, is his notion of complete utterance. This is productive of many effects splendid in themselves, but it is fatal to truth in so far as truth resides in fine shades and degrees.

In this intense constructive glow, M. Taine quite forgets his subject and his starting-point; the impetus of his rhetoric, the effort to complete his picture and reach forward to the strongest word and the largest phrase, altogether absorbs him. For ourselves, we confess that, as we read, we cease to hold him at all rigidly to his premises, and content ourselves with simply enjoying the superb movement of his imagination, thankful when it lights his topic at all truly, and mainly conscious of its radiance as color, heat, and force. Thus, while as a gallery of portraits the work demands constant revision and correction, as a sort of enormous *tableau vivant*, ingeniously and artificially combined, it is extremely rich and various. A phrase of very frequent occurrence with M. Taine, and very wholesome in its frequency, is *la grande invention;* his own tendency is to practise it. In effort and inclination, however, he is nothing if not impartial; and there is something almost touching in the sympathetic breadth of his admiration for a tone of genius so foreign to French tradition as the Scriptural inspiration of Bunyan and Milton. To passionate vigor he always does justice. On the other hand, when he deals with a subject simply because it stands in his path, he is far less satisfactory. His estimate of Swift is a striking example of his tendency to overcharge his portrait and make a picture at all hazards. Swift was a bitter and incisive genius, but he had neither the volume nor the force implied in M. Taine's report of him. We might add a hundred instances of the fatally defective perception of "values," as the painters say, produced by the author's foreign standpoint. M. Taine expresses altogether the "Continental" view of Byron, between which and the English view there is much the same difference as between the estimate Byron courted and the estimate he feared. A hundred special points may be conceded; but few modern Englishmen are prepared to accept him, as a whole, as the consistently massive phenomenon described by M. Taine. Touching the later poets, the author is extremely incomplete and fallacious; he pretends, indeed, merely to sketch general tendencies. On Wordsworth, however, he has some pertinent remarks from that protesting man-of-the-world point of

view to which the great frugal bard drives most Englishmen for
desperate refuge, let alone an epigrammatic Frenchman. We are
tempted to say that a Frenchman who should have twisted himself into a relish for Wordsworth would almost have forfeited
our respect. On Thackeray and Dickens he has two chapters of
great suggestiveness to those who know the authors, but on the
whole of excessively contracted outline. Of course, one cannot
pronounce upon important literary figures, of whatever dimensions, without a certain work of elimination; but a valid charge
against M. Taine is that, whereas your distinctly sensitive critic
finds this process to be an effort, M. Taine has the air of finding
it a relief. A compromise is perfectly legitimate so long as it is
not offered as a synthesis.

With all abatements, and especially in spite of one most important abatement, M. Taine's work remains a very admirable
performance. As a philosophical effort it is decidedly a failure;
as the application of a theory it is ineffective; but it is a great
literary achievement. The fruit of an extremely powerful, viva-
cious, and observant mind, it is rich in suggestive sidelights and
forcible aids to opinion. With a great many errors of detail, as
a broad expression of the general essence of the English genius
it seems to us equally eloquent and just. M. Taine has felt this
genius with an intensity and conceived it with a lucidity which,
in themselves, form a great intellectual feat. Even under this head
the work is not conclusive in the sense in which the author ten-
ders it, but it is largely and vividly contributive, and we shall
wait till we have done better ourselves before we judge it too
harshly. It is, in other words, very entertaining provisional criticism and very perfect final art. It is, indeed, a more significant
testimony to the French genius than to the English, and bears
more directly upon the author's native literature than on our
own. In its powerful, though arbitrary, unity of composition, in
its sustained æsthetic temper, its brilliancy, variety, and sym-
metry, it is a really monumental accession to a literature which,
whatever its limitations in the reach of its ideas, is a splendid
series of masterly compositions.

TAINE'S NOTES ON PARIS*

This is a very clever work, but it is by no means one of the author's most successful. Indeed, though a brilliant failure, no one, we believe, has ever pretended that it was anything but a failure. The author has tried a *tour de force*, and missed his effect. He has attempted to force his talent, but his talent has resisted and proved fatally inflexible. He has wished to be light and graceful, but he has succeeded only in being most elaborately and magnificently grave. For M. Taine to attempt lightness was, it seems to us, a most ill-advised undertaking. It is true that he has been charged, as the historian of English literature, with a certain presumptuous levity of judgment; but in form, at least, he is always solid, weighty, and majestic. There are few writers whom, as simple writers, we prefer; his style is full of color and muscle and savor; but we never suppose ourselves, in reading it, to be dabbling in light literature, and we rarely take it but in moderate quantities at a sitting. If M. Taine treats a subject at all, he bears heavily; the touch-and-go manner is a closed book to him. Here he has tried the touch-and-go manner, and the effect is very much like hearing a man with a deep bass voice trying to sing an air written for a thin tenor. There is such a thing as being too serious to succeed in a *jeu d'esprit,* and this has been M. Taine's trouble. A writer of half the value would have done much better with the same material, and, indeed, we remember that at the same time that M. Taine's work appeared, eight years ago, and was voted by all good critics a rather melancholy mistake, M. Gustave Droz was making his literary fortune with 'Monsieur, Madame et Bébé,' being acknowledged to have hit the nail on the head with his little silver hammer far more justly than the historian of English literature with his formidable battering-ram. Yet one reads the book, as a failure if not as success, and, all abatements made, we feel ourselves to be dealing with a man of extraordinary talent. It is very possible that

* *Notes on Paris.* The Life and Opinions of M. Frederic Thomas Graindorge, etc. By H. A. Taine. Translated by John Austin Stevens. New York: Henry Holt & Co. 1875. (*The Nation,* May 6, 1875).

it may have even more readers in English than in French, and to the American public seem decidedly entertaining. We apparently are capable of consuming an inordinate quantity of information, veracious or the reverse, about Paris, and the present volume is sufficiently free-spoken as to those social mysteries which are deemed typically Parisian. Many readers will take much satisfaction in reading in English what could not possibly with decency have originally been written in English. M. Taine is not easy to translate; but, well translated, he need be but a trifle less effective than in his own tongue. He loses very much less in a foreign version than his great fellow-critic Sainte-Beuve; for his chief characteristics are not subtlety and fugitive, idiomatic grace, but vigor and amplitude and a certain imaginative splendor, such as the English language is peculiarly qualified to render. To translate Taine, indeed, is in a measure to make him restore what he has borrowed, for there is a large English element in his style. The present translation has been very clevery done, and the right word often found where some taste was required to select it.

Exactly what M. Taine desired to do we hardly know; what he has done is to produce a singular compound of Stendhal and Théophile Gautier. Stendhal, as all readers of our author know, is the divinity of whom M. Taine is the prophet. Stendhal invented a method of observation which, in M. Taine's opinion, renewed the whole science of literary and social criticism. This method M. Taine has constantly applied—first to authors and books, then to works of art, and at last, in this case, to men and women, to a society. It was in this last fashion that Stendhal himself chiefly used his method; he was not a literary critic, he was a practical psychologist; he lived most of his life in Italy, and his work was the study and description of human nature in Milan, Florence, and Rome. He accumulated facts and anecdotes; he judged that there were none too trivial to serve as a stroke in the portrait; and he has left a storehouse of good, bad, and indifferent ones. M. Taine has proposed to do for Paris what Stendhal did for Milan; but he has come fifty years later, and he is consequently much more complex and needs a great deal more machinery. He is picturesque, for instance, both by necessity and by style, which Stendhal was not at all, in intention; his book overflows with the description of material objects—of face and hair, shoulders and arms, jewels, dresses, and furniture—and it is evident in all this description that, although M. Taine is a man of too individual a temperament to be an imitator, he has read Théophile Gautier, the master in this line, with great relish and profit. He is shooting in Gautier's premises, and when he brings down a bird we cannot help regarding it as Gautier's property.

M. Taine has endeavored to imagine a perfect observer, and he has given this gentleman's personality as a setting to his own extremely characteristic lucubrations. His observer is M. Frederic-Thomas Graindorge, a Frenchman, a bachelor, a man of fifty, who has made a fortune by hog-packing in Cincinnati, and returns to Paris in the afternoon of his days to take his ease, see the polite world in epitome, and systematize a little his store of observations. He has gone through the mill and been ground very fine; he was at school at Eton, as a boy; he was afterwards at the University of Jena; he has passed twenty years in our own great West, where his adventures have been of the most remarkable description. In his local color, as to this phase of his hero's antecedents, M. Taine is very much at fault; and this is the greater pity, as he has never failed to profess that one should speak only of that which one directly and personally knows. He knows the manners and customs of our Western States in a very roundabout and theoretical fashion; he seems to be under the impression, for instance, that the picturesque art of hog-packing (up to the time of our late war) was carried on in Cincinnati by slave-labor. "I desire only to listen and to look," says M. Graindorge; "I listen and I look; no woman is displeased at being looked at; nor any man at being listened to. Sometimes, as I button up my overcoat, an idea comes to me: I write it down when I go home; hence my notes. You see that this is not a literary matter." It is much more literary than M. Graindorge admits; and his notes have been for M. Taine quite as much an exercise of style as an expression of opinion. He writes admirably; he writes too well; he is simply the very transparent mask of the real author. He is, therefore, as a person, a decidedly ineffective creation, and it was hardly worth while to be at so much labor to construct him. But the point was that M. Taine desired full license to be sceptical and cynical, to prove that he had no prejudices; that he judged things not sentimentally but rationally; that he saw the workings of the *machine humaine* completely *à nu,* and he could do all this under cover of a fictitious M. Graindorge more gracefully than in his own person. M. Graindorge is the most brutal of materialists, and the more he watches the great Parisian spectacle, the greater folly it seems to him to be otherwise. He finds it all excessively ugly, except in so far as it is redeemed by a certain number of pretty women in beautiful dresses, cut very low. But though it is ugly, it is not depressing; exaltation and depression have nothing to do with it; the thing is to see—to see minutely, closely, with your own eyes, not to be a dupe, to find it very convenient that others are, to treat life and your fellow-mortals as a spectacle, to relish a good dinner, and keep yourself in as luxurious a physical good-humor as possible until the "machine" stops working. That of M. Graindorge ceases to operate in the course of the present volume, and the book closes with a statement of his "intimate" personal habits by his secretary, in lieu of a funeral oration.

TAINE'S ANCIENT REGIME*

I just now mentioned M. Taine's new book, which is the literary event of the day, and is very well worth speaking of. The history of the French Revolution, upon which he has so long been engaged, proves to be a work of the somewhat larger scope, which the title I quoted above would indicate. The first volume, a stout octavo of 550 pages, came out two or three

* Taine's *The Ancient Regime,* the first volume of *The Origins of Contemporary France* was translated by John Durand, and published in New York by Henry Holt and Company, in 1876. (*New York Daily Tribune,* Saturday, January 8, 1876).

days since; it is devoted to the "Ancien Régime." M. Taine has been so much translated that he is now, to English eyes, a tolerably distinct physiognomy. With the exception of M. Renan, he is now the most brilliant French writer, albeit that he is not in the Academy. But in truth, with his extraordinary store of general knowledge and his magnificent skill in that office, which is considered the peculiar function of academies—presentation, exhibition, harmonious arrangement—M. Taine is an academy in himself. He is very far from infallible, and so are academies; but like them, right or wrong, he always speaks with a certain accumulated authority. I speak of him advisedly as a "writer," for although he is also a logician, a metaphysician, a thinker, and a scholar, it is the literary quality of his genius that I most highly relish. I suspect, moreover, that it is the side that he most relishes himself, and that, on the whole, it is the most valuable side. Some of his theories have been severely riddled by criticism, but at the worst he is capital reading. His style in his present work flows in as ample a current as ever; one sees that it has been fed from many sources. His theories here, moreover, are not obtrusive. His work has been chiefly one of narration and exposition. He has given a complete picture of the structure and condition of the French society that preceded the Revolution—its organization, its habits, its occupations, its public and private economy, its diet, its costume, its temper, its ideas, its ways of feeling. The picture is extraordinarily complete, and is executed with that sustained vigor of which M. Taine only is capable. The eighteenth century in French literature has been turned inside out, sifted and resifted, explored in its minutest detail; but the thing has never been done with the method and energy of M. Taine; there is no other such rich and vivid *résumé*. He has disinterred new facts, possessed himself of new documents, illuminated a variety of points with a stronger light, and made a most interesting book. It is amazing how well we have come to know the eighteenth century; there was never such a labor of revivification. The defunct is standing upon his feet again; he wears his clothes as he used to put them on himself, and his wig as his valet used to powder it; he has the cares of life in his cheeks and the look of sympathy in his eyes; not a wrinkle on his brow, not a detail of his costume is wanting; he can almost speak, or if he cannot speak he easily can listen. If he listens to M. Taine he will hear some painful truths. M. Taine is supposed to intend to take a reactionary view of the French Revolution, and to devote himself chiefly to that somewhat neglected province of history, the injury it did to France. It is high time, certainly, that this work were done, from the liberal and philosophical standpoint. In this volume, however, the author is by no means reactionary; a more damning indictment than his picture of the social orders that the Revolution swept away cannot be imagined. The criticism of what it in turn established will come later. The book is a curious mine of facts about the old royal and aristocratic habits—about the expenditure of the court and of those who frequented it. I had marked a great many passages for quotation. Page after page is filled with accounts of the sinecures under Louis XIV. and Louis XV. Gentlemen and ladies drew ten and twenty thousand francs a year for performing functions which had not even a name, and others for performing functions which had names which we do not pronounce in English (they do in French), though the functions themselves were strictly nominal. The analysis of the temper and intellectual condition of society is as complete as might have been expected from so keen a psychologist as M. Taine. This is accompanied by a great many characteristic anecdotes. Louis XIV. loved to centralize; he wished the whole aristocracy to be perpetually at court, paying him its respects. He was therefore much gratified, I suppose, when a certain M. de Vardes, (the name deserves to be preserved) remarked to him that, "When one is away from your Majesty, one is not only unhappy; one is ridiculous." One might be ridiculous, it appears, even within speaking distance of his Majesty. M. Taine speaks of course of the reign of "sensibility," which set in about the middle of the last century and continued during the Revolution, without the least detriment to that of Terror. It produced a great deal of vaporous sentimentality, but it sometimes gave a very delicate point to the feelings. "We meet thus," says our author, "with actions and expressions of a supreme grace, unique of their kind, like some tiny little masterpiece in Sèvres china." One day that the Countess Amélie de Bouffiers was speaking rather lightly of her husband, her mother-in-law said, "You forget that you are speaking of my son." "It is true," she answered, "I thought I was speaking only of your son-in-law." The virtuous and temperate Madame Elizabeth had sixty thousand dollars allowed her annually for her food. There was doubtless a good deal of reason in Talleyrand's saying that "He who had not lived before 1789 did not know the sweetness of living." There was another point of view, however; the last division of M. Taine's volume, and the most interesting is on the people. But the whole book is to be read.

SAINTE-BEUVE'S PORTRAITS*

THE ESSAYS collected in the volume introduced to American readers by Miss Preston in this very agreeable translation (to which the translator has prefixed a well-written and discriminating preface) belong to the early period of the distinguished writer's career, and may be said, moreover, to treat of persons not especially dear to the American public. And yet on this occasion we have no hesitation in speaking of the book and its author; for M. Sainte-Beuve still lives and writes, and so long as he has not gone to join those illustrious departed spirits to whom in this modern world he has given a voice and a shape, he may be deemed in literature one of the subjects of the day. Miss Preston's translation, we say, is agreeable; but is it always exactly faithful? In the article on Mme. de Sévigné, the author, commenting in a note on a description of his heroine by a contemporary, writes: *"Que c'est bien elle!"* etc., which Miss Preston renders, "This is worth while." This is the first error on which our eyes fell; we have not pursued the search; perhaps it is the only one.

Of the nine women whose lives are here sketched, three alone are known even by name to American ears—Mesdames de

---

* "Portraits of Celebrated Women." By C. A. Sainte-Beuve. Translated from the French by H. W. Preston. Boston: Roberts Bros. 1868. (*The Nation*, June 4, 1868).

Sévigné, Roland, and De Staël. Who is Mme. de Duras, Mme. de Krüdener, Mme. de Rémusat? Each of these ladies, in the early part of our century, wrote two or three novels which thirty years ago—the date of these articles—were in a fair way to be forgotten in France. M. Sainte-Beuve, in his inimitable manner, said a good word for each; but did he arrest the wave of oblivion? On the contrary, his word was doubtless felt to be the last word, and his heroines received their quietus. It is not as that of a novelist that the mystical Krüdener's ghost of a name appears to us. To read and enjoy his various articles must have seemed to ordinary readers an all-sufficient tribute to these departed women of talent. They read M. Sainte-Beuve's extracts, and this was quite enough. Who nowadays sits down to a perusal of "Edouard" or "Valerié?" M. Sainte-Beuve himself, in the current year, would admit that we can make a better use of our time. There is, to our sensibilities, something sad and spectral in the sight of these poor old French ladies, summoned from their quiet graves, deep in the warm and comfortable soil of oblivion, and clad afresh in the chilly drapery of our American speech. With all deference to the translator's opinion, we cannot help thinking that this was not a book to translate. For our own part, we should have wholly deprecated any translation at all; but if such a work had been determined upon, we should have suggested a selection of articles from the immense repository of the "Causeries du Lundi," where the translator would have found at once greater perfection of manner and heroines more generally interesting. The article on Mme. Roland in the present collection is extremely good, but it is wholly inferior to the admirable paper on the new edition of her memoirs contained in the eighth volume of the "Nouveaux Lundis." And so any one of the essays before us, with the exception of the first, the fourth, and the fifth, might have ceded its place to the sketch in the "Derniers Portraits" of Mme. de Staal-Dalaunay, the author of one of the most deeply-interesting volumes of memoirs ever written. To induce an intelligent reader to go through the memoirs of Mme. de Staal-Delaunay would be a better service than to lead him (or her, we may say, as Miss Preston chiefly covets female readers) to rest content with a few extracts from three or four feeble and elegant tales of fifty years ago. Let us add the expression of our regret that the translator has judged best to omit the article on Mme. de Charrière, a lady no better known indeed than her sisters, but far more deserving of our modern attention. This person, a Dutch woman by birth, and for a long time a resident in Switzerland—it is doubted that she ever visited Paris—was perfect mistress of a delightful French style, in which she composed two excellent novels as well as several inferior ones. From these two works M. Sainte-Beuve gives a number of extracts, all remarkable for strength and truthfulness. Mme. de Charrière looks like the first of the realists. But with the realists, as we have learned, one must proceed cautiously, and it is very possible that with all her merits Mme. de Charrière could not logically hope to figure in these chastened English pages.

"The quiet fairness," says Miss Preston in her preface, "with which M. Sainte-Beuve estimates feminine effort and achievement in letters, as contrasted alike with the indulgent praise and considerable blame which they ordinarily receive, is to a woman, at least, absolutely affecting." This is doubtless perfectly true, and yet after all the author's tone is by no means the pure judicial one. On the title-page of the French edition of the work before us is the following bit of dialogue, by way of an epigraph: " 'Have you ever been a woman, sir, that you should pretend in this way to know us?' 'No, madam, I am not Tiresias the soothsayer; I am only a humble mortal who has loved you much.' " He has loved them much—this is the motive and the secret of M. Sainte-Beuve's deep appreciation of the characteristics of women. To our mind it is not his fairness that is affecting, but his devotion; the exquisite humility of his intellect—its servility, one may call it—under the charm of feminine grace and talent. In one sense it is a deeper and more disinterested devotion than that of the great poets and romancers. These writers construct lovely women by the dozen, and lose their hearts to their own creations; but their heroines are emphatically their creatures; they bear the stamp of their own passions and prejudices; they flatter their genius. M. Sainte-Beuve takes women as they come, neither ideally beautiful nor ideally gifted, full of foibles and disenchantments and incompleteness, and places his faculties at their service to act upon society; waits upon them, interprets them, exhibits them, repeats their faint accents in a louder key. It is decidedly as they are—as they have been, even in the past—and not as they may be and as many of them wish to be, that he studies and admires them. The translator, we think, forces a point when she intimates that M. Sainte-Beuve has caught a glimpse of that luminous future which shines from afar in the eyes of the more sober and strenuous of her sex. She even goes so far—*horrescimus referentes*—as to mention in this connection the word suffrage. This terms suggests an order of facts and ideas to which we may be sure the mind of the illustrious critic is a stranger. We may best express at once the extent and the limitation of his conception of the feminine nature—of *das ewige Weibliche*—by saying that he deals only with women as established in society, and that he uses the word society in its artificial and modern sense of *good company*. If we regard this circumstance in connection with the fact indicated in the epigraph —the fact that he maintains an emphatically sentimental relation to the ladies of his choice—we shall see that it is no easy task to enlist him on the side of reform, progress, emancipation, or any tendency foreshadowed in these formidable words. Society, in the sense necessarily attached to the word by M. Sainte-Beuve, does not exist, and is not likely to exist, in this country. To M. Sainte-Beuve it has, as much as anything can have, probably, an absolute sanctity and meaning. In France, from the time of Madame de Sévigné down to the present day, it has gradually assumed form and substance, and has constituted the only possible medium of life and action for superior women. Each of the ladies described in the present volume was a woman of the world —of the nine no less than seven were members of what is called the great world, of the inner circle of society. This inner circle was composed of many elements, among which it would be unfair not to mention literature. But the further one penetrates into it, it seems to us, the more those complex elements tend to reduce themselves to two simple ones—in the first place the *salon,* and in the second place love, or, as it would be more correct to say, lovers. Miss Preston admits, correctly, that what our author chiefly values in woman is the "capacity for passion." Of course the love indicated in our quotation is not all on one side. M. Sainte-Beuve repays himself for his own effusion of sentiment by detecting and pursuing the emotion in the lives of his heroines. Assuredly, it is not directed towards himself; but this is of small account. Provided it is really the process, the act of love, he is quite content to be but a spectator. The translator has, of necessity, omitted from her volume the last of the original portraits, a sketch of a certain Madame de Pontivy. This lady, who flourished in the first half of the last century, was in no sense of the word a celebrated woman; she was not even a literary woman, and we remain in ignorance of the documents in which her history is revealed. Her sole claim to our interest is her love story—the fact that for a large number of years, a whole lifetime indeed, in the midst of a faithless and licentious society, she maintained privately, and yet in all its fulness, a passion of the most exquisite quality. There is nothing in the story but that; no wit, nor wisdom, nor action—nothing but happy love, pure and simple. M. Sainte-Beuve relates it with excellent skill, and with the most generous sympathy and unction. But that he should relate such a story in such a manner is conclusive evidence that he is very little of a moralist and, in a really liberal sense of the word, not overmuch of a thinker. We are half sorry that the translator might not have ventured to retain the sketch. To a serious mind it offers perhaps more matter for reflection than any of the other essays.

What we ourselves most enjoy in the writings of M. Sainte-Beuve is their numerous literary merits. The literary merit of the present volume so far exceeds its merits in other particulars that it seems futile to look upon it as anything but a contribution to pure literature. A writer and a psychologist—an empiric, if you will, in each case, but a most successful one—these seem to us the terms which best describe M. Sainte-Beuve. We admit that it is dangerous to assume aught of a trenchant tone in speaking of the constitution of his genius. He contains a little of so many things in a degree that sadly puzzles the critic's mind and leads him to forswear the attempt to classify and label him. He is a little of a poet, a little of a moralist, a little of a historian, a little of a philosopher, a little of a romancer. But successively, with patience and care, you detect each of these characters in its littleness—you detect the wonderful man in flagrant default of imagination, of depth, of sagacity, of constructive skill, and you feel that he is reduced to logical proportions. At the same time you feel that there is another element of his mind which looks small from no point of view, but which remains immeasurable, original, and delightful. This is his passion for literature—in which we include both his insatiable curiosity and his eternal gift of expression—his style.

SAINTE-BEUVE'S FIRST ARTICLES*

The acutest critic the world has seen spent much of the latter part of his life in revising his published writings, amending them, minutely annotating, and generally re-editing them. Everything that had ever come from his pen retained his interest to the last, and he thought that anything that was worth doing at all was worth doing well. He had a passion for exactitude, and he wished, as it were, to make a certain toilet for his productions, on their appearance before posterity. This is the sentiment of a man who feels that he has done good work; it is only solid objects that will bear free handling, and Sainte-Beuve had a comfortable sense that in his essays and *causeries* there was no want of pegs to hang notes and appendices upon. He prepared, therefore, during his last years, a series of "authorized editions" of all his principal performances—beginning with the later and proceeding back to the earlier ones. The editor of the present volume quotes from him a passage in which he expresses his general theory on these undertakings:

"I save what I can of the damaged baggage; I wish that what I reject might perish wholly and leave no trace. Unfortunately, this cannot absolutely be; what one collects into

* 'Premiers Lundis' Par C. A. Sainte-Beuve, de l'Académie Française. Tome I. Paris: Michael Lévy; New York: F. W. Christern. 1874. (*The Nation*, February 18, 1875).

stout volumes is not saved by that fact, and what remains in scattered sheets is not so completely lost that it does not drag in one's track and weigh down, if need be, one's literary march and, later, one's memory (if a memory there is to be), with a multitude of confused and straggling reminiscences. It is proper, then, to answer only for what one has admitted, and, without disavowing the rest, to send it to the bottom. In a word, if one has a care for the future; if, without having the vanity of believing in anything in the way of glory, one feels at least the lawful desire to be in some rank or other an honorable witness to one's time, one has all precautions to take: one cannot too much act as a ship (*faire navire*), and keep one's course straight, to pass, without foundering, the perilous straits."

Sainte-Beuve republished his early poems and his youthful novel 'Volupté,' but he did not live to collect his first critical articles, his groping experiments in the line in which he subsequently became a master. It is a vast pity that, since they were to be exhumed, he himself should not have presided at the ceremony. He would have supplied them with a number of entertaining notes, and given many valuable glimpses of the history of the formation of his opinions. It is a strange and uncomfortable thing to find one's self reading Sainte-Beuve uncommented by himself; the absence of the familiar footnotes, generally more characteristic and pointed than the text itself, has something melancholy and almost cruel; it reminds one afresh of his departure, and is like seeing a person thrust half-dressed into company. The present volume has been put together by one of his literary executors, and the work has apparently been carefully done, as far as the searching out and identification of his pieces are concerned. Sainte-Beuve had, after much solicitation, announced his intention of doing this work himself; they seem to come under the head of those things which would not go to the bottom, even if one threw them overboard. They were contributed to the *Globe* newspaper during a series of years beginning with 1824, when the author was a half-hearted medical student of twenty. The title of 'Lundis' is of course a device of the publisher, but the subjects are the same in character as those he treated later—literary figures of the day, and of the seventeenth and eighteenth centuries.

It is interesting to observe his first trustful impressions of writers on whom he subsequently expatiated with such ripe sagacity and, in some cases, with such polished irony. This especially strikes us in reading his youthfully glowing tribute to the early poetry of Victor Hugo and Lamartine. As to Victor Hugo indeed, as years advanced, Sainte-Beuve maintained a portentous silence; he let him alone, as he let alone Madame Sand and Balzac (to the latter of whom he never did justice), and when he withheld an opinion one might know there was a good reason for it. But Lamartine, on various occasions, he handled with unsparing acerbity; the poet had relaxed and the critic had hardened. The merit of these papers is evidently greater than was to be expected; they seem to us to contain the distinct promise of the author's future. There are things excellently said throughout, and which would be worth quoting; but the main thing is the general manner, the general firmness, the certainty and maturity of touch. The author writes as if he felt that, without abrupt transitions, he was going to become a master; if we had been his editor we should certainly have kept an eye on him. The article on the Memoirs of Madame de Genlis is, for a young man of twenty-two, extremely remarkable, and if he does not yet speak with the authority with which, many years after, he alluded to the lady's being *de veine verbeuse et mensongère*, there is no lack of a really penetrating perception of her foibles. The talent for incisive irony is apparent from the first. "At Modena, the Prime Minister, M. de Lascaris, threw himself at her feet, with a little air of triumph which she contrived very well to repress. At Rome, she saw the Cardinal de Bernis, whom they called there the King of Rome. . . . He assisted regularly at the baths of Madame de Genlis, and enlivened them by his charming conversation. The Chevalier de Bernis, his nephew, was her guide in her nocturnal promenades among the ruins of the Coliseum, but 'he was at least fifty years old.' At Naples, she ravished the whole court by the sound of her harp—and the queen especially, who kissed her hands; she saw also some lazzaroni, all naked, and some superb figs and pine-apples—and

81

there ends the journey in Italy." These lines, from a charming paper on Diderot, of the date of 1830, might have been written at the close of the author's life; they have quite his final tone and rhythm: "That Diderot should grow fat, that his paunch should define itself, that he should have indigestion and take medicine, that Mlle. Voland herself should 'pay a bad fortnight for a little glass of wine and the thigh of a partridge too much,' this shocks us, in turn, for a long time, and spoils for us many effusions still living, many fresh reminiscences of love. For noble, ideal love, as for poetry, there are but two periods of life, youth and old age; in the interval, when profound and passionate love exists, it must hide itself and beware of witnesses; it does not easily interest a third person; it is complicated with a thousand petty miseries of body and mind, with obesity, with ambition; one can hardly believe in it, one can't admire it." These reflections savor of the wisdom that comes of much observation of the world, and, if anything might have qualified our confidence in the wisdom of the shrewd young critic, it would have been the suspicion that he was *too* shrewd, too old, too *posé;* that his taste was too good. Youthful genius is, traditionally at least, a trifle more erratic.

English readers will glance with especial interest at the articles on Scott's 'Life of Napoleon' and on Fenimore Cooper. The former is remarkable for its very delicate and sympathetic discrimination between Scott's charm as a romancer and his culpable weaknesses as a historian. For a young Frenchman of 1827 to declare so eloquently that he esteemed the author of 'The Bride of Lammermoor,' *as such,* none the less for having compiled that melancholy work, 'The Life of Napoleon,' indicates a striking measure of critical generosity. But young Frenchmen of that period took romancers on easy terms if we may judge by the extreme friendliness of the author's remarks on 'Le Corsaire Rouge'—that fast friend of our school-days, 'The Red Rover.' Cooper's magnificent popularity in France has always seemed to us a half-amusing, half-touching spectacle, and there could be no better proof that people, in judging a foreigner, should never be sure they have not made a mistake in *proportion.* The "cultivated American" at the present day has an old-time fondness for

Cooper, which makes the smile in which he indulges on finding that there are people who still read him a very kindly smile; but though we have a healthy disposition to make the most of our literary luminaries, we are not commonly addicted to speaking of the author of the 'Last of the Mohicans' as a first-rate man, and we are puzzled on finding ardent allusions to him in such writers as Balzac and Madame Sand. But, of course, if we take his trappers and his Indians in good faith, Europeans could hardly do less, and the prairie and the virgin forest, as he portrayed them, had, when contemplated from the Boulevard, a prodigiously natural air. We are inclined to believe, however, that Sainte-Beuve made, first and last, almost no other mistake than this, and these slight papers give us, as we have hinted, an impression of almost formidable sagacity. We confess that, touching such a man as Sainte-Beuve, our curiosity is infinite; we feel as if we could never learn enough about him. His intellectual fecundity was so unbounded that one imagines that the history of his individual opinions would throw a preternaturally brilliant light upon the laws of the human mind at large. We are thankful to learn from his present editor that such a history is to receive a valuable contribution in the publication of his letters, as completely as possible. We had a couple of years since a taste of his epistolary faculty in his published notes to the Princess Mathilde. These were not elaborate letters; they were emphatically notes— notes on life, on people, on books—but they had a point, an acuteness, a savor which make one eager for the sequel. They will set the seal of completeness on a truly magnificent literary record. We may add that there is apparently to be another volume of these 'Nouveaux Lundis.' and that there is much so-called "ripe criticism" at the present hour which has less flavor than these verdant first-fruits of a man of extraordinary genius. The grasp may here and there lack firmness, but the hand is already the hand of a master.

SAINTE-BEUVE'S ENGLISH PORTRAITS*

It may be said that if it is of no particular profit to translate
Sainte-Beuve into English, it at least does no harm. Those who
care to read him will be sure to be able, and to prefer, to read
him in his own tongue, and those who do not will let him alone,
as before. To this may be answered, we think, that a performance
like the present volume sins in being a spurious rather than a
real service to culture; that Sainte-Beuve, of all men, was devoted
to culture in its purest and most incorruptible forms; and that it
is therefore paying him a poor compliment to present him in a
fashion based on a compromise with sound taste. Sainte-Beuve's
was not in the least an English mind, in spite of his partially
English ancestry; he was a Frenchman to his finger-tips; and his
intellect, his erudition, his taste, his tone, his style, were of a
deeply national stamp. It cannot be said that he spoke without
authority on any subject whatever; but his authority in speaking
of foreign writers was diminished by half. He spoke of them
rarely; he *happened,* so to say, at wide intervals to have touched
upon Franklin, Chesterfield, Gibbon, Cowper, and Pope. The
articles are charming, but even in the original they are not
among his best; and in the present translation (which is yet
extremely good) they offer an almost painfully dim and ineffective
image of the brilliant qualities familiar to those who greatly
admire him. The part of culture—the part of that penetrating
and initiated taste of which Sainte-Beuve was so eminent a
representative—is to say: "You are not really reading the great
critic in this form; you are only half reading him; you are seeing
him through a glass, very darkly; you are not doing him justice."
The part of the translator of these essays, on the other hand,
of the compiler of the volume for which circulation and popularity are sought, is to say, naturally: "You *are* doing him justice;
the glass is a glass, but it is very clear; what you lose is, after
all, not the essential." And this is why to serve up half-a-dozen

---

* 'English Portraits. By C. A. Sainte-Beuve. Edited and translated from
the 'Causeries du Lundi.' With an Introductory Chapter on Sainte-Beuve's
Life and Writings.' New York: Henry Holt & Co. 1875. (*The Nation,*
April 15, 1875).

of Sainte-Beuve's second-best *Causeries* as an English book is to be at odds with the very spirit of Sainte-Beuve. We may be thought rather cynically fastidious; but we may affirm that if there is a touch of ill-humor in our restrictions we are not without an excuse for it. If the voluminous introductory essay prefixed to the present volume had been a strikingly felicitous performance—had offered us any new information or any especially suggestive reflections—we do not think that we should have been less disposed to hold the translator to an account. But the essay strikes us as having little value. It is both meagre and clumsy—extremely diffuse in manner and yet very chary of real characterization, of that finer, subtler characterization of which one strikes the note in the simple mention of Sainte-Beuve's name. The author alludes to a great many books and writers, and institutes a vast number of laborious, commonplace comparisons and *rapprochements,* but we honestly think that a reader whose sole knowledge of the great critic should be derived from these pages would carry away an extremely vague and formless image. And why should the translator utter a judgment so unaccountable as the following? "Though it is hardly doubtful that Sainte-Beuve's 'Causeries du Lundi' will gratify and inform future generations of Frenchmen, yet the universality and endurance of his renown might have been still assured had he produced one work, of moderate compass, supplying a complete impression of his power." If the 'Causeries' do not supply a complete impression of his powers, these are even larger than our large estimate of them, and if through "one work of moderate compass" he would have become more easily the intellectual companion, the ever-present, suggestive, inspiring friend of those who love letters, surely the admirably consistent, available, unimportunate form of the 'Causeries' is ingenuity sadly wasted. We are grateful to the author, however, for his quotation from Taine, which, in its admirable definiteness, stands out in high relief in the midst of his own vague portraiture.

If M. Taine has succeeded in portraying Sainte-Beuve, it is not that the task was an easy one. He himself was more complex than any figure he ever drew, and he could only have been adequately painted in colors from his own palette. There are so many things to say about him that one hardly knows where to begin, and whatever we say, we feel that we have omitted something essential. The truly essential thing, we take it, is that he worked, as Taine happily says, "for lettered and delicate men." These are Sainte-Beuve's real public—the public which would find something indelicate in Sainte-Beuve Anglicized. But even this is true only if taken in a certain cautious sense. The great critic had as much of what is called human nature as of erudition, and the proof of his genius was the fashion in which he made them go hand-in-hand. He was a man of books, and yet in perception, in divination, in sympathy, in taste, he was consummately a man of the world. It is a marvel to see the way in which he effects this subtle interfusion of science and experience. He appeals to the cultured man, to the highly civilized and finished social unit, but he appeals to him in behalf of something which demands no sacrifice of points of contact with the world, but an increase and a higher sensibility in each. Most erudition beside Sainte-Beuve's seems sterile and egoistic; none was ever turned to such infinite account, so put to use, so applied, so controlled by life. These are his general characteristics, and the portrait would be only more interesting in going down into detail. Then would appear his patience, his religious exactitude, his marvellous memory, his exquisite fancy—all the accomplishments and virtues and graces of the literary passion. On the other hand, we should touch in a dozen different directions his limitations and his defects, and these perhaps would be most interesting of all. They would be limitations of temper, of morality, of generosity, and they would also now and then be limitations of taste. This it takes some courage to say; but readers who have really suffered in a tender part of their mental organism from certain baser moments, as they may call them, in the great critic, will feel as if they had paid for the right to be positive. We allude here to the vices of temper, to his two volumes on Châteaubriand, to such an episode, for instance, as the long, interpolated diatribe against poor Gustave Planche—against his personal habits, his ugliness, his poverty—in the series of papers (in the *Nouveaux Lundis*) on Horace Vernet; as well as to many a thrust and scratch, quite out of the rules of the game, in the author's innumerable footnotes. We should fancy that among the people of the day, within range of Sainte-Beuve's reference, there must have been a certain special, well-known physical sensation associated with a glimpse of their names in these terrible notes. There was no knowing what was coming: he never spoke save by book; what documents had he got hold of now? Sainte-Beuve's faults of taste were those of omission, not of commission. Anything he admired was in some degree admirable; but there were also things to which he was constitutionally unable to do justice. He flourished side by side with Balzac, whom he detested, without ever suspecting, apparently, the colossal proportions of the great novelist's genius. It is true that what we all dislike in Balzac Sainte-Beuve disliked with an acuteness, with a power to measure the extent of its aberration, which few of us possess. He liked Pope and Cowper, as the present volume shows, more than the mind of the "period" just now finds easy. It would be most interesting to follow through his writings the vein of old French conservatism of taste—to see it wind and twist and double, making occasionally a startling deflection into dangerous places, taking a plunge into turbid waters, but never altogether, as simple *taste,* losing a certain remote family likeness to Philistinism. Sainte-Beuve, as a whole, is the least of a Philistine conceivable; but to the end of his life, in spite of passing fancies and sudden enthusiasms, in spite of his immense and constant intellectual hospitality and flexibility, what he most relished was temperance, perfect taste, measure. This fact of necessity makes him a partial and inadequate witness to English literature. All these points will be elucidated, harmonized, balanced against each other, when a really conclusive and adequate portrait is produced—a better portrait than that which M. d'Haussonville has lately been contributing to the *Revue des Deux Mondes* with so much pretended, and so little real, liberality. M. d'Haussonville's last word is that Victor Cousin once said to him, as the conclusion of a comparison they had been making together (they might have been better employed!) of Sainte-Beuve and Mérimée: "Mérimée is a *gentilhomme,* and Sainte-Beuve is not: that is why Mérimée is superior to Sainte-Beuve." This is as valueless as the majority of epigrams. Carlyle says of Mirabeau that he had swallowed all formulas; and we may say of Sainte-Beuve that he had swallowed all *gentilshommes* —M. Cousin, certainly, *quâ* gentilhomme, included. Sainte-Beuve's defects, we think, are not to be analyzed in that line, but on an even deeper and subtler one. The best essays in the present volume are those upon Franklin and Gibbon. It is also very well to see what an acute Frenchman can say on behalf of Chesterfield, who has been too long the victim of the pure Johnsonian view. The article on Mary Stuart is, in the present state of learning, rather antiquated. That on Taine's English literature is chiefly a sympathetic disquisition upon Pope. Even if Sainte-Beuve were, at the worst, twice the Philistine he escapes being, it would still be delightful to see a conservative opinion uttered with such happy tact as this:

"But apropos of Boileau, can I then accept this strange judgment of a clever man, this opinion which M. Taine assumes, and does not fear to take on his shoulders as he goes? 'There are two sorts of verses in Boileau: the most numerous, which seem by a good sophomore; the least numerous, which seem by a good senior.' The clever man who so speaks (M. Guillaume Guizot) does not feel Boileau as a poet, and I will go further and say that he does not feel any poet as a poet. I quite understand that you should not make all poetry lie in the *métier,* but I do not at all understand that when you are treating of an art you should take no account of the art itself, and should depreciate to this point the perfect workmen who excel in it. Suppress at a stroke all poetry in verse—that would be more expeditious; otherwise speak with esteem of those who have possessed its secrets. Boileau was of the small number of these; Pope equally."

GAUTIER'S WINTER IN RUSSIA*

We have observed for some time past an increasing mania
for translations. It is a very good fashion, but even the best
things may be overdone. Of course, dull books should never be
translated, but it by no means follows that because a book is
clever it should be interpreted into another tongue. A book
may be very clever in French or in German and very dull in
English, and translation, intended as a compliment, may become
in fact an unpardonable injury. There are certain cases, indeed,
in which it seems to us really immoral; when it deliberately
encumbers a foreign language, namely, with books of a light and
trivial order. Natives have a certain property in their language,
and though we may regret their using it for frivolous purposes,
one can hardly pretend to legislate against them. As a general
thing, a people may be trusted to produce its own padding, and
there is no good reason why our groaning English idiom should
be weighted with exotic commonplaces. A great many things
are said in society which it is very well to hear once, if you
happen to be sitting near the speaker; but he would be a very
officious master of ceremonies who should insist on repeating
and propagating them. In so far as we may lay down a general
rule in the case we should say that the books translatable were
books of *matter,* and books untranslatable books of *manner.*
If the substance of a book is light and its chief attraction is
in the way things are said, it had certainly better be left in the
closely-fitting garment of the original. This, of course, limits
very much the translation of merely entertaining and amusing
books, but the restriction in such cases is especially wholesome.
If a writer has nothing but sweetened froth to offer the public,
it is well that he should at least have been at pains to beat his
froth into the finest possible consistency; and just so it is well
that readers who have an appetite for the compound should be
forced to take such exercise as is involved in a walk to the
confectioner's. To read such a writer as Théophile Gautier, for

* 'A Winter in Russia.' From the French of Théophile Gautier. By M. M.
Ripley.' New York. Henry Holt & Co. 1874. (*The Nation.* November 12, 1874).

instance, is pure diversion, and a healthy-minded reader ought to pay for his pastime by making the very moderate effort required for reading him in the original. It is true that readers are becoming such abandoned Sybarites, and the aversion of the public at large to anything which compels attention to pause for an instant and touch her feet to the earth is so strikingly on the increase, that the "healthy mind" in question can be but rarely postulated. Gautier is precisely one of the writers who are everything in their own tongue, and nothing, or almost nothing, out of it. He is what the French call a *fantaisiste,* and his fantasies are four-fifths verbal to one-fifth intellectual. Half the charm of his writing is in the mere curl and flutter of his phrase, as he unreels it in long bright-colored ribands; but in an English version the air of spontaneity soon disappears, and this ceaseless play of style becomes rigid and awkward. Moreover, Gautier chose his words with an extraordinary fineness of instinct, and in his pictures, as they stand, every hair-stroke tells. A translator rarely chooses the foreign equivalent with the care with which such an artist as Gautier selects the original term, so that the phrase must often be at best but a rough approximation to the author's. In each case the deflection is slight, but in the whole is enormous. The house when it is finished is found to stand crooked. The translation before us is executed with commendable skill; its only fault is that it *is* a translation. It will have rendered a service, however, if it sends a few readers to its untranslated companions.

The 'Voyage en Russie' is one of Gautier's later works and not one of his best. It is not as full and compact as the 'Voyage en Espagne' or 'Italia,' the former of which has become in its way a sort of classic. Most of the writing is spread rather thin, and the art of the bookmaker is a trifle obvious. But the book is a charming one, and nothing approaching it in merit has been written on the outward face of things in Russia. Gautier was so true an artist that everything he wrote has a singular unity, and one may trust it from beginning to end to contain no false notes. And then the true notes are struck with such a masterly hand! As you close the 'Voyage en Russie' you seem to have before your eyes a sort of symbolic physical image composed of the white of glittering snows and the steely blue of northern air. The book is a verbal symphony on the theme *frost*. Gautier's winter in Russia was apparently one of the happiest seasons of his life, and the reader feels the contagion of his deep good-humor—of his luxurious enjoyment of his holiday, his fine friends and their dusky hot-house drawing-rooms, and his sleigh-rides beside pretty "Hyperborean" countesses, muffled in twenty thousand francs' worth of fur. He is the prince of travellers, taking the word in its simplest sense. He neither enquires nor investigates, nor dissents nor theorizes; he doesn't care a straw for politics, and if you had no notions of your own on the subject, you would never learn from his pages whether the Muscovite Empire is an absolute monarchy or a radical republic. He simply travels—that is, he looks and enjoys. His business is only with what comes within the jurisdiction of the eyes; but never were a pair of eyes so vigilant. One feels that from the moment he takes his seat in the railway carriage, facing the engine and next to a window, it behooves Mother Nature to be on her good behavior: Burns's "chiel" taking notes was nothing to this. He sees pictures where most people find mere dead surfaces, and where common eyes find the hint of a picture he constructs a complete work of art. His fancy is always on the alert. If he goes into an old crypt in the Kremlin at Moscow, he reflects that "here it was that, in an atmosphere heated to excess, the women, crouched in Oriental fashion upon piles of cushions, used to pass the long hours of the Russian winter looking out through the little windows to see the snow sparkle upon the gilded cupolas, and the ravens describe wild spirals around the belfries." He was an admirably descriptive poet, but we lately heard it truly, although somewhat uncivilly said, that his powers of reflection were about equivalent to those of an intelligent poodle. There is something characteristic in the way he here brings his journey and his book to a close—the way that, the play being over and the curtain dropped, the writer's mind feels no impulse towards a moment's musing—towards pointing any other moral than that "a coupé awaited me at the (Paris) station, and a quarter of an hour later I found myself surrounded by old friends and pretty women, before a table brilliant with lights, on which a fine supper was smoking, and my return was celebrated gaily until the morning." But if Gautier was not a moralist he was an incomparable painter, and there is no such good picture as this of St. Petersburg and Moscow.

CONSTANTINOPLE BY GAUTIER*

We had occasion, some months ago, on the appearance of the translation of Théophile Gautier's 'Russia,' to express our opinion as to the wisdom of depriving this extraordinary descriptive genius of the benefit of his own tongue. Gautier is above all a man of style, and one has no right to divest him of his own style without giving him another in exchange. The 'Winter in Russia' seemed to us carefully and not unskilfully translated, but the gentleman who has undertaken to do the present work into English has had a very imperfect idea of his responsibilities. To translate Gautier in the off-hand fashion in which you would transfer from one language to another the gist of a newspaper paragraph strikes us as a literary misdemeanor of the first magnitude, and yet of no less an offence has Mr. Robert Howe Gould, M.A., been guilty. 'Constantinople' is, next after the 'Voyage en Espagne,' its author's masterpiece, and to translate it with perfect verbal felicity would not have been easy. But to translate it with care, zeal, and respect was the least to be required of one who should put his hand to the task. Mr. Gould should, in the first place, have notified his readers that what he was giving them was an abbreviated and mutilated edition of the original. Omission in translation is rarely absolutely unjustifiable; but some intimation should always be given of the extent to which the privilege has been used. Mr. Gould uses it freely and constantly—indeed, we may say that whenever a passage is at all difficult to render he leaves

* *Constantinople*. From the French of Théophile Gautier. By Robert Howe Gould, M.A. (New York: Henry Holt & Co. 1875). (*The Nation*, July 15, 1875).

it out. Many passages, it is true, were better left out than
rendered as baldly and flatly as Mr. Gould renders them. His
infelicities swarm even in the opening pages of the book. The
great point with Gautier was to use at any hazard what he
calls the *mot propre*—to make an image. When he speaks of
the country round Marseilles as "ces beaux rochers couleur de
liége et de pain grillé"—the "color of cork and of toast"—Mr.
Gould insipidly renders it "rocks of rich brown." This is indeed
not only insipid, but false, inasmuch as it was obviously the
idea of dry and arid brown that the author wished to convey.
When he says that at Malta "il fait véritablement clair"—"it
is really light"—the best that Mr. Gould can do is to say the
"atmosphere is really clear." When the author uses so special
and picturesque a phrase as the sea being "gaufré de moires par
la brise," Mr. Gould translates vulgarly, "broken into ripples."
Mr. Gould always gives the vague epithet instead of the special
one. "Un bloc de rochers fauves, fendillés de sécheresse, calcinés
de chaleur," is a vivid picture: "a mass of rocks, tawny, con-
sumed by drought, burned by heat," is relatively none. Why
shuffle away the admirably expressive term *fendillé*—split into
chinks, cracked, chapped? Why in the next page interpolate
bodily a threadbare line from Byron which does not exist in
the original? In the chapter on the Golden Horn there is an
admirable passage about certain old houses—"ces bonnes vieilles
murailles empâtées, égratignées, lépreuses, chancies, moisies,
affritées, que la truelle de Decamps maçonne avec tant de
bonheur dans ses tableaux d'Orient, et qui donnent un si haut
ragoût aux masures." This is Gautier at his best, but as to
render the passage requires some little ingenuity, the translator
quietly drops it out. A still finer passage, a description of a der-
vish, is worth quoting, with Mr. Gould's version of it: "Je
n'oublierai jamais ce masque court, camard, élargi, qui semblait
s'être écrasé sous la pression d'une main puissante, comme ces
grotesques de caoutchouc qu'on fait changer d'expression en
appuyant le pouce dessus; de grosses lévres bleuâtres, épaisses
comme celles d'un négre; des yeux de crapaud, ronds, fixes,
saillants; un nez sans cartilage, une barbe courte, rare et frisée,
un teint de cuir fauve, glacé de tons rances et plus culotté de ton

qu'un Espagnolet. . . ." What Mr. Gould offers us instead of
this is: "His whole aspect and the mould of his features were
among the most remarkable, as well as the most hideous, that
I have ever beheld." Even for a single word the translator will
not brighten his wit a little. If a casket of jewels is scattered
"dans un désordre chatoyant," for Mr. Gould it is merely a
"picturesque disorder." We have encountered those inexcusable
shortcomings in a very rapid examination of the volume. It is
evident that a vast number more may be found. The work, in
short, has been translated by a person totally destitute of appreciation of his author, and in whose hands its essential merit,
its vividness, its incisiveness, its gaiety, have evaporated. No one
reads Gautier for information; we read him for the vivacity of
his phrase, for his imagery. If you suppress this, you deliberately
suffocate him. It is to be hoped that if it is intended to offer
a translation of the 'Voyage en Espagne,' the services of some
other literary artist than Mr. Gould will be obtained. A good
translation might be made by a person who would give care,
and taste, and imagination to it; but to subject the work to
the process which has spoiled this unfortunate 'Constantinople'
would be simply cruel.

GAUTIER'S POSTHUMOUS WORKS*

The admirers of Théophile Gautier will be pleased to hear
that a well-earned honor is to be bestowed on his literary remains.
The immense number of short articles—criticisms, *feuilletons,*
sketches, notices—scattered through the newspapers and magazines in which he earned his daily bread are to be gathered into
volumes and given to the world under an intelligent and sympathetic editorial supervision. Two volumes have already ap-

---

* *Théophile Gautier, Souvenirs Intimes.* Par Ernest Feydeau. Paris: E.
Plon. 1874.

Histoire du Romantisme, Suivie de Notices Romantiques, etc. Par.
Théophile Gautier. Paris. Charpentier. 1874. (*North American Review*,
October 1874).

peared: one entitled *Les Jeunes-France,* the second and more important baptized for the occasion as we have indicated. We ourselves rejoice greatly in this undertaking, for we confess to a peculiar and, in its nature, almost inexpressible kindness for the author of the *Voyage en Espagne* and *Emaux et Camées.* His writings present themselves with such modest pretensions that it is easy to underestimate them. He wrote from day to day, from hour to hour (in the morning paper and the evening paper), his exquisite prose, flanked on one side by the telegraphic gossip of the Agence Havas, and on the other by the advertisement of the Révalescière Dubarry. His work was a lifelong, ceaseless, restless improvisation, and his themes for the most part, at best, but a nine days' wonder. And yet it may really be said of him, that he has hardly written a line that is not worth reprinting. We never read ten consecutive lines from his pen,— tossed off though they may have been on the most trivial occasion,—without feeling irresistibly charmed, without seeming to hear the tread of the Muse, if in but a single footfall. Gautier was blessed with a perception of material beauty so intense and comprehensive that he was unable to write five lines without creating a lovely image or ministering in some odd fashion to the delight of the eyes. Art was his divinity, and he worshipped her by example as well as by dogma. He forged himself, at the outset of his career, a perfect style, and his lavish application of it has always reminded us of the conduct of the heroes of old-fashioned romances, who pay their debts by breaking off a bit of their gold chain. Gautier paid out his chain, as it were, in larger and smaller pieces, but the fragment, whatever its size, always contained a portion of the original metal. For many minds —minds of an ascetic and utilitarian temper—he will always have a limited interest, or rather an unlimited repulsiveness; but for the happy majority, as we imagine it, who are blessed with an eternal relish for the pictorial, whether rendered by the pen or by the brush, this projected complement to his published volumes will give a larger outline to his genius. As we recede from him with the lapse of time, and his figure is lighted by this intensified glow, we more freely perceive how rare and perfect a genius it was. Nothing probably is easier than to exaggerate Gautier's merits, or rather to pervert his claims; but to our sense we should lose more by making light of them than by commemorating them in unstinted measure. In his own way, Gautier was simply perfect, and we have had not many great talents in these latter years of whom the same can be said. Few have been so wholly of one piece, of so unmingled a strain; so pure, compact, serene, so in tune with themselves. This was the case with Gautier from the first, and there is something extremely respectable in the way in which through forty years of possible intellectual corruption he preserved the beautiful unity of his inspiration. He had an extraordinary intellectual simplicity. The late M. Feydeau, in a volume of *Souvenirs Intimes,* painfully compounded of triviality and pretentiousness, has attempted to render his friend the cruel service of establishing the contrary. He talks of him as a great thinker and a profound scholar. M. Feydeau's indiscreet adulation will provoke a smile in those who have breathed the atmosphere, so unweighted with a moral presence, so unstirred by the breath of reflection, which pervades equally our author's most ardent verse and most deliberate prose. Gautier's simplicity is his alpha and his omega, and the all-sufficient explanation of much that, in a complex nature, would have savored of offence. He never judged morality; he knew no more about it than a Fiji-Islander about coal-smoke. His sole mission in the world was to make pictures, and he discharged it with a singleness of sympathy which even his possibly more spiritualized ghost will shudder to see his posthumous eulogists attempting to discredit. His pictorial faculty was unsurpassed; he was one of the first descriptive poets. This surely is glory enough, and in the very interest of refined enjoyment we protest against all extension or qualification of it. For it is not in the least paradoxical to say that Gautier would have been a much less estimable writer if he had been in the least a more edifying one. Nature had furnished him with an unequalled apparatus for æsthetic perception and verbal portraiture, and she had attempted, in the intellectual line, to do nothing else. To preserve the balance she had contented herself with giving him an imperturbable moral amenity. Those who have read to any purpose the *Voyage en Espagne* and the *Capitaine Fracasse,*

to say nothing of that tremendous monument of juvenile salubrity, *Mademoiselle de Maupin,* in which the attempt to seem
vicious is like a pair of burnt-cork mustaches smirched over lips
still redolent of a mother's milk, will know what we mean when
we say that Gautier is almost grotesquely *good*. His temperament
is as full of *bonhomie* as his imagination of refinement. He
occasionally pointed a period with a dash of sarcasm; but such
a missile, in his hands, did execution hardly less gentle than a
feather pillow. This almost helpless-looking moral simplicity and
benignity in Gautier, as it shows in union with his lifelong appeal
to all the delightful material influences of life, is the source
of that part of our good-will for our author which we just now
called inexpressible. In one's admiration for him, in this spirit,
there is something of compassion. He seems to be, in a manner,
the unretributed sport of Nature. He gives her all his attention,
his love, and his zeal; year in and year out he gazes at her, waits
on her, catches her every image and mood and tone; and she,
sitting there in her splendors and seeing herself mirrored in a
style which never ceased to develop till its polished surface had
reflected her from head to foot, never drops into his conscience,
by way of reward, a single vivifying germ; never by her grateful
breath transforms him for a day from the poet who merely observes and describes into the poet who conceives and creates.
All this, to our sense, if we are not over-fanciful, gives Gautier
an odd sort of isolated, unsupported, unfriended air in the midst
of the beautiful material world to which he spent his life in
paying exquisite compliments. We do not really react upon
natural impressions and assert our independence, until these
impressions have been absorbed into our moral life and become
a mysterious part of moral passion. Poor Gautier seems to stand
forever in the chill external air which blows over the surface
of things; above his brilliant horizon there peeped no friendly
refuge of truth purely intellectual, where he could rake over
the embers of philosophy, and rest his tired eyes among the
shadows of the unembodied.

M. Feydeau was, according to his own account, for many
years an intimate friend of Gautier and the confidant of his most
personal pleasures and pains. It was his habit to take notes dur-

ing this period of all noteworthy incidents, and he aspires in his little volume to play the part of a miniature Boswell. Unfortunately, we get a more lively sense of M. Feydeau's own personality than of that of his weightier friend; and we may say in parenthesis, and without an infraction of charity, considering on this and on other occasions the frankness of the author's self-exposure, that a less attractive personality has rarely sought to exhibit itself in literature. His volume, however, reminds us pertinently enough of the intellectual atmosphere in which Gautier lived and worked. It was an atmosphere which imperiously urged all who breathed it to the cultivation of the picturesque in some form or other,—painting or the drama, the *feuilleton* or the novel. "Art," says M. Flaubert, was his friend's master-passion: his life was passed in the zealous appreciation of clever pictures and new plays; in going from the studio to the theatre and from the theatre to the printing-office. There have doubtless been circles far more prolific in valuable generalizations about art,—circles in Berlin and Düsseldorf, in which the philosophy of the matter was opened up in a far more abysmal fashion over pipes and *Schoppen* any night in the year; but there has probably been in our time no more exquisite and penetrating a sentiment of the subject than was to be found in the half-Bohemian *coterie* of which M. Feydeau's "Théo" was the high-priest. From this *coterie* every human consideration not immediately bearing upon some possible artistic interpretation of sensuous pleasure seems to have been unanimously excluded. "Politics" were religiously tabooed, the sense of the company being unexceptionally that producers in their line should have a good strong money-spending, picture-ordering government to take care of them and guard them well against the rising tide of democracy and utilitarianism, but never be bothered with principles and details. When, on the close of the war (which brought to Gautier a good deal of personal misfortune), he has occasion, like any other good citizen, to treat his friend to a little talk (very sensible talk) about the prospects of France, the duties of Frenchmen, and the question of the *"revanche,"* he thinks it necessary, according to M. Feydeau's report, to make an elaborate apology for venturing upon such unfamiliar ground, even in the freedom of a *tête-*

à-tête. But perhaps the strongest impression we get from M. Feydeau is of the uninterrupted laboriousness of our author's career. Gautier was to the end a poor man. His exquisite literary work, though relished by the delicate of taste all over the world, never procured him anything but a decent subsistence. He could never treat himself to that supreme luxury of the artist,—the leisure to do a certain fine thing to please himself. He was chained to the newspapers; to the hour of his death he was hammering with his golden mallet on the resonant anvil of the daily press. His vivid images, his charming fancies, his wealth of color and metaphor and perception, his polished perfection and unerring felicity of style, through all of which, as we read, there seems to circulate such a current of joyous spontaneity and leisurely appreciation, were to the writer's own sense all mere daily drudgery, paid for by the line,—the goaded effort of a mind haunted by visions of hungry mouths and unpaid bills. In this daily pressure of labor and need, it is immensely to Gautier's credit that he never, for three words together, was false to his rigid literary conscience. The work, under the spur, was not only done, but perfectly done. It was often done in the printing-office on the edge of a smutted table, with a dozen people talking; but there is never a case in which the reader of the finished article is not free to fancy it may have been excogitated in luxurious leisure, amid the fumes of a perfumed pipe, by a genius in a Persian dressing-gown reclining under a bower of roses. The conjunction of Gautier's hurried, overworked, oppressed manner of life with the indescribably exquisite, chiselled quality ("chiselled" is the word that always comes to us) of his prose, is one of the interesting facts of literature. It is just such a fact as the Academy was bound to take cognizance of, but he knocked more than once in vain at the door of rusty hinges; it remained his privilege to complete, with Balzac and Madame Sand for his companions, the trio of the great excluded imaginative writers.

We should like to quote, for curiosity's sake, a few lines from a letter of M. Gustave Flaubert, the author of *Madame Bovary.* M. Flaubert was an intimate friend of Gautier, and M. Feydeau prints a note received from him at the time of the poet's death:—

"Je ne plains pas notre ami défunt. Au contraire, je l'envie profondément. Que ne suis-je pourrir à sa place? Pour l'agrément qu'on a dans ce bas monde, autant s'en aller le plus vite possible. Le 4 Septembre a inauguré un état de choses qui ne nous regarde plus. *Nous sommes de trop.* On nous hait et on nous méprise. Voilà le vrai. Donc, bonsoir! Pauvre cher Théo! C'est de cela qu'il est mort (du dégoût de l'infection moderne). C'etait un grand lettré et un grand poëte."

M. Feydeau gives his friend's letter with the reverse of an invidious intention, but its effect is the same as that of his own reflections throughout his volume when he quotes himself or speaks *in propria persona*. Gautier's younger comrades are a corrupt generation, and their arid cynicism only serves to throw into relief the admirable geniality of the elder writer,—the happy salubrity of a temperament which could spend forty years in the lap of tendencies predestined to all manner of ultimate morbid efflorescence, and yet preserve its sweetness to the end. MM. Feydeau and Flaubert, M. Dumas *fils,* and a dozen others are the dregs of a school,—the running to seed of the famous generation of 1830. Gautier had the good fortune to belong to the elder race, and to enjoy the good health which, if it came from nothing else, would come from his being original.

The second of the volumes which serve as the text of our remarks may be regarded as his contribution to the history of that extraordinary literary revolution. A "History of Romanticism" is a rather ambitious title for what is hardly more than a string of picturesque anecdotes and reminiscences of the author's early comrades, reinforced by a series of obituary notices of the veterans in the grand army, published as they dropped one by one out of the march. But it was to the picturesque side of the movement of 1830 that Gautier was especially attached, and its hundred outward eccentricities could not have found a more sympathetic and amusing chronicler. The great flood-tide which, with the coming in of Louis Philippe, detached from their immemorial anchorage so many of the old divinities and dogmas in French art and letters has, by this time, wellnigh subsided; has, in fact, in great part retreated into various quiet coves and corners, under watch of the declining star of genius which has earned its rest. But, it behooves us to remember well what a mighty tide it was, and what a wondrous work it achieved. The eighteen years of the reign of Louis Philippe were certainly, for art and letters, one of the great moments of the human mind, and quite worthy, proportions observed, to rank with the age of Pericles, the age of Elizabeth, or the Florentine Renaissance. It offers a splendid list of names, as Gautier here strings them together: "Lamartine, Victor Hugo, Alexandre Dumas, Alfred de Musset, George Sand, Balzac, Sainte-Beuve, Auguste Barbier, Delacroix, Louis Boulanger, Ary Scheffer, Dévéria, Decamps, David d'Angers, Barye, Hector Berlioz, Frédéric Lemaître, and Madame Dorval." He omits Prosper Mérimée, Michelet, and himself from the writers, Horace Vernet from the painters, and Mademoiselle Rachel from the actors. All these great talents worked together, lived together very much, and had a multitude of common passions, hopes, and aspirations. They were young and poor, and conscious of their strength; all herded together in the attics and *entresols* of a brilliant, inspiring capital, and inflamed with a generous comradeship as well as with artistic ardor. The band of the young *romantiques* had its wild oats to sow, and it scattered a plentiful crop; but English readers, in judging the explosive temper of this Parisian *Sturm und Drang,* must remember how long art and letters in France had groaned under the weight of inanimate tradition. Literature was like Sinbad the Sailor with the Old Man of the Sea on his back. It resorted naturally enough to the most frolicsome pace and most fantastic gambols to unseat the monstrous incubus. Gautier says, in all but perfect earnest, that the old French theatre contained but two picturesque lines. Corneille had risked

"Cette obscure clarté qui tombe des étoiles."
And in Moliére's Tartuffe Cléante had remarked that
"La campagne à présent n'est pas beaucoup fleurie."

To protest against the uniform grayness of classicism, it seemed to Gautier himself but half enough to write the glowing pictorial scenes of *Albertus* and take the liberties of *Mademoiselle de Maupin;* to be consistent, he thought it proper to let his hair grow down to his waist, to wear yellow Turkish slippers in the street, and to go to the first representation of Victor Hugo's *Hernani* in the crimson waistcoat which afterwards became legendary. He gives in the present volume the history of the crimson waistcoat, disentangled from legendary perversion, and informs us that the garment in question was composed of the finest scarlet satin and was laced behind like a woman's corset. Of information of this calibre the present chapters are largely composed; they make no pretensions to being a philosophic history. Philosophy, indeed, was so scantily represented either at that or at any period in the career of literary romanticism, that we wonder, as we think of it, whence came the saving discretion which kept it from submersion in its own excesses. All the intellectual force of the movement seemed concentrated in a passionate sense of the "plastic," —of a plastic which should especially embody color. But all this unballasted æstheticism gives one a lively idea of the quantity of clear genius diffused through the group. The intuitive, instinctive side of art was magnificently exemplified. In spite of the lightness of Gautier's treatment of his theme, his chapters may provoke a good deal of serious reflection. The list of the romanticists who drew the prize and grasped the laurel is very short, compared with that of their innumerable comrades who, as the French say, never "arrived." Gautier's allusions to these abortive careers are rather melancholy reading: so many were called, and so few chosen; so many were young and ardent and confident, and so few, relatively, lived and matured to exchange the young confidence for the old certainty. But we see here, as in the history of every important intellectual movement, that the failures fertilized the soil for success, that nothing great is done without a school, and that to produce a hundred finished masterpieces there must be ten thousand vain attempts. However many the masterpieces, it is always a pity there are not more; but one must nevertheless pronounce happy in its day the generation which, while the verdict was yet in abeyance, cared so universally and ardently to win the good cause. We have had great pleasure, we may say in conclusion, in reading the last division of the present volume, the *Tableau des Progrés de la Poésie Française depuis 1830*. The work was drawn up by request of the Imperial government with a series of cognate reports from other hands on the occasion of the Exhibition of 1867. It was perfectly in character that it should be "genial," and the place of criticism is kept throughout by exquisite, sympathetic, and, in the literal sense of the word, imaginative description. It is not often, we suppose, that in a government report one stumbles on such a passage as these lines upon Théodore de Banville:—

"La chaste pâleur et le contour tranquille des marbres ne suffisaient pas à ce coloriste. Les décesses étalaient dans l'onde ou dans la nuée des chairs de nacre, veinées d'azur, fouettées de rose, inondées de chevelures rutilantes au ton d'ambre et de topaze, et des rondeurs d'une opulence qu'eût évité l'art grec. Les roses, les lys, l'azur, l'or, la pourpre, l'hyacinthe abondent chez Banville; il revêt tout ce qu'il touche d'un voile tramé de rayons, et ses idées, comme des princesses de féeries, se promènent dans les prairies d'emeraude, avec des robes couleur du temps, couleur du soleil, et couleur de la lune."

MAURICE DE GUÉRIN*

We have had occasion more than once in these columns, to speak of Eugénie de Guérin, and in so doing to touch upon her less famous but even more remarkable brother. The opportunity to-day is afforded us to dwell at greater length upon Maurice de Guérin. A gentleman well fitted for the task has executed a translation of the most valuable portion of Guérin's literary remains—his "Journal"—and promises us a version of his letters and his fragmentary pieces. When these shall have been published, American readers who are acquainted with the writings of Eugénie de Guérin, and whose curiosity has been stimulated by the important although silent part played therein by her brother, will find themselves in possession of all such evidence

* The Journals of Maurice de Guérin. Translated by Edward Thornton Fisher. New York: Leypoldt & Holt. 1867. (*The Nation*, March 6, 1867).

as exists of the young man's extraordinary powers. Let us say immediately a good word for the present translation. It bears marks of fidelity, sympathy, and intelligence, the three essential requisites of a translator; and it strikes us, moreover, as the work of one possessing a good English style. We have observed two or three slight aberrations from the lines of the French text, where it is somewhat ambiguous; but these are pardonable, since the spirit of the whole is not falsified. We should add that the editor has prefixed to the "Journal" a translation of Sainte-Beuve's "Causerie" on Guérin, an example of his best manner; and Mr. Matthew Arnold's essay, an example of his poorest. It was chiefly for the good taste of his selections—always one of Mr. Arnold's great merits—that his essay was valuable; and as Mr. Fisher has suppressed the extracts and given us only the commentary, the character of the essay suffers not a little.

The facts of Guérin's life are soon told. He was born at the château of Cayla, in Languedoc, in the year 1810, of a family noble, religious, and poor. His first studies were prosecuted at the *petit seminaire* of Toulouse; his subsequent ones, from the age of thirteen, at the Collége Stanislas, in Paris. On the completion of these latter, he spent a short interval in Paris, undecided as to a profession and in search of temporary work; but, finally, in mid-winter of 1832, in accordance with the wishes of his family, he entered a small quasi-religious brotherhood, founded and governed by La Mennais, at La Chenaié, in Brittany. This step was taken with a view of preparing himself for an ecclesiastical career. Guérin possessed the least conceivable fitness (short of positive aversion) for such a career. There is every appearance, however, that he derived great benefit from his sojourn and his daily contact with La Mennais. These were brought to a sudden conclusion by La Mennais' dissension with the Church and the consequent dispersion of his little group of disciples. Guérin's attitude throughout this critical period is that of cordial sympathy with his instructor. Nine months of religious seclusion and study, however, have convinced him that the Church is not his vocation, and he is again thrown upon the world for support. Before returning to Paris, he spends a number of weeks in the house of a friend on the coast of Brittany, and it is here that some of the finest passages of his journal are written. In January, 1834, he takes up his residence in Paris, where he remains until his early death in 1839. Destitute of all resources save such as he himself creates, his life during this interval is one of hard and often distasteful labor. He gives lessons of Latin and Greek and contributes articles to magazines and newspapers. His lessons, however, are ill paid and his literary connections not extensive, and the first real ease which he knows he obtains through a marriage which he allows to be arranged for him in his twenty-eighth year. Judging from the evidence of his letters and of those of his sister, these words do not mis-represent the nature of Guérin's marriage. His wife was young, charming, and mistress of an income, but Guérin did not live to enjoy his good fortune. He died of consumption in the course of a few months.

Such are the external facts of his history—facts few and simple. To what does he owe, it may be asked, the reputation which, twenty-seven years after his death, causes his writings to be translated into a foreign tongue? What are the names of his works? What idea has he given to the world? There is something very odd in the answer to these questions. Guérin's "works" are a private journal of a hundred duodecimo pages; a half-dozen copies of verses, some twenty-odd letters, and two short prose compositions on mythological subjects. He produced, moreover, a number of book-notices and of miscellaneous articles for periodicals, but these have never been disentombed, and it is by the scanty relics of his private history that his reputation is upheld. So solid a reputation has seldom rested on a basis so accidental. As for Guérin's "ideas," the task of enumeration is easy; or, rather, it is impossible. We are unable to associate a single idea with his name. His gift to the world was the gift of himself, of his own history; or, in other words, of the documents in which this history is reflected—documents as exquisite in quality as they are few in number.

Guérin's history may be briefly described as that of a mel-ancholy man who overcomes his melancholy. The reader of his journal and letters is made a spectator of this delicate process of self-education. He watches the gradual decline of the writer's sadness, the successive diminution of each of its multifold elements, its backward retreat before the advance of the positive cares of life, and its final extinction at the moment when the young man engages in the most rational of marriages and embraces for the second time the most paternal and comfortable of creeds. It may be that Guérin's struggles were not really over at this moment, but it is certain that the reader's perception of them is satisfied.

When we speak of Guérin's sadness, of his melancholy, of his *tristesse*, we feel straightway bound to qualify our language and to explain the force of these terms. Save in a single particular, Guérin was not built on a large scale; he possessed an extraordinary sense of style; he was a master of the use of words. His melancholy has nothing profound and organic. It is not complicated with intellectual curiosity and intellectual doubts. His objects of interest are few in number, and easily approached. His dejection, therefore, is not the prodigious sadness of Pascal, nor, to take another example from among his own countrymen, the ceaseless weariness of Rousseau. It is an egotistical, a sentimental sadness. It is not the apprehension that the world is wrong, that life is worthless, that everything is nothing; it is the impression that *he* is wrong, that his own life is worthless, that his own powers are null. From the beginning to the end of his journal there is no trace of that penetrating (and penetrated) observation of the manners and motives of men which imparts a large portion of their value to the pages of Pascal and Rousseau. Guérin's outward gaze is for physical nature alone. When it deserts this field it reverts to his own mind. Here it lingers with a patience, a vigilance, which have never been surpassed. We quote an illustration:

"Day before yesterday, in the evening, I had passed my arm round the trunk of a lilac and was singing softly J. J.'s song, 'Que le jour me dure.' This touching, melancholy air, my posture, the calm of evening, and, more than all, this habit that belongs to my soul of taking up at evening all its sadness, of surrounding itself with pale clouds towards the end of the day, threw me back upon the deep vast consciousness of my inner poverty. I saw myself miserable, very miserable, and utterly incapable of a future. At the same time, I seemed to hear murmuring, far and high above my head, that world of thought and poetry toward which I so often spring without the power ever to attain to it."

On this occasion he experiences a reaction; that is, he extracts a species of consolation, a whisper of encouragement, from the very depths of his dejection. At other times his depression is complete:

"My soul shrinks and recoils upon itself like a leaf touched by the cold; it has abandoned all the positions from which it looked out. After some days of struggle against social realities, I have been obliged to fall back and retire within. Here I am circumscribed and blockaded until my thought, swollen by a new inundation, rises above the dike and flows freely over all the banks. I know of few events of my internal life so formidable for me as this sudden contraction of my being after extreme expansion. In this condensation, the most active faculties, the most unquiet, the most bitter elements find themselves seized and condemned to inaction, *but without paralysis, without decrease of vitality;* all their vehemence is confined and compressed with them. Pressed and crowded, they struggle against each other and altogether against their barrier. At these times all the feeling of life I have is reduced to a deep dull irritation, alternating with paroxysms; it is the fermentation of so many various elements, becoming inflamed and exasperated by their forced contact, and making repeated efforts to burst forth. All the faculties which place me in communication with outside space, with distance—those bright and faithful messengers of the soul, which go and come continually from the soul to nature and from nature to the soul—finding themselves pent within, I remain isolated, cut off from full participation in universal life. I become, like an infirm old man deficient in all his senses, alone and excommunicated from the world of nature."

These lines strike us as a forcible example of clear insight into moral phenomena, and of clear and masculine writing. We might multiply examples on both of these points, but want of space forbids us. The value and interest attached to Guérin's introspective habits reside in the fact that his self-scrutiny was so honest and unsparing, and that he really brought back positive data from his incursions into his soul. But perhaps the source of their main interest is in the intimate connection which existed between his constant self-appreciation and his sympathies with the world of external nature. It is upon this last phase of his character that Mr. Matthew Arnold chiefly dwells; and it is to the exquisite delicacy of his feeling for the life of the earth that we owe some of the finest pages of his journal. Many of them have been quoted and requoted, so that we hardly know which to choose. It is not, in our opinion, when he deliberately describes in its fulness a landscape or a bit of scenery that his style attains to its greatest beauty; this happens more particularly when a vague and general sense of the bounding, inexhaustible forces of nature, as contrasted with his own slow-beating pulses, imparts an almost special rhythm to his language, or when an irresistible memory of spring or of midsummer breaks into the tissue of his prose and suffuses it with light and heat and sound:

"Leave there," he cries at the end of a noble passage in which he registers an impression of growing strength, through the contact of the spreading idea of liberty,—"leave there those men and their sayings, and steep yourself in the memory of those days of freedom when you roamed at will through the country, with your heart swollen with joy, and singing full-voiced hymns of liberty; or when you spent a day all idleness from one end to the other, from the joyous breezes of morning to the warm odors of evening; lying under a pear tree, careless of everything, and bidding defiance in your insolent ease to the tyrants of every kind, bound like vultures upon the flanks of the human race."

Here is another fine passage:

"Let us abjure the worship of idols; let us turn our backs on the deities of art, decked with paint and false finery, on all these images with mouths that speak not. Let us adore nature, frank, ingenuous, and in no respect exclusive. Great God! how can men make poetry in face of the broad poem of the universe? Your poetry! The Lord has made it for you; it is the created world."

But it is in the short prose poem entitled "The Centaur" that we find the richest fruits of Guérin's constant communion with the silent processes of nature, and of his unquenchable curiosity as to her secrets. The centaur relates the story of his long life, recalls the memories of his early years, and enumerates his sensations, at once so simple and so complex. Guérin's style in this composition reaches a breadth and elevation which are truly remarkable when we consider the age at which it was written. There is no loose flinging of epithets, no confounding of crude colors. The whole piece is marked by a classical unity and simplicity. What poetry is more impetuous at once and more serene than this?

"My glances travelled freely and reached the most distant points. Like the shores of rivers, for ever wet, the mountain ranges in the west remained stamped with spaces of light, but half wiped out by the shadows. There, in the pale clearness, survived the pure, bare peaks. There I saw at one time the descent of the god Pan, always alone, and at another the choir of the secret divinities, or the passage of some mountain nymph, intoxicated by the night. Sometimes the eagles of Mount Olympus crossed the upper sky and vanished among the far-off constellations or in the depths of the inspired woods. The presence of the gods, overtaken by sudden trouble, would break the quiet of the old oaks."

There is a hyper-criticism which consists in burrowing for small beauties quite as offensive as that which consists in picking out insignificant faults; but we trust we shall not be held guilty of this vice when we say that the simple words "always alone," in the above passage, taken in their connection, strike us as more thoroughly imbued with the spirit of poetry than the brightest of those floral chains of adjectives with which the poets of a later day have grown used to festoon the naked surface of their verse. Guérin was, in truth, an incomparable writer, and it is for this reason that his name deserves to stand. It is great praise to say of a man, deceased at the age of twenty-eight, that his style possesses something of that authority which will enable one to imitate it with impunity; but this praise may be given to Guérin. With so much about him that was weak, he must have felt that here he was strong. He has written pages which will live as long as his language.

DUMAS FILS AND GOETHE*

The French have long been reproached with their ignorance of foreign languages and their indifference to foreign literatures, and their best friends have lately had no hesitation in telling them that it is high time they should mend their ways, and learn what is going on in those parts of the world which do not happen to be included in the Paris *banlieue*. It is a matter of life and death, say these wholesome advisers; their salvation depends upon it; and if five years ago the various Frenchmen responsible in their respective degrees for the security of their country had known a fiftieth part as much German as the corresponding personages in Germany knew French, Alsace and Lorraine might not at this day be enslaved to the masters of the former idiom. It would lead us too far to enquire why it is that, more than any other people in the world, the French have considered their speech and their writings as the normal tongue and the classic literature, and rather regarded the acquisition of English and German as an eccentric and superfluous accomplishment, but a degree removed from a curious attention to local dialects and vulgar variations. The fault is their neighbors' as well as their own; indeed, the fault may be brought home to a very occult historic cause. It has been the mingled blessing and bane of the French nation that it possesses a language which all the world has found it a pleasure to learn—an education, in a certain sense,

---

* 'Le Faust de Goethe, Traduction nouvelle, par H. Bacharach. Préface de M. Alexandre Dumas fils.' Paris: Michel Lévy. New York: F. W. Christern. 1873. (*The Nation*, October 30, 1873).

to use—a piece of intellectual grossness not, in some degree or other, to have felt the influence of. For very many years this has been true, and it has not altogether ceased to be true at the present moment. But for a hundred reasons it is not so true as it was. We may say roughly, that so long as the refinements of civilization were of a tolerably simple order, there was very little that the French language was not capable of saying about them, and of saying better than any other. But of late the world has been getting to look very complex, and we hear a great many ideas buzzing away at our ears which answer, when addressed, neither to *Monsieur* nor to *Madame*. The French is not a large language; we have greatly loved it; we may claim even to have zealously *used* it, and we pretend to speak without prejudice. Its very charm and the secret of its long prosperity is its compactness, its convenience, the half-a-dozen virtues which it even now helps us out of our bungling by calling its *netteté*. On many points, for a long time, it seemed as much more civilized to express one's self in French rather than in English or German, as it seems to pay for an article in silver crowns rather than in eggs and chickens, in cattle and corn. These points are still standing, but other points have become visible all around them, which the silver crown, when applied, but insufficiently covers, so that we are obliged to have recourse to a larger coinage. Of course, to stretch our metaphor, the French are interested in insisting that the only wares worth owning are the wares their money will buy; for it is certainly not agreeable, in the supposed heyday of one's prosperity, to be left with a depreciated coinage on one's hands. For this we make large allowance and we therefore note the more promptly all symptoms of an ungrudging attention to foreign markets, as we may say.

These remarks are suggested by the volume whose title we have transcribed—a volume noteworthy in both its aspects. It contains primarily a new translation of 'Faust,' more perfect, more adequate, its author affirms, than any of its predecessors. This is very possible; the translation strikes us as excellent, and it may fairly seem to its publishers a very proper *pièce de circonstance*. There was presumably a good deal of reading of Voltaire in the original beyond the Rhine before the events of

1870, and it is part of the humorous logic of history that there should be such reading as may be of Goethe, in the best attainable translation, on the hither side of it at this late period, which is better than never at all. But what Michel Lêvy & Co. count upon to sell their book, even more than the war of 1870, is the preface furnished to the volume by M. Alexandre Dumas fils. This gentleman's readers have of course observed that with the progress of events he has become more and more of a moralist. Every few months, for some time now, he has found himself with something edifying to say, and he has preached his little sermons with increasing gusto and skill. Every one has heard of the pamphlet on adultery in which the writer's wisdom seemed to have said its last word. This last word, it will be remembered, was *Tue-la!*—"Shoot her dead!" It made quiet thinkers jump, like a pistol-shot at the circus. But the seasons have revolved, and M. Dumas has arrived at new results. This time it is not the treacherous wife that we are to kill, but the author of 'Faust' whom we are to sit and behold ground into small, inanimate pieces before us. M. Dumas frankly confesses that he has never had a finer opportunity to hold his tongue. He is ignorant of the German language, and he comes after a host of commentators who had eluded this reproach. But his desire to paint a moral is irresistible, and he bravely embarks upon his theme.

M. Dumas is an excellent dramatist. There have been few greater pleasures for the theatre-goers of our time than to listen to the 'Demi-Monde' and the 'Question d'Argent.' These are considerable performances, and they imply in their author, in some points at least, a sound judgment and a lively imagination. They prove, certainly, that he knows how to present his ideas. His theory (very well stated in one of his prefaces), that in a drama every word uttered should *count* mathematically, here stands him in excellent stead, and makes him extremely readable. But apart from the presumption that there is something in M. Dumas's ideas, there is a great deal that holds one's attention in his sincerity. Evidently the various items of his philosophy are the result of no small amount of ardent emotion; he believes what he says, and he believes that a foolish generation which does not heed it will go to the bad all the faster for its indifference. For that we are going very directly to the bad, unless we radically amend our morals, is M. Dumas's intimate conviction. We are fatally fond of unclean things, and unless we pull up short in our reckless carnival, we shall find ourselves in the bottomless pit. M. Dumas should know, for he has made an especial study of the unclean; he has an infallible scent for it, and a singularly cunning hand in depicting it. He has apparently received his original impetus in his present undertaking from the discovery that there are a number of unclean things in the history of the author of 'Faust.' He begins his argument, however, by a vigorous plea for the diffusion of the masterpieces of foreign literature among his countrymen, and insists especially that the best works of the English and German stage ought to be occasionally represented at the Théâtre Français. He made the acquaintance of 'Faust' with a view to judging whether a literal translation of it might be successfully represented in Paris, but he was led to conclusions of a far larger scope. These were in great measure the result of a comparison between the poem and the poet's personal history, and they were flattering, on the whole, neither to the author nor to the man. Goethe, twenty years old, made near Strasbourg the acquaintance of a country parson's daughter; readers of his 'Autobiography' will remember the episode of Frederica. Goethe loved her, seduced her, left her, and carried away the germ of the story of *Margaret;* he loved again repeatedly, and M. Dumas counts off his successive sweethearts on his fingers with a critical commentary worthy of his best performances in this line; but he never loved with the same good faith; everything else was rank grossness; he had got his *Margaret,* his passport to posterity, and this was all he cared about. He began his poem, and wrote a bit here, and a bit there—having found his legend ready-made to his hand; but on the whole he got on rather lamely, and would very likely have hobbled along into utter oblivion, had not Schiller one fine day made his appearance—Schiller, who, like M. Dumas, could really serve you up a drama. Schiller set him, poetically, on his feet, prompted, suggested, invented, took charge of him intellectually, to the dénouement. But Schiller, unfortunately, could not last for ever; he died in harness, and left his friend with the second part of 'Faust' on his hands. What Goethe made of it shows us all that Schiller had done for the first part.

> "Meanwhile, as death might grow tired of waiting till Goethe found the good (*le bien*), as his intellectual sense became weaker every day, according to the laws of nature, as the moral sense could not come to his assistance and Schiller could no longer advise him, as this poem, commenced with a cry of the heart, ought to have finished with a cry of the soul, as the heart had gone and the soul had never come, Goethe heaped up in his work episodes upon episodes, formulas upon formulas, symbols upon symbols. History, mythology, science, arts, politics, agriculture, industry, everything is summoned, everything comes in without connection, without reason. If Goethe were still living, he would be adding railway, the electric telegraph, chloroform, postal orders, and the *fumier impérial*. What fine verses he would use himself up in making about them all! For this labyrinth is enamelled here and there with charming bowers, where you pause to wipe your forehead; this low, opaque sky, which suffocates and asphyxiates you, is suddenly streaked with phosphorescent flashes which cross it and brighten it; but *'ce n'est pas le jour, ce n'est pas l'alouette';* they are nothing but spontaneous combustions of air, blue aerolites, which fall and are quenched in deserts of granite and oceans of lead."

M. Dumas gives us the second part of 'Faust' as it should have been, as surely, he declares, as two and two make four. We have no space for his ingenious synopsis, which culminates in the tableau of Faust presenting himself before the Lord, "holding with one hand Mephistopheles chained at his feet, with the other, Margaret, the eternal spouse, recovered and saved, leaning on his bosom." "Humanity," the author adds, "will be thus represented as she is to be some day, after all her errors, revolts, and falls, victorious over evil, man redeemed by his conscience, woman redeemed by her love, making only one in a God integral, eternal, and infinite. This is the fatal, inevitable deduction which the idea contained in the first 'Faust,' imposed upon the second. Good or bad, there was no other, as there is no other solution than *four* to two multiplied by two." But the great Goethe was incapable of putting two and two together, having, in the first place, too little imagination, and, in the second, too little morality. That he lacked imagination sounds like a terrible heresy, but nothing is more obvious. He could conceive of no event without the warrant of a particular example; in order to conceive Faust seducing Margaret, he had first himself to seduce Frederica—in order to know that Werther would shoot himself, he had to wait two years, after first planning the tale, for Jerusalem to put a real bullet into a real pistol. He had, therefore, a very dull fancy. Morally, however, he was unfortunately none the better, as sometimes happens for this peculiar intellectual torpor. Into the history of Goethe's *mœurs* M. Dumas penetrates bravely, but we have no desire to follow him. They were as bad as bad could be; he was a very nasty fellow; he came near dying of vexation at seventy-four because a virtuous young lady would not listen to him; he ended his days, in short, as a *polisson vénérable*. M. Dumas touches these points with indescribable vivacity, and this whole phase of his subject elicits the choicest treasures of his wit. We especially recommend his account of Goethe's marriage and of his wife's eccentricities. As a *tirade*, it has really not elbow-room in the midst of the author's hard-pressing logic; uttered before the foot-lights at the Gymnase, it would bring down the house. M. Dumas, however, we suppose, is as free to expatiate on these matters in his own manner, and with his own object, as the poet's admirers have been to do so from the opposite point of view. They have to our mind usurped a much larger place in literary history than their merits entitle them to, and, offence for offence, we perhaps prefer M. Dumas's irony to the complaisance of friendlier critics. It is certainly more entertaining. Its purpose is to establish the position that Goethe was all of a piece, and that both in his life and writings he was criminally indifferent to *le bien*. But we may rest in peace, for God has already chastised him. He condemned 'Faust,' as a whole, to be a decidedly poor affair—a thing of intellectual shreds and patches, fluttering in every breath of criticism, and showing the daylight (or rather the inner darkness) at every rent; and he cut down the author's remaining literary baggage to a very light parcel indeed. After summing up his hero's infirmities—his poetic incompetence and his personal licentiousness, the terrible dulness and depravity of his second 'Faust,' and his going to bed with poultices and gruel on discovering that young ladies had ceased to find him irresistible—M. Dumas concludes:

> "In short, of this strange tissue of errors, of faults, of researchers, of egotism, of pride, of levity, of emotions, of weakness, of shadows, of lights, of science, of want of conscience, and of genius, there remains, with a few remarkable poems, two superior works, 'Werther' and 'Hermann and Dorothea,' and a masterpiece—the first 'Faust'—after sixty years of daily labor."

And then M. Dumas proceeds to remind us how the great poets of the Latin race have produced their masterpieces at a far faster rate, to declare that the great representative of the other race, "in its cold deduction, fragmentary, dusky genius, born of tenacious labor, of slow, mysterious, step-by-step progression, without original inspiration, without an ideal, without probity," may do very well for the humanity he so complacently embodies, "the mechanical humanity of functionaries and soldiers who believe that the world will accept their ideas, bear their yoke, and speak their language"; but that he, M. Dumas, speaking briefly, in the name of all Latinity, must give him, once for all, a piece of his mind. "Posterity will do her duty. She will write on her brazen tablets: 'Goethe, born at Frankfort, 1749; died at Weimar, 1832; great writer, great poet, great artist.' And, when the fanatics of form, of art, of love *quand même* and materialism, come and ask her to add 'Great man,' she will answer, 'No.'"

As far as proving a case and settling a question is concerned, M. Dumas's preface is of very small value. His acquaintance with Goethe is evidently of the slightest, and his judgment, even so far as it is based on his meagre information, is ludicrously perverted by national prejudice. The reader who is informed that the author of 'Faust' had no imagination, no intuition, we would recommend simply to read 'Faust' itself—even in the French translation which follows M. Dumas's essay, and which, in spite of its merit, is such a palpable underfit to the swelling, straining volume of the original; to read 'Wilhelm Meister,' 'Iphigenia,' 'Egmont,' 'Torquato Tasso'—works which M. Dumas has apparently not thought it worth his while to look into. Goethe certainly had an immense respect for reality, and no man was ever a greater collector and conservator, as one may say, of facts; but given the multifarious use he made of them—the mysterious music he drew from them—this was not a limitation but an extension of the poetic faculty. As for his having been or not been a *grand homme,* the question seems to us beside the mark, even from M. Dumas's point of view, and he reaches his conclusion by a perplexing *lapsus* in his argument. Very likely he was not; this would be our own impression; but M. Dumas ought to know that it is likely to be a waste of time to look for great men among prolific *littéateurs.* He ought, moreover, to have defined his term, and chosen near home an example of eminent moral virtue and eminent poetic genius. The real interest of his essay is, to our sense, quite an uncalculated one, and comes from our seeing a peculiarly Latin mind—or at least an intensely characteristic Gallic one—treating itself to a wholesome effusion of spleen against a peculiarly Germanic one. Our author's pamphlet has a really historic value. We do it injustice, moreover, by calling it splenetic; it is the voice of instinctive, deep-seated protest, dissent, and distaste, passing under the pressure of circumstances from the chronic to the acute form. M. Dumas, with his peculiar qualities and defects, is a happy mouthpiece for this dissenting voice. His mind is a very small one, but in its way it is very perfect; a larger mind, of the same stamp, would probably have found more points of contact in the author of 'Faust' than points of difference. How, indeed, was M. Dumas to endure Goethe for an hour? He seems to us to have been wonderfully patient, and to have handled him more gently than was to be expected. When the reader has followed our advice and refreshed his memory of 'Faust,' let him—we speak without the slightest intention of irony—go and read the 'Demi-Monde.' This clever drama will suffer, and yet it will not suffer. The reader will find it all form, compactness, roundness, smoothness, polish, art; but he will not find in it, without a rare amount of good will, a single word that echoes in the soul, that provokes the shadow of a reverie. "Faust" is another affair: it is slow reading for its very suggestiveness and intellectual resources. Of course, as M. Victor Hugo would say, the one hates the other; that is, when the one is in a greater hurry to hate than to understand. We may be sure that there are plenty of M. Dumas's fellow-thinkers who consider that he is making a rather indecent exposure of the Latin mind. And as for the "other," we suspect that if Goethe were living he would be at some pains to treat M. Dumas and his plays as one more *fact*—and a very entertaining one

SCHÉRER'S LITERARY STUDIES*

We have often wondered why M. Edmond Schérer, a critic whose privilege it sometimes is, by the acuteness of his insight or the felicity of his expression, to remind his readers of Sainte-Beuve, has never undertaken a work of larger proportions than the short journalistic articles in which he has hitherto been content to record his opinions. Such an enterprise seems at present more remote than ever, for M. Schérer has for some time past been devoting himself with increasing zeal to practical politics, and has lately been elected one of the seventy-five life members (on the Republican side) of the new French Senate. Moreover, the present volume perhaps explains in a measure why the author has remained a desultory critic. Clever as he is, brilliant also, abundant in knowledge and excellent in style, he stops short at a certain point. He tends to fall within the limit that the reader has set for him. He often disappoints, he lacks imagination, and he is subject to odd lapses and perversities of taste. He is one of the very few French writers who give the reader a sense of any serious first-hand acquaintance with English literature; and yet we remember his speaking some time since of the remarkable faculty of the English people for agreeing at a given moment

---

* 'Etudes Critiques de Littérature.' Par Schérer. Sixième Série. Paris: Michael Lévy; New York: F. W. Christern. 1876. (*The Nation*, April 6, 1876).

to get excited or infatuated over a nothing or a trifle, as the
necessary explanation of the popularity of Thackeray, "a cold,
ennuyeux writer." A literary critic who does not enjoy Thackeray
has certainly a limp in his gait. This impediment in his own
carriage however, M. Schérer manages on the whole very skilfully
to conceal, and some of the best pages in the present volume are
devoted to English authors. They contain, among other things,
one of the best criticisms of Taine's 'English Literature' that we
remember to have seen—that extraordinary work in which a
superb energy has vainly done its best to conceal a fatal want
of familiarity with the subject. M. Schérer resents this want of
familiarity almost as roundly as a native Englishman, and has in
particular some excellent remarks about the author's perverse
magnification of Byron. There are indeed few things more
singular than the way in which M. Taine steps over the heads
of the whole literary group ushered in by the present century—
Wordsworth, Shelley, Keats, Scott—and fastens himself upon
Byron for the reason that he is more an "Englishman" than
the others—more a Viking, a Berserker, a product of north-winds
and seafog! M. Schérer well observes that, with regard to Byron,
M. Taine stands just where French criticism stood thirty years
ago. The author has a long, entertaining, and well-informed
article upon Milton, whom he greatly admires, though perhaps
the average English reader will wince at his summing-up of his
judgment of 'Paradise Lost':

> " 'Paradise Lost' is a false, grotesque, tiresome poem; not one
> reader in a hundred can go, without smiling, through the
> ninth and tenth books, or without yawning through the
> eleventh and twelfth. It does not hold together, it is a
> pyramid balancing on its point, the most frightful of prob-
> lems resolved by the most puerile of means. And yet, never-
> theless, 'Paradise Lost' is immortal. It lives in virtue of some
> episodes which will remain for ever famous. In opposition
> to Dante, whom we must read altogether if we wish really
> to possess his beauties, we must read Milton only in frag-
> ments. But these fragments are part of the poetic patrimony
> of the human race."

In English we express the foregoing sentiments less trenchantly; every one is waiting for some one else to begin. But even among ourselves it has been for some time tacitly admitted that with regard to 'Paradise Lost' some of the cargo must be thrown overboard to save the ship. In an article on Bossuet and some of his recent editors, M. Schérer has some equally downright remarks upon sermons in general. "I conclude as I began: the sermon is a false style, and it is false in particular because it has grown old. It has so little human and general truth that it is difficult to interest one's self in it even retrospectively. In vain we consent to place ourselves at the desired point of view, make allowance for time and change, take tradition into account. We must be very fond of eloquence to enjoy it when it is in the condition of pure form—that is to say, of empty form, of rhetoric." On Bossuet in general M. Schérer makes some remarks which have a rather wholesome freshness as against the conventional, superstitious deference to their great classics which has so long prevailed among the French.

"The fact is that Bossuet has no *stock* (*pas de fonds*), or, what amounts to the same thing, that his stock doesn't belong to him. He is neither a *savant*, a thinker, nor a moralist. He never has what we call views, still less audacities. He lacks invention, observation, intelligence. He has a great imagination, a consummate knowledge of the oratorical style, an abundant, magnificent movement of phrase, but he uses these things only to paraphrase the commonplaces of the ecclesiastical dogma and the ecclesiastical morality. His exposition, in spite of its amplitude of form, remains essentially scholastic."

The longest of M. Schérer's papers, and the one we have found most interesting, is upon Goethe; its interest is the greater from the fact that it appeared after the Franco-Prussian war. Better than anything else, however, it illustrates what we have called the author's limitations and in particular his want of imagination. He remarks upon the fact that since the war the French have begun to pay a good deal of attention to German literature, and he thinks it an excellent sign.

"The Germans," to quote, "have revived against us the right of conquest; they have attacked us with envious hatred and cowardly insult; they have placed between us and themselves such offences as cannot be forgiven. But if it is just to detest Germany, it would be puerile on that account to seek to ignore her. It is at an end, we know; the charm that formerly drew us towards her is for ever broken; we shall no longer expect from her a single one of the ideas that elevate, of the sentiments that ennoble. So be it, we shall be but better placed to judge her. There had mingled itself with our inclination for German science and literature an enthusiasm which excluded discernment; in future it will be easier to see things in their true proportions . . . . If we are able to preserve ourselves from the other extreme—deliberate and intentional disparagement—we shall have obtained the noblest of enjoyments: that of judging impartially those who themselves defy all justice."

If M. Schérer has made an effort to be impartial, it is evident that it has cost him something. It may be said, too, that he decidedly exaggerates the "charm" which the French public found, before the war, in German literature. If he speaks of a small coterie of highly cultivated men, his observations have a certain justice; but French readers in general have certainly never given themselves the least trouble about the literature of the land of Goethe. If they find good reason to hate the Germans now, it is not that they ever loved them. The French have never been duped by the Germans or any one else; for to be duped implies attention and acquaintance. They have never been duped by any people but themselves. Upon Goethe M. Schérer says a great many discriminating and excellent things, and his article is a very vivid piece of portraiture. But he is guilty of a strange dullness of vision when he declares that he can see nothing but dreariness in 'Wilhelm Meister,' and, indeed, in all the author's literary works except the lyrics and 'Faust.' "Goethe remains none the less," he says in conclusion, "one of the greatest among the sons of man. 'After all,' " he said to one of his friends, " 'there are here and there some honest people who will be enlightened by my works, and whoever reads them and takes the trouble to understand me will recognize that he has gained by it a certain inward liberty.' I would write these words on the pedestal of Goethe's statue; one can give him no juster praise, and, indeed, one can make of no man a higher or more enviable eulogy." We alluded just now to Sainte-Beuve, and it is in place to add that we have often wished that he might have witnessed and survived the late war, if for no other purpose than to show us how he would have spoken of the Germans. The situation would have been a most interesting test of that subtilized and almost etherealized faculty of impartiality which had developed in him in his later years. It would have given play to all his *finesse*—to that strange mixture of fatal compliments and flattering blame. Unfortunately, Saint-Beuve's acquaintance with German literature was very limited; one cannot know absolutely everything. He had written about Goethe and two or three other German authors, but he had evaded with characteristic skill any indication of whether he read them in translations or in the original.

GEORGE SAND'S
MADEMOISELLE MERQUEM*

MADAME SAND's last novel—the last in a very long list, the reader will remember—is decidedly not one of the best of her works; but as it has enjoyed the rare fortune of being translated in this country, a few critical remarks may not fall amiss. The time was when Madame Sand's novels were translated as fast as they appeared, and circulated, half surreptitiously, as works delightful and intoxicating, but scandalous, dangerous, and seditious. To read George Sand in America was to be a socialist, a transcendentalist, and an abolitionist. You may obtain from the biography of Margaret Fuller an impression of the sort of

---

* "Mademoiselle Merquem: A Novel, By Madame George Sand," New York: G. W. Carleton & Co. 1868. (*The Nation*, July 16, 1868).

influence which she exercised in certain circles, and of the estimation in which she was held; of the large credit attached to her philosophical and didactic pretensions, which seem to us somewhat vain; and of the apparent indifference bestowed upon her vast imaginative and descriptive powers. One of Miss Fuller's first acts on reaching Paris, we learn from her life, was to call upon Madame Sand, effecting thereby, as it seems to you in reading the life, a very curious and anomalous conjunction. It may be added, however, that although George Sand figures in Miss Fuller's memoirs, the brilliant American is not mentioned in those of her illustrious sister. For ourselves, the first occasion on which Madame Sand became to us something more than a name was on the perusal of a chapter in Thackeray's "Paris Sketch Book," in which the author, in a moralizing mood, pulls to pieces one of her novels. The work in question was "Spiridion," from which, unfortunately for his intent, he translates a passage of some length. We cherished the passage in our memory—and indeed the writer admits its great beauty—but we retained a very vague impression of the drift of Mr. Thackeray's sermon. The impression was vivid enough, however, when subsequently we came to read "Spiridion" (which we must premise to be a tale of a purely religious cast, without incidents and without love, without the mention, indeed, throughout of a woman's name) forcibly to suggest the reflection that it was a piece of signal impertinence in the author of the "Sketch Book," holding, as he obviously did, the lightest and most superficial religious opinions, to measure his flimsy convictions against the serious and passionate ideas propounded in Madame Sand's work. We can perfectly well understand that Thackeray should not have liked "Spiridion"—to ourselves it is not an agreeable book—but there can be no better instance of that superficial and materialistic quality of mind which constantly chafes the serious reader of his novels, than his gross failure to appreciate the relative dignity of Madame Sand's religious attitude and of his own artificial posture. But these are things of the past, and possibly best, forgotten. The last of Madame Sand's novels translated in America was one of her prettiest tales "Teverino," which, we believe, had but little success. Since "Teverino" the author has produced a vast number of romances, and exhibited a greater fecundity, we think, considering the quality of her work, than any writer of our day. With all her precipitation, not one of her tales (we believe we have read them all) can be said to have forfeited the claim to literary excellence. This is certainly more than can be said for the productions of her *confrères*, Messrs. Dumas and Eugene Sue.

Your foremost impression, we fancy, on reading the work before us, "Mademoiselle Merquem," is of the extraordinary facility in composition begotten by the author's incessant practice. Never has a genius obtained a more complete and immediate mastery of its facilities. In the pages before us they seem to move not, as in common minds, at its express behest and injunction, but in harmony with its very instincts, and simultaneously with the act of inspiration. This perfect unity of the writer's intellectual character, the constant equilibrium of the powers reigning within its precinct, the confidence with which the imagination appeals to the faculty of utterance, and the radiant splendor which the latter reflects so gratefully from the imagination—these things, more than any great excellence of form in particular works, constitute the author's real claim to admiration and gratitude. These things it is which bestow an incomparable distinction on this actual "Mademoiselle Merquem" far more than any felicity of selection in the way of events and characters. The narrative gushes along copious and translucent as a deep and crystalline stream, rolling pebbles and boulders and reflecting all the convex vault of nature. Madame Sand's style, as a style, strikes us as so far superior to that of other novelists, that while the impression of it is fresh in your memory, you must make up your mind to accept her competitors wholly on the ground of their merits of substance, and remit for the time the obligation of writing properly. The great difference between the author of "Consuelo" and "Mademoiselle Merquem," and the authors (let us say) of "The Newcomes" and of "David Copperfield," is, that whereas the latter writers express in a satisfactory manner certain facts, certain ideas of a peculiar and limited order, Madame Sand expresses with equal facility and equal grace ideas and facts the most various and the most gen-

the luminous growth of the moon. Nevertheless, as we say, we have a vague preference for the earlier tales, in which an occasional crudity or a fitful turgidity of diction appeared to remind us that we were dealing with literary and not with vital phenomena. Madame Sand's masterpieces, however, are scattered throughout her career, and in many cases stand cheek to cheek with some of her most trivial works. "Simon" appeared in the same year with "Mauprat," and "Les Beaux Messieurs de Bois-Doré" about the same time as that marvellous romance of "La Daniella." But taking it as a whole, and judging it in a liberal fashion, what a splendid array does this career exhibit! What a multitude of figures, what an infinite gallery of pictures! What a world of entertainment and edification! From our own point of view there has been none in modern years to compare with it, and to find a greater magician we must turn to the few supreme names in literature. Madame Sand is said to have celebrated but a single passion—the passion of love. This is in a great measure true; but in depicting it she has incidentally portrayed so many others that she may be said to have pretty thoroughly explored the human soul. The writer who has amply illustrated the passion of love has, by implication, thrown a great deal of light on the rest of our nature. In the same way, the writer who has signally failed to achieve an adequate conception of this vast object, must be said to remain an incomplete and partial witness. This is the case with Balzac, in so many respects Madame Sand's superior, and who is never to be considered as slighted by any praise bestowed upon his comrade. Balzac's merits form a very long story, and he is not to be dealt with in a parenthesis. An intelligent reader of both authors will, at times, be harassed with the feeling that it behooves him to choose between them and take up his stand with the one against the other. But, in fact, they are not mutually inimical, and the wise reader, we think, will take refuge in the reflection that choosing is an idle business, inasmuch as we possess them both. Balzac, we may say, if the distinction is not too technical, is a novelist, and George Sand a romancer. There is no reason why they should not subsist in harmony. A large portion of the works of both will eventually be swept into oblivion, but several of the best productions of each will, we imagine, survive for the delight of mankind. Let us softly add the expression of our belief that for Balzac, booked as he is for immortality or thereabouts, this is a very happy circumstance. You may read "Consuelo" and "Mauprat," and not be ashamed to raise your eyes from the book to the awful face of Nature. But when you have been reading "Le Père Goriot" or "Un Ménage de Garçon," you emphatically need to graduate your return to life. Who at such a moment better than George Sand can beguile the remorseful journey, and with "Consuelo" and "Mauprat," or even with "L'Homme de Neige" and "Mademoiselle Merquem," reconcile you to your mortal lot?

LAST GLEANINGS FROM
GEORGE SAND'S WRITINGS

Madame Sand's industry was equal to her talent, and the quantity of her work was not less remarkable than the quality. Her diligence did not decline with age; the latter years of her life were indeed even more productive than the earlier ones. She wrote a large number of newspaper articles, and she was not above performing in this line the most modest functions. Obituary notices, short reviews of books, prefaces, fragmentary reminiscences—these things flowed constantly from her pen, and had always a certain value from being signed with her name. This was not their only value, for in every utterance of George Sand, however brief, there is always an appreciable touch of wisdom and grace of style. Every scrap that fell from her pen has now been collected, and the "Dernières Pages" contain the very last possible gleanings. Most of them are very slight, but the book is worth glancing through, for the author had this characteristic of a great mind, that her touch was never vulgar or vulgarizing, and that every now and then, even when the topic

---

* *Dernières Pages. Par George Sand.* (Paris: Calmann Lévy. 1877). (*The Nation*, October 25, 1878).

is the slightest, it strikes a charming gleam. Only three of the short articles of which this volume is composed deserve specification—the rest are mere trifles. One of these is of the most rambling character: beginning with an account of a walk in the woods in midwinter, and of some curious botanical observations, it terminates in an interesting and discriminating appreciation of the personal character of Napolean III., who at the time the article was written was on his death-bed. Madame Sand judges the late Emperor partly from personal impressions; she relates that, at one period, having twice had an interview with him on behalf of an unfortunate person (apparently a political prisoner), she made up her mind that he was deluding her with false pretensions and not keeping faith, and left Paris abruptly, without presenting herself at a third audience. She afterwards received news not that (as in the anecdote of Louis XIV.) the King had almost waited, but that the Emperor had waited altogether. She judges him leniently and liberally, thinks him above all a dreamer, a kind of sinister Don Quixote, and says, very justly, that the French people owes it to its own self-respect not to try to make out that the sovereign to whom they submitted for twenty years was an unmitigated villain. This is what Victor Hugo so loudly proclaims; and in this case, what does Victor Hugo make of complaisant Paris, the most amiable, the most high-toned, the most exemplary city in the world?

In another article Madame Sand gives an entertaining account of her granduncle, the Abbé de Beaumont, who figures in the early pages of 'L'Histoire de ma Vie,' and upon whose portrait, having received some fresh documentary evidence about her ancestor, she desires to bestow a few flattering touches. He was the robust and handsome bastard of a great nobleman of the old régime (the Duc de Bouillon), whose only legitimate child was a helpless and peevish cripple, and the account of his unrequited devotion to his at once more and less fortunate brother is sufficiently affecting. But the most charming thing in these pages is the history of the theatre of marionettes—in plain English, the puppet-show—which has been for many years a brilliant feature of the author's home at Nohant. Madame Sand has written few more delightful pages. There are puppet-shows and puppet-shows; Madame Sand takes the institution very seriously and earnestly pleads the cause of *fantoccini* as a domestic amusement. The account she gives of the gradual elaboration and finally brilliant perfection of the troupe of marionettes of which her son had constituted himself operator is peculiarly interesting, and all that she says about the possible extension of the development of the entertainment is full of a characteristic appreciation, both of artistic and human things. We recommend the perusal of these pages, and we urge their being acted upon. Or must we be French and frivolous to care about ingenious and artistic pastimes? We should almost recommend that the article be translated, and circulated as a tract, for the benefit of domestic circles infected with what Matthew Arnold calls "dreariness."

GEORGE SAND*

The newspapers, for the last fortnight, have contained a certain number of anecdotes about Madame Sand; but they have been generally of a rather trivial sort, and I have not gathered any that are worth repeating. Private life in France —more fortunate than among ourselves—is still acknowledged to have some rights which the reporter and the interviewer are bound to respect. A Frenchman often makes surprising confidences to the public about himself, but as a rule he is not addicted to telling tales about his neighbor. Madame Sand, in the memoirs which she published 20 years ago, lifted the vail from her personality with a tolerably unshrinking hand (though to the admirers of what is called scandal she gave very little satisfaction); and yet for the last 30 years of her life she was one of the most shade-loving and retiring of celebrities. Her life, indeed, was almost entirely in her books, and it is there that one must look for it. She was essentially a scribbler; she wrote unceasingly from the publication of her first novel to the day of

(* *New York Tribune,* July 22, 1876. Correspondence from Paris, June 28).

her death, and she had always been fond above all things of a
quiet life, even during that portion of her career in which our
Anglo-Saxon notions of "quietness" are supposed to have been
most effectively violated. She was very intimate at one time with
Alfred de Musset, and I have heard that this charming poet,
by right of his membership of the *genus irritabile* sometimes
found it more than his nerves could endure to see the author
of "Consuelo" sit down to her perpetual manuscript at the most
critical hours of their somewhat troubled friendship. But Madame Sand wrote for her bread, and her remarkable power of
imaginative abstraction must help to explain the very large
amount of work that she achieved. She was also very intimate
with Prosper Mérimée, and I have been told that very early one
cold Winter morning he perceived her, with a hankerchief on
her head, lighting the fire to resume her literary tasks. He also,
it appears, had nerves; the spectacle disturbed them—he himself
was not thinking of getting about his labors yet awhile—and from
that moment the intimacy ceased. Madame Sand had spent a
large portion of her life at Nohant, in the Berry, in the plain old
country-house, which she described so charmingly in "L'Histoire
de ma Vie," and for which and for its (I believe) rather meager
setting of natural beauty she appears to have had a singularly
intense affection. As she advanced in life, Nohant became more
and more her home, and her visits to Paris were brief. Her house
was very hospitable, and under her own roof she was never without society. She had worked very hard, and she had made no
fortune; she still earned her income—an income which at the
bottom, as they say, of an old French province is still considered
easy, but which in America, as in England, would not be thought
in fair proportion to the writer's industry and eminence. Madame
Sand made, I believe, between six and seven thousand dollars
a year. She was very silent, and had little assurance of manner.
People who knew her well have told me that she looked a great
deal on the ground, and seemed pre-occupied; that one felt shut
off from her by a sort of vail or film. Occasionally this vail was
lifted, she found her voice, and talked to very good purpose.
This characterization corresponds with a phrase which one of her
heroes, in I forget what novel, applies to one of her heroines—

the heroine being an idealized portrait of Madame Sand herself. He calls her a *sphinx bon enfant*—"a good-natured sphinx." In spite of her advanced age—she was 72—Madame Sand's vigor had not failed at the time of the sudden illness which ended in her death. Her activity was great, and her faculties unimpaired. I saw a letter, the other day, written a few weeks before she died, in which she declared that her eyesight was better than when she was 50, and that she went up stairs as fast as her dog. She was carried off by an acute attack of a malady which she had at first neglected. Her last audible words on her deathbed were characteristic of one who had loved nature passionately, and described it almost incomparably—"*Laissez verdure,*—" The allusion was apparently to some wild herbage in the corner of the village churchyard in which she expressed a wish to rest. In spite of her complete rupture, early in life, with Catholicism—in spite of "Spiridion," "Mademoiselle La Quintinie," and numberless other expressions of religious independence—Madame Sand was buried from the little church of Nohant, and the curé performed the service. Her family had the good taste to ask permission of the Bishop of Bourges, and the Bishop had the good taste to answer that if she had not positively refused the sacraments he saw no objection. What made it good taste in Madame Sand's family (it was poor logic), was the fact that she was greatly beloved by the country people, that she had been held in great esteem by the prior generation, that these people were numerically her chief mourners, and that it would have perplexed and grieved them not to see her buried in the only fashion of which they recognized the impressiveness. Alexandre Dumas did not pronounce a funeral oration, though he was, with Prince Napoleon, one of the pall-bearers. A short address by Victor Hugo was read —he not being personally present. It had all of his latter-day magniloquence, but it contained no phrase so happy in its eloquence as one that I find in a letter from Ernest Renan, published in the *Temps* a few days after Madame Sand's death. The last lines she had written were a short notice of M. Renan's new book, the "Dialogues Philosophiques." "I am touched to the bottom of my heart," he says, "to have been the last to produce a vibration of that sonorous soul which was, as it were, the

Æolian harp of our time." Persons who have read Madame Sand with a certain amount of sympathy will find it just, as well as fanciful, to call her soul "sonorous." It is an excellent description of her intellectual temperament. A few other fine lines in M. Renan's letter are worth quoting: "Madame Sand went through all visions, smiled at them all, believed in them all; her practical judgment may occasionally have gone astray, but as an artist she never deceived herself. Her works are truly the echo of our age. When this poor nineteenth century which we abuse so much is gone, it will be heard and eagerly looked into, and much one day will be forgiven it. George Sand then will rise up as our interpreter. The age has not had a wound with which her heart has not bled, not an ailment of which she has not harmoniously complained." I suspect that M. Renan has not perused any very great number of Madame Sand's fictions, but this is none the less very finely said.

I have been refreshing my memory of some of George Sand's earlier novels, which I confess I do not find as easy reading as I once did. But—taking the later ones as well—they are a very extraordinary and splendid series, and certainly one of the great literary achievements of our time. Some people, I know, cannot read Madame Sand; she has no illusion for them and but a moderate amount of charms; but I think such people are to be pitied—they lose a great pleasure. She was an *improvisatrice*, raised to a very high power; she told stories as a nightingale sings. No novelist answers so well to the childish formula of "making up as you go along." Other novels seem meditated, pondered, calculated, thought out and elaborated with a certain amount of trouble; but the narrative with Madame Sand always appears to be an invention of the moment, flowing from a mind which a constant process of quiet contemplation, absorption and reverie keeps abundantly supplied with material. It is a sort of general emanation, an intellectual evaporation. There had been plenty of improvisation before the author of "Consuelo," but it had never been—and it has never been in other hands—of so fine a quality. She had a natural gift of style which is certainly one of the most remarkable of our day; her diction from the first ripe and flexible, and seemed to have nothing to learn from practice. The literary form of her writing has always been exquisite, and this alone would have sufficed to distinguish it from the work of the great body of clever scribblers who spin their two or three plots a year. Some of her novels are very inferior to others; some of them show traces of weariness, of wandering attention, of a careless choice of subject; but the manner, at the worst, never sinks below a certain high level—the tradition of good writing is never lost. In this bright, voluminous envelope, it must be confessed that Madame Sand has sometimes wrapped up a rather flimsy kernel; some of her stories will not bear much thinking over. But her great quality from the first was the multiplicity of her interests and the activity of her sympathies. She passed through a succession of phases, faiths and doctrines—political, religious, moral, social, personal—and to each she gave a voice which the conviction of the moment made eloquent. She gave herself up to each as if it were to be final, and in every case she turned her steps behind her. Sainte-Beuve, who as an artist relished her but slenderly, says somewhere, in allusion to her, that "no one had ever played more fairly and openly at the great game of life." It has been said wittily, in reference to Buffon's well-known axiom that "the style is the man," (which by the way is a misquotation,) that of no one was this dictum ever so true as of Madame Sand; but I incline to believe, with the critic in whose pages I find this *mot*, that at bottom the man was always Madame Sand herself. She accepted as much of every influence as suited her, and when she had written a novel or two about it she ceased to care about it. This proves her, doubtless, to have been a decidedly superficial moralist; but it proves her to have been a born romancer. It is by the purely romantic side of her productions that she will live. It is a misfortune that she pretended to moralize to the extent that she did, for about moral matters her head was not at all clear. It had now and then capital glimpses and inspirations, but her didacticism has always seemed to me what an architectural drawing would be, executed by a person who should turn up his nose at geometry. Madame Sand's straight lines are straight by a happy chance—and for people of genius there are so many happy chances. She was without a sense of certain differences—the difference between the pure and the impure—the things that are possible for people of a certain delicacy, and the things that are not. When she struck the right notes, and so long as she continued to strike them, the result was charming, but a sudden discord was always possible. Sometimes the right note was admirably prolonged—as for instance in her masterpiece, "Consuelo," in which during three long volumes, if I remember rightly, the charming heroine adheres strictly to the straight line. After all, Madame Sand's "tendency" novels, as the Germans call such works, constitute but the minor part of her literary bequest; as she advanced in life she wrote her stories more and more for the story's sake, and attempted to prove nothing more alarming than that human nature is on the whole tolerably noble and generous. After this pattern she produced a long list of masterpieces. Her imagination seemed gifted with perpetual youth; the freshness of her invention was marvelous. Her novels have a great many faults; they lack three or four qualities which the realistic novel of the last thirty or forty years, with its great successes, has taught us to consider indispensable. They are not exact nor probable; they contain few living figures; they produce a limited amount of illusion. Madame Sand created no figures that have passed into common life and speech; her people are usually only very picturesque, very voluble, and very "high-toned" shadows. But the shadows move to such a persuasive music that we watch them with interest. The art of narration is extraordinary. This was Madame Sand's great art. The recital moves along with an evenness, a lucidity, a tone of seeing, feeling, knowing everything, a reference to universal things, a sentimental authority, which makes the reader care for the characters in spite of his incredulity and feel anxious about the story in spite of his impatience. He feels that the author holds in her hands a stringed instrument composed of the chords of the human soul.

HUGO'S LÉGENDE DES SIÈCLES

From the very flattering notices which the English journals have accorded to the new volumes of Victor Hugo's 'Légende des Siècles,' it is apparent that the writer has lately become almost the fashion in England—a fact to be attributed in a measure to the influence of the "æsthetic" school, or, to speak more correctly, probably, of Mr. Swinburne, who, as we know, swears by Victor Hugo, and whose judgments seem to appeal less forcibly to the English sense of humor than they do to a corresponding quality on this side of the Atlantic. Be this as it may, however, Victor Hugo's new volumes are as characteristic as might have been expected—as violent and extravagant in their faults, and in their fine passages as full of imaginative beauty. Apropos of the sense of humor, the absence of this quality is certainly Victor Hugo's great defect—the only limitation (it must be confessed it is a very serious one) to his imaginative power. It should teach him occasionally to kindle Mr. Ruskin's "lamp of sacrifice." This "nouvelle série" of the 'Légende des Siècles' is not a continuation of the first group of poems which appeared under this name: it is rather a return to the same ground, the various categories under which the first poems appeared being supplied with new recruits. These categories are too numerous to be mentioned here; they stretch from the creation of the world to the current year of grace. It is an immense plan, and shows on the author's part not only an extraordinary wealth of imagination, but a remarkable degree of research. It is true that Victor Hugo's researches are often rather pedantically exhibited; no poet was ever so fond of queer proper names, dragged together from dusty corners of history and legend, and strung together rhythmically—often with a great deal of ingenuity. He is too fond of emulating Homer's catalogue of the ships. But he has what the French call an extraordinary *scent* for picturesque subjects. These two volumes contain many examples of it; the story, for instance, of a certain king of Arragon who gives his son a blow on the cheek, whereupon

(*The Nation*, May 3, 1877).

the proud and sensitive young man, outraged, retires into the desert. The father, aggrieved at his desertion and greatly sorrowing, descends into the sepulchral crypt where his own father is buried, and there, apostrophizing the bronze statue on his tomb, complains of the young man's ingratitude and weeps. After this has gone on some time he feels, in the darkness, the statue stroke his cheek tenderly with its great hand. "L'Aigle du Casque," one of the best things in the two volumes, is the tale of a certain Northumbrian baron of the dark ages, Lord Tiphaine—Victor Hugo's English names are always very queer. He has a duel with a young Scotch noble—a delicate stripling many years his junior, and on the latter taking fright and fleeing from him, he pursues him a whole summer's day, over hill and dale, and at last overtakes him and murders him. The story of the chase and its various episodes is a specimen of Victor Hugo at his best. When the brutal Northumbrian has hacked his victim to death the brazen eagle perched upon his helmet suddenly becomes animate, utters in a rancorous scream its detestation of the dead, bends over and with its beak and talons tears his face to pieces, and then spreading its wings sails majestically away. Victor Hugo excels in leading a long narrative piece of verse up to a startling climax of this kind, related in the half-dozen closing lines. These volumes contain the usual proportion of fulsome adulation of Paris and of the bloodiest chapters in its history—that narrow Gallomania which makes us so often wonder at times, not whether the author is, after all, a great poet, but whether he is not very positively and decidedly a small poet. But, outside of this, this new series of what is probably his capital work contains plenty of proofs of his greatness—passages and touches of extraordinary beauty. No poet has written like Victor Hugo about children, and the second of these volumes contains a masterpiece of this kind. "Petit Paul" is simply the history of a very small child whose mother dies and whose father takes a second wife—a coarse, hard woman, who neglects the little boy. Before his father's second marriage he has been much with his grandfather, who delights in him—"Oh! quel céleste amour entre ces deux bonshommes." The grandfather dies and is buried, to Paul's knowledge, in the village churchyard. The stepmother comes; the child's life is miserably changed, and at last, one winter's night, he starts out, and not having been missed, is found the next morning dead in the snow at the closed gate of the cemetery. We must quote the lines in which the author describes him while he is meditating this attempt to rejoin his grandfather, the other *bonhomme;* on hearing his step-mother caress his step-brother, lately born:

> "Paul se souvenait avec la quantité
> De mémoire qu'auraient les agneaux et les roses
> Qu'il s'était entendu dire les mêmes choses.
> Il prenait dans un coin, à terre, ses repas;
> Il etait devenu muet, ne parlait pas.
> Ne pleurait plus. L'enfance est parfois sombre et forte,
> Souvent il regardait lugubrement la porte."

HUGO'S NINETY-THREE*

A new work from Victor Hugo may be considered a literary event of some magnitude. If the magnitude of the event, indeed, were measured by that of the work in chapters, books, and volumes, we should need one of the author's own mouth-filling epithets to qualify it. The present performance is apparently but a fragment—the first *"récit"* of a romance destined to embody on a vast scale the history of a single year. Like all the author's novels, it abounds in subdivisions and minor headings, which serve as a kind of mechanical symbolism of his passion for the moral enormous. It is nevertheless complete enough to give us a solid reminder of his strangely commingled strength and weakness. The 'Misérables,' we suppose, may have been called a great triumph; but we doubt if its successors—the 'Travailleurs de la Mer' and 'L'Homme qui Rit'—found many readers who were constant to the end. The verdict on the present work, however, so far as it has been pronounced, has been eminently favor-

---

* 'Quatrevingt-treize. Par Victor Hugo.' Paris: Michel Lévy. 1874.
'Ninety-three. By Victor Hugo. Translated by Frank Lee Benedict.' New York: Harper & Bros. (*The Nation,* April 9, 1874).

able, and we are assured that M. Hugo has rekindled his smolder-
ing torch at the pure flame of inspiration. The reader, indeed,
has only to open the volume at hazard to find that M. Hugo is
himself again with a vengeance. "Cimourdain was a conscience
pure but sombre. He had within him the absolute. He had been
a priest, which is grave. Man can, like the sky, have a black
serenity; it is enough that something should have made night
within him. The priesthood had made night in Cimourdain.
Who has been a priest, is one." Or further: "We approach the
great peak.—Here is the Convention.—The gaze becomes fixed
in the presence of this summit.—Nothing higher has ever appeared
on the horizon of man.—There is the Himalayah and there is
the Convention." Or elsewhere, of the cry of a mother who sees
her children in danger: "Nothing is more ferocious and nothing
is more touching. When a woman utters it, you think you hear
a wolf: when a wolf utters it, you think you hear a woman . . . .
Hecuba barked, says Homer." These few lines suffice to show
that the author has not flinched from his chosen path, and that
he walks escorted between the sublime and the ridiculous as
resolutely as his own most epic heroes. In truth, at M. Hugo's
venerable age, and with one's forehead aching with laurels, it
is not to be expected that one should ever drop a glance at the
swarm of nameless satirists; but the moral of the matter is that
the luxurious cultivation of his own peculiar manner, for which
our author continues remarkable, seems now not only the natural
thing, but on the whole the sagacious one. If you are sure of your
strength, the lesson seems to read, cleave to your ideal, however
arrogant, however perverted, however indifferent to the ideals
of others, and in the end even the fastidious will accept you.
We confess to a conservative taste in literary matters—to a relish
for brevity, for conciseness, for elegance, for perfection of form.
M. Hugo's manner is as diffuse as that of the young woman in the
fairy tale who talked diamonds and pearls would alone have a
right to be, and as shapeless and formless as if it were twenty
times the "grande improvisation" which is his definition of the
French Revolution. His prolixity, moreover, has the further
defect of giving one a nearly intolerable impression of conceit;
few great rhetoricians have the air of listening so reverently to

their own grandiloquence. And yet we frankly admit that the effect of these volumes has been to make us submit to the inevitable, and philosophically accept the author whose shoulders sustain so heavy a load of error. To many persons our experience will have a familiar air. There comes a time, in most lives, when points of difference with friends and foes and authors dwindle, and points of contact expand. We have a vision of the vanity of remonstrance and of the idleness of criticism. We cease to look for what we know people cannot give us—as we have declared a dozen times—and begin to look for what they can. To find this last and enjoy it undisturbedly is one of the most agreeable of intellectual sensations. We are doubtless wrong in breaking our yard-stick; for what is to become of the true and the beautiful without a "high standard"? We only say that we are natural, and we simply pretend that in this natural fashion we have been enjoying 'Quatrevingt-treize.'

M. Hugo has chosen a subject in which his imagination may revel at its ease; his inordinate relish for the huge and the horrible may feast its fill upon the spectacle of the French Revolution. One might have wondered indeed that he should not long ago have made it his own; but he has shown the instinct of the genuine epicure in such matters in keeping it in reserve. He has drawn from it effects of the most sinister picturesqueness, and, judging his work from the picturesque point of view merely, he is certainly to be congratulated on his topic. Judged from the rational point of view, the theme seems to us much less fortunate. If the French people could forget their Revolution for fifty years and forego all manner of allusion to it, we are sure the result would be most favorable to their intellectual health. The moral has been drawn again and again, for seventy years, the lesson has been learned, the last drop of sweetness has been drained from the hideous sediment of blood and error. The better part of the Revolution is by this time a divided heritage; European society has been living on it, paying its daily expenses with it, as we may say, for the last twenty years. Nothing could better illustrate the strange moral irresponsibility which is so often combined with a rich imagination than the reckless glee with which our author kindles the blue fire, touches off the rockets, and sets a-whizzing the catherine-wheels of this new apotheosis. If anything were wanted to prove that, as a philosopher, M. Hugo has nothing of the smallest consequence to say, the extraordinary intellectual levity with which he faces the unsolved problems of his theme would amply suffice. He has not attempted, however, to give us a picture of the whole Revolution, but, choosing a salient episode, has dramatized with characteristic vividness the sanguinary strife of the Royalists of Brittany and the Republican troops. As a story, M. Hugo's work as yet is meagre; it has no hero, no heroine, no central figure, none of the germs of a regular drama. The hero properly is the Republican army, the heroine the fanatical horde of the Vendéans. We are shifted from place to place, hurried through deserts of declamation and oceans of paradox, tossed, breathless, from a bewildering antithesis to an astounding "situation" with all that energy to which, from of old, M. Hugo's readers have received notice that they must accommodate their intellectual pace. Our author's characters are always more or less monstrous, either in virtue or vice, and he has given us here the usual proportion of heroic grotesques. Robespierre, Danton, and Marat figure, in their estimable persons, and we are treated to a conference in which, in the back shop of a café, they settle the affairs of the nation. We have seen this called one of the strong episodes of the work, but it is very disappointing. The leading members of the Committee of Public Safety talk altogether in disjointed epigrams and bristling antitheses, any one of which would be highly in keeping with M. Hugo himself on the frequent occasions when he appears as chorus to the drama. This scene, in which an immense effort has been attended with a meagre result, is ushered in by an elaborate picture of the streets of Paris during the high-pressure time of the Revolution. The author has collected an extraordinary multitude of small facts and anecdotes, and he strings them together with the effectiveness of a great painter. The chapter is well worth reading. Less vivid, but curious enough, is the account of the hall of session of the National Convention in the Tuileries and its surrounding precinct. In these pictures M. Hugo makes Revolutionary Paris really palpable to our senses. If he would only give us more pictures and fewer disquisitions! His pictures, however,

141

are vitiated by an affectation of the Rabelaisian fashion of long catalogues; we are deluged with proper names and useless enumerations.

The main action of the story consists of the adventures of a Paris battalion sent into Brittany to confront a certain Marquis de Lantenac, a superb old fanatic for the Royal cause, invincible among his savage peasantry, and conspiring to help the English fleet to effect a landing. The handful of tried Parisians is commanded by a nephew of the Marquis, a young Viscomte de Gauvain, who has torn up his pedigree and cast his lot with the Republic. From Paris, despatched by Robespierre to hold the young nobleman, whose thoroughgoing rigidity is suspected, to a strict account, is a certain Cimourdain, a *ci-devant* priest and actual radical of the deepest dye—one of the duskiest and most colossal of all M. Hugo's dusky and colossal heroes. Cimourdain is bound to Gauvain by ties of old affection, having been his preceptor and more than a father to him. Gauvain, in fact, is the apple of his eye; he loves him better even than the Revolution. Just so, Gauvain is bound to the Marquis de Lantenac, on whose head he sets a price, by ties of blood, and the relations of the three individuals are as fertile as may be expected in those terrific conflicts between the voice of nature and a cruel outward force which have formed the majority of our author's great dramatic situations. Out of all this comes an abundance of tragic suspense —and sometimes of comic surprise. For the rest, the story is chiefly a compound of blood and gunpowder, of long descriptions, geographical and genealogical, which are frequently mere strings of proper names drawn out through pages, and of infinite discourse on things in general by M. Hugo. The only really charming element in the work is the occasional apparition of three little children, whose adventures indeed are the *nodus* of the action. Very charming it is, and lighted up with the author's brightest poetry. With a genius at once powerful and eccentric, like M. Hugo, if one has great disappointments, one has great compensations. A writer in whom the poetic heat is so intense that he must be sublime under all circumstances and at any cost, makes many a strange alliance and produces many a monstrosity; but every now and then it befalls him to flash his lantern upon an object which, as one may say, receives transfiguration gracefully. These little children, whose poor peasant-mother is supposed to have been shot in a bloody *battue* of the Royalists, are picked up and adopted by the Parisian battalion. They are subsequently carried off by the Royalists, kept as hostages, and confined in an old feudal tower, in which Lantenac with a handful of men is besieged by the Parisians. The latter break into the castle, to which the others, escaping through a subterranean passage, have succeeded in setting fire. The children are left behind, but although we see them, in their rosy innocence, nestling in what the author happily calls a "grotto of flame," of course they are not destroyed. They are reserved obviously for future volumes, where their presence is the more needful that Gauvain and Cimourdain perish on the same occasion in all the sublimity of melodrama. If the work contained nothing else than the chapter in which the three chubby babies are described as playing, amid the impending carnage, in the old dusty library of the château, it would not have been ineffectually written.

The whole work is a mine of quotations—nuggets of substantial gold and strange secretions of the mere overflow of verbiage. M. Hugo's pretension is to say many things in the grand manner—to fling down every proposition like a ringing medal stamped with his own image. Hence, for the reader, an intolerable sense of effort and tension; he seems to witness the very contortions of ingenuity. But, as we say, the contortions are often those of the inspired sybil, and the poet utters something worth hearing. We care little for the Marquis de Lantenac and less for the terrible Cimourdain; but the author's great sense of the sad and tragic has rarely been exercised more effectively than in the figures of Michelle Fléchard, the poor stupid starving peasant-mother of the three children, and of Tellemarch, the philosophic beggar who gives her shelter in her desperate quest. Here the author deals with the really human and not with the mechanical and monstrous, aping the human. All this is Victor Hugo at his best. One judges a work of these dimensions and pretensions, however, not by its parts, better or worse, but by its general tone, by the spirit of the whole, by its leading idea. Expressed with perfect frankness, the leading idea of 'Quatrevingt-treize' seems to us to be that the horrible—the horrible in crime and suffering and folly, in blood and fire and tears—is a delightful subject for the embroidery of fiction. After this there is no denying that M. Hugo is really fond of horrors. He is an old man; he has written much and seen much; he may be supposed to know his own mind; yet he dives into this sea of blood for the pearl of picturesqueness with a truly amazing freshness of appetite. If we were inclined to interpret things rigidly, we might find a very sombre meaning in the strange complacency with which his imagination contemplates the most atrocious details of his subject. His fellow-countrymen lately took occasion to remind the world forcibly that they were of the same stock as their ancestors, and that when once they had warmed to the work again they could burn and kill on the same extensive scale. One would have said that, to a reflective mind, it might have seemed that the blood-stains and ashes of French history had, for some years to come, better be consigned to obscurity. The sublimely clear conscience with which M. Hugo drags them into the light proves, to say the least, an inordinate share of national vanity. To say, in combination with this, that we have enjoyed the work, may seem but an admission that we have been passing through an atmosphere of corrupting paradox. But what we have enjoyed is neither Cimourdain nor Marat, nor the woman-shootings of the Royalists, nor the ambulant guillotine of the Republicans. It is M. Hugo himself as a whole, the extraordinary genius that shines through the dusky confusion of repulsive theme and erratic treatment. It is the great possibilities of his style and the great tendencies of his imagination. The latter sometimes leads him astray; but when it leads him aright he is great.

FLAUBERT'S TEMPTATION OF
ST. ANTHONY*

SAINT ANTHONY, as most readers know, was an Egyptian monk who, toward the end of the third century, hid himself in the desert to pray, and was visited by a series of hallucinations painfully irrelevant to this occupation. His visions and his stout resistance to them have long been famous—so famous that here is M. Gustave Flaubert, fifteen hundred years afterwards, publishing a large octavo about them, and undertaking to describe them in every particular. This volume, we confess, has been a surprise to us. Announced for publication three or four years ago, it seemed likely to be a novel of that realistic type which the author had already vigorously cultivated, with Saint Anthony and his temptation standing simply as a symbol of the argument. We opened it with the belief that we were to find, not a ragged old cenobite struggling to preserve his virtue amid Egyptian sands, but a portrait of one of the author's own contemporaries and fellow-citizens engaged in this enterprise in the heart of the French capital. M. Flaubert's strong side has not been hitherto the portrayal of resistance to temptation, and we were much in doubt as to whether the dénouement of the novel was to correspond to that of the legend; but it was very certain that, whatever the upshot, the temptation itself would be elaborately represented. So, in fact, it has been; but it is that of the dim-featured founder of monasticism, and not of a gentleman beset by our modern importunities. The work has the form of a long monologue by the distracted saint, interrupted by voluminous pictorial representations of his visions and by his imagined colloquies with the creatures who people them. We may frankly say that it strikes us as a ponderous failure; but it is an interesting failure as well, and it suggests a number of profitable reflections.

In so far as these concern M. Gustave Flaubert himself, they are decidedly melancholy. Many American readers probably have

---

* 'La Tentation de Saint Antoine. Par Gustave Flaubert.' Paris: Charpentier; New York: F. W. Christern. 1874. (*The Nation*, June 4, 1874).)

followed his career, and will readily recall it as an extraordinary example of a writer outliving his genius. There have been poets and novelists in abundance who are people of a single work, who have had their one hour of inspiration, and gracefully accept the certainty that it would never strike again. There are other careers in which a great success has been followed by a period of inoffensive mediocrity, and, if not confirmed, at least not flagrantly discredited. But we imagine there are few writers who have been at such extraordinary pains as M. Flaubert to undermine an apparently substantial triumph. Some fifteen years ago he published 'Madame Bovary,' a novel which, if it cannot be said exactly to have taken its place in the "standard literature" of his country, must yet have fixed itself in the memory of most readers as a revelation of what the imagination may accomplish under a powerful impulse to mirror the unmitigated realities of life. 'Madame Bovary,' we confess, has always seemed to us a great work, and capable really of being applied to educational purposes. It is an elaborate picture of vice, but it represents it as so indefeasibly commingled with misery that in a really enlightened system of education it would form exactly the volume to put into the hands of young persons in whom vicious tendencies had been distinctly perceived, and who were wavering as to which way they should let the balance fall.

The facts in 'Madame Bovary' were elaborate marvels of description, but they were also, by good luck, extremely interesting in themselves, whereas the facts in 'Salammbô,' in 'L'Education Sentimentale,' and in the performance before us, appeal so very meagrely to our sympathy that they completely fail in their appeal to our credulity. And yet we would not for the world have had M. Flaubert's novels unwritten. Lying there before us so unmistakably still-born, they are a capital refutation of the very dogma in defence of which they appeared. The fatal charmlessness of each and all of them is an eloquent plea for the ideal. M. Flaubert's peculiar talent is the description—minute, incisive, exhaustive—of material objects, and it must be admitted that he has carried it very far. He succeeds wonderfully well in making an image, in finding and combining just the words in which the *look* of his object resides. The scenery and properties in his dramas are made for the occasion; they have not served in other pieces. "The sky [in St. Anthony's landscape] is red, the earth completely black; under the gusts of wind the sand-drifts rise up like shrouds and then fall down. In a gap, suddenly, pass a flight of birds in a triangular battalion, like a piece of metal, trembling only on the edges." This is a specimen, taken at random, of the author's constant appeal to observation; he would claim, doubtless, for his works that they are an unbroken tissue of observations, that this is their chief merit, and that nothing is further from his pretension than to conclude to philosophize or to moralize. He proceeds upon the assumption that these innumerable marvels of observation will hold together without the underlying moral unity of what is called a "purpose," and that the reader will proceed eagerly from point to point, stopping just sufficiently short of complete hallucination to remember the author's cleverness.

The reader has, at least, in *La Tentation de Saint Antoine,* the satisfaction of expecting a subject combining with a good deal of chance for color a high moral interest. M. Flaubert describes, from beginning to end, the whole series of the poor hermit's visions; the undertaking implies no small imaginative energy. In one sense, it has been bravely carried out; it swarms with ingenious, audacious, and erudite detail, and leaves nothing to be desired in the way of completeness. There is generally supposed to be a certain vagueness about visions; they are things of ambiguous shapes and misty edges. But vagueness of portrayal has never been our author's failing, and St. Anthony's hallucinations under his hands become a gallery of photographs, executed with the aid of the latest improvements in the art. He is visited successively by all the religions, idolatries, superstitions, rites and ceremonies, priests and potentates, of the early world—by Nebuchadnezzar and the Queen of Sheba, the Emperor Constantine and the Pope Calixtus, the swarm of the early Christian fanatics, martyrs, and philosophers—Origen, Tertullian, Arius, Hermogenes, Ebionites and Encratites, Theodotians and Marcosians, by Helen of Troy and Appollonius of Rhodes, by the Buddha in person, by the Devil in person, by Ormuzd and Ahriman, by Diana of the Ephesians, by Cybele, Atys, Isis, by the whole company of the gods of Greece and by Venus in particular, by certain unnamable Latin deities, whom M. Flaubert not only names but dramatizes, by the figures of Luxury and Death, by the Sphinx and the Chimæra, by the Pigmies and the Cynocephali, by the "Sadhuzag" and the unicorn, by all the beasts of the sea, and finally by Jesus Christ. We are not precisely given to understand how much time is supposed to roll over the head of the distracted anchorite while these heterogeneous images are passing before him, but, in spite of the fact that he generally swoons away in the *entr-acte*, as it were, we receive an impression that he is getting a good deal at one sitting, and that the toughest part of his famous struggle came off on a single night. To the reader who is denied the occasional refreshment of a swoon, we recommend taking up the book at considerable intervals. Some of the figures in our list are minutely described, others are briefly sketched, but all have something to say. We fancy that both as a piece of description and a piece of dramatization M. Flaubert is especially satisfied with his Queen of Sheba:

> "Her dress, in golden brocade, divided regularly by furbelows of pearls, of jet, and of sapphire, compresses her waist into a narrow bodice, ornamented with applied pieces in color representing the twelve signs of the zodiac. She wears high skates, of which one is black and spangled with silver stars, with the crescent of the moon, while the other is white, and covered with little drops in gold, with the sun in the middle. Her wide sleeves, covered with emeralds and with feathers of birds, expose the nakedness of her little round arm, ornamented at the wrist by a bracelet of ebony; and her hands, laden with rings, terminate in nails so pointed that the ends of her fingers look almost like needles. A flat gold chain, passing under her chin, ascends beside her cheeks, rolls in a spiral around her hair, which is powdered with blue powder, then, falling, grazes her shoulder and comes and fastens itself on her bosom in a scorpion in diamonds which thrusts out its tongue between her breasts. Two great blood pearls drag down her ears. The edges of her eyelids are painted black. She has on her left cheek-bone a natu-

ral brown mole, and she breathes, opening her mouth, as if her bodice hurt her. She shakes as she walks, a green parasol surrounded with gilt bells, and twelve little woolly-headed negroes carry the long train of her dress, held at the end by a monkey, who occasionally lifts it up. She says: '*Ah, bel ermite! bel ermite! mon cœur défaille!*' "

This is certainly a "realistic" Queen of Sheba, and Nebuchadnezzar is almost equally so. Going on from figure to figure and scene to scene in this bewildering panorama, we ask ourselves exactly what it is that M. Flaubert has proposed to accomplish. Not a prose-poem from the saint's own moral point of view, with his spiritual sufferings and vagaries for its episode, and his ultimate expulsion of all profane emotions for its dénouement; for St. Anthony throughout remains the dimmest of shadows, and his commentary upon his hallucination is meagre and desultory. Not, on the other hand, a properly historical presentment of the various types he evokes, for fancy is called in at every turn to supplement the scanty testimony of history. What is M. Flaubert's historic evidence for the mole on the Queen of Sheba's cheek and the blue powder in her hair? He has simply wished to be tremendously pictorial, and the opportunity for spiritual analysis has been the last thing in his thoughts. It is matter of regret that a writer with the pluck and energy to grapple with so pregnant a theme should have been so indifferent to its most characteristic side. It is probable that, after M. Flaubert's big volume, we shall not have, in literature, for a long time, any more 'Temptations of St. Anthony'; and yet there is obviously a virtue in the subject which has by no means been exhausted. Tremendously pictorial M. Flaubert has certainly succeeded in being, and we stand amazed at his indefatigable ingenuity. He has accumulated a mass of curious learning; he has interfused it with a mass of still more curious conjecture; and he has resolved the whole into a series of pictures which, considering the want of models and precedents, may be said to be very handsomely executed. But what, the reader wonders, has been his inspiration, his motive, his *souffle*, as the French say? Of any abundant degree of imagination we perceive little in the work. Here and there we find a touch of something like poetry, as in the scene of the Christian martyrs huddled in one of the vaults of the circus, and watching through the bars of the opposite vault the lions and tigers to whom they are about to be introduced. Here and there is a happy dramatic turn in the talk of the hermit's visionary interlocutor or a vague approach to a "situation" in the attitude of the saint. But for the most part M. Flaubert's picturesque is a strangely artificial and cold-blooded picturesque —abounding in the grotesque and the repulsive, the abnormal and the barely conceivable, but seeming to have attained to it all by infinite labor, ingenuity, and research—never by one of the fine intuitions of a joyous and generous invention. It is all hard, inanimate, superficial, and inexpressibly disagreeable. When the author has a really beautiful point to treat—as the assembly of the Greek deities fading and paling away in the light of Christianity—he becomes singularly commonplace and ineffective.

His book being, with its great effort and its strangely absent charm, the really painful failure it seems to us, it would not have been worth while to call attention to it if it were not that it pointed to more things than the author's own deficiencies. It seems to us to throw a tolerably vivid light on the present condition of the French literary intellect. M. Flaubert and his contemporaries have pushed so far the education of the senses and the cultivation of the grotesque in literature and the arts that it has left them morally stranded and helpless. In the perception of the materially curious, in fantastic refinement of taste and marked ingenuity of expression, they seem to us now to have reached the limits of the possible. Behind M. Flaubert stands a whole society of æsthetic *raffinés*, demanding stronger and stronger spices in its intellectual diet. But we doubt whether he or any of his companions can permanently satisfy their public, for the simple reason that the human mind, even in indifferent health, does after all need to be *nourished*, and thrives but scantily on a regimen of pigments and sauces. It needs sooner or later—to prolong our metaphor—to detect a body-flavor, and we shall be very much surprised if it ever detects one in 'La Tentation de Saint Antoine.'

HENRY BEYLE*

STENDHAL was a most singular character, but nothing surely
in his destiny was so singular as having Mr. Paton write his life.
Beyond his good-will and his industry, we are unable to perceive
that the biographer has a single qualification for his task, and
we should be curious to know whether it was undertaken spon-
taneously or to order. In speaking of the author's admirable
'Chroniques Italiennes,' and by implication of his masterpiece,
the 'Chartreuse de Parme,' Mr. Paton remarks that Beyle was
here quite off his beat, and that what he *might* have done was
something in the "pleasant, gossiping manner of Louisa Mühlbach"! In his review of his hero's works, Mr. Paton devotes eleven
pages to that forgotten fragment, the 'Vie de Rossini,' and not a
line to this same 'Chartreuse de Parme,' now recognized as Beyle's
chief title to the attention of posterity. Of the smallest capacity
to appreciate the author either on his moral or intellectual side
Mr. Paton is strikingly guiltless. He regards him as a shrewd,
amusing, eccentric gossip, determined to have his laugh at everything, and to offer his readers at any cost a light, frothy entertainment—a judgment about on a level with his speaking incidentally of the "naive Dutch realism of Balzac." A critic who
finds Stendhal amusing and Balzac "naif" must be left to his
own devices. Mr. Paton is, as a commentator, quite worthless,
and as a writer sadly slipshod and vulgar. We have seldom seen
a book more in need of a complete revision, both as to matter
and to manner. It contains hardly an opinion which is not
ludicrously erratic, and hardly a quotation, a foreign phrase, or
a proper name which is not misspelled and misprinted. But
the author writes with a garrulous *bonhomie*—that of an easy-
going cosmopolite, well advanced, apparently, in years—which
will soften the edge of the reader's displeasure; and he is to be
thanked at any rate for bringing Beyle once more before the
world, and giving occasion for that final sifting and summing

* 'Henry Beyle (otherwise De Stendahl) [sic!] A Critical and Biographical
Study. By Andrew Archibald Paton.' London: Trübner & Co. 1874. (*The
Nation*, September 17, 1874).

up of opinion which the world finds it constantly more needful
to practise expeditiously towards all claimants for permanent
attention. But it seems, we repeat, the crowning stroke of that
something perverse and melancholy which pervaded all Stendhal's
career, that these last proceedings in judgment should take place
in an English court and be carried on in English—and in English
in which Mr. Paton has a voice. Beyle was the most French of
Frenchmen, but he spent half his life in Italy, lauding the Italians
and denouncing his countrymen. He caused "Arrigo Beyle,
Milanese," to be inscribed upon his tombstone, and he falls
victim, thirty years after his death, to a biographer who discourses upon him in a strange, slovenly English, flavored with
Scotch and interlarded with disfigured fragments of French and
Italian. By denying that he was the flippant feuilletonist represented by Mr. Paton, we do not mean to intimate that he was a
dull writer. He is always interesting and often divertingly so,
but his merit, to our sense, is not in his powers of entertainment,
greater or less, but simply in his instinctive method. What this
method was, and how instinctive it was, is suggested by this passage in a letter to his sister, written in his twenty-first year:

> "I like *examples,* and not, like Montesquieu, Buffon,
> and Rousseau, systems . . . . Help me to know provincial
> manners and passions; describe me the manners in the draw-
> ing-room of Madame ———. I need examples and facts.
> Write quickly, without seeking fine phrases . . . . Contribute
> to my knowledge of women, facts, facts! I have a passionate
> desire to know human nature, and a great mind to live in
> a boarding-house, where people cannot conceal their real
> characters . . . . Borrow and read Sallust; you will find
> there thirty superb characters."

Later, he advises the same young lady to make a list of the
good and bad passions, and then to write opposite each category
a description of such examples as she had observed. By persever-
ance in this course, she would find that she had discovered
treasures of knowledge of human nature. It was this absorbing
passion for example, anecdote, and illustration that constituted
Beyle's distinctive genius, and is the ground of the fresh claims

put forth on his behalf by his recent eloquent apostle, M. Taine. Beyle felt, as soon as he began to observe, that character, manners, and civilization are explained by circumstances, and that in the way of observing and collecting circumstances there was a great work to be done. He devoted himself as far as possible to doing it, and on the whole, with his profound mistrust of systems, left the theory of the matter very much to take care of itself. M. Taine follows, with a genius for theory, and erects a symmetrical system on Beyle's unordered *data*. It is interesting to observe that in his attempts to theorize, Beyle is always flimsy and erratic; and that in his attempts to collect small facts in the manner of Beyle (as in *Monsieur Graindorge*), M. Taine is generally ponderous and infelicitous.

The only value of M. Paton's volume is in its distinterring a good many obscure facts of Beyle's personal history, and, in particular, in its offering us a number of extracts from the copious and intimate correspondence which he carried on in his early years with his sister Pauline. With his genius for observation, fortune led Beyle, happily, to see a good deal of the world. He was born at Grenoble in the year 1783. His father occupied an honorable position in the law, but his means were moderate, and Beyle's money-troubles were unceasing to the day of his death. In his own line, he had a fine start in life in having opportunities for close observation of the great Napoleonic drama. He obtained by family influence a cavalry commission in the army, and afterwards occupied some responsible posts in the commissariat. He was at the battle of Marengo and in the retreat from Moscow (as the reader of any given five pages of his writing will not fail to discover). He also discharged various small administrative functions in Germany. In his Italian campaign, he formed that passion for Italy and all things Italian which provided him with the occupation of a lifetime. He returned to Milan in 1811, and from that time to his death made repeated visits, of varying duration, amounting in all to more than twenty years. His last ten years (though he died while on leave of absence in Paris) were spent as consul to Civita Vecchia—a passion for Italy cherished certainly under difficulties. He died in 1842. Mr. Paton will enable an ingenious reader to construct a tolerably vivid

personal portrait. After the fall of the Empire, Beyle was continually poor, and his habits and tastes demanded money. His
writings were not popular, and have come into favor since his
death. He was extremely ugly, with a coarse, corpulent, plebeian
ugliness. Mr. Paton says characteristically that by one of his
friends "some rather offensive" traits are mentioned—"for instance, he wore stays." This is certainly not an Anglo-Saxon custom for gentlemen, but, except that, as Beyle was very fat, tight-
lacing may have often been uncomfortable to him, we are at
a loss to see to whom, besides himself, it was "offensive." Mr.
Paton adds that the same witness, whose name he misprints, pro-
nounces him "a *gentilhomme sans blason*," and translates the
phrase "a would-be gentleman, without armorial bearings." It
means, of course, the direct reverse—a real gentleman, though
he could show no arms. This judgment affords some relief to
the reader's imagination, which, by reflecting much upon Beyle's
poverty and his ugliness, has found itself unable to view in as
graceful a light as is desirable his unremitting and somewhat
pretentious love-affairs. It is an especial ill-fortune for Beyle
that his relations with women and his views on the whole matter
of love should be presented for judgment at an English tribunal,
unaccustomed to dealing either with such temperaments or with
such opinions. Beyle's temperament was apparently the French
temperament in a highly exaggerated form; and as for his opinions, they are scattered through all his writings, and especially
embodied in his voluminous treatise *De l'Amour*—his masterpiece, according to Mr. Paton, but to our taste that one of his
books which, with the exception perhaps of *Le Rouge et le Noir*,
comes nearest to being absolutely unreadable. As is generally the
case in regard to this matter in the lives of men of genius in which
it plays a part, we know at once too much and too little. We
know with more or less accuracy the number and succession of
the ladies to whom these gentlemen have been devoted, and
we know their published philosophy of such devotion, but we
are not able, for want of a general light, to appreciate justly
either the weak points in their philosophy or the strong points
in their conduct.

Stendhal was apparently very industrious, though he worked in a desultory and disjointed manner, wrote (or published, at least) because he had to do so for bread, and affected to be as little as possible a littérateur by profession. He ought to have considered, however, that the character was made honorable by the danger which he persisted in fancying attached to it. He published everything under a false name (he had half a dozen), travestied his own on his tombstone, and is known to fame by a disguise. He professed an entire indifference to literary fame, except as consisting in mere conciseness. He boasts that the *Chartreuse de Parme* is written in the style of the Civil Code. He borrowed largely, especially in his early writings, and transferred long passages from other books without acknowledgment. One may say roughly that his subject is always Italy. He had a number of affectations, but his passion for Italy is evidently profoundly sincere, and will serve to keep his memory sweet to many minds and his authority unquestioned. This subject he treated under a number of different forms; most successfully, toward the end of his life, in a novel which will always be numbered among the dozen finest novels we possess; in a number of short tales, founded on fact, and extracted from the manuscript archives of Italian families, of many of whom Stendahl purchased the privilege of transcribing for a certain number of mornings in their libraries—just as in some parts of the Rhineland one may obtain for a small fee the right to spend an hour in a vineyard or orchard, and retire carrying as much fruit as possible about one's person, as the phrase is; and in a series of loosely connected notes, descriptive, reflective, anecdotic, and epigrammatic, on monuments and pictures, manners and morals (such as *Rome, Naples et Florence* and the *Promenades dans Rome*). To these last may be added his *Histoire de la Peinture en Italie* and various pamphlets—the *Vie de Rossini* and *Racine et Shakespeare*. The *History of Painting* is an ambitious name for a string of desultory though often acute suggestive dissertations on matters nearly and remotely connected with Italian art. It is no history, and, with much suggestiveness, it has to our mind little value. Stendhal as an art-critic is inveterately beside the mark, and it is striking evidence of the development of the science of taste within the last forty years that with his extreme "sensibility," as he would call it, and his excellent opportunities for study, he should seem to us nowadays to belong to so false a school.

The letters placed in Mr. Paton's hands by Beyle's family, and unfortunately offered us here only in translated and condensed extracts, add much to our sense of intimacy with our author, but help us little to understand him better. He was a strange mixture of genius and pretension, of amiability and arrogance, of fine intuitions and patent follies. He condemned his genius to utter more foolish things than it seems to us a wise man was ever before responsible for. He practised contempt on a wholesale, a really grotesque scale, and considered, or pretended to consider, all mankind an aggregation of *"sots,"* except a small class endowed like himself with "sensibility." We have spoken of his method; it was excellent, but we may say on the whole that it was better than any use he made of it—save only when he wrote the *Chartreuse de Parme.* His notion was that *passion,* the power to surrender one's self sincerely and consistently to the feeling of the hour, was the finest thing in the world, and it seemed to him that he had discovered a mine of it in the old Italian character. In the French, passion was abortive, through the action of vanity and the fear of the neighbors' opinion—a state of things with which he is never weary of expressing his disgust. It is easy to perceive that this doctrine held itself quite irresponsible to our old moralistic canons, for *naïveté* of sentiment in any direction, combined with great energy, was considered absolutely its own justification. In the *Chartreuse de Parme,* where every one is grossly immoral, and the heroine is a kind of monster, there is so little attempt to offer any other, that through the magnificently sustained pauses of the narrative we feel at last the influence of the writer's cynicism, regard it as amiable, and enjoy serenely his clear vision of the mechanism of character, unclouded by the mists of prejudice. Among writers called immoral there is no doubt that he best deserves the charge; the others, beside him, are spotlessly innocent. But his immorality seems vicious and harsh only according to the subjects he handles. *Le Rouge et le Noir, L'Amour,* and certain passages in his other writings have an air of unredeemed corruption—a quality which in the novel amounts to a positive blight and dreariness. For the rest, Stendhal professed a passionate love of the beautiful *per se,* and there is every reason to suppose that it was sincere. He was an entertaining mixture of sentiment and cynicism. He describes his heroes and heroines in perfect good faith as "sublime," in appearance and fact, in the midst of the most disreputable actions, and it seems to him that one may perfectly well live a scandalous life and sit up half the night reading Dante in a glow of pure rapture. In repudiating Mr. Paton's assumption that he is a light writer, we would fain express that singular something which is fairly described neither as serious nor as solemn—a kind of painful tension of feeling under the disguise of the coolest and easiest style. It is the tension, in part, of conceit —the conceit which leads him with every tenth phrase to prophesy in the most trenchant manner the pass to which "les sots" will have brought things within such and such a period—and in part of aspiration, of deep enjoyment of some bold touch of nature or some fine stroke of art. This bespeaks the restlessness of a superior mind, and makes our total feeling for Beyle a kindly one. We recommend his books to persons of "sensibility" whose moral convictions have somewhat solidified.

MINOR FRENCH NOVELISTS:
THE GONCOURTS, ETC.*

A CRITIC has not spoken, fully of Gustave Flaubert unless he has spoken also of MM. de Goncourt. These gentlemen, brothers, collaborators, and extremely clever writers, have certainly plenty of talent of their own, but it may fairly be suspected that without Flaubert's example they would not have used their talent in just the way they have done. If we have nothing in

(* The Galaxy: February, 1876).

English like M. Flaubert, we are still further from having anything like Edmond and Jules de Goncourt. Their works have all been published under their associated names and produced by their united hands, according to a system best known to themselves. Everything they have written exhibits a perfect superficial unity. Jules de Goncourt, the younger brother, lately died; and since then the survivor has published nothing. MM. de Goncourt have written four or five novels, but it was not as novelists that they began their career. Their first labors were historical, and they produced a series of volumes at once solid and entertaining upon the French society of the last century and the early years of the present one. These volumes are a magazine of curious facts, and indicate a high relish for psychological research. In addition MM. de Goncourt are art students, and have published several elaborate monographs on painters. It has been very well said of them that the eighteenth century is their remotest antiquity; that for them the historical imagination ends there, after a long revel in sights of its goal. If time with these writers terminates at about 1730, space comes to a stop at the limits of Paris. They are the most Parisian thing I know. Other writers—Balzac, Sainte-Beuve, Edmond About—are intensely French; MM. de Goncourt are essentially Parisian. Their culture, their imagination, their inspiration, are all Parisian; a culture sensibly limited, but very exquisite of its kind; an imagination in the highest degree ingenious and, as the French say, *raffiné*—fed upon made dishes. Their inspiration is altogether artistic, and they are artists of the most consistent kind. Their writing novels strikes me as having been a very deliberate matter. Finding themselves in possession of a singularly perfect intellectual instrument—men of the study and of the drawing-room, with their measured and polished literary style, their acute observation of material things, their subtle Parisian imagination, their ingrained familiarity with questions of taste—they decided that in the novel of the most consummately modern type they could manifest themselves most completely. They inevitably went into "realism," but realism for them has been altogether a question of taste—a studio question, as it were. They also find the disagreeable particularly characteristic, and there is something ineffably odd in seeing these elegant erudites bring their highly complex and artificial method—the fruit of culture, and leisure, and luxury—to bear upon the crudities and maladies of life, and pick out choice morsels of available misery upon their gold pen-points. "Germinie Lacerteux" is the history of an hysterical servant girl. "Manette Salomon" introduces us to a depraved Jewess who follows the trade of model in painters' studios, and who entangles, bewitches, and ruins a young artist of high promise. "Sœur Philomène" is the story of a sister of charity in a hospital, who falls in love with one of the house surgeons; while he, having to perform an operation upon a woman of the town whom he has once loved, and who has been stabbed by a subsequent lover—an operation which proves fatal to the patient—drowns his remorse in absinthe, becomes an incurable drunkard, and finally, in self-loathing, deliberately infects himself, during a dissection, with some poisonous matter, and dies in horrible tortures. With MM. de Goncourt the whole thing is a spectacle, a shaded picture, and the artist's mission is to reproduce its parts in a series of little miniatures of the highest possible finish. A novel, for them, is a succession of minute paintings on ivory, strung together like pearls on a necklace. Their first tale, indeed—"Renée Mauperin," which is also their most agreeable—has more of the old-fashioned narrative quality. I use a "agreeable" here in a purely relative sense. The book is an attempt to portray the young girl "of the period" in France—but the young girl of the period at her best, the young girl whose instincts are pure and elevated. It proposes to show us what "l'éducation garconnière et artistique" of the day makes of such a character. It does this in a very pretty fashion. I remember no French novel in which the consequences of allowing a young girl a moderate amount of liberty are more gracefully and naturally presented. But it is the people and the doings with which the charming Renée is associated that make us open our eyes. She belongs to an honorable *bourgeois* family who have made a handsome fortune in trade, and she has a brother who is a rising young politician and endowed with irreproachable manners and a profound ambition. The brother, to push his fortunes, determines to make a rich marriage, and selects for this purpose the pretty Mlle. Bourjot, sole heiress of numberless millions. This young lady's family insist upon his changing his name to something noble; so he obtains governmental permission to call himself Mauperin de Villacourt—the name of a small estate belonging to his father. This is not at all to the taste of Renée, who thinks the proceeding snobbish and ignoble, and who, learning that a member of the old race of Villacourt still exists, denuded of everything but the family pride, sends him a copy of the newspaper in which her brother has given legal notice of his intention, in the hope that he will put in a protest. Meanwhile she learns, through Mlle. Bourjot herself, that young Mauperin has long been carrying on an intrigue with her mamma—a lady old enough, in vulgar phrase, to know better. To marry Henri Mauperin under these circumstances is naturally disagreeable to Mlle. Bourjot; but the mamma and the intended at last agree to bring their relations to a close; the daughter appears to be duly informed of their decision; she is reassured and satisfied, and things for a while go forward very comfortably. At last the necessary year has elapsed since Mauperin promulgated his intention to assume the name of Villacourt, and no one has contested his right. But on the eve of the wedding day the last of the Villacourts turns up. He is a rude, rustic nobleman, a mighty hunter and drinker, who lives in the woods, and never looks at the newspapers, even when posted to him by pretty feminine hands. The journal sent by Renée, however, has at last come under his dreamy eyes. He springs up in wrath, hastens to Paris, bursts into Mauperin's apartment, and by way of counterclaim smites him in the face. In the duel which follows Mauperin is killed, and Renée, with her brother's blood on her conscience, wastes away to death in a series of attitudes most gracefully described by MM. de Goncourt. Renée, as I have said, with her Parisian wit and her generous temper, is a very agreeable creation. Her talk throughout is excellent, though it is extremely difficult to translate. The following may serve as a specimen: "What a bore it is to be a young person—don't you think so? I would like to see you try it!" (She is bathing in the Seine, in company with a young man to whom these remarks are addressed. But of this anon.) "You would see what that bore comes to—

the bore of being 'proper.' Suppose we were dancing now, eh? Do you think we can talk with our partner? Yes, no, yes, no— that's all. We must stick to monosyllables. That's proper! That's the pleasure of life for us. And for everything it's the same. The only thing that is really proper is to sit and swing our heels. I don't know how. And then to sit and tittle-tattle with persons of one's own sex. If we have the misfortune to let them go for a man—oh, mamma has blown me up for that! Another thing that isn't at all proper is to read. It is only these last two years that they allow me the *feuilletons* in the newspapers. There are some of the crimes in the 'faits divers' that they make me skip; they are not sufficiently proper. It's like our 'accomplishments'; they must not go beyond a certain little mark. Beyond duets on the piano and heads in crayon, it becomes professional; one sets up for something. For instance, I paint in oil, and my family are in despair. I ought to do nothing but roses in water-colors." When "Renée Mauperin" first appeared, the opening pages (from which my quotation is made) had a great success. The description of the young girl in the water is very felicitous, and is also worth quoting. "The young girl and the young man who were talking thus were in the water. Tired of swimming, drawn along by the current, they had hooked themselves to a rope which fastened one of the great boats, alongside the island. The force of the water swayed them softly to and fro at the end of the tense and quivering rope. They sank a little, then rose again. The water broke against the breast of the young girl, rose in her woollen dress as high as her neck, and threw against her from behind a little wave which a moment later was nothing but a dewdrop ready to fall from her ear. Clasping the rope a little higher than the young man, her arms were raised and her wrists turned in, to hold the cable better; her back was against the black wood of the boat. Naturally, every moment, her body floated away from that of the young man, carried against her by the current. In this hanging, retreating posture she resembled those figures of sea gods twisted by wood-carvers along the sides of galleys. A little tremor, coming from the movement of the river and the cold of the bath, seemed to give her something of the undulation of the water."

That is admirable; we seem to see it. MM. de Goncourt have possessed themselves of every literary secret; they have made a devout study of style. "Sœur Philomène," as a piece of writing and of visual observation, is a masterpiece; refinement of observation, an unerring scent for the curious and morbid, can hardly go further. The book is worth reading, from beginning to end, for its exquisite art—although the art is, to my mind, superficial, and the subject both morally and physically unsavory. It required great skill to interest us during a whole volume in the comings and goings of a simple and ignorant man, around the sickbeds of a roomful of paupers. The authors have "got up" their subject, as the phrase is, with extraordinary care; I do not know what their personal experience of hospital wards has been, but the reader might suppose that they had spent years in one. MM. de Goncourt are *dilettanti;* they are *raffinés* and they write for *raffinés;* but they are worth attention because they are highly characteristic of contemporary French culture. They are even more characteristic than some stronger writers; for they are not men of genius; they are the product of the atmosphere that surrounds them; their great talent is in great part the result of sympathy, and contact, and emulation. They represent the analysis of sensation raised to its highest powers, and that is apparently the most original thing that the younger French imaginative literature has achieved. But from them as from Gustave Flaubert the attentive reader receives an indefinable impression of perverted ingenuity and wasted power. The sense of the picturesque has somehow killed the spiritual sense; the moral side of the work is dry and thin. I can hardly explain it, but such a book as "Sœur Philoméne," with all its perfection of manner, gives me an impression of something I can find no other name for than cruelty. There are some things which should be sacred even to art, and art, when she is truly prosperous, is comfortably contented to let them alone. But when she begins to overhaul the baser forms of suffering and the meaner forms of vice, to turn over and turn again the thousand indecencies and impurities of life, she seems base and hungry, starving, desperate, and we think of her as one who has wasted her substance in riotous living.

I said that MM. de Goncourt did not strike me as men of
genius, and I can think of but two names in the list of those
whom I have called the minor French novelists that suggest the
idea of genius. The first is that of Erckmann-Chatrian and the
second that of Gustave Droz. The two associated story-tellers
known to the world under the former of these names constitute
surely a genius of the purest water. Of all the French romancers
of the day they are the most simply delightful, and their exquisite sense of the decent, wholesome, human side of reality,
ought to balance a multitude of infectious researches in the
opposite direction. It is natural to believe, and it is impossible
not to hope, that "Le Conscrit de 1813," "Le Blocus," "L'Ami
Fritz," "Le Joueur de Clarinette" will be read by our children's
children. Gustave Droz is not by any means so clear or so complete a genius, but he has that spark of magic in his fancy, that
something lightly and easily human in his humor, which are
kindled in the glow of the sacred fire. One at least of the tales of
M. Droz ought to stand. "Le Cahier Bleu de Mlle. Cibot" is a masterpiece, and a capital example of the charm that intense reality
may have when it is reached by divination, by the winged fancy,
rather than by a system more or less ingenious. After this, there
are the brilliant talents—Octave Feuillet, Edmond About, Victor
Cherbueliez. These writers are all prodigiously clever, but the
cleverness of M. Cherbuliez, overtops that of his companions.
They are clever by nature, and he is clever by art, and yet he
wears his cleverness with a grace and gallantry that quite eclipses
theirs. He has deliberately learned how to write novels, and
he writes them incomparably well. Unfortunately he seems of
late to have come to the end of his lesson; his last two tales are
almost painfully inferior to their predecessors. Five-and-twenty
years ago, before the writers of whom these pages treat had (with
one exception) presented themselves to the public, Mme. Sand
was the first of French romancers. Five-and-twenty years have
elapsed: these writers have exhibited all their paces, and Mme.
Sand is still unsurpassed. Each of the novelists I have mentioned
can do something which she cannot; but she, at her best, has
resources which exceed the total aggregation of theirs. (I say
advisedly at her best, for between her best and her second best

there is a gulf.) She has the true, the great imagination—the metaphysical imagination. She conceives more largely and executes more nobly; she is easy and universal and—above all—agreeable.

EDMOND DE GONCOURT'S LA FILLE ELISA

The great success of Emile Zola's remarkable and repulsive novel, 'L'Assommoir,' which was lately described in these columns, has been, if not equalled, at least emulated, by 'La Fille Elisa' of Edmond Goncourt. 'L'Assommoir,' we believe, is going on toward its thirtieth edition, while the last copy of 'La Fille Elisa' that we have seen is stamped with the fainter glory of a tenth. On the other hand, M. Zola's novel had by some weeks the start of its companion, and the adventures of M. de Goncourt's heroine (a prostitute who murders a soldier) may after all be as widely disseminated as those of the fair protagonist of 'L'Assommoir,' the washerwoman who dies of drink. M. Edmond de Goncourt has gone into these matters in a more amateurish sort of way than his rival, who is thoroughly professional and business-like; and 'La Fille Elisa' is very inferior in ability to the history of Gervaise and Coupeau. It is equal, however, or perhaps even superior, in audacity. Edmond de Goncourt, we may remind the reader, is the elder and survivor of the two brothers De Goncourt, who, during the lifetime of the younger, Jules, published several novels of the realistic sort and several substantial works upon the history of France in the last century. 'La Fille Elisa' is the first production upon the title-page of which the name of one of the brothers has stood alone; and, curiously enough, it offers some enlightenment (for such readers as have wondered over the matter) as to the mystery of French "collaboration." The book is feebler, thinner, less clever than its predecessors; it seems to prove that there are some talents that need to "collaborate," and that they are fully themselves only on this condition. Like M. Zola, the author of the tale in

(*The Nation*, May 10, 1877).

question has written a preface, in which he calls attention to the edifying properties of his book—his "livre austère et chaste." Speaking seriously, the preface is the best part of the work. M. de Goncourt says, very justly, that it is an unwarrantable pretension on the part of certain critics to forbid the school of novelists to which he belongs—"la jeune école sérieuse"—to write anything but what may be read by young ladies in railway trains. This is really what the prohibitory legislation amounts to. The author asserts that the young serious school, if not interfered with, stands ready to divest the novel of its traditional frivolity, and make it co-operate with history and scientific research in the task of enlightening and instructing mankind. As an example, M. de Goncourt devotes himself to showing up the horrors of the régime of silence in prisons—the system which he appears to consider it the peculiar infamy of the American penal establishments to have invented and propagated. His heroine, convicted of manslaughter, is imprisoned for life, and, being never allowed to speak, becomes after a certain number of years idiotic and dies of a sort of chronic stupor. This part of the book, the last third, dealing with her prison life, shows most ability, and has doubtless a certain value. The author has evidently "studied up" his subject. The preceding chapters, which describe minutely the career of the unfortunate Elisa as a street-walker of the lowest class, and include an account of the circumstances of her childhood—as daughter of a *sagefemme* also of the lowest class—are not practically agreeable, however valid the theory upon which they have been composed. As we read them we wonder what is becoming of the French imagination, and we say that even readers who have flattered themselves that they knew the French mind tolerably well find that it has some surprisingly unpleasant corners. M. de Goncourt's theory is perfectly respectable; novelists are welcome to become as serious as they please; but are the mysteries of such a career as Elisa's the most serious thing in the list? M. de Goncourt's fault is not that he is serious or historical or scientific or instructive, but that he is intolerably unclean. The proof of the pudding is in the eating, and, in spite of its elevated intentions, "La Fille Elisa" must be profoundly distasteful to healthy appetites.

MÉRIMÉE'S LETTERS TO ANOTHER UNKNOWN

Our readers have probably not forgotten the review of Mérimée's 'Lettres à une Inconnue' which appeared in these columns some year and a half ago. The book had been largely read, but it was variously appreciated. Some people thought it very trivial, others deemed it very deep; upon its being entertaining, however, most people were agreed. Amid the criticism to which it gave rise, there was not a little animadversion upon the audacity of the lady to whom the letters were addressed, who, when her admirer had passed away, had not scrupled to make public some thirty years of their common very private history. We hardly know if it makes this lady's frankness more surprising or more natural to find another person capable of the same intrepidity. Here is another "unknown" with another bundle of confidential epistles. She has apparently very sagaciously reflected that to have been a correspondent of Mérimée is just now a remunerative situation, and that since the ice has been broken there is no harm in making a few more holes. About Mérimée himself everything worth saying seems to us by this time to have been said; he has received his dues, and more than his dues. So small an investment of talent has certainly never brought in a higher interest of fame. He wrote a dozen tales which will last, but there is something really paradoxical in talking much about them—so very reticent, and spare, and frugal of eloquence are they themselves. M. Blaze de Bury, a writer who is a great talker (and it must be added a very entertaining one), has endeavored in a long preface to the present volume to say something new about the author of 'Colomba,' but most of his novelties are of a sort that would evaporate in quotation. He has made one good point, however, on the subject of that masterly reserve for which Mérimée has been so much praised.

---

* *Lettres à une autre Inconnue*. Par Prosper Mérimée, de l'Académie Française. Avant-propos par H. Blaze de Bury. (Paris: Michel Lévy; New York: F. W. Christern.) (*The Nation*, January 27, 1876).

Mérimée never describes, he only narrates, and there is certainly often something very eloquent in his studied sobriety. It has always been assumed that if he did not describe it is because he would not, and not because he could not; but M. Blaze de Bury reminds us that there is another side to the question, and that there is such a thing as glorifying negative merits too highly. In the 'Chronique de Charles IX.,' when the king comes in, the author, who is apparently about to give a sketch of his person, suddenly stops short. "His portrait?—wait. Really you had better go and see it in the Museum at Angoulême; it is in the second room; number 98." "This is a convenient way of getting out of it," says M. Blaze de Bury; "is it the best way? Mérimée was a sly fox, depend upon it, and he had no need of La Fontaine and his fables to characterize the grapes that one cannot reach." It is certain, with all deference to what is called economy of effect, that the phrase above quoted could not have been written by a man of a rich genius, and Mérimée decidedly was not a man of a rich genius. There is fortunately a golden mean between bathos and blankness.

It is not, however, for their undue reticence that these new letters are remarkable. Mérimée's pen, in addressing his fair correspondents, was neither prudish nor cautious, and there are several passages in this little volume which seem to belong to a date much earlier than our modern proprieties. They will afford an extra satisfaction to those connoisseurs who consider Mérimée the last of the French writers who has to some extent preserved the last-century traditions of style. These letters are fifty in number; they are very short; and they are really not valuable. Persons seriously interested in the author will find in them something to complete their mental image of him; but those who should read them without having been otherwise introduced to Mérimée, would scarcely suppose them to be the productions of a superior man. They run, at wide intervals, through a space of five years, from 1865 to 1870, and the person to whom they were addressed is less of a mystery than the first unknown. She was a Polish lady of high rank, who seems to have been, like her correspondent, on a footing of familiarity at the court of Napoleon III. The Empress, during those laboriously brilliant years that preceded the war, had established certain "courts of love" for the entertainment of her social circle, and Mérimée's correspondent was "president," or judge, at one of these. Whether she had ever had to pass sentence on Mérimée as an offender is more than we can say, but it is in this character that he always addresses her. He deals chiefly in court gossip, and alludes to the trifles of the hour. Such slender value as the letters possess belong to the fact that the Imperial court, having become so thoroughly a thing of the past, a theme for the historian and the moralist, Mérimée's anecdotes and *cancans* have a sort of historical savor. "We have the happiness occasionally of seeing the Empress of Mexico. She is a *maîtresse-femme*, and as like as two peas to Louis Philippe. She has some ladies of honor with flaming eyes, but complexions like gingerbread, and a sort of look of orang-outangs. We expected to see the houris of Mahomet! It is supposed that her majesty has come to ask for money and soldiers; but I fancy they will give her nothing but fêtes, for which she seems to care little." That seems very far away from the present moment in France. Most of the proper names have been retained; the reader may judge of the practical results in some cases. "The Princess of Metternich is, on the contrary, all grace and amiability. Only, she has thrown herself into painting. I mean the *Samojivopistro* (the painting of one's self); and how this science has progressed! She has lips of the most delightful flame-color, with which she can drink tea without leaving them on the cup." Here is another specimen, from Biarritz: "We have here the Grand-Duchess Marie of Russia, and the Grand-Duke of Leuchtenberg, who is a very handsome fellow, and who would make ravages on this shore if there were a few beauties less thoroughly known than those we possess. Madame de Talleyrand, whose hair has become blond, the Duchess of Frias—such are the highest temptations we can offer. I don't speak of Madame Korsakof, in a yellow dress and a black jacket, black stockings, and boots with yellow rosettes, who leads about a great black dog (without any yellow), and a gentleman to protect her. She has still a charming figure, and with her back turned makes a great many conquests." The following is more interesting: "We have brought back the Emperor in very good health. He took long tramps on foot with us, which quite used us up. In truth, the more I see of princes, the more I perceive that they are made of another paste than common mortals. For myself, I have no fitness whatever for the profession, and I abstain absolutely from all pretension to sovereignty—even to that of Greece or the Moldo-Wallachian Principalities."

On the whole, the unprejudiced reader may conclude that, if these letters add nothing to Mérimée's reputation, they were at least good enough for the person to whom they were addressed, and who has seen fit to give them to the world.

MÉRIMÉE'S LAST TALES

Edmond About somewhere speaks of Madame Sand and Prosper Mérimée, "the two greatest French writers." Without exactly agreeing with M. About, the reader interested in literary matters in France may have a high enough opinion of the author of 'Colomba' and the 'Double Méprise' to be thankful for this posthumous volume of tales. Unfortunately, the stories before us will add little weight to the opinion; though, indeed, they remind us agreeably of the author's limited but singularly perfect talent. Mérimée had long ago given the measure of his power as a story-teller, and it was hardly to be hoped that this little collection of literary remnants would place it in a new light. His first successes date from the early years of the century; the 'Théâtre de Clara Gazul' and 'Colomba,' his masterpiece, as most people think, are already ancient literature. In the subject-matter of his tales he was a precursor of the *romantiques* of 1830, and it is greatly to be wished that they had taken example by his manner as well. Victor Hugo would have been none the worse poet for a little of Mérimée's conscious sobriety, and Madame Sand would have been none the less readable for occasionally emulating his

Dernières Nouvelles de Prosper Mérimée, de l'Académie Française. (Paris: Michel Lévy; New York: F. W. Christern. 1873.) (*The Nation,* February 12, 1874).

extraordinary conciseness. That M. About should couple the author of 'Lélia' with Mérimée, in the estimate just quoted, indicates a taste determined to be comprehensive at any cost; for the
shortest way to describe Mérimée would perhaps be to say that
he is the absolute reverse of Madame Sand. He is unlike her in
the *quantity* of his genius as well as the quality, his fecundity
being as limited as hers has been excessive. He wrote very short
tales, and produced them, one by one, at long intervals. Many
years before his death he ceased to produce stories at all, and
confined himself to publishing occasionally a short historical or
archæological sketch, so that a complete collection of his tales
would fill but three or four small volumes, and might be read
in a day. Such as they are, however, we confess that Mérimée's
chiselled and polished little fictions, and indeed, the whole manner and system of the author, have always had a great fascination
for us. He is, perhaps, the most striking modern example of
zealous artistic conciseness—of the literary artist who works in
detail, by the line, by the word. There have been poets who
scanned their rhythm as narrowly as Mérimée, but we doubt
whether there has ever been a prose writer. His effort was to
compress as large an amount of dramatic substance as possible
into a very narrow compass, and the result is that, though his
stories are few and short, one may read them again and again,
and perceive with each reading a greater force of meaning. Some
of the earlier ones are most masterly in this pregnant brevity;
the story seems to say its last word, as the reader lays it down,
with a kind of magical after-resonance. We have often thought
a selection might be made from these tales, and presented to
young narrators as a sort of manual of their trade—a guide for
the avoidance of prolixity. Mérimée's subjects are always of the
romantic and picturesque order, dealing in action, not in sentiment. They almost always hinge on a violent adventure or chain
of adventures, and are strongly seasoned with bloodshed and
general naughtiness. There are a great many sword-thrusts and
pistol-shots, and a good deal of purely carnal love-making. At
the beginning of his career the author had a great relish for
Spanish local color, and several of his early works are richly
charged with it. The 'Théâtre de Clara Gazul,' written, we be-

lieve, before he was twenty-three, is a series of short tragic dramas on the picturesque cruelties and immoralities of Old Spain. One of his masterpieces, 'Carmen,' published later, is the history of a wonderful *gitanilla*—a princess among the heroines who have dared much for love. With his brutal subjects and his cynical style, Mérimée is doubtless thoroughly disagreeable to such readers as are not fascinated by his artistic skill. To tell a terrible little story without flinching—without expressing a grain of reprobation for the clever rascal who escapes under cover of the scuffle in which his innocent rival has his brains blown out, or a grain of compassion for the poor guilty lady whose husband or father, brought upon the scene by the crack of pistols, condemns her to a convent cell for life; not to be sentimental, not to be moral, not to be rhetorical, but to have simply a sort of gentlemanly, epicurean relish for the bitterness of the general human lot, and to distil it into little polished silver cups—this was Mérimée's conscious effort, and this was his rare success.

Some of his best stories are those in which a fantastic or supernatural element is thrown into startling relief against a background of hard, smooth realism. An admirable success in this line is the 'Venus d'Ile'—a version of the old legend of a love-pledge between a mortal and an effigy of the goddess. Mr. Morris has treated the theme with his usual somewhat prolix imagery in his 'Earthly Paradise.' Mérimée, making his heroine an antique brozen statue, disinterred in the garden of a little château in Gascony, and her victim the son of the old provincial antiquarian who discovered her, almost makes us believe in its actuality. This was the first known to us of Mérimée's tales, and we shall never forget our impression of its admirable art. The first and much the best of the stories in the present volume, "Lokis," deals with a subject as picturesquely unnatural. A Polish lady is seized by a bear, and dragged for five minutes toward his hiding-place. She is rescued in time to save her life, but her reason has succumbed to her terror, and she remains for ever a monomaniac. A few months after her disaster she gives birth to a son. Mérimée tells us the son's story. We recommend it to readers not averse to a good stiff horror. Our author's last years were very silent, though "Lokis," indeed, was published shortly before his death. He broke his silence in a flimsier cause in producing the mildly scandalous tale of the 'Chambre Bleue.' Among the papers found at the Tuileries after the flight of the Empress, as the story goes, was the MS., tied with blue ribbons, of this little performance à la Crébillon Fils. Worthy, perhaps, of the circle for which it was composed, it adds little to the reputation of one of the "first French writers." But we strongly suspect that Mérimée's best things will be valued for many years to come. Among writers elaborately perfect in a somewhat narrow line he will hold a high place; he will always be admired by the votaries of "manner." Twenty years hence, doubtless, clever young men, reading him for the first time, will, in the flash of enthusiasm, be lending his volumes to appreciative female friends, and having them promptly returned, with the observation that they are "coarse." Whereupon, we suppose, the clever young men will fall to reading them over, and reflecting that it is quite right, after all, that men should have their distinctive pleasures, and that a good story by Mérimée is not the least of these. We should add that our author gave some attention to Russian literature, and that the best thing in the present volume, after "Lokis," the extremely energetic little tale called "Le Coup de Pistolet," is a translation from Pushkin.

OCTAVE FEUILLET'S CAMORS*

THIS latest novel of M. Octave Feuillet is already a year old, but we take occasion, from the recent appearance of an American translation of the work, to offer a few English comments. Let us say, to begin with, that the translation is perfectly bad; that it is equally pretentious, vulgar, and incorrect; and that we recommend no reader who has the smallest acquaintance with the French tongue to resort to it either for entertainment or for edification. M. Octave Feuillet has been known in France for the past

---

* "Camors: or, Life Under the New Empire. From the French of M. Octave Feuillet." New York: Blelock & Co. 1868. (*The Nation*, July 30, 1868).

fifteen years as a superior writer of light works—tales, proverbs, and comedies. Those of his plays which have been acted are among the most successful of the modern French theatre, and on perusal, indeed, they exhibit a rare union of strength and elegance. A couple of years ago M. Feuillet was admitted—on the plea, we fancy, rather of his elegance than of his strength—to the French Academy. He has apparently wished to justify his election by the production of a masterpiece. In "M. de Camors" he has contributed another novel to the superior literature of his country.

One of the most interesting things about M. Feuillet's career, to our mind, is his steady improvement, or, rather, his growth, his progression. His early works treat almost wholly of fine ladies, and seem as if they were meant to be read by fine ladies—to be half-languidly perused in the depths of a satin arm-chair, between a Sèvres coffee-cup and the last number of *Le Follet,* with the corner of a velvet prayer-book peeping out beneath it. M. Feuillet has a natural delight in elegance—elegance even of the most artifical kind—and this "M. de Camors," the ripest fruit of his genius, with all its nervous strength and energy, is one of the most highly elegant novels we have ever read. But whereas, in his first literary essays, elegance was ever the presiding spirit, she is now relegated to the second rank, and gazes serenely over the shoulders of force. M. Feuillet has gradually enlarged his foundations and introduced into his scheme of society a number of those natural factors which we find in real life to play as large a part as the artificial and conventional. Not that he has not retained, however, all his primitive arts and graces; only, they have lost their excessive perfume, and are reduced to comparative insignificance by being worn abroad in the open air of the world. The long play of "Rédemption" was much better than his short ones; "Dalila" was better still; and "Montjoie" and "M. de Camors" are best of all. Nevertheless, we confess that there is not one of M. Feuillet's comedies and proverbs—"scenes," as he calls them—that we have not read with extreme delight and that we are not willing to read again. It must have been from the first an earnest of future power for the close observer that the author, in spite of the light and unsubstantial character of his materials and the superficial action of his mind, should yet be so excellent a master of dramatic form; but for this excellence—a thoroughly masculine quality—there might have been some truth in the charge that M. Feuillet was a feminine writer. But women assuredly have no turn for writing plays. A play is action, movement, decision; the female mind is contemplation, repose, suspense. In "M. de Camors" the author has simply redeemed the promise, liberally interpreted, of the strong dramatic instincts of "Le Village" and "Alix."

In this work M. Feuillet has attempted to draw a picture of what he calls "one of the most brilliant Parisian lives of our time." He has endeavored to pull off the veil of brilliancy, and to show us his hero in all the nakedness of his moral penury. He has wished to effect a contrast between that face of a man's destiny which he presents to the world and that far other face which meets the eyes of his own soul. He has contrived for this purpose a narrative so dramatic and interesting that we shall briefly repeat its main outline. M. de Camors is the only son of the Count de Camors, who on the threshold of old age finds himself utterly disenchanted with the world. Feeling that he has come to the end of all things, and that his soul is equally indifferent to pleasure and to profit, he indites a long, didactic letter to his son and blows out his brains. This letter—an extremely clever performance—is the profession of faith of an aristocratic cynic. It declares that there are no such things as virtue and vice, and that the sole rule of life is the pursuit of agreeable physical sensations and the maintenance of a perfect equanimity. To be absolutely and consistently selfish is to come as near as possible to being happy. Wealth is essential to comfort and women are useful for pleasure. Children are an unmitigated nuisance—which, by the way, is not very civil to the count presumptive. "To be loved by women," writes the count, "to be feared by men, to be as impassible as a god before the tears of the former and the blood of the latter, to end your life in a tempest—this is the destiny which I have failed to grasp and which I bequeath to you." To cast off all natural ties, instincts, affections, sympathies, as so many shackles on his liberty; to marry only for valid reasons of interest and on no account to have children or friends, to perfect his fencing, to keep his temper, never to cry, and to laugh a little—these are the final injunctions of M. de Camors to his son. They are in many ways cold and pedantic, but they are conceived and expressed with great ingenuity. The young Count de Camors receives his father's bequest as a sacred deposit, and the story relates his attempts to apply practically these select principles. While his father has been occupied in drawing up his last will, he has been engaged in an act of supreme *rouerie* in the house of an intimate friend. So happy a start in the career of egotism is not to be thrown away, and M. de Camors says amen to the voice from beyond the grave. He forthwith prepares to enter political life, and, betaking himself with this view to a small estate in the country, presents himself as candidate for the Chamber of Deputies. In this region he meets two women—the heroines of the tale. The younger, his cousin, a poor girl in a servile position, and a great beauty, appeals to the reader's interest from the first by offering her hand in marriage to M. de Camors—an overture which he feels compelled to arrest. The young lady subsequently makes a splendid match with an old general of immense wealth. The second of M. de Camors's female friends is Mme. de Tècle, a young widow, a charming woman and an admirably-finished portrait. M. de Camors wins the love of Mme. de Tècle and returns it, but is unable, for good reasons, to obtain her hand, which he is not yet sufficient master of his emotions to abstain from soliciting. Mme. de Tècle, to whom virtue is comparatively easy, determines to stifle her passion, or at least to keep it smouldering, by means of a very odd and ingenious device. She offers to bring up her little daughter as the wife of M. de Camors, who in eight years' time, when the girl has arrived at maturity, will have reached the marrying age of a man of his society. This idea and the scene in which Mme. de Tècle unfolds it are, as we say, ingenious; delicate also, and almost poetical; but strike us as unreal, unnatural, and morbid. M. de Camors is by no means enchanted by his friend's proposition; he assents coldly and vaguely and takes his departure, thanking his stars, after all, that Mme. de Tècle had the wit to refuse him.

He becomes engaged in political life and lays the foundation of a large fortune by industrial manœuvres. He works hard, keeps his terms with elegant dissipation, and cherishes the cold precepts of his father. After a lapse of three or four years he renews his relations with his beautiful cousin, now Mme. de Campvallar, but in so depraved (although so dramatic) a fashion that we need not enter into particulars. Mme. de Campvallar is by nature, and with a splendid feminine insolence and grace, just such an audacious and heartless soul as M. de Camors has well-nigh become by culture. The two unite their sympathies, their passions, and their lives. Finally, however, their intrigue is on the point of being discovered by the husband of Mme. de Campvallar—a *naif* and honest old warrior, the soul of purity and honor, who esteems with an almost equal warmth his wife and his wife's lover— and an exposure is averted only by the tact and presence of mind of the impenitent marquise. Her husband is concealed and listening: Camors is expected. A motive for their meeting must be improvised within the minute, and a full intelligence of the situation flashed from her eyes into those of her lover. The latter arrives radiant. The pretext is ready. Mme. de Campvallar has sworn that she will not let M. de Camors depart until he has promised to marry—whom?—Mlle. de Tècle. In this way the prayers of Mme. de Tècle are fulfilled, and a third heroine is introduced—a third, and the most charming of all. The scene just indicated is in a dramatic sense, we may add, extremely effective; and if M. Feuillet ever converts his novel into a play (as it is the fashion to do in France), here is a situation made to his hand, strong enough, by itself, to ensure the success of the piece, and admirably fitted to exhibit good acting. M. de Camors, then, marries Mlle. de Tècle and loves Mme. de Campvallar. This is well enough for the latter lady; but the other (who has a passionate childish admiration of her rival) speedily discovers the facts of the matter, and signally fails to reconcile herself to them. M. de Campvallar, whose suspicions, once dispelled, have begun once more to congregate, eventually encounters the most damning confirmation of their truth, and expires under the hideous shock. Mme. de Camors and her mother, more and more alienated from the count, and infected with the most painful impressions touching his relations to the death of M. de Campvallar, no longer conceal their open horror of his character. M. de Camors, on his own side, weary of his mistress, writhing under the scorn of his wife, whose merits he has learned to appreciate, sick of the world and of his own life, dies, without remorse and without hope.

The reader may perceive nothing in this sad story, as we have told it, to justify us in deeming it worthy of repetition; but it is certain that, told by M. Feuillet with all the energy of his great talent, it makes a very interesting tale. The author, indeed, has aimed at making it something more—at writing a work with a high moral bearing. In this we think he has signally failed. To stir the reader's moral nature, and to write with truth and eloquence the moral history of superior men and women, demand more freedom and generosity of mind than M. Feuillet seems to us to possess. Like those of most of the best French romancers, his works wear, morally, to American eyes, a decidedly thin and superficial look. Men and women, in our conception, are deeper, more substantial, more self-directing; they have, if not more virtue, at least more conscience; and when conscience comes into the game human history ceases to be a perfectly simple tale. M. Feuillet is not in the smallest degree a moralist, and, as a logical consequence, M. de Camors is a most unreal and unsubstantial character. He is at the best a well appointed fop— what the French call a *poseur*. The lesson of his life is that you cannot really prosper without principles, and that although the strict observance of "honor"—the only principle which M. de Camors recognizes—is a very fine thing in its way, there are sore straits in life from which the only issue is (M. Feuillet would say) through the portals of the Church; or, in other words, that our lives are in our own hands, and that religion is essential to happiness. This is, doubtless, very true; but somehow it is none the truer for M. Feuillet's story. To be happy, M. de Camors apparently needed only to strike a becoming attitude. When M. de Campvallar discovers him in the small hours of the night in his wife's apartment and marches on him furious, he remembers to fold his arms. Another man might have done it instinctively; but we may be sure that M. de Camors did it consciously. And so with Mme. de Campvallar. She is essentially cold, artificial, and mechanical. She is pedantically vicious. For these reasons and many others; from our inability to sympathize either with the delusions or the mortifications of his hero, M. Feuillet's book strikes us simply, as a novel, like any other. Its chief merit, we think, lies in the portraits of Mme. de Tècle and her daughter. Here, too, the author is superficial; but here, at least, he is charming. The virtues—the virtue, we may say, of these two ladies is above all things elegant, but it has a touch of the breadth and depth of nature. The work as a whole is cold and light; but it is neither vulgar nor trivial, and would amply repay perusal if only as a model of neat, compact, and elaborate dramatic writing.

OCTAVE FEUILLET'S LES AMOURS DE PHILIPPE

M. Octave Feuillet's new novel reaches an eighth edition within a few weeks of its appearance; and this circumstance, combined with the reputation of the author, may fairly be held to indicate that it is worth reading. M. Feuillet usually lays his hand upon an interesting fable, and his execution is always extremely neat and artistic. His defect is a too obvious desire to be what we call in English a "fashionable" novelist. He relates exclusively the joys and sorrows of the aristocracy; the loves of marquises and countesses alone appear worthy of his attention, and heroes and heroines can hope to make no figure in his pages unless they have an extraordinary number of quarterings. But there are few storytellers of our day who know how to tell their story better than M. Octave Feuillet, though we must add that it may sometimes be a question whether his story was worth telling. This one is about a young man of very ancient lineage, who is predestined by his family to a union with a young girl of a proportionate pedigree. The young girl is his cousin; he is brought up side by side with her, and, knowing that she expects to be his wife, he conceives a violent aversion to her. This rebellious sentiment is

Les Amours de Philippe. Par Octave Feuillet. (Paris: Calmann Lévy; New York: F. W. Christern.) (*The Nation*, November 15, 1877).

so strong that when he comes of age he declares he will never look at her again, and departs for Paris, greatly to the distress of his aristocratic father. In Paris he takes a fancy to turn playwright, and manufactures an heroic drama, with a part especially intended for a brilliant and celebrated young actress with whom he has fallen violently in love. In the portrait of Mary Gerald M. Feuillet has evidently meant to suggest the figure of an actual artist, about whom "legend" has clustered thickly—Mlle. Sarah Bernhardt—but the image is rather vague; it lacks detail, and we should have advised the author either not to go so far or to go further. Philippe, however, goes very far in the company of his young actress. She takes a fancy to his play and to his person, and, staking everything upon his drama, he mortgages his financial future on her behalf. The drama proves a colossal failure, and Mary Gerald ceases to care for a lover who has been hissed.

Philippe has a cruel awakening, but the war of 1870 breaks out in time to distract his attention. He serves in it gallantly, and on the return of peace falls in love with Mme. de Talyas, the wife of an intimate friend. This lady is a fiend incarnate and a monster of corruption, but she has charms which are so highly appreciated by Philippe that he becomes her reluctant but abject slave. Mme. de Talyas is very cleverly described by M. Feuillet, who in the portraiture of diabolical fine ladies has a very skilful touch and a very practised hand. Meanwhile Philippe's cousin and intended, the amiable Jeanne de la Roche-Ermel, is pining away at the château, deeply attached to the young man, and sorrowing over the *spretœ injuria formœ*. Mme. de Talyas has learned from Philippe that his marriage with her has been the dream of both their families, but that he has a positive repugnance to the young girl. The moment comes when she commands him, in these circumstances, to pretend to have reconciled himself to the project, in order to throw dust into the eyes of her husband. He obeys her, and the result of his obedience is that, weary of Mme. de Talyas, and disgusted at the dishonorable part he is playing, both as regards his friend, her husband, and as regards Jeanne, he falls honestly and earnestly in love with Mlle. de la Roche-Ermel. Caught in her own trap, the unscrupulous Mme. de Talyas tries first to stop the marriage, and then to bring about the death of Jeanne. At the moment when she has almost succeeded in the latter attempt Philippe comes on the scene, and seeing his fiancée in a very bad way (her rival, having invited her out to walk, has tried to push her into a lake), demands an explanation. Jeanne looks at Mme. de Talyas for a moment, and then utters one of those magnanimous fibs in which, from Victor Hugo down, French romancers delight. She says that she has by her own awkwardness slipped into the water, and that Madame has tried to save her. Madame, overwhelmed and humiliated by such generosity, retires, leaving the coast clear.

Such are the loves of Philippe, which, if they are not very pretty, are very prettily told. The faults of the tale are a certain disjointedness, the want of connection between the episode of Mary Gerald and that of Mme. de Talyas, and the very unsubstantial and inestimable—character of the hero. The author tells us that he looked like one of the *mignons* of the court of the Valois king; and he really is hardly less contemptible. But French novelists are always addicted to making their heroes too unscrupulous first and too comfortable afterwards.

ALPHONSE DAUDET*

THE French have about many matters a way of feeling that is not ours, and M. Ernest Daudet's little volume[1] illustrates some of these differences. He is the brother of the brilliant author of the *Lettres de mon Moulin*, the *Rois en Exil,* and *Numa Roumestan,* and it has seemed to him natural to celebrate his kinship with so charming a writer in a volume published while the latter is yet in his prime, and in which biography and eulogy, admiration and tenderness, are gracefully blended. In England or in America, an artist's brother would, we think, hold himself less designated than another to discourse to the public about the great man of the family. The artist would be sure to dislike

---

[1] *Mon Frère et Moi: Souvenirs d'Enfance et de Jeunesse.* Par ERNEST Daudet. Paris: Plon. 1882. (*Atlantic Monthly,* June, 1882).

it, and the brother would have an awkward, and possibly morbid, fear of making two honest men ridiculous. But the French have never worshiped at the shrine of reticence, and it is fortunate that there should be a race of people who acquit themselves gracefully of delicate undertakings, and who have on all occasions the courage of their emotion. The French do such things because they *can;* we abstain because we have not that art. M. Ernest Daudet admires his brother as much as he loves him, and as he presumably knows him better than any one else, he may have regarded himself as the ideal biographer. His delightful volume is, to speak grossly, just a trifle too much of a *puff;* but if he was able to settle the matter with Alphonse Daudet (for whom he claims complete irresponsibility), we see no obstacle to his settling it with the public and with his own conscience. Our principle regret is the regret expressed by the subject of the work in a letter from which, in the preface, the author quotes a passage. M. Alphonse Daudet, who was in Switzerland at the time the chapters of which the present volume is composed were put forth in a periodical, protested against "being treated as people treat only the dead. I am living, and very living," he wrote, "and you make me enter rather too soon into history. I know people who will say that I have got my brother to advertise me." Alphonse Daudet is living, and very living; that is his great attraction. But after all, his too zealous biographer has not killed him. We hold, all the same, that there is little to please us in the growing taste of the age for revelations about the private life of the persons in whose works it is good enough to be interested. In our opinion, the life and the works are two very different matters, and an intimate knowledge of the one is not all necessary for a genial enjoyment of the other. A writer who gives us his works is not obliged to throw his life after them, as is very apt to be assumed by persons who fail to perceive that one of the most interesting pursuits in the world is to read between the lines of the best literature. Alphonse Daudet is but forty-two years of age, and we hope to read a more definitive life of him thirty years hence. By that time we shall know whether we really need it.

Once grant M. Ernest Daudet his premises, he tells his story with taste as well as with tenderness. The story is perhaps not intrinsically remarkable, but there is something so ingratiating in the personality of the hero that we follow his small adventures with a kind of affectionate interest. His youth was the youth of nineteen out of twenty French artists and men of letters, and he served the usual apprenticeship to poverty and disappointment. Born in a small provincial city, of parents more or less acquainted with chill penury, he picks up a certain amount of heterogeneous knowledge at the communal college or the *lycée;* becomes conscious of talents or of ambition; struggles more or less, in a narrow interior, with a family circle which fails to appreciate these gifts; and finally, with empty pockets and immense curiosities, comes up to Paris to seek a fortune. Nineteen out of twenty of these slender beginners never get any further; they never succeed in breaking open their little envelope of obscurity. Daudet was the twentieth, who takes all the prizes. He deserved them, if suffering is a title; for his childhood, in spite of a few happy accidents,—the brightness and sweetness both of his birthplace and of his temperament,—had been difficult, almost cruel. He was born in that wonderful Provence which he has so frequently and so vividly, though perhaps not so accurately, described; he came into the world in the picturesque old city of Nîmes, the city of Roman remains, of fragrant gardens, of beautiful views, of sun and dust, of Southern dullness and Southern animation. Much of his childhood, however, thanks to his father's reverses and embarrassments (his family had been engaged in the weaving of silk), was spent at Lyons, among gray, damp, sordid, sickening impressions,—a period described with touching effect in M. Daudet's first long story, the exquisite memoirs of *Le Petit Chose.* M. Ernest Daudet relates the annals of his family, which appears to have numbered several vigorous and even distinguished members, and makes no secret of the fact that in his own childhood its once considerable honors had been much curtailed. This period, for the two brothers, contained many dismal passages, and Alphonse, while still a mere boy (at least, in appearance), was obliged to earn a wretched livelihood as ill-paid usher in a small provincial college. We do not mean, however, to retrace the chapters of his life; we take him as we find him to-day, in the full enjoyment of his powers and his rewards, and we attempt, in a few rapid strokes, to sketch his literary physiognomy.

If we were asked to describe it in two words, we should say that he is beyond comparison the most *charming* storyteller of the day. He has power as well as charm, but his happy grace is what strikes us most. No one is so light and keen, so picturesque; no one pleases so by his manner, his movement, his native gayety, his constant desire to please. We confess to an extreme fondness for M. Alphonse Daudet; he is very near to our heart. The bright light, the warm color, the spontaneity and loquacity, of his native Provence have entered into his style, and made him a talker as well as a novelist. He tells his stories as a talker; they have always something of the flexibility and familiarity of conversation. The conversation, we mean, of an artist and a Frenchman; the conversation of a circle in which the faculty of vivid and discriminating speech exists as it has existed nowhere else. This charming temper, touched here and there with the sentiment of deeper things, is the sign of his earlier productions. As time has gone on, he has enlarged his manner,—enlarged with his field of observation. The Parisian has been added to the Provençal, fortunately without crowding him out. It is not M. Daudet's longest things that we like best, though we profess a great fondness for *Les Rois en Exil*. The *Lettres de mon Moulin,* the *Contes du Lundi, Le Petit Chose*, the exquisitely amusing history of Tartarin de Tarascon, the charming series of letters entitled Robert Helmont,—these contain, to our sense, the cream of the author's delicate and indescribable talent. Daudet sketches in perfection; he does the little piece—*il fait le morceau,* as the French call it—with a facility all his own. No one has such an eye for a subject; such a perception of "bits," as the painters in water-colors say. It is indeed as if he worked in water-colors, from a rich and liquid palette; his style is not so much a literary form as a plastic form. He is a wonderful observer of all external things,—of appearances, objects, surface, circumstances; but what makes his peculiarity is that the ray of fancy, the tremor of feeling, always lights up the picture. This perception of material objects is not uncommon to-day, and it has never been rare among the French, in whom quickness of vision, combined with a talent for specifying and analyzing what they see, is a national characteristic. The new fashion of realism has indeed taught us all that in any description of life the description of places and things is half the battle. But to describe them we must see them, and some people see, on the same occasion, infinitely more than others. Alphonse Daudet is one of those who see most. Among the French, moreover, the gift is cultivated, and the first canon of the "young school" of to-day is that to write a novel you must take notes on the spot. Balzac took notes, Gustave Flaubert took notes, Emile Zola takes notes. We are sure that Alphonse Daudet takes them, too, though in his constitution there is a happy faculty for which all the notes in the world are an insufficient substitute, namely, the faculty of feeling as well as seeing. He feels what he sees, and the feeling expresses itself in quick, light irony, in jocosity, in poetry. M. Daudet never sees plain prose. He discovers everywhere the shimmer and murmur of the poetic. He has described in a great many places the Provençal turn of mind, the temperament of the man of the South; his last novel in particular—*Numa Roumestan*—being an elaborate picture of this genial type, for which M. Daudet does not profess an unlimited respect. He feels it so strongly, perhaps, because he feels it in himself; it is not to be denied that his own artistic nature contains several of the qualities on which he has expended his most charming satire. The weak points of the man of the South, in M. Daudet's view, are the desire to please at any cost, and, as a natural result of this, a brilliant indifference to the truth. There is a good deal of all this, in its less damaging aspects, in the author of *Numa Roumestan*. We have spoken of his desire to please, which is surely not an unpardonable fault in an artist, though M. Zola holds it to be so. M. Daudet likes to entertain, to beguile, to gratify, to mystify, to purchase immediate applause. For ourselves, we give the applause without the slightest reluctance. May it be a fault in a writer of fiction to be very fond of fiction? In this case it seems to us that M. Daudet is distinctly culpable. M. Zola, to quote him again, holds that the love of fiction is the most evil passion of the human heart; and yet he has most inconsistently found many civil things to say of his *confrére* Daudet, whom he would represent as one of the standard-bearers of naturalism. M. Daudet is fond of fiction as Dickens was fond of it,—he is fond of the picturesque. His taste is for oddities and exceptions, for touching *dénoûments,* for situations slightly factitous, for characters surprisingly genial. There is nothing uncompromising, nothing of a depressing integrity, in his love of the real. Left to himself, he takes only those parts of it that happen to commend themselves to his fancy, which, as we have already said, is, in his intellectual economy, the mistress of the house. But he has not always been left to himself. He has lived in Paris, he has become a disciple of Balzac, he has frequented Flaubert, he has known Zola, he has been made to feel that there are such things as responsibilities. There are, indeed,—those terrible responsibilities which M. Zola carries with such a ponderous tread. He himself recalls Alphonse Daudet to a sense of them in a passage which we may quote from his lately published volume, entitled *Une Campagne.* He is more troubled, we suspect, than he ventures to say by Daudet's taint of the factitious, and he speaks with a good dead of point of the very different aspect which the Provence of *Numa Roumestan* wears from the Provence of his own young memories,—he being also a son of that soil. "Alphonse Daudet seems to me to see the country of Provence in one of the gilded falsehoods of his hero. I don't speak of the inhabitants, whom he treats with even too much cruelty; I speak of the look of the land, of that perpetual dream of sunshine, which he manages to fill with all the romance of the troubadours. He softens down the very *mistral,* which he calls 'the wholesome, vivifying blast, spreading its jovial influence to the furthest edge of the horizon.' My own Provence, that of which the heated harshness still blows into my face, is a much rougher affair, and the mistral cracks my lips, burns my skin, fills the valley with a devastation so terrible that the blue sky grows pale. I remember the extinguished look of the sun in the pure, bleached air, through that roaring breath which sometimes ruins the country-side in a day. The Provence of Alphonse Daudet is therefore, for my sensations, too good-natured; I should like it stronger and more scorched, with that perfume of which the violence turns to bitterness under the hard and cloudless blue."

It was inevitable, we suppose, that our author should sooner or later become a Parisian; should attempt to master the great

city, in the manner of successful Frenchmen. This capitalization
of his talent, as we may call it, has been extremely fruitful, has
produced a multitude of admirable chapters; but, on the other
hand, it has made Alphonse Daudet much less perfect. The
sketches and stories we mentioned at the beginning of this article
all have the stamp of perfection. There is nothing to add to them,
nothing to take from them, nothing to correct in them. In his
later and larger works there have been great inequalities, though
the successful portions, we admit, have become more and more
brilliant. It is an odd thing that though it is as a peculiarly
imaginative writer that we reckon him, he is not at his best when
he gives his imagination the reins. At such moments he is very
apt to become false and unnatural; his charming fancy is an
excellent companion, but an uncertain guide. His great successes
(in his longer works) have been portraits of known individuals.
Fromont Jeune et Risler Aîné, the first in date of these later
things, and perhaps the most popular, is by no means the one
we prefer; with all its keenness of touch, it has perhaps even more
than its share of the disparities of which we speak. The accessories, the details, the setting of the scene, the art of presentation,
the three or four subordinate characters, furnish the strong points
of the book. The portrait of the depraved and dangerous heroine
(there is a virtuous female figure to balance her) is wanting to
our sense in solidity, and the main interest of the novel suffers
from thinness. Sidonie Chèbe strikes us as a study at once elaborate and shallow; and indeed the elaboration of the frivolous and
perfidious wife, in French fiction, has grown to be inevitably
and indefinably stale. The best figure in the book is the old
humbugging tragedian Delobelle,—a type of which we have had
glimpses elsewhere. In Delobelle and in his daughter Désirée,
English readers find an echo, at once gratifying and tormenting,
of our own inimitable Dickens. Dickens is dying, they say; Dickens is dead (though we don't believe it), and nothing is more
generally admitted than that Dickens's absent qualities were as
striking as those he had. But on his own ground he was immeasurable, and when we are reminded of him by another writer, the
comparison suggested is not likely to be to the advantage of
the latter. We speak, of course, from the point of view of a gen-

eration impregnated with Dickens's humor, and our remark has no application to French readers, who have no idea, when they smile or sigh over the fortunes of the famille Joyeuse (in *Le Nabab*), or drop a tear upon the childish miseries of Jack, that they are tasting of an ingenious dilution of the violent humor of Nickleby and Copperfield. We do not mean in the least that Alphonse Daudet is a conscious copyist of Dickens; he has denied the charge, we believe, in definite terms. But the English writer is certainly one of his sympathies, and we suspect that if he had never opened (even in a translation) one of those volumes which constitute the great cockney epic, one of the effective notes of his scale would be absent. In *Jack* the influence of Dickens is very visible, and it has not, we think, made the story more natural. That falsetto note, in pathos, which was the fatal danger of the author of *Dombey and Son,* is sounded with a good deal of frequency in *Jack,* and the portrayal of innocent suffering, through the intensification of the innocence, is also overdone. Neither do we care very much for the famille Joyeuse, in *Le Nabab,* finding in them, as we do, too sensible a reflection of that rather voluntary glow of satisfaction with which Dickens invites us to contemplate such people as the Brothers Cheeryble. *Le Nabab,* is on the whole, however, a brilliant production, and contains some of the author's strongest pages. It is a gallery of portraits, like all of his later stories,—portraits of contemporary Parisian figures, in which the intelligent reader is always able to detect a more or less distinguished model. The hero himself is a study of the "man of the South," but in his more robust and fruitful aspects, and is an exceedingly vivid picture of a great industrial and commercial *parvenu.* The picture takes a tragical turn, for the great fortune of M. Daudet's ex-dock-porter crumbles away through a series of events as remarkable as those which have helped to build it up. It is the analysis of a coarse, powerful, vulgar, jovial, florid, energetic temperament, which has known the two extremes of human experience; and it is no secret that the author has reproduced the history—or at least the physiognomy—of the remarkable M. Bravais, whose rapid rise and fall were one of the innumerable queer incidents of the later years of the Empire.

This period is embodied even more effectively in the figure of the Duc de Mora,—a thin modification of the once impressive title of the Duc de Morny, who is presented in M. Daudet's pages in company with several members of his circle. This is the historical novel applied to the passing hour. The author has expended his best pains on the portrait of the Duc de Mora, and if the picture fails of vividness it is not for want of the multiplication of fine touches. It has great color and relief,—the mark of that brush-like quality of pen which is a specialty of M. Daudet. Is Felicia Ruys intended for Mademoiselle Sarah Bernhardt? The answer to the question hardly matters, for the personage belongs to the rank of the author's half-successes. We mention her, because, like the other characters, she is an example of the manner which Alphonse Daudet may be said to have invented. This manner, the reproduction of actualities under a transparent veil, the appropriation of a type embodied in a living specimen, with the peculiarities much accentuated, is an inspiration which, when it is most fruitful, Alphonse Daudet induces rather to condone than to welcome. Cultivated by a writer of his tact and talent, it would probably produce a plentiful crop of vulgarities. M. Daudet is never vulgar, but he is sometimes rather false. Many of his readers doubtless hold that his best guarantee against falsity is this very practice of drawing not only from life, but from the special case. They remark, justly enough, that in *Le Nabab,* in the *Rois en Exil,* the best things are the things for which he has had chapter and verse in the world around him. When he has attempted to generalize, as in the more technically romantic episodes, he has gone astray, and become fantastic. We incline to agree to this, though it may seem to contradict what we have said about his great charm being his element of fancy. We should explain that we have not used fancy here in the sense of invention; we have used it to denote the faculty which projects the unexpected, irresponsible, illuminating day upon material supplied out of hand. If there were nothing else to distinguish Alphonse Daudet from Emile Zola, his delicate, constant sense of beauty would suffice. Zola of course consoles himself, though he does not always console others, with his superior sense of reality. Daudet is a passionate observer,—an observer not perhaps

of the deepest things of life, but of the whole realm of the immediate, the expressive, the actual. This faculty, enriched by the
most abundant exercise and united with the feeling of the poet
who sees all the finer relations of things and never relinquishes
the attempt to charm, is what we look for in the happiest novelist
of our day. Ah, the things he sees,—the various, fleeting, lurking,
delicate, nameless human things! We have spoken of his remarkable vision of accessories and details; but it is difficult to give
an idea of the artistic "go" with which it is exercised. This beautiful vivacity finds its most complete expression in *Les Rois en
Exil,* a book that could have been produced only in one of these
later years of grace. Such a book is intensely modern, and the
author is in every way an essentially modern genius. With the
light, warm, frank Provençal element of him, he is, in his completeness, a product of the great French city. He has the nervous
tension, the intellectual eagerness, the quick and exaggerated
sensibility, the complicated, sophisticated judgment, which the
friction, the contagion, the emulation, the whole spectacle, at
once exciting and depressing, of our civilization at its highest,
produces in susceptible natures. There are tears in his laughter,
and there is a strain of laughter in his tears; and in both there
is a note of music. What could be more modern than his style,
from which every shred of classicism has been stripped, and
which moves in a glitter of images, of discoveries, of verbal gym-
nastics, animated always by the same passion for the concrete?
With his merits and short-comings combined, Alphonse Daudet
is the charming writer we began by declaring him, because he is
so intensely living. He is a thoroughly special genius, and in our
own sympathies he touches a very susceptible spot. He is not so
serious, not to say so solemn, as Emile Zola, and we suspect that
in his heart he finds the doctrine of naturalism a good deal of
a bore. He is free from being as deep and wise and just as the
great Turgenieff. But with his happy vision, his abundant expression, his talent for episodes and figures that detach themselves, his sense of intimate pleasures and pains, his good-humor,
his gayety, his grace, and that modern quality of intensity that
he throws into everything, he is really a great little novelist.

IVAN TURGENEV'S VIRGIN SOIL*

There are only two living novelists the appearance of whose new productions constitutes anything that can be called a literary event. If one of these writers is that blessing of reviewers the author of *Daniel Deronda*, the other is certainly the distinguished Russian whose name we have inscribed at the head of these remarks, and who has now for some time been recognized, even among those people who are condemned to know him only in imperfect translations, as one of the profoundest of observers and one of the most fascinating of story-tellers. It had been known for some months past that Ivan Turgenef was engaged upon a new novel, which was to be in plan and purpose one of the most considerable of his productions, and the impatience of his admirers was increased by the fact that—Russian scholars being few—the book would be for some time before the world and yet be inaccessible. *Nov* appeared in Russia during the first weeks of the present year; but it has been translated into French with commendable promptitude—with what degree of accuracy we are unable to say, though we may suppose that as the translation was made under the eyes of the author it is fairly satisfactory. This is a very good moment for a Russian novel to appear—at least out of Russia. As a *pièce de circonstance* we can imagine nothing except a Turkish novel which would be more opportune. We believe that in M. Turgenef's own country the prospective clash of arms has to a certain extent deadened the public ear to the voice of the artist; but among ourselves, disinterested yet observant spectators of what is going on in the East, we imagine the author will find the attention he commands has rather been quickened by circumstances. The designs, ambitions, prospects, and characteristics of Russia form a great spectacle, in which M. Turgenef's literary activity has its place. This is all the more the case that the subject of his new novel connects the work with an element in the spectacle which we

* 'Terres Vierges. Par Ivan Tourguéneff. Traduit par E. Durand-Gréville.' Paris. 1877. New York: F. W. Christern. (*The Nation*, April 26, 1877).

hear a great deal about, and which is, perhaps, especially what appeals to our curiosity. The outside world knows in a vague way of the existence of certain "secret societies" in Russia, and of the belief entertained by some people that their revolutionary agitation forms a sufficient embarrassment at home to keep the Government of the Czar from extending his conquests abroad. Of one of these secret societies M. Turgenef has given a picture, though it must be said that the particular association he describes hardly appears to be of a nature seriously to alarm the powers of order. Whether it is because it is a characteristic of his genius to throw a sort of ironical light over all things—even to some extent over the things that have his deepest sympathy; to see with peculiar vividness the side on which human effort is comical, and helpless, and ineffectual; or whether it is that revolutionary propagandism in Russia is really too crude, and youthful, and vague to be, as the phrase is, counted with; certain it is, the impression left by Neshdanoff and Markeloff, by Ostrodumoff and Mashurina, even by Marianne and Solomin, is not so much of a sinister as a touching and melancholy, or even of a softly-exhilarating cast. Ivan Turgenef always shows his superiority in the choice of his subjects; his themes are never conventional and stale; he is certain to select a *donnée* which means and reveals something. He has shown this admirable instinct here—shown it much more strongly than by producing, as the mention of his subject may have suggested, a story of mysteries and surprises, excitements and escapes. He has approached his ground on the moral and psychological side, and made, as is usual with him, a profound study of character. The vulgar capacities of the theme have not been taken advantage of, but the finer ones have been handled in a masterly manner. The author's wisdom is shown in his deep perception of the fact that the clandestine movements of which he gives a sketch is particularly fertile in revelations of character—that it contains inevitably the seeds of an interesting psychological drama. The opposition of different natures convoked together by a common ideal—this ideal being one which appeals with peculiar force to youthful generosity, accompanied by a due share of that "little knowledge" which is a dangerous thing; such, roughly speaking, is the subject of *Terres Vierges*.

The story is a picture of a certain portion of the "young generation" in Russia, the generation of which we had a glimpse in *Fathers and Sons,* and of which the "nihilist" Bazaroff was so robust an exponent—the young people of liberal instincts who find no legitimate channel of expression, and who expend their ardor in aimless machinations, compounded in equal parts of puerility and heroism. The central figure in the present tale is a young man named Neshdanoff, selected, like most of the author's central figures, on account of his being a particularly good subject for irony. Ivan Turgenef's heroes are never heroes in the literal sense of the word, rather quite the reverse; their function is to be conspicuous as failures, interesting but impotent persons who are losers at the game of life. The utmost that the heroic can hope for is to be obscurely embodied in some secondary figure whose quiet robustness helps to satirize its companions. Upon M. Turgenef's predilection for failures, losers at the game, his acute observation and extensive knowledge of them, there would be a great deal to say; in the eyes of foreign readers he has almost made them the Russian type *par excellence*. We suspect that if they are not this, they are at least, in Russia, a very characteristic class of persons; though whether such persons are always as interesting as the art of Ivan Turgenef renders them is possibly doubtful. Their interest, in his hands, comes in a great measure from the fact that they are exquisitely conscious of their short-comings, thanks to the fine and subtle intelligence, that "subjective" tendency, with which he represents all Russians who are not positive fools and grotesques as being endowed. His central figure is usually a person in a false position, generally not of his own making, which, according to the peculiar perversity of fate, is only aggravated by his effort to right himself. Such eminently is the case with young Neshdanoff, who is the natural son of a nobleman, not recognized by his father's family, and who, drifting through irritation and smothered rage and vague aspiration into the stream of occult radicalism, finds himself fatally fastidious and sceptical and "æsthetic"—more essentially an aristocrat, in a word, than any of the aristocrats he has agreed to conspire against. He has not the gift of faith, and he is most uncomfortably at odds with his companions, who have it in a high degree—these types of "faith" which surround Neshdanoff being most vividly portrayed. He accepts a place as resident tutor in the house of a certain Sipiagin, a liberal of the discreet and official sort, whose ideal of conduct, costume, and manner is the English country gentleman of large fortune, Parliamentary training, and "progressive" tendencies. One of the features of the story is the contrast between the passionate fermentation of the four young revolutionists and the urbane and patronizing sympathy with progress of this happy proprietor, whose liberalism is hardly more than an affair of the toilet. In his house lives his niece, Marianne Sinetzkaia, who forms, with Neshdanoff, the connecting link between genteel society and the little group of propagandists. Turgenef's young girls are always remarkable creations, and this striking figure of the young lady by birth, who is an ardent democrat by temperament and aspiration, is perhaps the great success of 'Terres Vierges.' Like all Turgenef's heroines, Marianne is both very original and very real; never was there less of a portrait in pastel. She crops her hair short and keeps her own counsel; very soon, of course, living under the same roof with Neshdanoff, the preceptor of her little cousin, she discovers his propagandist affiliations and falls more or less in love with him. We say "of course"; but, in fact, in Turgenef's novels events never take the conventional and expected course; there is always some deeper complexity—some closer "twist." Marianne and Neshdanoff exchange ideas and expressions of sympathy, admire each other greatly, become very intimate, and have secret nocturnal interviews. At last they agree to leave the house together and throw themselves into the revolutionary movement, and they wander forth like brother and sister, hand in hand, like the Babes in the Wood, and take up their abode with a certain Solomin, a radical of the sturdy and practical type, who can bide his time. (This Solomin is an admirable portrait.) There is something very beautiful and very characteristic of Turgenef in the idea of the mutual purity of these two young people. They have started on a wild-goose chase, and would be quite at a loss to say what they propose to do, and how they propose to do it; but the delicacy of their enthusiasm is such that they do not even desire to possess each other, and in their moments of tenderest *épanchement* they only shake hands affectionately, like plighted comrades.

There is another young man, Markeloff by name, a character directly opposed to Neshdanoff—a revolutionist whose perceptions are narrow and whose faith is absolute, so that his attitude towards constituted powers and beliefs is very much that of a projectile emitted from a cannon-mouth. In his dogged, dusky, unlovely, but unshrinking and fatally consistent figure there is a certain tragic impressiveness. He has but one touch of inconsistency—he is in love with Marianne, and he therefore finds himself for a moment in apparent rivalry with the younger, handsomer, more agreeable Neshdanoff. The finest scene in the book is that in which his jealousy of Neshdanoff, who is engaged with him in a common and sacred cause, breaks out in the course of a jolting drive which they take together at night. One has, of course, read Turgenef to little purpose if one has not observed that the Russian character, as he portrays it, differs strikingly at a dozen points from that of other peoples with which we are more familiar; but we remember no incident in all his novels that more forcibly illustrates this difference. Markeloff, in his wrath, suddenly reminds Neshdanoff of his irregular birth, and declares that his gaining Marianne's favor is nothing, after all, but the "usual good luck of the d—d race of bastards!" This affront is mortal, and is felt in the keenest manner by Neshdanoff, who declares that it can only be washed out in blood, and prepares immediately to part company with his companion. But the latter has hardly uttered the words before he repents of them; he entreats his rival to remain, and offers to go down on his knees and beg his pardon. This is a most extraordinary scene, and it is evident that the author feels it to be such. Neshdanoff shakes hands with his insulter, and the author explains that before three minutes were over the two were addressing each other with *thee* and *thou*, as if nothing had happened; all of which seems to prove that Russians have not the idea of "honor" as strongly developed as some races, though, in that very phase of their character upon which this episode throws light there is something very interesting, spontaneous, and human.

We will not spoil the reader's entertainment by disclosing the solution of poor Neshdanoff's difficulties further than to say that it is a solution to which Ivan Turgenef's heroes have more than once resorted. Of course, his career receives the final tragic stamp; the "æsthetic" young man, venturing to play with revolution, finds it a coarse, ugly, vulgar, and moreover very cruel thing; the reality makes him deadly sick. Very happily invented is the incident which completes his disillusionment— his being brought home dead-drunk from a propagandist excursion among the peasantry, who have insisted on his proving himself a good fellow by swallowing long draughts of their pestilent brandy. Marianne, who is not æsthetic nor addicted to hair-splitting, loses no illusions and we feel that she never will. The author leaves her with the excellent Solomin, in whom she finds her proper counterpart as a type of one of the latent forces of the future, in a country in which these will probably let themselves loose on a great scale. Marianne, as we said, is very real so far as she goes; but we confess that we find her the least agreeable of Ivan Turgenef's young girls; and this, we think, contrary to the author's intention. She lacks sweetness and softness; she is somewhat too acrimonious, too pert, in her dealings with Mme. Sipiagin, her highly uncongenial aunt. The book contains a great number of other figures, which we have not left ourselves space to pick out for special commendation. Particularly good is the female devotee of the "common cause," Mashurina, who is big, ugly, and awkward, but profoundly pure and sincere. She has taken her diploma in obstetrics, and she is privately in love with Neshdanoff, who never knows it and would be horrified if he were to do so; she is one of those intensely individual figures which form Turgenef's great strength. We must also pass over Mme. Sipiagin, the lady remarkable for her resemblance to Raphael's Dresden Madonna, who represents the feminine side of cultivated liberalism—represents it in a manner to make the reader shudder. We have seen the episode of Zimushka and Zomushka, the grotesque old couple living among their rococo coffee-cups and snuff-boxes, condemned as a *hors d'œuvre*—an excrescence; but this strikes us as an inattentive judgment. The picture of their ancient superstitions, their quaintness, and mellowness and serenity is intended as a dramatic offset to the crude and acrid unrest of the young radicals who come to see them; it has a "value," as the painters say. It is, moreover, very charming in itself. Subtle intentions are far from wanting in *Terres Vierges*; there are always more of these in Ivan Turgenef than even the acutest critic can gather together the threads of. In the present work they all throw into relief the author's great quality—the union of the deepest reality of substance, of *fonds*, as the French say, with the most imaginative, most poetic, touches.

ESSAYS ON AMERICAN AND
ENGLISH LITERATURE

HOWELLS'S ITALIAN JOURNEYS*

UNDER favor of his work on "Venetian Life," Mr. Howells took his place as one of the most charming of American writers and most satisfactory of American travellers. He is assuredly not one of those who journey from Dan to Beersheba only to cry out that all is barren. Thanks to the keenness of his observation and the vivacity of his sympathies, he treads afresh the most frequently trodden routes, without on the one hand growing cynical over his little or his great disappointments, or taking refuge on the other in the well-known alternative of the Baron Munchausen. Mr. Howells has an eye for the small things of nature, of art, and of human life, which enables him to extract sweetness and profit from adventures the most prosaic, and which prove him a very worthy successor of the author of the "Sentimental Journey."

Mr. Howells is in fact a sentimental traveller. He takes things as he finds them and as history has made them; he presses them into the service of no theory, nor scourges them into the following of his prejudices; he takes them as a man of the world, who is not a little a moralist,—a gentle moralist, a good deal a humorist, and most of all a poet; and he leaves them,—he leaves them as the man of real literary power and the delicate artist alone know how to leave them, with new memories mingling, for our common delight, with the old memories that are the accumulation of ages, and with a fresh touch of color modestly gleaming amid the masses of local and historical coloring. It is for this solid literary merit that Mr. Howells's writing is valuable,—and the more valuable that it is so rarely found in books of travel in our own tongue. Nothing is more slipshod and slovenly than the style in which publications of this kind are habitually composed. Letters and diaries are simply strung into succession and transferred to print. If the writer is a clever person, an observer, an explorer, an intelligent devotee of the picturesque, his work will

* *Italian Journeys*. By W. D. Howells, author of "Venetian Life." New York: Hurd and Houghton. 1867. (*North American Review*, January, 1868).

doubtless furnish a considerable amount of entertaining reading; but there will yet be something essentially common in its character. The book will be diffuse, overgrown, shapeless; it will not belong to literature. This charm of style Mr. Howells's two books on Italy possess in perfection; they belong to literature and to the centre and core of it,—the region where men think and feel, and one may almost say breathe, in good prose, and where the classics stand on guard. Mr. Howells is not an economist, a statistician, an historian, or a propagandist in any interest; he is simply an observer, responsible only to a kindly heart, a lively fancy, and a healthy conscience. It may therefore indeed be admitted that there was a smaller chance than in the opposite case of his book being ill written. He might notice what he pleased and mention what he pleased, and do it in just the manner that pleased him. He was under no necessity of sacrificing his style to facts; he might under strong provocation—provocation of which the sympathetic reader will feel the force—sacrifice facts to his style. But this privilege, of course, enforces a corresponding obligation, such as a man of so acute literary conscience as our author would be the first to admit and to discharge. He must have felt the importance of making his book, by so much as it was not to be a work of strict information, a work of generous and unalloyed entertainment.

These "Italian Journeys" are a record of some dozen excursions made to various parts of the peninsula during a long residence in Venice. They take the reader over roads much travelled, and conduct him to shrines worn by the feet—to say nothing of the knees—of thousands of pilgrims, no small number of whom, in these latter days, have imparted their impressions to the world. But it is plain that the world is no more weary of reading about Italy than it is of visiting it; and that so long as that deeply interesting country continues to stand in its actual relation, æsthetically and intellectually, to the rest of civilization, the topic will not grow threadbare. There befell a happy moment in history when Italy got the start of the rest of Christendom; and the ground gained, during that splendid advance, the other nations have never been able to recover. We go to Italy to gaze upon certain of the highest achievements of human power,—

achievements, moreover, which, from their visible and tangible nature, are particularly well adapted to represent to the imagination the *maximum* of man's creative force. So wide is the interval between the great Italian monuments of art and the works of the colder genius of the neighboring nations, that we find ourselves willing to look upon the former as the ideal and the perfection of human effort, and to invest the country of their birth with a sort of half-sacred character. This is, indeed, but half the story. Through the more recent past of Italy there gleams the stupendous image of a remoter past; behind the splendid efflorescence of the Renaissance we detect the fulness of a prime which, for human effort and human will, is to the great æsthetic explosion of the sixteenth century very much what the latter is to the present time. And then, beside the glories of Italy, we think of her sufferings; and, beside the masterworks of art, we think of the favors of Nature; and, along with these profane matters, we think of the Church,—until, betwixt admiration and longing and pity and reverence, it is little wonder that we are charmed and touched beyond healing.

In the simplest manner possible, and without declamation or rhetoric or affectation of any kind, but with an exquisite alternation of natural pathos and humor, Mr. Howells reflects this constant mute eloquence of Italian life. As to what estimate he finally formed of the Italian character he has left us uncertain; but one feels that he deals gently and tenderly with the foibles and vices of the land, for the sake of its rich and inexhaustible beauty, and of the pleasure which he absorbs with every breath. It is doubtless unfortunate for the Italians, and unfavorable to an exact appreciation of their intrinsic merits, that you cannot think of them or write of them in the same judicial manner as you do of other people,—as from equal to equal,—but that the imagination insists upon having a voice in the matter, and making you generous rather than just. Mr. Howells has perhaps not wholly resisted this temptation; and his tendency, like that of most sensitive spirits brought to know Italy, is to feel—even when he does not express it—that much is to be forgiven the people, because they are *so* picturesque. Mr. Howells is by no means indifferent, however, to the human element in all that he sees.

Many of the best passages in his book, and the most delicate touches, bear upon the common roadside figures which he met, and upon the manners and morals of the populace. He observes on their behalf a vast number of small things; and he ignores, for their sake, a large number of great ones. He is not fond of generalizing, nor of offering views and opinions. A certain poetical inconclusiveness pervades his book. He relates what he saw with his own eyes, and what he thereupon felt and fancied; and his work has thus a thoroughly personal flavor. It is, in fact, a series of small personal adventures,—adventures so slight and rapid that nothing comes of them but the impression of the moment, and, as a final result, the pleasant chapter which records them. These chapters, of course, differ in interest and merit, according to their subject, but the charm of manner is never absent; and it is strongest when the author surrenders himself most completely to his faculty for composition, and works his matter over into the perfection of form, as in the episode entitled "Forza Maggiore," a real masterpiece of light writing. Things slight and simple and impermanent all put on a hasty comeliness at the approach of his pen.

Mr. Howells is, in short, a descriptive writer in a sense and with a perfection that, in our view, can be claimed for no American writer except Hawthorne. Hawthorne, indeed, was perfection, but he was only half descriptive. He kept an eye on an unseen world, and his points of contact with this actual sphere were few and slight. One feels through all his descriptions, —we speak especially of his book on England,—that he was not a man of the world,—of this world which we after all love so much better than any other. But Hawthorne cannot be disposed of in a paragraph, and we confine ourselves to our own author. Mr. Howells is the master of certain refinements of style, of certain exquisite intentions (intentions in which humor generally plays a large part), such as are but little practised in these days of crude and precipitate writing. At the close of a very forcible and living description of certain insufferable French *commis-voyageurs* on the steamer from Genoa to Naples. "They wore their hats at dinner," writes Mr. Howells; "but always went away, after soup, deadly pale." It would be difficult to give in three lines a better picture of unconscious vulgarity than is furnished by this conjunction of abject frailties with impertinent assumptions.

And so at Capri, "after we had inspected the ruins of the emperor's villa, a clownish imbecile of a woman, *professing to be the wife of the peasant who had made the excavations,* came forth out of a cleft in the rock and received tribute of us; why, I do not know." The sketch is as complete as it is rapid, and a hoary world of extortion and of stupefied sufferance is unveiled with a single gesture. In all things Mr. Howells's touch is light, but none the less sure for its lightness. It is the touch of a writer who is a master in his own line, and we have not so many writers and masters that we can afford not to recognize real excellence. It is our own loss when we look vacantly at those things which make life pleasant. Mr. Howells has the qualities which make literature a delightful element in life,—taste and culture and imagination, and the incapacity to be common. We cannot but feel that one for whom literature has done so much is destined to repay his benefactor with interest.

HOWELLS'S A FOREGONE CONCLUSION*

THOSE who, a couple of years ago, read "A Chance Acquaintance" will find much interest in learning how the author has justified the liberal fame awarded that performance. Having tried other literary forms with remarkable success, Mr. Howells finally proved himself an accomplished story-teller, and the critic lurking in even the kindliest reader will be glad to ascertain whether this consummation was due chiefly to chance or to skill. "A Chance Acquaintance" was indeed not only a very charming book, but a peculiarly happy hit; the fancy of people at large was vastly tickled by the situation it depicted; the hero and heroine

---

A Foregone Conclusion. By W. D. Howells. Boston: J. R. Osgood & Co. (*North American Review*, January, 1875).

were speedily promoted to the distinction of types, and you became likely to overhear discussions as to the probability of their main adventures wherever men and women were socially assembled. Kitty Ellison and her weak-kneed lover, we find, are still objects of current allusion, and it would be premature, even if it were possible, wholly to supersede them; but even if Mr. Howells was not again to hit just that nail, he was welcome to drive in another beside it and supply the happy creations we have mentioned with successors who should divide our admiration. We had little doubt ourselves that he would on this occasion reach whatever mark he had aimed at; for, with all respect to the good fortune of his former novel, it seemed to us very maliciously contrived to play its part. It would have been a question in our minds, indeed, whether it was not even too delicate a piece of work for general circulation,—whether it had not too literary a quality to please that great majority of people who prefer to swallow their literature without tasting. But the best things in this line hit the happy medium, and it seems to have turned out, experimentally, that Mr. Howells managed at once to give his book a loose enough texture to let the more simply-judging kind fancy they were looking at a vivid fragment of social history itself, and yet to infuse it with a lurking artfulness which should endear it to the initiated. It rarely happens that what is called a popular success is achieved by such delicate means; with so little forcing of the tone or mounting of the high horse. People at large do not flock every day to look at a sober cabinet-picture. Mr. Howells continues to practise the cabinet-picture manner, though in his present work he has introduced certain broader touches. He has returned to the ground of his first literary achievements, and introduced us again to that charming half-merry, half-melancholy Venice which most Americans know better through his pages than through any others. He did this, in a measure, we think, at his risk; partly because there was a chance of disturbing an impression which, in so far as he was the author of it, had had time to grow very tranquil and mellow; and partly because there has come to be a not unfounded mistrust of the Italian element in light literature. Italy has been made to supply so much of the easy picturesqueness, the crude local color of poetry and the drama, that a use of this expedient is vaguely regarded as a sort of unlawful short-cut to success,—one of those coarsely mechanical moves at chess which, if you will, are strictly within the rules of the game, but which offer an antagonist strong provocation to fold up the board. Italians have been, from Mrs. Radcliffe down, among the stock-properties of romance; their associations are melodramatic, their very names are supposed to go a great way toward getting you into a credulous humor, and they are treated, as we may say, as bits of coloring-matter, which if placed in solution in the clear water of uninspired prose are warranted to suffuse it instantaneously with the most delectable hues. The growing refinement of the romancer's art has led this to be considered a rather gross device, calculated only to delude the simplest imaginations, and we may say that the presumption is now directly against an Italian in a novel, until he has pulled off his slouched hat and mantle and shown us features and limbs that an Anglo-Saxon would acknowledge. Mr. Howells's temerity has gone so far as to offer us a priest of the suspected race,—a priest with a dead-pale complexion, a blue chin, a dreamy eye, and a name in *elli*. The burden of proof is upon him that we shall believe in him, but he casts it off triumphantly at an early stage of the narrative, and we confess that our faith in Don Ippolito becomes at last really poignant and importunate.

"A Venetian priest in love with an American girl,—there's richness, as Mr. Squeers said!"—such was the formula by which we were first gossipingly made acquainted with the subject of "A Foregone Conclusion." An amiable American widow, travelling in Italy with her daughter, lingers on in Venice into the deeper picturesqueness of the early summer. With that intellectual thriftiness that characterizes many of her class (though indeed in Mrs. Vervain it is perhaps only a graceful anomaly the more), she desires to provide the young girl with instruction in Italian, and requests the consul of her native land (characteristically again) to point her out a teacher. The consul finds himself interested in a young ecclesiastic, with an odd mechanical turn, who has come to bespeak the consular patronage for some fanciful device in gunnery, and whose only wealth is a little store of English, or rather Irish, phrases, imparted by a fellow-priest from Dublin. Having been obliged to give the poor fellow the cold shoulder as an inventor, he is prompt in offering him a friendly hand as an Italian master, and Don Ippolito is introduced to Miss Vervain. Miss Vervain is charming, and the young priest discovers it to his cost. He falls in love with her, offers himself, is greeted with the inevitable horror provoked by such a proposition from such a source, feels the deep displeasure he must have caused, but finds he is only the more in love, resists, protests, rebels, takes it all terribly hard, becomes intolerably miserable, and falls fatally ill, while the young girl and her mother hurry away from Venice. Such is a rapid outline of Mr. Howells's story, which, it will be seen, is simple in the extreme,—is an air played on a single string, but an air exquisitely modulated. Though the author has not broken ground widely, he has sunk his shaft deep. The little drama goes on altogether between four persons,—chiefly, indeed, between two,—but on its limited scale it is singularly complete, and the interest gains sensibly from compression. Mr. Howells's touch is almost that of a miniature-painter; every stroke in "A Foregone Conclusion" plays its definite part, though sometimes the eye needs to linger a moment to perceive it. It is not often that a young lady in a novel is the resultant of so many fine intentions as the figure of Florida Vervain. The interest of the matter depends greatly, of course, on the quality of the two persons thus dramatically confronted, and here the author has shown a deep imaginative force. Florida Vervain and her lover form, as a couple, a more effective combination even than Kitty Ellison and Mr. Arbuton; for Florida, in a wholly different line, is as good—or all but as good—as the sweetheart of that sadly incapable suitor; and Don Ippolito is not only a finer fellow than the gentleman from Boston, but he is more acutely felt, we think, and better understood on the author's part. Don Ippolito is a real creation,—a most vivid, complete, and appealing one; of how many touches and retouches, how many caressing, enhancing strokes he is made up, each reader must observe for himself. He is in every situation a distinct personal image, and we never lose the sense of the author's seeing him in his habit as he lived,—"moving up and down the room with his sliding step, like some tall, gaunt, unhappy girl,"—and verging upon that quasi-hallucination with regard to him which is the law of the really creative fancy. His childish mildness, his courtesy, his innocence, which provokes a smile, but never a laugh, his meagre experience, his general helplessness, are rendered with an unerring hand: there is no crookedness in the drawing, from beginning to end. We have wondered, for ourselves, whether we should not have been content to fancy him a better Catholic and more intellectually at rest in his priestly office,—so that his passion for the strange and lovely girl who is so suddenly thrust before him should, by itself, be left to account for his terrible trouble; but it is evident, on the other hand, that his confiding her his doubts and his inward rebellion forms the common ground on which they come closely together, and the picture of his state of mind has too much truthful color not to justify itself. He is a representation of extreme moral simplicity, and his figure might have been simpler if he had been a consenting priest, rather than a protesting one. But, though he might have been in a way more picturesque, he would not have been more interesting; and the charm of the portrait is in its suffering us to feel with him, and its offering nothing that we find mentally disagreeable,—as we should have found the suggestion of prayers stupidly mumbled and of the *odeur de sacristie*. The key to Don Ippolito's mental strainings and yearnings is in his fancy for mechanics, which is a singularly happy stroke in the picture. It indicates the intolerable *discomfort* of his position, as distinguished from the deeper unrest of passionate scepticism, and by giving a sort of homely practical basis to his possible emancipation, makes him relapse into bondage only more tragical. It is a hard case, and Mr. Howells has written nothing better—nothing which more distinctly marks his faculty as a story-teller—than the pages in which he traces it to its climax. The poor caged youth, straining to the end of his chain, pacing round his narrow circle, gazing at the unattainable outer world, bruising himself in the effort to reach it and falling back to hide himself and die unpitied,—is a figure which haunts the imagination and claims a permanent place in one's melancholy memories.

The character of Florida Vervain contributes greatly to the dusky, angular relief of Don Ippolito. This young lady is a singularly original conception, and we remember no heroine in fiction in whom it is proposed to interest us on just such terms. "Her husband laughed," we are told at the close of the book, "to find her protecting and serving [her children] with the same tigerish tenderness, the same haughty humility, as that with which she used to care for poor Mrs. Vervain; and he perceived that this was merely the direction away from herself of that intense arrogance of nature which, but for her power and need of loving, would have made her intolerable. What she chiefly exacted from them, in return for her fierce devotedness, was the truth in everything; she was content they should be rather less fond of her than of their father, whom, indeed, they found much more amusing." A heroine who ripens into this sort of wife and mother is rather an exception among the tender sisterhood. Mr. Howells has attempted to enlist our imagination on behalf of a young girl who is positively unsympathetic, and who has an appearance of chilling rigidity and even of almost sinister reserve. He has brilliantly succeeded, and his heroine just escapes being disagreeable, to be fascinating. She is a poet's invention, and yet she is extremely real,—as real, in her way, as that Kitty Ellison whom she so little resembles. In these two figures Mr. Howells has bravely notched the opposite ends of his measure, and there is pleasure in reflecting on the succession of charming girls arrayed, potentially, along the intermediate line. He has outlined his field; we hope he will fill it up. His women are always most sensibly women; their motions, their accents, their ideas, savor essentially of the sex; he is one of the few writers who hold a key to feminine logic and detect a method in feminine madness. It deepens, of course, immeasurably, the tragedy of Don Ippolito's sentimental folly, that Florida Vervain should be the high-and-mighty young lady she is, and gives an additional edge to the peculiar cruelty of his situation,—the fact that, being what he is, he is of necessity, as a lover, repulsive. But Florida is a complex personage, and the tale depends in a measure in her having been able to listen to him in a pitying, maternal fashion, out of the abundance of her characteristic strength. There is no doubt that, from the moment she learns he has dreamed she might love him, he becomes hopelessly disagreeable to her; but the author has ventured on delicate ground in attempting to measure the degree in which passionate pity might qualify her repulsion. It is ground which, to our sense, he treads very firmly; but the episode of Miss Vervain's seizing the young priest's head and caressing it will probably provoke as much discussion as to its verisimilitude as young Arbuton's famous repudiation of the object of his refined affections. For our part, we think Miss Vervain's embrace was more natural than otherwise—for Miss Vervain; and, natural or not, it is admirably poetic. The poetry of the tale is limited to the priest and his pupil. Mrs. Vervain is a humorous creation, and in intention a very happy one. The kindly, garrulous, military widow, with her lively hospitality to the things that don't happen, and her serene unconsciousness of the things that do, is a sort of image of the way human levity hovers about the edge of all painful occurrences. Her scatter-brained geniality deepens the picture of her daughter's brooding preoccupations, and there is much sustained humor in making her know so much less of the story in which she plays a part than we do. Her loquacity, however, at times, strikes us as of a trifle too shrill a pitch, and her manner may be charged with lacking the repose, if not of the Veres of Vere, at least of the Veres of Providence. But there is a really ludicrous image suggested by the juxtaposition of her near-sightedness and her cheerful ignorance of Don Ippolito's situation, in which, at the same time, she takes so friendly an interest. She *overlooks* the tragedy going on under her nose, just as she overlooks the footstool on which she stumbles when she comes into a room. This touch proves that with a genuine artist, like Mr. Howells, there is an unfailing cohesion of all ingredients. Ferris, the consul, whose ultimately successful passion for Miss Vervain balances the sad heart-history of the priest, will probably find—has, we believe, already found—less favor than his companions, and will be reputed to have come too easily by his good fortune. He is an attempt at a portrait of a rough, frank, and rather sardonic hu-

morist, touched with the *sans gêne* of the artist and even of
the Bohemian. He is meant to be a good fellow in intention
and a likeable one in person; but we think the author has rather
over-emphasized his irony and his acerbity. He holds his own
firmly enough, however, as a make-weight in the action, and it is
not till Don Ippolito passes out of the tale and the scale descends
with a jerk into his quarter that most readers—feminine readers
at least—shake their heads unmistakably. Mr. Howells's conclusion
—his last twenty pages—will, we imagine, make him a good many
dissenters,—among those, at least, whose enjoyment has been an
enjoyment of his art. The story passes into another tone, and the
new tone seems to *jurer*, as the French say, with the old. It passes
out of Venice and the exquisite Venetian suggestiveness, over to
Providence, to New York, to the Fifth Avenue Hotel, and the
Academy of Design. We ourselves regret the transition, though
the motive of our regrets is difficult to define. It is a transition
from the ideal to the real, to the vulgar, from soft to hard, from
charming color to something which is not color. Providence and
the Fifth Avenue Hotel certainly have their rights; but we doubt
whether their rights, in an essentially romantic theme, reside in
a commixture with the suggestions offered us in such a picture
as this:—

> "The portal was a tall arch of Venetian Gothic, tipped
> with a carven flame; steps of white Istrian stone descended
> to the level of the lowest ebb, irregularly embossed with
> barnacles and dabbling long fringes of soft green sea-mosses
> in the rising and falling tide. Swarms of water-bugs and
> beetles played over the edges of the steps, and crabs scuttled
> sidewise into deeper water at the approach of a gondola.
> A length of stone-capped brick wall, to which patches of
> stucco still clung, stretched from the gate on either hand,
> under cover of an ivy that flung its mesh of shining green
> from within, where there lurked a lovely garden, stately,
> spacious for Venice, and full of a delicious half-sad surprise
> for whoso opened upon it. In the midst it had a broken
> fountain, with a marble naiad standing on a shell, and look-
> ing saucier than the sculptor meant, from having lost the
> point of her nose; nymphs and fauns and shepherds and

shepherdesses, her kinsfolk, coquetted in and out among the greenery in flirtation not to be embarrassed by the fracture of an arm or the casting of a leg or so; one lady had no head, but she was the boldest of all. In this garden there were some mulberry and pomegranate trees, several of which hung about the fountain with seats in their shade, and, for the rest, there seemed to be mostly roses and oleanders, with other shrubs of the kind that made the greatest show of blossom and cost the least for tendance."

It was in this garden that Don Ippolito told his love. We are aware that to consider Providence and New York not worthy to be mentioned in the same breath with it is a strictly conservative view of the case, and the author of "Their Wedding Journey" and "A Chance Acquaintance" has already proved himself, where American local color is concerned, a thoroughgoing radical. We may ground our objection to the dubious element, in this instance, on saying that the story is Don Ippolito's, and that in virtue of that fact it should not have floated beyond the horizon of the lagoons. It is the poor priest's property, as it were; we grudge even the reversion of it to Mr. Ferris. We confess even to a regret at seeing it survive Don Ippolito at all, and should have advocated a trustful surrender of Florida Vervain's subsequent fortunes to the imagination of the reader. But we have no desire to expatiate restrictively on a work in which, at the worst, the imagination finds such abundant pasture. "A Foregone Conclusion" will take its place as a singularly perfect production. That the author was an artist his other books had proved, but his art ripens and sweetens in the sun of success. His manner has now refined itself till it gives one a sense of pure *quality* which it really taxes the ingenuity to express. There is not a word in the present volume as to which he has not known consummately well what he was about; there is an exquisite intellectual comfort in feeling one's self in such hands. Mr. Howells has ranked himself with the few writers on whom one counts with luxurious certainty, and this little masterpiece confirms our security.

HOWELLS'S A FOREGONE CONCLUSION*

(Second Article)

MR. HOWELLS in his new novel returns to his first love, and treats once more of Venice and Venetian figures. His constancy has not betrayed him, for 'A Foregone Conclusion' is already rapidly making its way. A novelist is always safer for laying his scene in his own country, and the best that can be said of his errors of tone and proportion, when he deals with foreign manners, is that the home reader is rarely wise enough to measure them. But in Venice Mr. Howells is almost at home, and if his book contains any false touches, we, for our part, have not had the skill to discover them. His Venetian hero is not only a very vivid human being, but a distinct Italian, with his subtle race-qualities artfully interwoven with his personal ones. We confess, however, that in spite of this evidence of the author's ability to depict a consistent and natural member of the Latin family, we should have grudged him a heroine of foreign blood. Not the least charm of the charming heroines he has already offered us has been their delicately native quality. They have been American women in the scientific sense of the term, and the author, intensely American in the character of his talent, is probably never so spontaneous, so much himself, as when he represents the delicate, nervous, emancipated young woman begotten of our institutions and our climate, and equipped with a lovely face and an irritable moral consciousness. Mr. Howells's tales have appeared in the pages of the *Atlantic Monthly,* and the young ladies who figure in them are the actual young ladies who attentively peruse that magazine. We are thankful accordingly, in 'A Foregone Conclusion,' for a heroine named after one of the States of the Union, and characterized by what we may call a national aroma. The relation of a heroine to a hero can only be of course, to be adored by him; but the specific interest of the circumstance

---

* 'A Foregone Conclusion. By W. D. Howells, author of 'Their Wedding Journey,' 'A Chance Acquaintance,' etc.' Boston: J. R. Osgood & Co. (*The Nation,* January 7, 1875).

in this case resides in the fact that the hero is a priest, and that one has a natural curiosity to know how an American girl of the typical free-stepping, clear-speaking cast receives a declaration from a sallow Italian ecclesiastic. It is characteristic of Mr. Howells's manner as a story-teller, of his preference of fine shades to heavy masses, of his dislike to *les grands moyens,* that Florida Vervain's attitude is one of benignant, almost caressing, pity. The author's choice here seems to us very happy; any other tone on the young girl's part would have been relatively a trifle vulgar. Absolute scorn would have made poor Don Ippolito's tragedy too brutally tragical, and an answering passion, even with all imaginable obstructions, would have had a quality less poignant than his sense that in her very kindness the woman he loves is most inaccessible. Don Ippolito dies of a broken heart, and Florida Vervain prospers extremely—even to the point of marrying, at Providence, R. I., an American gentleman whom, in spite of his having in his favor that he does not stand in a disagreeably false position, the reader is likely to care less for than for the shabby Venetian ecclesiastic.

This story is admirably told, and leads one to expect very considerable things from Mr. Howells as a novelist. He has given himself a narrow stage, or rather a scanty *dramatis personæ* (for he has all glowing Venice for a back scene), and he has attempted to depict but a single situation. But between his four persons the drama is complete and the interest acute. It is all a most remarkable piece of elaboration. Mr. Howells had already shown that he lacked nothing that art can give in the way of finish and ingenuity of manner; but he has now proved that he can embrace a dramatic situation with the true imaginative force— give us not only its mechanical structure, but its atmosphere, its meaning, its poetry. The climax of Don Ippolito's history in the present volume is related with masterly force and warmth, and the whole portrait betrays a singular genius for detail. It is made up of a series of extremely minute points, which melt into each other like scattered water-drops. Their unity is in their subdued poetic suggestiveness, their being the work of a writer whose observation always projects some vague tremulous shadow into the realm of fancy. The image of Don Ippolito, if we are not mistaken, will stand in a niche of its own in the gallery of portraits of humble souls. The best figure the author had drawn hitherto was that charmingly positive young lady, Miss Kitty Ellison, in 'A Chance Acquaintance'; but he has given it a very harmonious companion in the Florida Vervain of the present tale. Miss Vervain is positive also, and in the manner of her positiveness she is a singularly original invention. She is more fantastic than her predecessor, but she is hardly less lifelike, and she is a remarkably picturesque study of a complex nature. Her image is poetical, which is a considerable compliment, as things are managed now in fiction (where the only escape from bread-and-butter and commonplace is into golden hair and promiscuous felony). In the finest scene in the book, when Florida has learned to what extent Don Ippolito has staked his happiness upon his impossible passion, she, in a truly superb movement of pity, seizes his head in her hands and kisses it. Given the persons and the circumstances, this seems to us an extremely fine imaginative stroke, for it helps not only to complete one's idea of the young girl, but the fact of the deed being possible and natural throws a vivid side-light on the helpless, childish, touching personality of the priest. We believe, however, that it has had the good fortune to create something like a scandal. There are really some readers who are in urgent need of a tonic regimen! If Mr. Howells continues to strike notes of this degree of resonance, he will presently find himself a very eminent story-teller; and meanwhile he may find an agreeable stimulus in the thought that he has provoked a discussion.

A matter which it is doubtless very possible to discuss, but in which we ourselves should be on the protesting side, is the felicity of the episodes related in the last twenty pages of the tale. After the hero's death the action is transplanted to America, and the conclusion takes place in the shadow of the Fifth Avenue Hotel. We have found these pages out of tune with their predecessors, and we suspect that this will be the verdict of readers with the finer ear. The philosophy of such matters is very ethereal, and one can hardly do more than take one's stand on the "I do not like you, Doctor Fell" principle. One labors under the disadvantage, too, that the author's defence will be much more categorical than the reader's complaint, and that the complaint itself lays one open to the charge of siding against one's own flesh and blood. We should risk it, then, and almost be willing, for the sake of keeping a singularly perfect composition intact, to pass for a disloyal citizen. And then the author can point triumphantly to 'A Chance Acquaintance' as proof that a very American tale may be also a very charming one. Of this there is no doubt; but everything is relative, and the great point is, as the French say, not to *mêler les genres*. We renounce the argument, but in reading over 'A Foregone Conclusion' we shall close the work when the hero dies—when old Veneranda comes to the door and shakes her hands in Ferris's face and smites him, as it were, with the announcement. The author, however, is thoroughly consistent, for in stamping his tale at the last with the American local seal he is simply expressing his own literary temperament. We have always thought Mr. Howells's, in spite of his Italian affiliations, a most characteristically American talent; or rather not in spite of them, but in a manner on account of them, for he takes Italy as no Italian surely ever took it—as your enterprising Yankee alone is at pains to take it. American literature is immature, but it has, in prose and verse alike, a savor of its own, and we have often thought that this might be a theme for various interesting reflections. If we undertook to make a few, we should find Mr. Howells a capital text. He reminds us how much our native-grown imaginative effort is a matter of details, of fine shades, of pale colors, a making of small things do great service. Civilization with us is monotonous, and in the way of contrasts, of salient points, of chiaroscuro, we have to take what we can get. We have to look for these things in fields where a less devoted glance would see little more than an arid blank, and, at the last, we manage to find them. All this refines and sharpens our perceptions, makes us in a literary way, on our own scale, very delicate, and stimulates greatly our sense of proportion and form. Mr. Lowell and Mr. Longfellow among the poets, and Mr. Howells, Bret Harte, and Mr. Aldrich among the story-tellers (the latter writer, indeed, in verse as well as in prose), have all pre-eminently the instinct of style and shape. It is true, in general, that the conditions here indicated give American writing a limited authority, but they often give it a great charm—how great a charm, may be measured in the volume before us. 'A Foregone Conclusion' puts us for the moment, at least, in good humor with the American manner. At a time when the English novel has come in general to mean a ponderous, shapeless, diffuse piece of machinery, "padded" to within an inch of its life, without style, without taste, without a touch of the divine spark, and effective, when it is effective, only by a sort of brutal dead-weight, there may be pride as well as pleasure in reading this admirably-balanced and polished composition, with its distinct literary flavor, its grace and its humor, its delicate art and its perfume of poetry, its extreme elaboration and yet its studied compactness. And if Mr. Howells adheres in the future to his own standard, we shall have pleasure as well as pride.

HOWELLS'S POEMS*

The many readers who find in Mr. Howells's charming prose one of the most refined literary pleasures of the day will open his volume of *Poems* with a good deal of curiosity as well as a good deal of confidence. The author's habit of finished workmanship is in itself an assurance of delicate entertainment; but those who have relished as we have the lurking poetical intuitions of "Italian Journeys" and "Suburban Sketches" will ask themselves what a fancy which finds so happy an utterance in natural, flexible prose has left itself to say in verse. As it turns out, Mr. Howells's verse is as natural and unforced as his prose; and we are left wondering what law it is that governs his occasional preference of one vehicle of expression to the other, until at last we forget our wonderment in envy of this double skill. Double it is, this delicate skill, and yet characteristically single, too; for, whatever he writes, *style* somehow comes uppermost under Mr. Howells's hand, and what is poetry when it charms us

---

* Poems. By William D. Howells. Boston: James H. Osgood & Co. 1873. (*The Independent,* January 8, 1874).

most but style? We have taken much of our pleasure over these light lyrics and grave hexameters in recognizing and greeting again the manner and the sentiment which our author's sketches and tales have made familiar to us. His inspiration throughout seems very much akin to itself; the only visible rule we detect in the matter being that, when a prompting of his fancy is just a trifle too idle, too insubstantial, too unapologetically picturesque, as it were, for even the minute ingenuities of his own prose manner, the trick of the versifier steps in and lends the charming folly its saving music. In prose, indeed, the reader knows the author of "A Chance Acquaintance" to be much of a humorist—there are few writers now in whose pages there is more of a certain sort of critical, appreciative exhilaration; and to his humor he has given, happily, we think, little play in his verse. Versified jokes, except in rare cases, spoil, to our tase, good things. But for the rest, prose and poetry with Mr. Howells strike very much the same chords and utter the same feelings. These feelings in the volume before us are chiefly of a melancholy strain; pathetic pieces we should call most of the poems. It is for the most part a very fine-drawn melancholy. We should, perhaps, find it hard to determine, at times, the whence, the whither, the wherefore of the author's melodious sighs.

But this light irresponsibility of sadness is, we confess, the great charm of his verse. Poetry was made to talk about vague troubles and idle hopes, to express the thinnest caprices of thought, and when sensitive people meddle with it it is certain to be charged with the more or less morbid overflow of sadness. There is almost nothing of this sort that the poetic form, in its happiest moods, may not justify and make sweet. We must hasten to add, however, that Mr. Howells has laid no such very heavy burden upon it. His melancholy is the melancholy of reflection, not of passion; and his bitterness has an indefinable air, which becomes it vastly, of being turned to mild good humor by the glimpses it enjoys of its graceful poetized image. One always feels free to doubt of the absolute despondency of a genuine artist. Before his sorrow is nine days old he is half in love with its picturesqueness; everything in his experience, dark or bright, is a passable "subject." The artistic element in Mr. Howells's talent is inveterate; with him, as with many of our modern singers, it is often a question for the reader whether the pain of feeling is not outbalanced by the relish of exquisite form. They have not been simple people as a general thing, the best of our recent poets; and this is one of their many complexities. They are the product of many influences; of their own restless fancy and sensitive tempers, to begin with; of the changing experience of life; of the culture that is in the air, of the other poets whom they love and emulate; of their New World consciousness (when they are Americans) and their Old World sympathies; of their literary associations, as well as their moral disposition. Half our pleasure, for instance, in Mr. Longfellow's poetry is in its *barkish* flavor, its vague literary echoes. So in its own measure Mr. Howells's verse is a tissue of light reflections from an experience closely interfused with native impulse. Discriminating readers, we think, will enjoy tracing out these reflections and lingering over them. They speak of the author's early youth having been passed in undisturbed intimacy with a peculiarly characteristic phase of American scenery; and then of this youthful quietude having expanded into the experience, full of mingled relief and regret, of an intensely European way of life. Ohio and Italy commingle their suggestions in Mr. Howells's pages in a harmony altogether original. We imagine, further, that the author has read a great many German lyrics, and has during a season cherished the belief that Heine's "Lieder" were the most delightful things in the world.

We infer that, as a deposit, as it were, from this and other impressions, he has retained a zealous affection for light literature, and has come to believe no time wasted which is spent in exploring the secrets of literary form. To conclude our running analysis, we fancy him writing fewer verses than formerly, but turning over his old ones with a good deal of tender sympathy, feeling how many impressions once vivid and convictions once intense, how many felicities of phrase, how many notes happily struck, how much true poetic inspiration is stored away in them; and saying to himself that, sifted, revised, retouched, they may be read with something of the pleasure with which they were written.

He has certainly been right—right to collect his verses and right to have sifted them; for, thanks to the latter circumstance, the volume gives us a peculiarly agreeable sense of evenness of merit. There are no half successes to remind us harshly of the inevitable element of effort contained in all charming skill. Three of the poems are narratives in hexameter—a measure for which Mr. Howells's has an evident relish. Half our pleasure in English hexameter has always seemed to us to be the pleasure of seeing them done with proper smoothness at all; and this pleasure is naturally greater with the poet than with his readers. But there have been too many fine English hexameters written to have solid ground for skepticism, and Mr. Howells's may rank with the best. None have been more truly picturesque or found a poet apter for their needful ingenuities. Both in poetry and prose the chance to be verbally ingenious has a marked attraction for our author, and we may safely say that the occasion never outwits him.

> "That time of year, you know,
>   when the summer, beginning to sadden,
> Full-mooned and silver-hearted, glides from the heart
>   of September,
> Mourned by disconsolate crickets and iterant grass-
>   hoppers, crying
> All the still nights long from the ripened abundance
>   of gardens;
> Then ere the boughs of maple are mantled
>   with earliest autumn,
> But the wind of autumn breathes from the orchards
>   at nightfall,
> Full of winy perfume and mystical yearning
>   and languor;
> And in the noonday woods you hear the foraging
>   squirrels,
> And the long, crashing fall of the half-eaten nut
>   from the tree-top;
> When the robins are mute and the yellow-birds,
>   haunting the thistles,
> Cheep and twitter and flit through the dusty lanes
>   and the loppings,

When the pheasant hums from your stealthy foot
  in the cornfield;
And the wild pigeons feed, few and shy,
  in the scokeberry bushes;
When the weary land lies hushed, like a seer
  in a vision,
And your life seems but the dream of a dream
  that you cannot remember—
Broken, bewildering, vague, an echo
  that answers to nothing!
That time of year, you know."

These few lines from "Clement" are an excellent specimen both of the author's graceful management of a meter which easily becomes awkward and of that touching suggestiveness of image and epithet which we find especially characteristic of him. The diction here seems to us really exquisite. If the essence of poetry is to make our muse a trifle downhearted, our quotation is richly charged with it. "Clement" is the most finished of the longer pieces and the fullest of this charm of minute detail. "The Faithful of the Gonzaga" is a very pretty version in ballad measure of a picturesque Mantuan legend; and "Bo-Peep; A Pastoral" is a *pastiche,* a trifle too elaborate perhaps for the theme, of the fairy tale or Spenserian style of poem. It is the only piece in the volume that is not serious; but in its jocose picturesqueness it is full of lovely, half-serious lines. The author has been vigorously in earnest, on the other hand, in the painful tale of "Avery," one of the dismal legends of Niagara. This is an excellent piece of rapidly moving poetic narrative. It might aptly replace certain threadbare favorites in the repertory of public "readers." The things, however, which have given us most pleasure are the shorter and slighter poems— poems about nothing, as we may almost call some of them; slender effusions of verse, on themes to which you can hardly give names, and which you would scarcely think phraseable in song unless the singer prunes it. The smallest pretexts have sufficed for these things, and half their substance is in the way they are said. Some vague regret, felt or fancied; some idle, youthful hope or longing; a hint, a conjecture, a reminiscence, a nameless pulsation of youth; the bitter-sweet sense of a past and a future—these are the author's poetic promptings—half emotion, half imagination, and, in their own peculiarly delicate way, all style. They are the expression of a sensitive mind; but of a mind happy beyond the fortune of many of the numerous spirits who take things hard in having this exquisite esthetic compensation. The moral melancholy at the source of the little poem of "Lost Beliefs" is transitory, but the charm of the poem is permanent. We leave the reader to judge:

> "One after one they left us;
>   The sweet birds out of our breasts
> Went flying away in the morning:
>   Will they come again to their nests?
> "Will they come again at nightfall,
>   With God's breath in their song?
> Noon is fierce with heats of summer
>   And summer days are long!
> "O my life, with thy upward liftings,
>   Thy downward-striking roots,
> Ripening out of thy tender blossoms
>   But hard and bitter fruits!
> "In thy boughs there is no shelter
>   For the birds to seek again.
> The desolate nest is broken
>   And torn with wind and rain!"

This seems to us altogether a little masterpiece, and we can offer the reader no kindlier wish than for a frequent occurrence of those quiet moods—not melancholy, but tolerant of melancholy, in which he may best enjoy it—one of the moods, *par excellence,* in which Mr. Longfellow, in those charming verses which every one knows, expresses a preference for the small suggestive singers over the grandly oppressive ones. It has a dozen companions—"The First Cricket," "Bubbles," "The Mulberries"—in which a moral shadow resolves itself into a lovely poetic fantasy. We intend no illiberal praise when we say that the fifth stanza of the "Elegy" on the author's brother seems to us the very perfection of good taste. It reverberates with all possible tenderness in the reader's conscience, and yet in its happy modulation it troubles him with no uneasy effort to reach beyond itself. The reminiscences of Heine which we have alluded to the reader will recognize for himself; they are charming turns of verse and very venial cynicism. We have no space for further specifications; we can only recommend our author's volume to all lovers of delicate literary pleasures. To literature, with its modest pretensions, it emphatically belongs. It has no weak places. It is all really classic work. The reader, as he goes, will count over its fine intuitions and agree with us that Mr. Howells is a master of the waning art of saying delicate things in a way that does them justice.

FRANCIS PARKMAN: THE JESUITS IN NORTH AMERICA*

Mr. Parkman gives in the present volume the second part of his history of the short-lived French dominion in North America. His first volume describes the abortive attempt of the Huguenots to establish themselves in Florida, the cruel destruction of their colony by the Spaniards, and the vengeance wrought upon them in turn by the Frenchman de Jourgue, together with a narrative of the gallant and useful career of Samuel de Champlain, the founder of Quebec. His third volume is to be devoted to that French exploration of the Valley of the Mississippi of which the memory still subsists in so many mispronounced names, from the Gulf of Mexico to Lake Superior. But whatever may be the interest of these narratives, and the importance of the facts on which they rest, it is certain that this touching story of the Jesuit missions in Canada is no less dramatic and instructive. It has peculiar and picturesque interest from the fact that the enterprise was, in a great measure, a delusion and a failure—a delusion con-

---

* "The Jesuits in North America in the Sevententh Century. By Francis Parkman." Boston: Little, Brown & Co. 1867. (*The Nation*, June 6, 1867).

secrated by the most earnest conviction and the most heroic effort, a failure redeemed by the endurance of incalculable suffering. The Jesuit undertaking as it stands described in Mr. Parkman's pages has an indefinably factitious look—an expression intensely *subjective*, as we call it nowadays. Its final results were null, and its success at no time such as to gratify the reason of the missionaries. Nevertheless they persisted through unprecedented hardship and danger, baptizing, preaching, rebuking, exploring, and hoping. Their faith, patience, and courage form a very interesting chapter in the history of the human mind, and it is to our perception more as contributions to that history than as a stage of the process of our American civilization that their labors are valuable. It is very true that these labors were not without a certain permanent and wholesome effect. The missionaries aimed at the sky, and their missiles reached the tree-tops. Their example and exhortations, if they failed to elevate the Indians to the practice of even the simpler virtues, or to make them good Catholics, made them to a certain extent bad heathens, and softened their most characteristic usages. But, on the whole, we repeat it is when regarded as a portion of the history of the Church and the ecclesiastical spirit that their exploits are most interesting. It is our impression that they share this character with most of the various Jesuit missions—certainly with those of the great Xavier. When the human mind wishes to contemplate itself at its greatest tension—its greatest desire for action, for influence and dominion—when it wishes to be reminded of how much it is capable in the direction of conscious hope and naked endurance, it cannot do better than read the story of the early Jesuit adventurers.

Mr. Parkman's narrative is founded chiefly on the reports regularly transmitted to France by the active members of the order, and from which, frequent as are his citations, we cannot help wishing that he had given more copious extracts. These reports were minute, frequent, and rigorously truthful—that is, if the writers told of miracles and portents they told of none but such as they themselves believed. The *relations* are marked apparently by great simplicity of tone, great credulity, and very great discrimination with regard to the Indian character. The missionaries were keen observers of the manners and impulses of the savages, as, indeed, it was of vital importance to their own personal safety that they should be. The Indians were the most unpromising material for conversion. Generally they were obstinate, intractable, and utterly averse to the reception of light; occasionally, however, they would consent to become Christians; but on such a basis! Their piety was more discouraging than their obduracy. Mr. Parkman gives a very vivid picture of the state of the savage populations at the time of the early settlements —a picture beside which the old-fashioned portrait of the magnanimous and rhetorical red man is a piece of very false coloring. Mr. Parkman knows his subject, and he mentions no single trait of intelligence, of fancy, or of character by which the Indian should have a hold on our respect or his fate a claim to our regret. The cruelty of the Canadian tribes is beyond description. They had no imagination in their religion; they confined what little they possessed to the science of torture. A prominent feature of this science was their voracious cannibalism, for in the enthusiasm of the practice they frequently neglected to await the death of their victim. When perchance they did, they danced about him as he stood in the stocks, shouting into his ears who would eat this morsel and who the other. Add to this their incredible squalor, their ignorance of any rule of decency, however elastic, the utterly graceless and sterile character of their legends and traditions, and finally the dismal severity of the climate in which they managed to support existence—their ceaseless struggle with winter, famine, and pestilence—and we have a conception as accurate as it is painful of the life of our aboriginal predecessors, and of the civilization which flourished on this continent during the long black ages in which Europe lay basking in light—such as it was. Let us not despair of our literature. During the lifetime of those great writers and adventurers about whom French and English critics write the brilliant articles which occasionally minister to our discouragement, Hurons and Iroquois were biting off each other's finger-ends on the shores of the St. Lawrence, and Mohawks, in the beautiful valley which perpetuates their virtues, were laying open the skulls of pious Frenchmen.

We have no space to trace in detail the various incidents and vicissitudes of the Jesuit mission. It lasted for forty years; and during this period was made illustrious by every form of heroism and martyrdom. Its failure was the result of several causes—of the purely religious character of the French establishments, of the superficial and mechanical nature of the conversions, and of the ceaseless internecine warfare of the different tribes, terminating in the supremacy of the Iroquois, the most cruel and intractable of all, and the extirpation of the Hurons, among whom the Jesuits had found their best proselytes. Quebec and Montreal were wholly priest-governed—the latter, indeed, priest-settled. The emigrations from France were under ecclesiastical auspices, and entirely wanting in any desire to turn the material resources of the country to account. On the contrary, all excessive prosperity, all superfluous comfort, were discouraged and prohibited. The motive of emigration was a strictly sentimental one, and the enterprise undertaken only for the greater glory of God. The interests of this life were consulted at most only in so far as to secure proper defence from attack. Agriculture was neglected, trade restricted, and the neophytes were instructed only in the Catechism. An Ursuline convent was founded at Quebec, and a number of enthusiastic volunteers were recruited among the ladies of France. To the female members of the mission Mr. Parkman has devoted a vividly-written chapter. The reader will readily understand that among those grim celibates in those snow-choked pine forests the interests of population were left to take care of themselves; and he will transfer a glance of approval down the map to the latitudes where prolific Dutch farmers and Puritan divines were building up the State of New York and the Commonwealth of Massachusetts. In 1650 Gabriel Druilletes, one of the Jesuit brothers, made an expedition across the country from Quebec to Boston, where he had occasion to be forcibly struck with the difference in the character of the French and English settlements.

"He says," writes Mr. Parkman, "that Boston (meaning Massachusetts) could alone furnish four thousand fighting men, and that the four united colonies could furnish forty thousand souls. His numbers may be challenged; but, at all events, the contrast was striking with the attenuated and suffering bands of priests, nuns, and fur-traders on the St. Lawrence. About forty thousand persons had come from Old to New England with the resolve of making it their home; and, though this immigration had virtually ceased, the natural increase had been great. The necessity, or the strong desire, of escaping from persecution had given the impulse to Puritan colonization; while, on the other hand, none but good Catholics, the favored class of France, were tolerated in Canada. These had no motive for exchanging the comforts of home and the smiles of fortune for a starving wilderness and the scalping-knives of the Iroquois. The Huguenots would have emigrated in swarms, but they were rigidly forbidden. The zeal of propagandism and the fur trade were, as we have seen, the vital forces of New France. Of her feeble population, the best part was bound to perpetual chastity, while the fur-traders rarely brought their wives to the wilderness . . . . To the mind of the Puritan heaven was God's throne; but no less was the earth his footstool . . . . He held it a duty to labor and to multiply, and, building quite as much on the Old Testament as on the New, thought that a reward on earth as well as in heaven waited on those who were faithful to the law . . . . On the other hand, those who shaped the character and, in great measure, the destiny of New France, had always on their lips the nothingness and the vanity of human life."

In heaven alone, then, they found their reward. Their story is far more romantic and touching than that of their Protestant neighbors; it is written in those rich and mellow colors in which the Catholic Church inscribes her records; but it leaves the mind profoundly unsatisfied. Like all sad stories, it carries a moral. What is this moral? However well disinterestedness and self-immolation may work for individuals, they work but ill for communities, however small. The Puritans were frank self-seekers. They withdrew from persecution at home and they practised it here. They have left, accordingly, a vast, indelible trace of their passage through history. The Jesuits worked on a prepared field, in an artificial atmosphere, and it was, therefore, easy for them to be sublime. However they, as a group—a very small group

—might embrace suffering and martyrdom, the paternal Church courted only prosperity and dominion. The Church was well aware of the truth at which we just hinted—that collective bodies find but small account in self-sacrifice; and it carefully superintended and directed the fervent passion of the Jesuits. The record of these latter in Canada is unstained by persecution, for the simple reason that French Protestants were not allowed to enter their circle. In this circle they freely burned themselves out. The Church could afford it on the part of the Catholic world at large, and as for individuals each had but his own case to manage. Of how well each performed his task, Mr. Parkman's pages are an excellent record. They furnish us, too, with a second inference, more gratifying to human vanity than the other, and that is, that religion, in spite of the commonplace, intellectual form which it has recently grown to assume in many quarters, is essentially bound up with miracles. Only the miracles are a tribute of man to God, and not of God to man. It may be fairly said of the Jesuit missionaries that, in the firmness of their endurance of horrible sufferings, they fairly broke the laws of nature. They broke at least those of their own temperaments. The timid man hourly outfaced impending torture, and the weak outlasted it. When one can boast of such miracles as these, what is the use of insisting on diseases cured by the touch of saintly bones, or of enthusiasts visibly transported in the arms of angels?

LATER LYRICS BY JULIA WARD HOWE: POEMS BY ELIZABETH AKERS (FLORENCE PERCY); POEMS BY AMANDA T. JONES; WOMEN OF THE GOSPELS: THE THREE WAKINGS AND OTHER POEMS BY THE AUTHOR OF THE SCHÖNBERG — COTTA FAMILY

OF the volumes whose titles are here set forth, the first two in order are also the first two in character. Mrs. Howe's verses, however, are very unequal. Those of Mrs. Akers, on the other hand, maintain throughout the same level of unassuming good taste. If Mrs. Howe is occasionally unsuccessful, it is because she is urged by a generous ambition and a more imperious fancy. The titles of some of her pieces will give a notion of the heights to which she sometimes aspires. Here are several in succession: "Philosophy," "Kosmos," "First Causes," "The Church," "The Christ." It is true that, on examination, we find these great topics to be dealt with in a more cursory fashion than might have been apprehended. The first-named piece, for instance, is a declaration of the author's willingness to share, for the sake of its glorious compensation, the discredit and discomfort attached to the pursuit of philosophy. The poet forgets that this is no longer the age in which Galileo was imprisoned, or Bruno was burned, and that indeed as a generation we are nothing if not philosophical. On the second of the pieces just cited our most lively impression is that the sun is there assumed to be of the feminine gender. But besides these, Mrs. Howe handles an immense

1. *Later Lyrics.* By Julia Ward Howe. Boston: J. E. Tilton & Co. 1866. 12 mo. pp. 326

2. *Poems.* By Elizabeth Akers (Florence Percy). Boston: Ticknor and Fields. 1866. 16 mo. pp. 251.

3. *Poems.* By Amanda T. Jones. New York: Hurd and Houghton. 12 mo. pp. 203.

4. *The Women of the Gospels: The Three Wakings, and other Poems.* By the Author of "The Schönberg-Cotta Family." New York: M. W. Dodd. 1867. 12 mo. pp. 275.

(*The North American Review*, April, 1867).

variety of profane subjects, and with very various felicity. She is most successful, to our mind, when her theme is simple and objective, as in the case of the War Poems which open the volume; although even the effect of the very best of these is marred by the introduction of some recondite fancy or some transcendental allusion. The fifth stanza of the "Battle Hymn of the Republic" is an instance in point. The first four stanzas are rapid and passionate; the last is cold-blooded and literary, and utterly at odds with the dignity of the Republic in whose name the whole is spoken. So in the lyric entitled "Our Orders," we regret that the author should not have suppressed the obscurely worded invocation to the "Sibyl Arts." The absence of any such impertinent matter in the "Harvard Students' Song," together with the animated measure of the poem, give it, in our opinion, the first place among the author's patriotic verses. Very forcible, too, are several of the series entitled "Lyrics of the Street," especially the little poem called "The Fine Lady." Under the head of "Poems of Study and Experience," Mrs. Howe has included three morsels of blank verse,—"studies," we ought perhaps to call them, in the fashion of the day,—which we fancy to have been inspired by certain of the pregnant monologues of Robert Browning. One of these compositions is a soliloquy by the Emperor Caligula,

> "the monster Caius, loathed of men,
> Him whose foul record women may not read."

It was a bold undertaking on the part of Mrs. Howe, in view of the fact here asserted, to unveil the heart of the profligate Roman; and it is perhaps, after all, to the credit of her fancy that her effort has fallen short of the mark. The same may be said of her attempt to reconstruct the character of the Emperor Claudius, whose

> "Tastes in blood were moderate, but nice."

Mrs. Howe's prevailing fault is that she is too vague, too general, too lax; and it requires a more constant patience of facts, of linear divisions, and of shades of meaning, than properly belongs to her genius, to call back into being phases of life and of character so alien to our actual circumstances as the humors of Claudius and Caligula.

Mrs. Akers, as we have said, sails much nearer to the shore. She is fluent, pensive, and tender, and exhibits a very genuine love for physical nature, and a sympathy with its slighter phenomena, which in Mrs. Howe's volume is almost conspicuous by its absence. "Violet Planting," "Spring at the Capitol," and "Among the Laurels," are all good examples of graceful versification. They are nowhere disfigured by that painful straining for effect, that ludicrous dislocation of the members of the phrase, which we are apt to encounter in the compositions of writers in whom the poetic heat is not intense. Mrs. Akers is content to gather the thoughts and images that are within easy reach, and such as will subsist on good terms with her vocabulary. Occasionally her fancy and her language are charmingly mated. Speaking, for instance, of the indifference of Nature to the civil strife of men, she writes:—

> "When blood her grassy altar wets,
>   She sends the pitying violets
>   To heal the outrage with their bloom,
>   And cover it with soft regrets."

Of the two remaining volumes on our list it is hard to write many words, Miss Jones is patriotic, bellicose, and slightly erudite; but both in her patriotic, and her domestic pieces she is verbose and rhetorical, rather than earnest and truly lyrical. We confess to a lively mistrust of collections of verse presenting a frequent recurrence of those metres which require twice the breadth of the page. The chief merit of a great deal of the versification of the day lies in the brevity of its lines, as compared to the line of prose; but this merit is absent from Miss Jones's pages. They present a most formidable and impartial diffusion of matter. We conjecture that the praise most after this lady's heart would be the bestowal upon her performance of the epithet "spirited." This epithet we cordially concede. It is decidedly spirited, for example, on the part of a soldier's mother, to speak of being "impaled" by terror as to her son's fate. Miss Jones's analogies and metaphors are throughout of a terrible description. "Ghouls," "fiends," "tigers," and "scorpions" all play a prominent part. Occasionally, however, Miss Jones imparts a singular subtlety to her portrayal of terrible sensations; as when she represents the cry of the whippoorwill as "taxing the sense with a dulcitude fearfully keen."

The poetic style of the author of "The Schönberg-Cotta Family," on the other hand, is colorless to a fault. Her work is essentially common, destitute alike of the fervor of piety and the graces of poetry. We should be sorry to impugn the sincerity of the author's devotional feelings; but if devotional poetry owes something to religion, it also owes something to art, or at least to taste; and when it is indifferent to art and taste, it suffers the penalty of being unreadable.

THE PROPHET. A TRAGEDY.

BY BAYARD TAYLOR*

Mr. Bayard Taylor presents us with another example of his versatility. He has written a great deal of almost everything, but we are not aware that he had hitherto produced a tragedy. The present one is in blank verse, in five acts, and fills a considerable volume. There is a great deal of talk about American art, the American novel, and the American drama, but as a general thing we are treated, in the matter, to vastly more precept than example. Mr. Taylor, however, whose large acquaintance with foreign lands might have given him an excuse for evading the problem, has taken the bull by the horns and attempted to fling a veil of romance over an episode intensely characteristic of our local conditions of life. He has written the tragedy of Mormonism, and taken Joe Smith and Brigham Young for his heroes. His experiment has not, to our taste, been remarkably successful, but it is creditable to his intellectual pluck. If he had succeeded, he would have achieved an extra-

---

The Prophet. A Tragedy. By Bayard Taylor. Boston: James R. Osgood & Co. 1874. (*The North American Review,* January, 1875).

ordinary feat; but it must be confessed that, though we should certainly have boasted of his performance, we would not perhaps have admitted that he had attempted it at his peril. Of course Mr. Taylor has had in a measure to adapt his material to poetic conditions. He has changed the names of his personages, elaborated his plot, left certain details gracefully vague, and, for the most part, steered clear of local color. But his desire has evidently been to adhere to reality as much as was practically convenient and to enjoy whatever benefit there might be in leaving to his drama the savor of the soil.

His idea was decidedly a tempting one, for he had the great advantage of finding a really massive subject ready made to his hands. New religions are tolerably common in our age and country, and, as things stand, they impress the imagination hardly more than the usual objects of registration in the Patent Office; yet it remains true that a revelation which events have handsomely justified is a rather solider theme for the dramatist than he often encounters, in this day of microscopic literature. We believe greatly, for our own part, in the importance of the subject; a large one, to our mind, promises more than a small one, and when a poet has secured for a hero a veritable prophet, with the bloom not yet rubbed off by literature, he has our heartiest congratulations. It perturbs our faith a little to learn that the prophet is Mr. Joe Smith, and the *dénouement* is to be the founding of Salt Lake City by Mr. Brigham Young; we reflect that there is a magic in associations, and we are afraid we scent vulgarity in these. But we are anxious to see what the author makes of them, and we grant that the presumption is in favor of his audacity. Mormonism we know to be a humbug and a rather nasty one. It needs at this time of day no "showing up," and Mr. Taylor has not wasted his time in making a poetical exposure. He assumes that the creed was founded in tolerable good faith, and he limits his view to its early stages, which already, at Western rates of progression, have faded into the twilight of tradition. His design has been to show how a religion springs into being, and how an honest man may be beguiled into thinking himself a prophet. He must of course be naturally of a rather attitudinizing turn, fond of brooding and spouting and riding a theological hobby. He must be half sincere and half shrewd,—sincere enough to desire his aim greatly, and shrewd enough to catch any capful of wind that may offer to swell his sails. He must make a figure in his neighborhood, and pass among his friends for a very remarkable young man,—a young man with more in him than simple folks can exactly give a name to. But folks about him must be remarkably simple, and the great point apparently is that his friends should be uncommonly well disposed. Mr. Taylor's idea is that, if this is the case, the prophet expands to his full proportions by a process that one may call *reaction*. A certain temperament must be postulated and a certain *milieu* conceded; after this the unfolding is logical. David Starr, Mr. Taylor's hero, would hardly have become a full-blown hierarch if his early lot had been cast in Boston or New York, unless indeed he had had the courage of his opinions in a greater degree than Mr. Taylor represents. His honors are forced upon him by the importunate credulity of his companions, and opportunity becomes so tempting as to resolve itself into a kind of law. He is not simply persuaded to pretend, he is persuaded, himself, to believe: first, as it were, to see how it feels; then, on finding that it feels very comfortable, because retreat is awkward and the fascination irresistible. All this implies a good deal of complexity of character, for there are prophets and prophets. Mr. Taylor's is neither a fierce monomaniac nor a clever charlatan, but a mysterious mixture of the two. The author's intention here, and, indeed, throughout the book, has a great deal of psychological subtlety, though unfortunately it is rather unskillfully served by his execution. He has chosen a theme which belongs to the province of Mr. Browning, and to which Mr. Browning alone of living writers could have rendered minute justice. This, however, is but half Mr. Taylor's idea; the remainder is equally analytic. David Starr is at once an imposter and a dupe, at once hammer and anvil; and after dealing various blows for his own ends, he receives several crushing ones for others. In Nimrod Kraft, the high-priest of David's undefined creed, Mr. Taylor represents the profane and worldly element which rarely fails to cling to the skirts of a great enthusiasm, and get what is vulgarly called a lift on its own journey.

Nimrod is a shrewd politician and a more powerful engine in the long run than David, whom he "works," as it were, deliberately and scientifically, as he would a vein of metal. David's revelation, which has acquired, with mysterious facility it must be confessed, a great following, is maliciously led into aggression and sedition, and incurs the displeasure of a certain Colonel Hyde, sheriff of the county, who, after various animadversions, shoots the prophet and breaks into the temple. There is a general scramble, in the midst of which Nimrod Kraft snatches the ark from the altar and rushes off to become the theocratic millionnaire of Salt Lake City. Upon this the curtain descends, for Mr. Taylor is right in suspecting that even the hungriest appetite for "national" subjects would find a poetization of that enterprise a rather tough morsel to swallow. This is the rough outline of a story which Mr. Taylor has been careful to supply with a due proportion of detail; but it is true of the details as of the outline, that they are better in idea than in the use he makes of them. The prophet has a wife who has loved and trusted him in the days of his obscurity, and who, loving him still, is sadly puzzled to adapt her faith to his new pretensions. This figure of Rhoda is the best in the drama, and the poor woman's situation is certainly pathetic: her mingled devotion and bewilderment, her vague sense of something evil in the whole matter, the purity of her own instincts, and her final submission to polygamy. Mr. Taylor has not balked at the peculiar institution of Mormonism; he has only tried to explain it rationally, as he, after a fashion, explains the other steps in the scheme. How far his explanation tallies with traditional fact we are unable to say; but it helps along the drama, which is decidedly in need of it. A certain Livia Romney, a so-called "woman of the world," makes her appearance, becomes the Egeria of the new Pompilius, and, with a certain grotesque analogy with the abbreviated fox who wished his comrades to put him in the fashion by the sacrifice of their tails, brings about the plurality of wives in order to legitimate her own connection. Livia is not as good as Rhoda; but Mr. Taylor is right in feeling that the imagination demands that the prophet shall have some ardent female associate. It is a happy conception of the author that Rhoda, with a woman's characteristic preference of the near kindness to the remote, has ministered to the delusion she deprecates. The best passage in the volume is the one in which her husband learns from her that if it was an angel who supplied him with food when he had gone forth to fast in the wilderness, it was a strictly human angel.

> When morning came,
> And lapped in faint indifference to life
> I lay, the barren rock before mine eyes
> Was as a table, spread by angel hands!
> He gave me food; I ate and I was saved.
> As well refuse the food he offers now,
> And let faith, starving, die!

RHODA, *eagerly.*

> Who saved you then
> May save again! 'Tis naught to offer food;
> But I obeyed a voice this moment clear,
> And charged, I feel, with all the Lord's high will
> In woman manifest. I pray you, take,
> Even from my hands which then were hid from you,
> Now, openly, my evidence from Him!

DAVID.

> What double sense is in your words? I hear,
> Not comprehending.

RHODA.

> How could I refrain?
> Two days had passed: I dared not interrupt
> Your solitude of soul, and prayers that fed
> Upon the life of your forgotten frame;
> But, guided near you, O, thank Him for that!
> I left the food.

DAVID.

> You? You?

RHODA.

> As was His will.
> What ails you, David?

(Aside.)

> He is deadly pale;
> There's something fierce and strange within his eyes:
> He frightens me.

DAVID.
You brought me food?
RHODA.

                                         I did.

DAVID.
What else? What more have you in secret done?
Who taught you so to counterfeit the Lord?
Woman! To burrow underneath my feet,
And make a hollowness where rock should be!
How dared you cheat me?
RHODA.

                      Slay me with your hand,
Not with such face and words. If I but saved
(You say it saved you), how could love refrain?
I have obeyed, believed all else in you,
As I believe and worship still: forgive!
            (*She falls on her knees before him.*)
DAVID.
Not unto me, your husband, David, man;
But if I be a prophet of the Lord,
Yes, *if!* It seems to you a little thing:
Rise up: I cannot answer now: the house
Rocks to and fro, the temple's pinnacles
Dance in the air like devil's shuttlecocks:
There's nothing stable. Rise, I say again!
            (*She rises to her feet.*)
Now take your seat and sew. I've heard it said
Women think better when the hand's employed.
If 't is so, think.
            (*He moves toward the door.*)
RHODA.

        David!

DAVID.
            I go to pray.
RHODA.
Come back! He's gone. O God, what have I done?

These lines represent Mr. Taylor at his best, and we are
unable to gainsay the reader's inference that a work in which
they are strikingly prominent is, as a general thing, rather wanting
in relief. Mr. Taylor writes with such extreme good-will, and

235

gives so little positive offence, that it seems ungrateful to criticise him; but it is impossible to deny that "The Prophet" does not take hold of the imagination. It is the reverse of vulgar in conception, it is careful in execution, it has a dozen commendable qualities, and we have seen better books which in some respects might take example by it. But it wants style, it lacks heat, it misses the nameless something which Sir Joshua Reynolds, in the anecdote, indicated by a snap of his fingers. The people are shadows, and the whole manner is prosaic. This is partly because of a want of warmth in the author's imagination, but partly also, we think, because a defect inherent in his plan makes it impossible (and would still make it impossible in other circumstances) that the reader's own imagination should kindle. If his book has no atmosphere, the fault is not only Mr. Taylor's but his subject's. It is very well to wish to poetize common things, but here as much as ever, more than ever, one must choose. There are things inherently vulgar, things to which no varnish will give a gloss, and on which the fancy contents only grudgingly to rest her eyes. Mormonism is one of these; an attempt to import Joseph Smith into romance, even very much diluted and arranged, must in the nature of things fall flat. The reason why is the reason the rhymist didn't like Doctor Fell. His associations are fatal to him and to all his companions. Mr. Taylor's Livia Romney is a capital example of this. He bravely sets her down in the *dramatis personæ* as a "woman of the world"; but we see her in our mind's eye, we hear her accent, we know her phraseology, and we guess in what world she flourished. There would be much to say on this matter of vulgarity and distinction; and if Mr. Taylor's volume lacks the prime requisite of success, it may at least be called a suggestive failure.

NERO: AN HISTORICAL PLAY
BY W. W. STORY*

MR. Story here offers us another proof of his remarkable versatility and facility. This would be a clever production for any one, but it is especially clever for a man who has found so much besides to do with his imagination. And yet, after all, this long drama is the work of a man who has made a specialty of the picturesque; if Mr. Story were not a distinguished sculptor, we should say it was the work of a painter. It is the picture in his subject that has most taken his fancy, and if a poet is always made up of a painter and a moralist, it is quite the painter that is predominant here. The history of Nero is certainly a subject to fix the attention of a dramatist, overcharged as it is with tragic incident—horror outstripping horror, and deepening, as it does, to an extraordinarily dramatic catastrophe. If, too, the dramatist has lived long in Rome, and has formed the habit of peopling mentally the old scenes with the old figures, and seeing imperial ghosts in the sunny stillness of the Palatine, it is easy to conceive that the figures of Nero and Agrippina, of Poppæa and Tigellinus, may have come to haunt and importune him. Mr. Story has breathed for many a year that densely-weighted Roman air; he has read and re-read his Tacitus and his Suetonius; he has lingered often among the portentous Roman busts in the Vatican and the Capitol, and at last the images of writer and sculptor have become vividly real to him, and he has reproduced them with conviction and energy. He has crowded his stage, laid his hand upon every incident and detail that seemed characteristic, and painted a goodly picture. He has painted a picture, in fact, rather than written a play; and indeed we think that, to the dramatist's second thought, there was no play here to write. The subject, especially as Mr. Story presents it, is too complete a monotony of horror. There is little contrast, little complexity or development, though indeed there is a constant progression— the progression from bad to worse, from one atrocity to another.

* Nero: an Historical Play. By W. W. Story (Edinburgh and London: Blackwood & Sons. 1875). (The Nation, November 25, 1875).

But it is all bad and all hideous, and there is no dramatic pivot, as it were, on which the story may turn and show its diverse faces. If Mr. Browning, for instance, had written the play, we should have probably had certain scenes in which Nero would have been made to show us not only the fine fellow (this indeed Mr. Story in some degree represents) but the altogether high-toned and superior gentleman which the pedantic young butcher presumably considered himself to be. Mr. Story has attempted contrast in some of the accompanying figures—in Octavia, Poppæa, and Seneca—in Poppæa very happily; but we think that the dramatic instinct of Racine was the true one when he decided that, in his 'Britannicus,' a single episode of Nero's history was an available subject, but not the whole career. In that master-piece of the formal and harmonious style there is a certain mixture of elements—a struggle, a conflict. We see the young man passing from good to bad and back again, and the interest of the drama lies in our curiosity as to which side the catastrophe will deposit him on.

Mr. Story has given us rather a panorama of the whole reign—a rolling chronicle. His play is Tacitus and Suetonius piece by piece, in verse and dialogue. He has great precedent for this in Shakspere's dramatizations of Plutarch. 'Antony and Cleopatra' is apparently none the worse play because it takes everything that Plutarch gives it. Of course it takes a great many things besides, and so also does Mr. Story in his 'Nero.' He has not been afraid of giving himself a great deal to do, and he moves easily and gracefully among his multitudinous figures. He has desired to be as complete as, in such a case, poetry can be, and in one or two instances he has not shrunk from a formidable realism. He has gone as far as Tacitus beckoned. He has repre-sented Agrippina, in one scene, striving to regain her lost dominion over her son by the exercise of those charms which she had found potent in cases of an altogether different kind—a scene such as, to the best of our knowledge, no modern dramatist has attempted, and which must look for its mate among the early audacities of the Elizabethans. In his picture of Nero he has been forcible and abundant in color rather than especially sub-tle—as Nero, compounded of numerous elements, and with his strange jumble of brutality and æsthetics, of the ferocious and the maudlin, might have offered the poet a chance to be. But Mr. Story has wished simply, we take it, to give an effective picture of prodigious, grotesque, fantastic vanity and cruelty, gorging themselves, as it were, upon impurity, and his picture is decidedly effective. Even more so is the portrait of Agrippina—a dramatic interpretation of one of those formidable imperial female busts, the hard, superb great Roman lady, low-browed, inexorable, and insatiable. Mr. Story's phrase is easily vivid and picturesque—it is naturally that of an artist; but we think it is sometimes too diffuse, and that the whole work would have gained by compression and by occasional cancellings on a final revision. The dramatic point is sometimes diluted. For instance, when Nero makes the unsuccessful attempt to put an end to his mother's life by the disaster to her galley off Baiæ, he is shown us waiting on shore for news of the result of his plot. The galley has gone to pieces, but the empress has been rescued. A messenger arrives with this information, and relates that he has seen Agrippina:

"To you, great Cæsar, her first thought was given.
'Go. Agerinus, go,' she said, 'and bear
This message to my son—His mother lives;
But bid him calm his fears.—I am not hurt,' " etc.

It would have been much better here, surely, that the message should have simply been, "His mother lives." It would, in the situation, have been more eloquent and portentous. The lines which follow weaken the effect.

HONEST JOHN VANE: A STORY BY J. W. DE FOREST*

Mr. De Forest, who has written several entertaining novels, offers us in this volume a political satire. His tale was published more than a year ago, we believe, in the *Atlantic Monthly,* and

* *Honest John Vane.* A Story. By J. W. Forest, author of, 'Kate Beaumont,' 'The Wethered Affair,' etc. (New Haven: Richmond & Palten, 1875). (*The Nation,* December 31, 1874).

he has judged it worthy after this considerable interval of being resuscitated. Mr. De Forest is capable of writing a story which holds the attention, but we should not have said, from our acquaintance with his works, that he possessed the cunning hand of a satirist. We have heard him called an American Charles Reade, and, *mutatis mutandis,* the analogy might stand. We know that when Mr. Charles Reade shows up a public abuse, his irony does not suffer from being drawn too fine, nor his moral go a-begging for want of being vigorously pointed. Mr. De Forest's colors are laid on not exactly with a camel's-hair pencil, and he has the drawback of pleading for political purity with a phraseology which is decidedly turbid. "The lobby proved to be every way more imposing and potent than he had imagined it. True, some of its representatives were men whom it was easy for him to snub—men of unwholesome skins, greasy garments, brutish manners, filthy minds, and sickening conversation; men who so reeked and drizzled with henbane tobacco and cockatrice whiskey that a moderate drinker or sucker would recoil from them as from a cesspool; men whose stupid, shameless boastings of their trickeries were enough to warn away from them all but the very elect of Satan." This is painting black black with a good will, and the most heedless reader will know whither he is being led. His hero's "pulpy pink face," the author tells us, when the wages of sin seem falling due for this recreant functionary, "wore an air of abiding perplexity which rivalled that of his Dundrearyish friend Ironman. At times it seemed as if its large watery features would decompose entirely with irresolution, and come to resemble a strawberry-ice which has been exposed to too high a temperature." The work contains an unclean and unscrupulous lobbyist, Darius Dorman by name, of whom it is told us, in like manner, that he "started up and paced the room briskly for some seconds, meanwhile tightly grasping his dried-up blackened claws across his coat-skirts, perhaps to keep his long tail from wagging too conspicuously inside his trousers—that is, supposing he possessed such an unearthly embellishment." The author's touch, in this and similar cases, has more energy than delicacy, and even the energy aims rather wildly. Did Mr. De

Forest refresh his memory of Swift before writing the adventures of John Vane? He would have been reminded that though that great master of political satire is often coarse and ferocious, he is still oftener keenly ingenious.

'Honest John Vane,' however, may pass as a tract for popular distribution, and the important thing with tracts is that they be printed in big letters and be adapted for a plain man's comprehension. Mr. De Forest's cause is so good and his temper apparently so fervid that, as matters stand with us, it will be no harm if they make their way even at the cost of a good deal of loose writing and coarse imagery. The work records the career of a (presumably) Republican Representative in Congress from the town of Slowburgh, and traces his progress from primitive integrity to corruption inevitable for an irresponsible barbarian. As a portrait of one of our average "self-made men" and usual legislators, the picture has a good deal of force, and will renew the familiar blush in the cheek of the contemplative citizen of this unwieldy Republic. John Vane, who has begun life as a country joiner, and risen to local eminence as a manufacturer of refrigerators, is a large, bland, cautious, and unsophisticated personage, whose benevolent visage and pastoral simplicity have earned him his honorable sobriquet. His intellectual culture is limited to the arts of writing and ciphering, but he is a promising national legislator, from the caucus point of view, and his election to Congress is triumphantly carried. He marries the showy and belated daughter of the mistress of a students' boarding-house, and repairs to Washington to breast the mingled political and social tide. Of how little use to him, under direct pressure, his uninstructed, mechanical, empirical probity turns out to be, and of how he goes into the great Sub-Fluvial Tunnel swindle and becomes shrewder in his turpitude than he ever was in his virtue, the volume offers a sufficiently lively recital. The most artistic stroke it contains is the history of his successful hocus-pocussing of the committee of investigation, and his ignobly triumphant evasion of disgrace. Mr. De Forest did well not to sacrifice to the vulgar need for a dénouement, but to leave his hero's subsequent career to the irritated conscience of the reader.

He is a national legislator at this hour, with his precious out-fit and his still more precious experience, and of this interesting circumstance the tale is a pertinent reminder. Otherwise, there is little "story" in the book; the dramatic element expires before it has really tried its paces, and the narrative becomes chargeable with a certain flatness. Several characteristic political types are sketched, coarsely from the artistic point of view, but wholesomely, it may appear, from the moral. In Darius Dorman, the "smutty" wire-puller, as Mr. De Forest is fond of calling him, the author has tried his hand at the grotesque and fantastic; but if he recalls Hawthorne, it is not altogether to his own advantage. We might repeat, however, that, *par le temps qui court*, his flag should be suffered to cover his cargo, if it were not for some such final reflection as this. Whether accidentally or intentionally we hardly know, 'Honest John Vane' exhales a penetrating aroma of what in plain English one must call vulgarity. Every note the author strikes reverberates with a peculiarly vulgar tone; vulgarity pervades the suggestions, the atmosphere of his volume. This result has doubtless been in a great measure designed; he has wished to overwhelm the reader with the evil odor of lobbyism. But the reader, duly overwhelmed, and laying down the volume with a sense of having been in irredeemably low company, may be excused for wondering whether, if this were a logical symbol of American civilization, it would not be well to let that phenomenon be submerged in the tide of corruption.

WE AND OUR NEIGHBORS: RECORDS OF AN UNFASHIONABLE STREET BY HARRIET BEECHER STOWE*

It would be rather awkward to attempt to tell what Mrs. Stowe's novel is about. There is a young woman married to an editor of "three papers—a monthly magazine for the grown

---

* *We and Our Neighbors*: Records of an Unfashionable Street. By Harriet Beecher Stowe (New York: J. B. Ford & Co. 1875). (*The Nation*, June 22, 1875).

folk, another for the children, and a weekly paper." This well-occupied personage, in a moment of easily conceivable bewilderment, invites an Englishman to dinner on washing-day, and this is how his wife, who is introduced to us as a model of the womanly graces, informs her cook of the circumstances (the lady, by the way, was one of the Van Arsdels, conspicuous among the first families of New York): "Mr. Henderson has invited an English gentleman to dinner, and a whole parcel of folks with him. . . . It's just sweet of you to take things so patiently, when I know you are feeling so bad, but the way it comes about is this." Mr. Henderson's dinner is one of the principal events of the book, and Mrs. Stowe's second manner, as we may call it, comes out strongly in the description of it. It proved a greater success than was to have been hoped—thanks to the accommodating disposition of the British guest. "Mr. Selby proved one of that delightful class of English travellers who travel in America to see and enter into its peculiar and individual life, and not to show up its points of difference from old-world social standards. He seemed to take the sense of a little family dinner, got up on short notice, in which the stereotyped doctrine of courses was steadfastly ignored, where there was no soup or fish, and only a good substantial course of meat and vegetables, with a slight dessert of fruit and confectionery. . . . A real high-class English gentleman," under these circumstances, the author goes on to remark (not oppressed, that is, by a sense of repletion), ". . . makes himself frisky and gamesome to a degree that would astonish the solemn divinities of insular decorum." In this exhilaration "soon Eva and he were all over the house, while she eloquently explained to him the working of the furnace, the position of the water-pipes, and the various comforts and conveniences which they had introduced into their little territories." They—who? The water-pipes? The phrase is ambiguous, but it is to be supposed that this real high-class English gentleman understood everything; for—" 'I've got a little box of my own out at Kentish Town,' Mr. Selby said, in a return burst of confidence, 'and I shall tell my wife about some of your contrivances.' " It should be added in fairness that the conversation was not all in this dangerously familiar key, for we are presently informed that Eva "introduced the humanitarian questions of the day."

There are a great many other people, of whose identity we have no very confident impression, inasmuch as they never do anything but talk—and that chiefly about plumbing, carpet-laying, and other cognate topics. We cannot perhaps give chapter and verse for the discussion of these particular points, but the reader remains in an atmosphere of dense back-stairs detail which makes him feel as if he were reading an interminable file of tradesmen's bills. There is in particular a Mrs. Wouvermans, an aunt of the Eva just commemorated, who pervades the volume like a keeper of an intelligence office, or a female canvasser for sewing-machines. This lady, we know, is intended to be very unpleasant, but would it not have been possible to vary a little, for the relief of the reader, the form of her importunity? She also belongs to one of the first families of New York, and this is a specimen of her conversational English. She is talking about the Ritualists and their processions: "I'd process 'em out in quick time. If I were he (the Bishop) I'd have all that sort of trumpery cleaned out at once." But none of Mrs. Stowe's ladies and gentlemen open their mouths without uttering some amazing vulgarism, and if we were to believe her report of the matter, the language used by good society in New York is a singular amalgam of the rural Yankee dialect (so happily reproduced by Mrs. Stowe in some of her tales), the jargon of the Southern negroes, and the style of the paragraphs in the *Home Journal* about such-and-such a lady's "German." "Never mind, I'll get track of them," says the exemplary Eva, alluding to the ghosts which her husband jestingly assures her she will find in the house of certain opposite neighbors; "and if there's a ghost's chamber I'll be into it!" Hereupon (she has never called at the house in question before) she throws over her head "a little morsel of white fleecy worsted, darts across the street, and kisses her hand to her husband on the door-step." What would those personages whom she somewhere calls "the ambitious lady leaders of our time" say to that?

EIGHT COUSINS: OR THE AUNT-HILL
BY LOUISA M. ALCOTT*

IT is sometimes affirmed by the observant foreigner, on visiting these shores, and indeed by the venturesome native, when experience has given him the power of invidious comparison, that American children are without a certain charm usually possessed by the youngsters of the Old World. The little girls are apt to be pert and shrill, the little boys to be aggressive and knowing; both the girls and boys are accused of lacking, or of having lost, the sweet, shy bloom of ideal infancy. If this is so, the philosophic mind desires to know the reason of it, and when in the course of its enquiry the philosophic mind encounters the tales of Miss Alcott, we think it will feel a momentary impulse to cry Eureka! Miss Alcott is the novelist of children—the Thackeray, the Trollope, of the nursery and the school-room. She deals with the social questions of the child-world, and, like Thackeray and Trollope, she is a satirist. She is extremely clever, and, we believe, vastly popular with infant readers. In this, her latest volume, she gives us an account of a little girl named Rose, who has seven boisterous boy-cousins, several grotesque aunts, and a big burly uncle, an honest seaman, addicted to riding a tilt at the shams of life. He finds his little niece encompassed with a great many of these, and Miss Alcott's tale is chiefly devoted to relating how he plucked them successively away. We find it hard to describe our impression of it without appearing to do injustice to the author's motives. It is evidently written in very good faith, but it strikes us as a very ill-chosen sort of entertainment to set before children. It is unfortunate not only in its details, but in its general tone, in the constant ring of the style. The smart satirical tone is the last one in the world to be used in describing to children their elders and betters and the social mysteries that surround them. Miss Alcott seems to have a private understanding with the youngsters she depicts, at the expense of their pastors and

* *Eight Cousins: or, The Aunt-Hill.* By Louisa M. Alcott. Boston: Roberts Bros. 1875. (*The Nation,* October 14, 1875).

masters; and her idea of friendliness to the infant generation seems to be, at the same time, to initiate them into the humorous view of them taken by their elders when the children are out of the room. In this last point Miss Alcott does not perhaps go so far as some of her fellow-chroniclers of the nursery (in whom the tendency may be called nothing less than depraved), but she goes too far, in our opinion, for childish simplicity or paternal equanimity. All this is both poor entertainment and poor instruction. What children want is the objective, as the philosophers say; it is good for them to feel that the people and things around them that appeal to their respect are beautiful and powerful specimens of what they seem to be. Miss Alcott's heroine is evidently a very subjective little girl, and certainly her history will deepen the subjective tendency in the little girls who read it. She "observes in a pensive tone" that her health is considered bad. She charms her uncle by telling him, when he intimates that she may be vain, that "she don't think she is repulsive." She is sure, when she has left the room, that people are talking about her; when her birthday arrives she "feels delicate about mentioning it." Her conversation is salted with the feminine humor of the period. When she falls from her horse, she announces that "her feelings are hurt, but her bones are all safe." She certainly reads the magazines, and perhaps even writes for them. Her uncle Alec, with his crusade against the conventionalities, is like a young lady's hero of the "Rochester" school astray in the nursery. When he comes to see his niece he descends from her room by the water-spout; why not by a rope-ladder at once? When her aunts give her medicine, he surreptitiously replaces the pills with pellets of brownbread, and Miss Alcott winks at the juvenile reader at the thought of how the aunts are being humbugged. Very likely many children are overdosed; but this is a poor matter to tell children stories about. When the little girl makes a long, pert, snubbing speech to one of her aunts, who has been enquiring into her studies, and this poor lady has been driven from the room, he is so tickled by what would be vulgarly called her "cheek" that he dances a polka with her in jubilation. This episode has quite spoiled, for our fancy, both the uncle and the niece. What have become of the "Rollo" books of our infancy and the delightful "Franconia" tales? If they are out of print, we strongly urge that they be republished, as an antidote to this unhappy amalgam of the novel and the story-book. These charming tales had, relatively speaking, an almost Homeric simplicity and "objectivity." The aunts in "Rollo" were all wise and comfortable, and the nephews and nieces were never put under the necessity of teaching them their place. The child-world was not a world of questions, but of things, and though the things were common and accessible to all children, they seemed to have the glow of fairy-land upon them. But in 'Eight Cousins' there is no glow and no fairies; it is all prose, and to our sense rather vulgar prose.

IDOLATRY BY JULIAN HAWTHORNE*

It has been more than once remarked that, on the whole, the penalties attached to bearing an eminent name are equal to the privileges. To be the son of a man of genius is at the best to be born to a heritage of invidious comparisons, and the case is not bettered if one attempts to follow directly in the paternal footsteps. One's name gets one an easy hearing, but it by no means guarantees one a genial verdict; indeed, the kinder the general sentiment has been toward the parent, the more disposed it seems to deal out rigid justice to the son. The standard by which one is measured is uncomfortably obtrusive; one is expected *ex officio* to do well, and one finally wonders whether there is not a certain felicity in having so indirect a tenure of the public ear that the report of one's experiments may, if need be, pass unnoticed. These familiar reflections are suggested by the novel lately published by Mr. Julian Hawthorne, a writer whose involuntary responsibilities are perhaps of an exceptionally trying kind. The author of The

* (*Atlantic Monthly*, December, 1874).

Scarlet Letter and Twice-Told Tales was a genius of an almost morbid delicacy, and the rough presumption would be that the old wine would hardly bear transfusion into new bottles; that, the original mold being broken, this fine spirit had better be left to evaporate. Mr. Julian Hawthorne is already known (in England, we believe, very favorably) as author of a tale called Bressant. In his own country his novel drew forth few compliments, but in truth it seemed to us to deserve neither such very explicit praise nor such unsparing reprobation. It was an odd book, and it is difficult to speak either well or ill of it without seeming to say more than one intends. Few books of the kind, perhaps, that have been so valueless in performance have been so suggestive by the way; few have contrived to impart an air of promise to such an extraordinary tissue of incongruities. The sum of Bressant's crimes was, perhaps, that it was ludicrously young, but there were several good things in it in spite of this grave error. There was force and spirit, and the suggestion of a perhaps obtrusively individual temper, and various signs of a robust faculty of expression, and, in especial, an idea. The idea—an attempted apprehension, namely, of the conflict between the love in which the spirit, and the love in which sense is uppermost—was an interesting one, and gave the tale, with all its crudities, a rather striking appearance of gravity. Its gravity was not agreeable, however, and the general impression of the book, apart from its faults of taste and execution, was decidedly sinister. Judged simply as an attempt, nevertheless, it did no dishonor to hereditary tradition; it was a glance toward those dusky psychological realms from which the author of The Scarlet Letter evoked his fantastic shadows.

After a due interval, Mr. Hawthorne has made another experiment, and here it is, rather than as applied to Bressant, that our remarks on the perils of transmitted talent are in place. Idolatry, oddly enough, reminds the perspicacious reader of the late Mr. Hawthorne's manner more forcibly than its predecessor, and the author seems less to be working off his likeness to his father than working into it. Mr. Julian Hawthorne is very far from having his father's perfection of style, but even in style the analogy is observable. "Suppose two sinners of our daylight world," he writes, "to meet for the first time, mutually unknown, on a night like this. Invisible, only audible, how might they plunge profound into most naked intimacy, read aloud to each other the secrets of their deepest hearts! Would the confession lighten their souls, or make them twice as heavy as before? Then, the next morning, they might meet and pass, unrecognizing and unrecognized. But would the knot binding them to each other be any the less real, because neither knew to whom he was tied? Some day, in the midst of friends, in the brightest glare of the sunshine, the tone of a voice would strike them pale and cold." And elsewhere: "He had been accustomed to look at himself as at a third person, in whose faults or successes he was alike interested; but although his present mental attitude might have moved him to smile, he, in fact, felt no such impulse. The hue of his deed had permeated all possible forms of himself, thus barring him from any stand-point whence to see its humorous aspect. The sun would not shine on it!" Both the two ideas, here, and the expression, will seem to the reader like old friends; they are of the family of those arabesques and grotesques of thought, as we may call them, with which the fancy that produced the Twice-Told Tales loved so well to play. Further in the story, the author shows us his hero walking forth from the passionate commission of a great crime (he has just thrown a man overboard from the Boston and New York steamer), and beginning to tingle with the consciousness of guilt. He is addressed caressingly by a young girl who is leaning into the street from a window, and it immediately occurs to him that (never having had the same fortune before) her invitation has some mysterious relation to his own lapse from virtue. This is, generically, just such an incident as plays up into every page of the late Mr. Hawthorne's romances, although it must be added that in the case of particular identity the touch of the author of The House of the Seven Gables would have had a fineness which is wanting here. We have no desire to push the analogy too far, and many readers will perhaps feel that to allude to it at all is to give Mr. Julian Hawthorne the benefit of one's good-will on too easy terms. He resembles his father in having a great deal of imagination and in exerting it in ingenious and capricious forms: but, in fact, the mold, as might have been feared, is so loose and rough that it often seems to offer us but a broad burlesque of Mr. Hawthorne's exquisite fantasies. To relate in a few words the substance of Idolatry would require a good deal of ingenuity; it would require a good deal on our own part, in especial, to glaze over our imperfect comprehension of the mysteries of the plot. It is a purely fantastic tale, and deals with a hero, Balder Helwyse by name, whose walking costume, in the streets of Boston, consists of a black velveteen jacket and tights, high boots, a telescope, and a satchel; and of a heroine, by name Gnulemah, the fashion of whose garments is yet more singular, and who has spent her twenty years in the pre-cincts of an Egyptian temple on the Hudson River. This is a singular couple, but there are stranger things still in the vol-ume, and we mean no irony whatsoever when we say they must be read at first-hand to be appreciated. Mr. Hawthorne has proposed to himself to write a prodigiously strange story, and he has thoroughly succeeded. He is probably perfectly aware that it is a very easy story to give a comical account of, and serenely prepared to be assured on all sides that such people, such places, and such doings are preposterously impossible. This, in fact, is no criticism of his book, which, save at a certain number of points, where he deals rather too profusely in local color, pursues its mysterious aim on a line quite distinct from reality. It is indiscreet, artistically, in a work in which enchanted rings and Egyptian temples and avenging thunderbolts play so prominent a part, to bring us face to face with the Tremont House, the Beacon Hill Bank in School Street, the Empire State steamboat, and the "sumptuous residence in Brooklyn"—fatal combination!—of Mrs. Glyphic's second husband. We do not in the least object, for amusement's sake, to Dr. Glyphic's minia-ture Egypt on the North River; but we should prefer to ap-proach it through the air, as it were, and not by a conveyance which literally figures in a time-table. Mr. Hawthorne's story is purely imaginative, and this fact, which by some readers may be made its reproach, is, to our sense, its chief recommendation. An author, if he feels it in him, has a perfect right to write a fairy-tale. Of course he is bound to make it entertaining, and if he can also make it mean something more than it seems to mean on the surface, he doubly justifies himself. It must be confessed that when one is confronted with a fairy-tale as bulky as the volume before us, one puts forward in self-defense a few vague reflections. Such a production may seem on occasion a sort of *reductio ad absurdum* of the exaggerated modern fashion of romancing. One wonders whether pure fiction is not running away with the human mind, and operating as a kind of leakage in the evolution of thought. If one decides, as we, for our part, have decided, that though there is certainly a terrible number too many novels written, yet the novel itself is an excellent thing, and a possible vehicle of an infinite amount of wisdom, one will find no fault with a romance for being frankly romantic, and only demand of it, as one does of any other book, that it be good of its kind. In fact, as matters stand just now, the presumption seems to us to be rather in favor of something finely audacious in the line of fiction. Let a novelist of the proper temperament shoot high by all means, we should say, and see what he brings down. Mr. Hawthorne shoots very high indeed, and bags some strangely feathered game; but, to be perfectly frank, we have been more impressed with his length of range than with his good luck. Idolatry, we take it, is an allegory, and the fantastic fable but the gayly figured vestment of a poised and rounded moral. We are haunted as we read by an uncomfortable sense of allegorical intention; episodes and details are so many exact correspondences to the complexities of a moral theme, and the author, as he goes, is constantly drawing an incidental lesson in a light, fantastic way, and tracing capricious symbolisms and analogies. If the value of these, it must be said, is a measure of the value of the central idea, those who, like ourselves, have failed to read between the lines have not suffered an irreparable loss. We have not, really, the smallest idea of what Idolatry is about. Who is the idol and who is the idolizer? What is the enchanted ring and what the fiddle of Manetho? What is the latent propriety of Mr. MacGentle's singular attributes, and what is shadowed forth in the blindness of Gnulemah? What does Salome stand for, and what does the hoopoe symbolize? We give it up, after due reflection; but we give it up with a certain kindness for the author, disappointing as he is. He is disappointing because his second novel is on the whole more juvenile than his first, and he makes us wonder whether he has condemned himself to perpetual immaturity. But he has a talent which it would be a great pity to see come to nothing. On the side of the imagination he is distinctly the son of his illustrious father. He has a vast amount of fancy; though we must add that it is more considerable in quantity than in quality, and finer, as we may say, than any use he makes of it. He has a commendable tendency to large imaginative conceptions, of which there are several noticeable specimens in the present volume. The whole figure of Balder Helwyse, in spite of its crudities of execution, is a handsome piece of fantasy, and there is something finely audacious in his interview with Manetho in the perfect darkness, in its catastrophe, and in the general circumstances of his meeting with Gnulemah. Gunlemah's antecedents and mental attitude are a matter which it required much ingenuity to conceive and much courage to attempt to render. Mr. Hawthorne writes, moreover, with a conscience of his own, and his tale has evidently been, from his own point of view, elaborately and carefully worked out. Above all, he writes, even when he writes ill, with remarkable vigor and energy; he has what is vulgarly called "go," and his book is pervaded by a grateful suggestion of high animal spirits. He is that excellent thing, a story-teller with a temperament. A temperament, however, if it is a good basis, is not much more, and Mr. Hawthorne has a hundred faults of taste to unlearn. Our advice to him would be not to mistrust his active imagination, but religiously to respect it, and, using the term properly, to cultivate it. He has vigor and resolution; let him now supply himself with culture—a great deal of it.

GARTH BY JULIAN HAWTHORNE*

It is difficult to know how to speak of Mr. Julian Hawthorne, and it may certainly be said that this hesitation and
perplexity are a practical compliment. They prove, at least, that
he is not commonplace. He is not, indeed; and, in addition to
this negative merit, the work before us may lay claim to several
positive ones in a much higher degree than its predecessors.
'Garth' strikes us as a decided improvement upon 'Bressant'
and 'Idolatry'; it is a very much riper and wiser work. We
must add that we use these terms in a strictly relative sense;
for Mr. Hawthorne's standing fault seems to be a certain incurable immaturity and crudity. Even about 'Garth' there is something strangely sophomorical. What we spoke of just now as
puzzling is the fact that, in spite of this unripe tone, Mr. Hawthorne continues to remind us of a genius as finished and mellow
as his illustrious father's. His imagination belongs to the same
family as that which produced the 'House of the Seven Gables';
and the resemblance is singular, considering the marked tendency of talent in the second generation to "react" rather than
to move on in the same line. Mr. Julian Hawthorne, who is
doubtless weary of being contrasted with his father, has not
the latter's profundity or delicacy; but he looks at things in
the same way—from the imagination, and not from observation—and he is equally fond of symbolisms and fanciful analogies.
He has a merit, indeed, which his father lacked; though it
must be added that the presence of the quality is not always a
virtue or its absence always a defect. There is a kind of positive masculinity in 'Garth,' a frank indication of pleasure in
the exercise of the senses, which makes the book contrast agreeably with that type of fiction, much of it pervaded, as it were,
by the rustle of petticoats, in which the imagination is as dry as a
squeezed sponge. 'Garth' is a very long story, and we have not
the space to recite its various entanglements. Like many of Na-

* *Garth*. By Julian Hawthorne. (New York: D. Appleton & Co., 1877).
(*The Nation,* June 21, 1877).

thaniel Hawthorne's tales, it is the history of a house—an old human dwelling which serves as the central figure of the story. A house, in being founded and erected, has involved bloodshed and wrong, and its future inhabitants have had to expiate these things in perplexity and suffering. Such, briefly expressed, is the idea of Mr. Julian Hawthorne's novel. It is a very pretty, picturesque idea, but it is not what we should call a "strong" subject and strikes us as not necessarily involving any very direct portraiture of reality. Such portraiture the author has not given us; what he has given us is a bit of picturesque romance, lodged in a New England village, which remains gracefully vague and unobtrusive. He deserves credit for what he has attempted in the figure of his hero; for it is kinder to speak of Garth Urmson as an attempt than as success. The attempt, however, was difficult, inasmuch as the author's design was to represent a hero with a strongly brutal side which should be, potentially, as disagreeable as his normal side was noble and beautiful. Mr. Julian Hawthorne's taste is constantly at fault, and he has thrown too much misdirected gusto into the portrayal of young Urmson's scowlings and snortings, his ferocity, his taciturnity, and his bad manners. It was an odd idea, too, to have made him an artist; we confess to having here quite lost the thread of Mr. Hawthorne's intention. Garth begins by thinking that art is "irreverent" and that he must therefore leave it alone; but he gets over this and takes up the brushes, which he handles with great success in the attic of the village house above mentioned. The author has evidently meant him for a pugilistic young Puritan who mistrusts æsthetics; but he has indicated the contradiction too much and described the struggle too little. We remain under the impression that Garth harnessed the family horse better than he painted pictures. He is surrounded by a great many figures which will not strike the usual reader as "natural," but which are all ingenious and touched by a certain imaginative coloring. Mr. Hawthorne cares for types, evidently, and he has suggested various types with a good deal of fanciful truth. His greatest success, perhaps, is with Golightly Urmson, the wicked uncle of the hero, who represents plausible rascality as against innocent and unvarnished virility.

Mr. Hawthorne, as we said just now, has something indefinably immature and provincial in his tone; but he has two or three merits which make us believe that with the lapse of time he will do things much better than 'Garth.' He has an imagination —a rare gift. With Mr. Hawthorne it is unmistakable; he sees everything in the imaginative light, and his fancy sports and experiments with a warranted confidence in its strength. He has also a literary ideal, and this long and complicated story of 'Garth' has evidently been composed with a great deal of care, reflection, and artistic intention. The author's great fault, we should say, is a want of observation. The absence of observation in these pages amounts, indeed, to a positive quality. Why should Mr. Sam Kineo, the fashionable young sharper who is represented as having passed muster in the most "fashionable circles" of Europe, always express himself in the English of a newsboy or a bootblack? But the manners and customs of Mr. Julian Hawthorne's *dramatis personæ* are throughout very surprising. The graceful heroine, for instance, while on a visit to the house of the interesting hero, is invited to clean out the cellar!

SAXON STUDIES BY JULIAN HAWTHORNE*

Mr. Hawthorne is decidedly disappointing. He strikes us as having inherited a certain portion of his father's genius. He writes with vigor and vivacity, and his style has a charm of its own; but he perpetually suggests more than he performs, and leaves the reader waiting for something that never comes. There is something masculine and out of the common way in his manner of going to work, but the use he makes of his talent is not characterized by a high degree of wisdom, and the reader's last impression is of a strange immaturity of thought. 'Saxon Studies'

* *Saxon Studies*. By Julian Hawthorne. J. R. Osgood & Co. 1876. (*The Nation*, March 30, 1876).

is such a book as a very young man might write in a season of combined ill-humor and conscious cleverness; but it is a book which most young men would very soon afterwards be sorry to have written. We suspect that this intelligent compunction will never be Mr. Hawthorne's portion, and the feeling makes us judge his volume with a certain harshness. The author fairly convinces us that he is not likely ever to understand why the tone in which he has chosen to talk about the worthy inhabitants of Dresden is not a rational, or a profitable, or a philosophic, or a really amusing one. Mr. Hawthorne spins his thread out of his own fancy, and at the touch of reality it would very soon snap. He had a perfect right, of course, to produce a fanciful book about Dresden; but such a book, as it gives our imagination some trouble, is more than usually bound to justify itself. It must have a graceful, agreeable, and pliable spirit to reward us for the extra steps we take. But Mr. Hawthorne has quite violated this canon and has been fanciful only to be acrimonious, and reflective only to be—it is not too strong a word—unwholesome. He has written a *brooding* book, with all the defects and none of the charms of the type. His reveries are ill-natured, and his ingenuity is all vituperative.

He declares, in an amusing preface, that "his interest in Saxony and the Saxons is of the most moderate kind—certainly not enough to provoke a treatise upon them. They are as dull and featureless a race as exists in this century, and the less one has to do with them, the better. But the plan of his work requiring some concrete nucleus round which to group such thoughts and fancies as he wished to ventilate, and the Saxon capital chancing to have been his residence of late years, he has used it rather than any other place to serve his turn in this respect." This strikes us as an explanation after the fact. In so far as 'Saxon Studies' had a "plan," we suspect it consisted of the simple desire on the author's part to pour forth his aversion to a city in which, for several years, he had not been able to guard himself against being regrettably irritable and uncomfortable. Dresden has served his turn, and enabled him to write his book; he ought at least in fairness to admit that there was something to say about her. But in truth, of what there was to say about her, even for ill, Mr. Hawthorne strikes us as having made but little. Of "plan" his volume contains less than the pardonable minimum; it has little coherency and little definiteness of statement. It is taken for granted in the first few pages, in an off-hand, allusive manner, that the Saxons are an ignoble and abominable race, and this note is struck at desultory intervals, in the course of a good deal of light, rambling talk about nothing in particular, through the rest of the volume; but the promise is never justified, the aversion is never explained, the story is never told. Before we know it we have Mr. Hawthorne talking, as of a notorious fact, about "the cold, profound selfishness which forms the foundation and framework of the national and individual character in every walk of life, the wretched chill of which must ultimately annul the warmth of the most fervent German eulogist," etc. This is a sweeping but an interesting charge, and the reader would have been glad to have the author go a little into the psychology of the matter, or at least into the history of his opinion—offer a few anecdotes, a few examples of Saxon selfishness, help us to know more exactly what he means. But Mr. Hawthorne is always sweeping and always vague. We can recall but two definite statements in his volume—that bearing upon the fact that the Germans, indoors, are pitifully ignorant of the charms of pure air, and the other upon the even more regrettable circumstance that they condemn their women to an infinite amount of hard labor. Here is an example of some of the reflections provoked in Mr. Hawthorne by the first-mentioned of these facts: "As might be imagined, such lung-food as this gets the native complexion into no enviable state; in fact, until I had examined for myself the mixture of paste and blotches which here passes for faces, I had not conceived what were the capacities for evil of the human skin. I have heard it said—inconsiderately—that the best side of the Saxon was his outside; that the more deeply one penetrated into him, the more offensive he became. But I think the worst damnation that the owner of one of these complexions could be afficted with would be the correspondence of his interior with his exterior man."

In spite of Mr. Hawthorne's six years' residence in Dresden, his judgments appear to be formed only upon those matters which limit the horizon of a six weeks' sojourner—the tramways, the cabmen, the policemen, the beer-saloons. When he invites us to penetrate into a Dresden house, we find he means only to gossip rather invidiously about the parties, and to talk about the way the doors open and the rooms are disturbed. The most successful pages in his volume are an extremely clever and amusing supposititious report, from a local newspaper, of the appearance of the first street-car, and a charming sketch of a beer-maiden, or waitress in a saloon, who invites the author and his friend to be her partners at a ball. These are the only cases we can recall in which Mr. Hawthorne's humor is not acrid and stingy. For the rest, he gives us no report of his social observations proper, of his impressions of private manners and morals; no examples of sentiments, opinions, conversations, ways of living and thinking. Upon those other valuable sources of one's knowledge of a foreign country—the theatre, literature, the press, the arts—Mr. Hawthorne is entirely dumb. The only literary allusion that his volume contains is the observation that the relation of Schiller and Goethe to the Germans of the present day may be described as sublimity reflected in mud-puddles. The absence of those influences to which we have alluded makes 'Saxon Studies' seem unduly trivial and even rather puerile. It gives us the feeling that the author has nursed his dislikes and irritations in a dark closet, that he has never put them forth into the open air, never discussed and compared and intelligently verified them. This—and not at all the fact that they *are* dislikes —is the weak point of Mr. Hawthorne's volume. He had a perfect right to detest the Saxons, and our strictures are made not in the least in defence of this eminent people, but simply in that of good literature. We are extremely sorry, indeed, that so lively an aversion should not have been better served in expression. Even if Mr. Hawthorne had made the Saxon vices much more vivid, and his irritation much more intelligible, we should still find fault with his spirit. It is the spirit which sees the very small things and ignores the large ones—which gives more to fancy than to observation, and more to resentment than to reflection.

CHARLES NORDHOFF'S COMMUNISTIC
SOCIETIES*

MR. NORDHOFF offers us here a copious volume on a subject deserving of liberal treatment. His researches have been minute and exhaustive, and he makes a very lucid and often an entertaining exposition of their results. He writes in a friendly spirit and tends rather, on the whole, to dip his pen into rose-color; but he professes to take the rigidly economical and not the sentimental view; and certainly the Rappists and the Shakers, the Perfectionists and the Bethel people, make their accounts balance with an exactness very delightful to a practical mind. It would have been possible, we think, for an acute moralist to travel over the same ground as Mr. Nordhoff and to present in consequence a rather duskier picture of human life at Amana, Mount Lebanon, and Oneida; but his work for our actual needs would doubtless have been less useful. Mr. Nordhoff, too, has not neglected the moral side of his topic, and much of the information he gives us has an extreme psychological interest. His purpose, however, was to investigate communistic life from the point of view of an adversary to trades-unions, and to see whether in the United States, with their vast area for free experiments in this line, it might not offer a better promise to workingmen than mere coalitions to increase wages and shorten the hours of labor. Such experiments would be worth examining if they did nothing more for the workingman than change the prospect ahead of him into something better than a simple perpetuity of hire—a prospect at the best depressing and irritating. "Hitherto," says Mr. Nordhoff, "very little, indeed almost nothing definite and precise, has been made known concerning these societies; and Communism remains loudly but very vaguely spoken of, by friends as well as enemies, and is commonly either a word of terror or contempt in the public prints . . . . I desired to discover how

* The Communistic Societies of the United States from Personal Visit and Observation, etc. By Charles Nordhoff. With illustrations. New York: Harper & Brothers. 1875. (The Nation, January 14, 1875).

the successful Communists had met and overcome the difficulties of idleness, selfishness, and unthrift in individuals, which are commonly believed to make Communism impossible . . . . I wished to see what they had made of their lives; what was the effect of communal living upon the character of the individual man and woman; whether the life had broadened or narrowed them, and whether assured fortune and pecuniary independence had brought to them a desire for beauty of surroundings and broader intelligence; whether, in brief, the Communist had any-where become more than a comfortable and independent day-laborer, and aspired to something higher than a mere bread-and-butter existence." As to some of these points, the author must have been satisfied at an early stage of his researches: beauty of surroundings and breadth of intelligence were nowhere striking features of communistic life. This life was everywhere, save at a very few points, nakedly practical; and at these excep-tional points, as in the case of the "spiritualism" of the Shakers, their celibacy, in a measure, as well, and in that of the inter-changeableness of husbands and wives in the Oneida Community, the ideal element is singularly grotesque and unlovely. The Shakers and the Perfectionists have certainly not been broadened; whether they have been narrowed or not is a different question. Mr. Nordhoff inclines to believe not, and he constantly reminds us that, in judging the people he describes, we must be careful that we do not compare them with a high ideal. They are for the most part common, uneducated, unaspiring, and the ques-tion is whether they are not, for the most part, more complete and independent than if they had struggled along in individual ob-scurity and toil. They are certainly more prosperous and more comfortable, and if their ignorance has often hardened into queer, stiff, sterile dogmas, the sacrifice of intelligence has not been considerable. Even the Shakers have, indeed, a sort of angular poetry of their own, and the human creature for whom it was a possibility to become a Shaker doubtless wears in that garb a grace which would otherwise have been wanting.

Mr. Nordhoff's field was extensive, stretching as it does from Maine to Oregon, and southward down to Kentucky. It contains some eight distinct communistic societies, but these are composed of a large number of subdivisions; the Shakers alone having no less than fifty-eight settlements. Mr. Nordhoff begins with the Amana Society, whose present abode, or cluster of abodes, is in the State of Iowa. Like most of its fellows, with the exception of the Perfectionists and Shakers this commune is of German origin. It established itself in this country in 1842; it contains something less than fifteen hundred members; it possesses twenty-five thousand acres of land; it has a rigidly religious character; it allows marriage, but keeps the sexes as much as possible apart, and thinks rather poorly of women. It supports itself by farming and by the manufacture of woollen stuffs; "lives well after the hearty German fashion, and bakes excellent bread"; has, indeed, at some seasons of the year five meals a day; keeps its affairs in very prosperous order, and finds an eager market for its produce of all kinds. Religion here, as in most of the communities, is of a strictly ascetic sort; they seem generally to find it needful to be girded up by some tight doctrinal bond. "Inspiration" is the *cheval de bataille* at Amana; the ministers, male and female, are called "instruments"; "the hymns are printed as prose, only the verses being separated." This congregation seems to have produced upon the author a strong impression of easy thrift, of the "well-to-do." Even better in this respect are the Rappists or Harmonists at Economy, near Pittsburgh. "Passing Liverpool, you come to Freedom, Jethro (whose houses are both lighted and heated with gas from a natural spring near by), Industry, and Beaver." You must feel yourself to be on the native soil of social experimentalism, and have a sort of sense of living in a scornfully conservative parody or burlesque. The experiment of Father Rapp, however, who came to America in 1803, and to this region in 1825, has been a solid, palpable success. The Harmonists, who number one hundred and ten persons, hold property to the amount of between two and three million of dollars. Mr. Nordhoff makes a point of the importance, in communistic ventures, of a strong-headed, strong-handed leader; and this, indeed, with a very definite religious tendency seems essential to success. The Harmonists had both; and Father Rapp, the Moses who led them out their house of bondage (the kingdom of Würtemberg), seems to have been a man of excellent sense and energy. He died in 1847, and, though he has had successors, the society is resting on its gains, making few recruits, and awaiting, in a sort of eventide tranquility and security, the second coming of Christ. The Rappists are celibates; and that the institution has been successful with them may be inferred from Mr. Nordhoff's remark that he has "been assured by older members of the society, who have, as they say, often heard the period described by those who were actors in it, that this determination to refrain from marriage and from married life originated among the younger members."

One is struck, throughout Mr. Nordhoff's book, with the existence in human nature of lurking and unsuspected strata, as it were, of asceticism, of the capacity for taking a grim satisfaction in dreariness. One would have been curious to have a little personal observation of these "younger members" who were so in love with the idea of single blessedness. "The joys of the celibate life," says one of the author's Shaker informants, "are far greater than I can make you know: They are indescribable." The Shakers, on this point, go further than the Catholic monks and nuns, who profess merely to find celibacy holy, and salutary to the spirit—not positively agreeable in itself. Mr. Nordhoff found in a Shaker Community near Rochester several French Canadians of the Catholic faith, and in another in Ohio several more Catholics, one of whom was a Spaniard and an ex-priest. A French Canadian Shaker strikes one as the most amusing imbroglio of qualities conceivable until one encounters the Spanish priest. One wonders how ineffable *they* deemed the joys of celibacy. At the village of Zoar, in Ohio, the author found a community of three hundred persons, of German origin, calling themselves "Separatists," owning seven thousand acres of very fertile land," together with other property, representing more than a million of dollars. "The Zoar Communists belong to the peasant class of Southern Germany. They are, therefore, unintellectual, and they have not risen in culture beyond their original condition . . . . The Zoarists have achieved comfort—according to the German peasant's notion—and wealth. They are relieved from severe toil, and have driven the wolf permanently from their doors. More they might have accomplished; but they have not been taught the need of more. They are sober, quiet, and orderly, very industrious, economical, and the amount of ingenuity and business skill they have developed is quite remarkable. Comparing Zoar and Aurora with Economy, I saw the extreme importance and value in such an experiment of leaders with ideas at least a step higher than those of their people." The Zoarites disapprove of marriage, but they permit it, which seems rather an oddity. "Complete virginity," say their articles of faith, "is more commendable than marriage." It is also, of course, more economical, and, though the Communistic creeds generally do not say this, it is pretty generally what they mean. At Bethel and Aurora, however, two German Communes of four hundred members apiece, in Missouri and Oregon respectively, Mr. Nordhoff found marriage not discountenanced, and affairs in general fairly prosperous. Of Dr. Keil, a Prussian, the head of the society at Aurora, Mr. Nordhoff gives an interesting account. He had been a man-milliner in his own country, but his present character, in spite of these rather frivolous antecedents, is a very vigorous and sturdy one. Mr. Nordhoff stands with him beside the graves of his five children—all of whom he had lost between the ages of eighteen and twenty-one. "After a minute's silence he turned upon me with sombre eyes and said: 'To bear all that comes upon us in silence, in quiet, without noise, or outcry, or excitement, or useless repining—that is to be a man, and that we can only do with God's help.'" Mr. Nordhoff gives further some account of several smaller and more struggling Communes —the Icarians, a French society in Iowa; a Swedish settlement, at Bishop Hill, in Illinois; a cluster of seven hopeful Russians (one of them a "hygienic doctor") at Cedar Vale, in Kansas; and, lastly, of an experiment in Virginia, embodying as "full members" two women, one man, and three boys. The three boys have a great responsibility on their shoulders; we hope they are duly sensible of it. There is also a sketch of some colonies— notably that of Mr. E. V. Bossière, of Bordeaux, in Kansas—not strictly communistic. Mr. Nordhoff thinks, with regard to this last settlement, that its members sacrifice too many of the advantages of private life without securing in a sufficient degree those of association.

The volume is largely occupied with a very complete and exhaustive report on the various Shaker settlements. Everything is told here about Shakerism that one could possibly desire to know. There are in the country eighteen societies, with something less than twenty-five hundred members, and possessing some fifty thousand acres of land. The Shakers seem to us by far the most perfect and consistent communists, and Mr. Nordhoff's account of them is very interesting. He explains everything indeed in the matter but one—how twenty-five hundred people, that is, can be found to embrace a life of such organized and theorized aridity. But to comprehend this one must reflect not only on what people take but on what they leave, and remember that there are in America many domestic circles in which, as compared with the dreariness of private life, the dreariness of Shakerism seems like boisterous gaiety. "It was announced," Mr. Nordhoff quotes from a Shaker record, "that the holy prophet Elisha was deputized to visit the Zion of God on earth. The time at length arrived. The people were grave, and concerned about their spiritual standing. Two female instruments from Canterbury, N. H., were at length ushered into the sanctuary. Their eyes were closed, and their faces moved in semi-gyrations. . . . One or two instances occurred in which a superhuman agency was indubitably obvious. One of the abnormal males lay in a building at some distance from the infirmary where the female instruments were confined." These few lines strike the note of Shaker civilization; and it requires no great penetration to perceive that it cannot be a very rich civilization. It proceeds, indeed, almost entirely by negatives. "The beautiful, as you call it," said Elder Frederick to Mr. Nordhoff, "is absurd and abnormal. It has no business with us." And he proceeded to relate how he had once been in a rich man's house in New York, where he had seen heavy picture-frames hung against the walls as "receptacles of dust." The great source of prosperity with the Shakers has evidently been their rigid, scientific economy, carried into minute details, and never contravened by the multiplication of children or non-producing members. Mr. Nordhoff says that they do not toil severely (this is his testimony as to most of the communes); but they work steadily, unremittingly, and, above all, carefully,

264

and they spend nothing on luxury or pleasure. The author emphasizes strongly the excellent quality of their work and their produce (this, too, is a general rule), and the high esteem in which they are held as neighbors and fellow-citizens. They "avoid all speculative and hazardous enterprises. They are content with small gains, and in an old-fashioned way study rather to moderate their outlays than to increase their profits . . . . Their surplus capital they invest in land, or in the best securities, such as United States bonds." There is a kind of wholesome conservatism in the Shaker philosophy, as Mr. Nordhoff depicts it, which we confess rather takes our fancy. It is grotesque and perverted in many ways, but at its best points it is both the source and the fruit of a considerable personal self-respect. Mr. Nordhoff gives a number of long extracts from the publications of the Shakers expository of their religious views, from which it appears that they are "spiritualists" in the current sense of the term. But their manifestations and miracles strike us as rather feeble and third-rate. They ought to come up to town occasionally, and take a few lessons at some of the more enterprising repositories of the faith. They have, however, a sacrament of confession to their elders of evil thoughts and deeds which seems to us respectable from their own point of view. It is rigidly enforced, apparently, as far as is possible, and it is a testimony to their sense of the value of discipline. The more accomplished "spiritualists," we are afraid, don't confess. We think of the Shakers as sitting in their more brilliant moods "with their faces moving in semi-gyrations"; but we regret nevertheless to learn that their number is decidedly not increasing. That they do not continue to make recruits is perhaps a sign that family life among Americans at large is becoming more entertaining.

The most interesting, or at least the most curious, section of Mr. Nordhoff's book is his report on the Oneida Perfectionists:

> "We have built us a dome
>   On our beautiful plantation,
> And we have all one home,
>   *And one family relation.*"

If the lines we quoted just now gave the key-note of culture among the Shakers, this charming stanza gives the key-note of culture among the ladies and gentlemen at Oneida. The line we have italicized seems to us to have a delightful naiveté, shadowing forth as it does the fact that these ladies and gentlemen are all interchangeably each other's husbands and wives. But Mr. Nordhoff chronicles many other facts besides this; as that the ladies wear short hair, and jackets and trowsers; that the community numbers nearly three hundred persons; that it is worth half a million of dollars; that it has "faith-cures"; and that it assembles of an evening in the parlor and devotes itself to "criticism" of a selected member. It is on a very prosperous footing, and it has in Mr. J. H. Noyes a very skilful and (as we suppose it would say) "magnetic" leader. Propagation is carefully limited, and there are, as may be imagined, many applications for admission. "If I should add," says Mr. Nordhoff, "that the predominant impression made upon me was that it was a commonplace company, I might give offence." Very likely; and the term is not one we should select. Such a phenomenon as the Oneida Community suggests many more reflections than we have space for. Its industrial results are doubtless excellent; but morally and socially it strikes us as simply hideous. To appreciate our intention in so qualifying it the reader should glance at the account given by Mr. Nordhoff of the "criticism" he heard offered upon the young man Henry. In what was apparent here, and still more in what was implied, there seem to us to be fathomless depths of barbarism. The whole scene, and all that it rested on, is an attempt to organize and glorify the detestable tendency toward the complete effacement of privacy in life and thought everywhere so rampant with us nowadays. For "perfectionists" this is sadly amiss. But it is the worst fact chronicled in Mr. Nordhoff's volume, which, for the rest, seems to establish fairly that, under certain conditions and with strictly rational hopes, communism in America may be a paying experiment.

CARLYLE'S TRANSLATION OF GOETHE'S
WILHELM MEISTER*

THIS new edition of Goethe's great novel will give many
persons the opportunity of reading a work which, although
introduced to the English public forty years ago, is yet known
to us chiefly by hearsay. We esteem it a matter for gratitude
that it should now invite some share of attention as a novelty,
if on no other ground; and we gladly take advantage of the occasion thus afforded to express our sense of its worth. We hope this
republication may help to discredit the very general impression
that *Wilhelm Meister* belongs to the class of the great unreada-
bles. The sooner this impression is effaced, the better for those
who labor under it. Something will have been gained, at least,
if on experiment it should pass from a mere prejudice into a
responsible conviction; and a great deal more will have been
gained, if it is completely reversed.

To read *Wilhelm Meister* for the first time is an enviable
and almost a unique sensation. Few other books, to use an expression which Goethe's admirers will understand, so steadily and
gradually *dawn* upon the intelligence. In few other works is so
profound a meaning enveloped in so common a form. The slow,
irresistable action of this latent significance is an almost awful
phenomenon, and one which we may vainly seek in those imaginative works in which the form of the narrative bears a direct,
and not, as it appears here to do, an inverse, relation to its final
import; or in which the manner appeals from the outset to the
reader's sympathy. Whatever may be the lesson which Goethe
proposes to teach us, however profound or however sublime, his
means invariably remain homely and prosaic. In no book is the
intention of elegance, the principle of selection, less apparent.
He introduces us to the shabbiest company, in order to enrich
us with knowledge; he leads us to the fairest goals by the longest

---

* *Wilhelm Meister's Apprenticeship and Travels. From the German of
Goethe.* By Thomas Carlyle. In two volumes. Boston: Ticknor and Fields.
1865. pp. 399, 388. (*The North American Review,* July, 1865).

and roughest roads. It is to this fact, doubtless, that the work owes its reputation of tediousness; but it justifies the reputation only when, behind the offensive detail, the patient reader fails to discover, not a glittering, but a steadily shining generality. Frequently the reader is unable to find any justification for certain wearisome *minutiæ*; and, indeed, many of the incidents are so "flat," that the reader who comes to his task with a vague inherited sense of Goethe's greatness is constrained, for very pity, to supply them with a hidden meaning. It would not, therefore, be difficult to demonstrate that the great worth of *Wilhelm Meister* is a vast and hollow delusion, upheld by a host of interested dupes. The book is, indeed, so destitute of the quality of cleverness, that it would be comparatively easy for a clever man to make out any given case whatsoever against it; do anything with it, in short, except understand it. The man who is only clever may do much; but he may not do this. It is perhaps one of the most valuable properties of *Wilhelm Meister* that it does not react against this kind of manipulation. We gladly admit, nay, we assert, that, unless seriously read, the book must be inexpressibly dull. It was written, not to entertain, but to edify. It has no factitious qualities, as we may call them; none of those innumerable little arts and graces by which the modern novel continually and tacitly deprecates criticism. It stands on its own bottom, and freely takes for granted that the reader cannot but be interested. It exhibits, indeed, a sublime indifference to the reader,—the indifference of humanity in the aggregate to the individual observer. The author, calmly and steadily guided by his purpose, has none of that preoccupation of *success* which so detracts from the grandeur of most writers at the present day, and leads us at times to decide sweepingly that all our contemporaries are of the second class.

Of plot there is in this book properly none. We have Goethe's own assertion that the work contains no central point. It contains, however, a central figure, that of the hero. By him, through him, the tale is unfolded. It consists of the various adventures of a burgher youth, who sets out on his journey through life in quest, to speak generally, of happiness,—that happiness which, as he is never weary of repeating, can be found only in the subject's perfect harmony with himself. This is certainly a noble idea. Whatever pernicious conclusions may be begotten upon it, let us freely admit that at the outset, in its virginity, it is beautiful. Meister conceives that he can best satisfy his nature by connecting himself with the theatre, the home, as he believes, potentially at least, of all noble aims and lessons. The history of this connection, which is given at great length, is to our mind the most interesting part of the whole work; and for these reasons: that those occasional discussions by which the action is so frequently retarded or advanced (as you choose to consider it), and of which, in spite of their frequency, we would not forfeit a single one, are here more directly suggestive than in subsequent chapters; and that the characters are more positive. The "Apprenticeship" is, in the first half, more of a story, or, to state it scientifically, more dramatic than in the last. If Goethe is great as a critic, he is at least equally great as a poet; and if *Wilhelm Meister* contains pages of disquisition which cannot be too deeply studied, it likewise contains men and women who cannot be forgotten. Meister's companions bear no comparison with the ingenious puppets produced by the great turning-lathe of our modern fancy.

There is the same difference between them and the figures of last month's successful novel, as there is between a portrait by Velasquez and a photograph by Brady. Which of these creations will live longest in your memory? Goethe's persons are not lifelike; that is the mark of our fashionable photographic heroes and heroines: they are life itself. It was a solid criticism of certain modern works of art, that we recently heard applied to a particular novelist: "He tells you everything except the very thing you want to know." We know concerning Philena, Aurelia, Theresa, Serlo, and Werner none of those things of which the clever story-teller of the present day would have made hot haste to inform us; we know neither their costume, nor their stature, nor the indispensable color of their eyes; and yet, for all that, they *live*,—and assuredly a figure cannot do more than that.

The women in *Wilhelm Meister* are, to our mind, truer even than the men. The three female names above mentioned stand for three persons, which abide in our memory with so unquestioned a right of presence that it is hard to believe that we have not actually known them. Is there in the whole range of fiction a more natural representation of a light-hearted coquette than that of the actress Philena,—she who, at the outset of an excursion into the country, proposes that a law be passed prohibiting the discussion of inanimate objects? Where, too, is there as perfect an example of an irretrievable sentimentalist as her comrade Aurelia, she who, as herself declares, bears hard upon all things, as all things bear hard upon her, and who literally dies for the sake of poetic consistency? What an air of solid truth, again, invests the practical, sensible, reasonable Theresa!

Wilhelm's purpose being exclusively one of self-culture, he is an untiring observer. He listens to every man, woman, and child, for he knows that from each something may be learned. As a character, he is vague and shadowy, and the results of his experience are generally left to the reader's inference. Indeed, as his lessons are mostly gathered from conversations for which he furnishes the original motive, the reader may place himself in the hero's position of an eminently respectful auditor, and judge of the latter's impressions by his own.

Although incidentally dramatic, therefore, it will be seen that, as a whole, *Wilhelm Meister* is anything but a novel, as we have grown to understand the word. As a whole, it has, in fact, no very definite character; and, were we not vaguely convinced that its greatness as a work of art resides in this very absence of form, we should say that, as a work of art, it is lamentably defective. A modern novelist, taking the same subject in hand, would restrict himself to showing the sensations of his hero during the process of education; that is, his hero would be the broad end, and the aggregate of circumstances the narrow end, of the glass through which we were invited to look; and we should so have a comedy or a tragedy, as the case might be. But Goethe, taking a single individual as a pretext for looking into the world, becomes so absorbed in the spectacle before him, that, while still clinging to his hero as a pretext, he quite forgets him as a subject. It may be here objected, that the true artist never forgets either himself or anything else. However that may be, each reader becomes his own Wilhelm Meister, an apprentice, a traveller, on his own account; and as his understanding is large or small, will Wilhelm and the whole work be real or the contrary. It is, indeed, to the understanding exclusively, and never, except in the episode of Mignon, to the imagination, that the author appeals. For what, as we read on, strikes us as his dominant quality? His love of the real. "It will astonish many persons," says a French critic, "to learn that Goethe was a great scorner of what we call the ideal. Reality, religiously studied, was always his muse and his inspiration."

The bearing of *Wilhelm Meister* is eminently practical. It might almost be called a treatise on moral economy—a work intended to show how the experience of life may least be wasted, and best be turned to account. This fact gives it a seriousness which is almost sublime. To Goethe, nothing was vague, nothing trivial,—we had almost said, nothing false. Was there ever a book so dispassionate, or, as some persons prefer to call it, cold-blooded? In reading it, we learn the meaning of the traditional phrase about the author's calmness. This calmness seems nearly identical with the extraordinary activity of his mind, as they must both indeed have been the result of a deep sense of intellectual power. It is hard to say which is the truer, that his mind is without haste or without rest. In the pages before us there is not a ray of humor, and hardly a flash of wit; or if they exist, they are lost in the luminous atmosphere of justice which fills the book. These things imply some degree of passion; and Goethe's plan was *non flere, non indignari, sed intelligere.*

We do not know that in what we have said there is much to lead those who are strangers to this work to apply themselves to the perusal of it. We are well aware that our remarks are lamentably disproportionate to the importance of our subject. To attempt to throw a general light upon it in the limits here prescribed would be like striking a match to show off the *Trans-figuration.* We would therefore explicitly recommend its perusal to all such persons, especially young persons, as feel that it behooves them to attach a meaning to life. Even if it settles nothing in their minds, it will be a most valuable experience to have read it. It is worth reading, if only to differ with it. If it is a priceless book to love, it is almost as important a one to hate; and whether there is more in it of truth or of error, it is at all events *great*. Is not this by itself sufficient? *Wilhelm Meister* may not have much else that other books have, but it has this, that it is the product of a great mind. There are scores of good books written every day; but this one is a specimen of the grand manner.

MR. FROUDE'S SHORT STUDIES*

MR. FROUDE'S two volumes, here reprinted in one, consist of a series of articles contributed to magazines and journals or delivered as lectures. They are collected probably rather in deference to a prevailing fashion than because they have been thought especially valuable. Valuable they are not in any high degree. The subjects treated are historical and theological. The historical papers are written in the popular manner and addressed to the popular judgment, which is but another way of saying that they are very superficial. The articles on religious subjects, "The Philosophy of Catholicism," "Criticism and the Bible History," "The Book of Job," are vitiated by a feeble sentimentalism which deprives them of half their worth as liberal discussions. Mr. Froude appears, therefore, to decidedly better advantage in his "History of England" than in these short essays. Here the faults which in the larger work are in a great degree concealed and redeemed by its distinguished merits—the energy of spirit, the industry of execution, the dignity of tone, the high pictorial style—are strangely obtrusive. What these faults are—what, at least, we hold them to be—may be gathered from our remarks.

Mr. Froude's volume opens with a lecture on the science of history, a very loose piece of writing for one who has made the study of history the business of his life. "One lesson, and

* "Short Studies on Great Subjects. By James Anthony Froude." New York: Charles Scribner & Co. 1868. (*The Nation*, October 31, 1867).

one only," says Mr. Froude, "history may be said to repeat with distinctness, that the world is built somehow on moral foundations; that in the long run it is well with the good; in the long run it is ill with the wicked." If this is all that history teaches, we had better cease to trouble ourselves about it. But it is hard to see how Mr. Froude is competent to make this assertion, and wherein his " long run" differs from those great cycles, defying human measurement, in which he affirms history must be organized if it is organized at all. If there is one thing that history does not teach, it seems to us, it is just this very lesson. What strikes an attentive student of the past is the indifference of events to man's moral worth or worthlessness. What strikes him, indeed, is the vast difficulty there is in deciding upon men's goodness and their turpitude. It is almost impossible to pronounce an individual whom we know only by written testimony positively good or positively bad without bodily detaching him from his *entourage* in a way that is fatal to the truth of history. In history it is impossible to view individuals singly, and this point constitutes the chief greatness of the study. We are compelled to look at them in connection with their antecedents, their ancestors, their contemporaries, their circumstances. To judge them morally we are obliged to push our enquiry through a concatenation of causes and effects in which, from their delicate nature, enquiry very soon becomes impracticable, and thus we are reduced to talking sentiment. Nothing is more surprising than the alertness with which writers like Mr. Froude are ready to pronounce upon the moral character of historical persons, and their readiness to make vague moral epithets stand in lieu of real psychological facts. All readers of history—or of histories, rather—know how this process has been followed *ad nauseam* touching the all-important figure of Martin Luther. There is every evidence to show that Luther must have been one of the most serious men of his age—the man of all men with his thoughts most strongly centred on an outward object. But in the hands of writers of Mr. Froude's school he is smothered to death under a mass of vague moral attributes—bravery, honesty, veracity, tenderness, etc.—as under a heap of feathers.

The lecture on "The Science of History" is followed by

three lectures on "The Times of Luther and Erasmus," and then by another on "The Influence of the Reformation on the Scottish Character." Here is a sentence from the last: "It had been arranged that the little Mary Stuart should marry our English Edward VI., and the difficulty was to be settled so. They would have been contented, they said, if Scotland had had the 'lad' and England the 'lass.' As it stood, they broke their bargain and married the little queen away into France to prevent the Protector Somerset from getting hold of her." There is something in the style of this short passage which reminds us forcibly of Dickens's "Child's History of England," and of a dozen other works for the instruction of the young; and it is not too much to say that these lectures are written in a style not essentially different from that of the crude narrative we have mentioned. The following passage might have proceeded equally well from such a source, and it is a better illustration, inasmuch as not only the manner but the sentiment is puerile. Mr. Froude relates, of course, the famous visits of the devil to Luther during his confinement in the Wartburg castle. The devil came one night and made a noise in the room; Luther got up and lit his lamp and looked for him, but being unable to find him went back into bed. Whereupon Mr. Froude: "Think as you please about the cause of the noise, but remember that Luther had not the least doubt that he was alone in the room with the actual devil, who, if he could not overcome his soul, could at least twist his neck in a moment; *and then think what courage there must have been in a man who could deliberately sleep in such a presence!*" To such odd shifts as this are historians of the sentimental school reduced.

Nothing can be more unphilosophical than such a method of exhibiting the development of a great race and a great cause. When once Mr. Froude and his associates have placed themselves on the same side as a given individual, the latter is allowed to have neither foibles nor vices nor passions; and because he was a powerful instrument in the civilization of his age he is also assumed to have been a person of unsullied private virtue. Mr. Froude thinks it necessary to enter upon an elaborate apology for Luther's marriage—an act for which no apology is needed—and in doing so he deprives his hero of the very best reason he could plead. "The marriage," he says, "was unquestionably no affair of passion." If it was not, so much the worse for Luther. There is a want of logic on Mr. Froude's part in affirming that feeling and emotion entered so largely into Luther's attitude towards the corruptions of the Church and into his own purifying desires, and in yet denying him the benefit of this same element of feeling on an occasion which so perfectly justifies its interference, simply because it may compromise a thoroughly fanciful and modern notion of personal purity. Upon the "Dissolution of the Monasteries under Henry VIII.," and upon "England's Forgotten Worthies" Mr. Froude has two articles of greatly superior merit to those we have mentioned. There is no doubt that the English monasteries at the time of their suppression were the abode of a vast deal of dissipation and incontinence, and that the regular clergy had become extremely demoralized. It is unfortunate, however, that both in his history and in the essay before us our author should prefer to tell us of the dreadful things which, if he were disposed, he *might* tell us out and out, to laying the evidence directly before us. His answer, of course, would be, that the evidence is too bad to print. But such being the case, the only fair method of proceeding, it strikes us, is to effect a dispassionate logical synthesis of the material at hand, and not to content one's self with lifting one's hands and rolling up one's eyes. Bad as the monasteries may have been, moreover, it is certain that the manner in which Henry VIII. went to work to sift them out was in the last degree brutal and unmerciful. This Mr. Froude is totally unwilling to admit. He finds the greatest ingenuity at his service to palliate acts for which, in the annals of Catholic governments, he finds only the eloquence of condemnation. Henry VIII., in Mr. Froude's view, was a very good man; and Mr. Froude's good men can do no wrong. The account of "England's Forgotten Worthies" is, we think, the best article in the collection. It is a piece of pure narrative, and narrative is Mr. Froude's best point. The brave men who in Queen Elizabeth's time set the first great examples to English enterprise and to the grand English passion for voyage and adventure, have been made the theme of a great deal of fine writing and of a kind of psychological exercise which is essentially at variance with the true historical and critical spirit. But the theme is great and beautiful, and we can easily forgive Englishmen for growing somewhat maudlin over it.

HISTORICAL NOVELS:* THE HOUSEHOLD OF SIR THOMAS MORE; JACQUES BONNEVAL, OR THE DAYS OF THE DRAGONNADES BY THE AUTHOR OF MARY POWELL (ANNE MANNING)

THAT this species of composition still retains its hold on the popular taste may be inferred from the fact that two New York publishing houses have constituted themselves agents for the supply of the commodity. One of these houses offers a series of translations from the works of a prolific German authoress, which unveil to our democratic gaze the *vie intime* of a dozen monarchial courts, from that of Henry VIII. downward. The other deals in the historical tales of the author of "Mary Powell," a writer of extraordinary fecundity, of a most comprehensive range of information, and of a degree of "reconstructive" skill upon which Mr. Andrew Johnson may look with envy. We have not read the novels of Madame Mühlbach, and are unable to discuss their merits; but we have a sufficient acquaintance with those of the second-mentioned lady to warrant us in saying that they are neither so good nor so bad as they might easily be. We take it that they belong to the large class

---

* "The Household of Sir Thomas More. By the Author of 'Mary Powell.'" New York: M. W. Dodd. 1867.

"Jacques Bonneval; or, The Days of the Dragonnades. By the Author of 'Mary Powell.'" M. W. Dodd. 1867. (*The Nation*, August 15, 1867).

of works designed for the use of "young persons," and that if
their purpose is to be commended, their effect, on the whole,
and considering the abuse that is made of them, is rather to
be deplored. They attempt to give the reader an idea of a
given phase of the past in a degree less abstract than the manner of professed historians, and less rudely and dangerously
concrete than that of the original documents of which text-
books are composed. The result, of course, is somewhat anomalous. Histories are very long and dull; chronicles, memoirs, and
reports, besides being inaccessible, are far too heavily charged
with local colors. So the writer extracts the moral from the one
source, and expresses the story from the other, and shakes
them up together into a gentle and wholesome potion. The
common expedient is to rescue from oblivion a supposititious
diary or note-book, or collection of letters written in troublous
times by some one of the supernumeries of the play. The great
novelists, Scott, Bulwer, Victor Hugo, Dumas, boldly lay hands
on the principals (Elizabeth, Mary, Rienzi, Louis XI., Richelieu,
etc.) and compel them to serve their unscrupulous purposes.
But the author of "Mary Powell" wisely approaches the famous
persons through the medium of their relations and dependants.

Sir Thomas More, as we all remember, had a daughter, a
Mrs. Roper, of whom he was extremely fond, and who bore
him company during his imprisonment. Our authoress accordingly takes this lady for her heroine, and relates—*a grand renfort*
of capitals, italics, terminal e's, and other simple antiquarian-
isms—the history of her early days. The effect is sufficiently
pleasing, even if it is somewhat insipid, and it would seem
that if the shades of Sir Thomas and his daughter exhibit no
signs of offence, we disinterested moderns might allow the harmless device to pass without protest. A protest addressed to the
author, indeed, we have no desire to make; we take it rather
that the reader should here be put on his guard. Young girls
divide their reading, we believe, into two sharply distinguished
provinces—light and heavy; or, in other words, into novels and
histories. No harm can come to them from the most assiduous
perusal of our authoress so long as they read her books as
stories pure and simple. They will find some difficulty, doubt-

less, in doing so, but the sacrifice is no more than a just one to the long suffering historic muse. It requires some strength of mind on a young girl's part to persuade herself that a book with red edges, with archaic type, and with the various syntactical and orthographical quaintness which characterizes the volumes of which we speak—a book, in short, in which the heroine speaks familiarly of "dear old Erasmus"—does not possess some subtle and infallible authority with regard to the past. This, of course, is not the case. Such books embody a great deal of diligence and cleverness and fancy, but it is needless to say that history is quite a different matter. The reader who bears this in mind may spend a pleasant half-hour over the fortunes of Mrs. Mary Powell and her various companions.

If the books in question are extensively read, slight as are their merits, it is logical to suppose that people are still kindly disposed toward the real historical novel; and that if in these latter days it has had but few representatives, the fault is rather among writers than readers. The study of history has in recent times acquired an impetus which would greatly facilitate the composition of such works. We know very much more at present than we knew thirty years ago about manners in the Middle Ages and in antiquity. Novel-writing, too, has taken a corresponding start. For one novel that was published thirty years ago, there are a dozen published to-day. But, on the whole, the two streams have kept very distinct, and are, perhaps, not destined to be forced into confluence unless the second half of the century turns out a second Walter Scott. Both history and romance are so much more disinterested at the present moment than they were during Scott's lifetime, that it will take a strong hand to force either of them to look upon the other with the cold glance of the speculator. The great historians nowadays are Niebuhr and Mommsen, Guizot and Buckle, writers of a purely scientific turn of mind. The popular novelist is Mr. Anthony Trollope, than whom it is certainly difficult to conceive a less retrospective genius. It is hard to imagine minds of these dissimilar types uniting their forces; or, rather, it is hard to imagine a mind in which their distinctive elements and sympathies should be combined; in which a due appreciation of the multifold details of human life and of the innumerable sentiments and passions which lie in ceaseless fermentation on its surface, should coexist with the capacity for weighing evidence and for following the broad lines of progress through the almost irreclaimable chaos of political movements and counter-movements. Historians and story-tellers work each in a very different fashion. With the latter it is the subject, the cause, the impulse, the basis of fact that is given; over it spreads the unobstructed sky, with nothing to hinder the flight of fancy. With the former, it is the effect, the ultimate steps of the movement that are given; those steps by which individuals or parties rise above the heads of the multitude, come into evidence, and make themselves matters of history. At the outset, therefore, the historian has to point to these final manifestations of conduct, and say sternly to his fancy: So far thou shalt go, and no further. A vast fabric of impenetrable fact is stretched over his head. He works in the dark, with a contracted forehead and downcast eyes, on his hands and knees, as men work in coal-mines. But there is no sufficient reason that we can see why the novelist should not subject himself, as regards the treatment of his subject, to certain of the obligations of the historian; why he should not imprison his imagination, for the time, in a circle of incidents from which there is no arbitrary issue, and apply his ingenuity to the study of a problem to which there is but a single solution. The novelist who of all novelists was certainly the most of one—Balzac—may be said, to a certain extent, to have done this, and to have done it with excellent profit. At bottom, his incidents and character were as fictitious as those of Spenser's "Fairy Queen;" yet he was as averse from taking liberties with them as we are bound to conceive Mr. Motley, for instance, to be from taking liberties with the history of Holland. He looked upon French society in the nineteenth century as a great whole, the character of which would be falsified if he made light of a single detail or episode. Although, therefore (if we except his "Contes Drolatiques"), he wrote but a single tale of which the period lay beyond the memory of his own generation or that preceding it, he may yet in strictness be called a historical novelist, inasmuch as he was the historian of contemporary manners. In Balzac's day and in Balzac's country, there was a fixedness and sacredness about social custom and reputation which furnished his critics with a measure of his fidelity. This fixedness and sacredness are daily growing less, but they will always exist among civilized people in a sufficient degree for a novelist's purposes. The manners, the ideas, the tone of the *moment,* may always be seized by a genuine observer, even if the moment lasts but three months, and the writer who siezes them will possess an historical value for his descendants.

These remarks, however, will be thought to confer an undue extension upon the meaning of our term, and we hasten to restrict it to those works of fiction which deal exclusively with the past. Every one is familiar with the old distinction among historical tales into those in which actual persons are introduced, and those in which actual events are transacted by merely imaginary persons, as is the case, for instance, (if we are not mistaken), with Charles Dickens's "Tale of Two Cities," in which a very vivid impression is given of the French Revolution without the assistance of any of the known actors. Novels of the former class are certainly the more difficult to write (for a man of conscience, at least), and novels of either class are more difficult to write than works which require no preparation of mind, no research. But story-tellers are, for the most part, an illogical, loose-thinking, ill-informed race, and we cannot but believe that this same research and preparation constitute for such minds a very salutary training. It is, of course, not well for people of imagination to have the divine faculty constantly snubbed and cross questioned and held to account: but when once it is strong and lusty, it is very well that it should hold itself responsible to certain uncompromising realities. There are a number of general truths of human nature to which, of course, it professes itself constantly amenable; but in many cases this is not enough, and particular facts of history are useful in completing the discipline. When the imagination is sound, she will be certain to profit; and so, on the other hand, history will be likely to profit. We speak, of course, of a first-class imagination—as men occasionally have it, and as no woman (unless it be Mme. Sand) has yet had it; for when the faculty is weak, although the practice of writing historical tales may strengthen it, it will be almost certain to dilute or to pervert the truth of history. George Eliot's "Romola" is a very beautiful story, but it is quite worthless, to our mind, as a picture of life in the fifteenth century. On the other hand, Thackeray's "Esmond," although it may abound in those moral anachronisms which a historian proper may almost as little hope to avoid as an historical novelist, yet, on the whole, is almost as valuable as an historical picture as it is a work of sentiment. Of the two writers, one would hardly have said, *à priori*, that in an attempt of this kind the latter would have been more likely to succeed. He, doubtless, owes his success in a great measure to the fact that he did not venture too far from the shore. He, too, would have made poor work of the days of the Medici. In treating of Queen Anne's times, he only humored a natural predilection. At the present time men of literary tastes may be said to be born with historical sympathies and affinities, just as men are said to be born Platonists or Aristotelians. Some of us find an irresistible attraction in the Greeks, some in Feudalism, some in the Renaissance, some in the eighteenth century, some in southern and some in northern civilizations. To *humor* these sympathies, as we say, and still to respect them, may be an act fruitful in charming results. Let men of imagination go for their facts and researches to men of science and judgment, and let them consult the canons of historical truth established by the latter, and both parties can hardly fail to be the better for it. Proof of this has already been offered more than once in English letters. Mr. Charles Reade's "Cloister and the Hearth" is an historical panorama to which no intelligent man, however learned he may be, need be ashamed to attach credit. This writer has extraordinary powers of divination—we can't express it otherwise; and the most judicious historian, we sincerely believe, cannot read the tale in question without confessing that there is a light there thrown upon the past which is eminently worth being thrown, and which it was not in his own province to produce. He will return to his own more austere labors with a renewed sense of dignity, and both parties will thus be the wiser.

THE SPANISH GYPSY* BY GEORGE ELIOT

THE appearance of a new work by George Eliot is properly cause of no small satisfaction to the lovers of good literature. She writes little compared with most of her distinguished comrades, and, still compared with them, she writes admirably well. She has shown no inclination to trade upon her popularity by anticipating—precipitating, one may say—the promptings of her genius, the moment of inspiration, or to humor the inconsiderate enthusiasm of that large body of critics who would fain persuade her, against her excellent sagacity, that she is at once a great romancer, a great poet, and a great philosopher. She is, as we have said, to our mind, one of the best of English writers; she is, incidentally to this, an excellent story-teller—a real novelist, in fact—and she is, finally, an elegant moralist. In her novels she had never struck us as possessing the poetic character. But at last, to-day, late in her career, she surprises the world with a long poem, which, if it fails materially to deepen our esteem for her remarkable talents, will certainly not diminish it. We should have read George Eliot to but little purpose if we could still suppose her capable of doing anything inconsiderable. Her mind is of that superior quality that impresses its distinction even upon works misbegotten and abortive. "The Spanish Gypsy" is certainly very far from being such a work; but to those who have read the author's novels attentively it will possess no further novelty than that of outward form. It exhibits the delightful qualities of "Romola," "The Mill on the Floss," and even "Silas Marner," applied to a new order of objects, and in a new fashion; but it exhibits, to our perception, no new qualities. George Eliot could not possess the large and rich intellect which shines in her writings without being something of a poet. We imagine that the poetic note could be not unfrequently detected by a delicate observer who should go through her novels in quest of it; but we believe, at the same time, that it would be found to sound

* "The Spanish Gypsy: a Poem by George Eliot." Boston: Ticknor & Field. 1868. (*The Nation*, July 2, 1868).

neither very loud nor very long. There is a passage in the "Mill on the Floss" which may illustrate our meaning. The author is speaking of the eternal difference between the patient, drearily-vigilant lives of women, and the passionate, turbulent existence of men; of the difference having existed from the days of Hecuba and Hector; of the women crowding within the gates with streaming eyes and praying hands; of the men without on the plain (we quote only from recollection) "quenching memory in the stronger light of purpose, and losing the sense of battle and even of wounds in the hurrying ardor of action." Elsewhere, in "Romola," she speaks of the purifying influence of public confession, springing from the fact that "by it the hope in lies is for ever swept away, and *the soul recovers the noble attitude of simplicity.*" In these two sentences, if we are not mistaken, there is a certain poetic light, a poetic ring. The qualities are not intense—they gleam, tremble, and vanish; but they indicate the manner in which a brilliant mind, when reason and sense guard the helm and direct the course, may yet, without effort, touch and hover upon the verge of poetry. "The Spanish Gypsy" contains far finer things than either of these simple specimens—things, indeed, marvellously fine; but they have been gathered, in our opinion, upon this cold outer verge—they are not the glowing, scented fruit that ripens beneath the meridian.

The poem was composed, the author intimates, while Spain was yet known to her only by descriptions and recitals; it was then, after a visit to the country, rewritten and enlarged. These facts correspond somehow to an impression made upon the reader's mind. The work is primarily—like the author's other productions, we think—an eminently intellectual performance; not the result of experience, or of moral and sensuous impressions. In this circumstance reside at once its strength and its weakness; its want of heat, of a quickening central flame; and its admirable perfection of manner, its densely wrought, richly embroidered garment of thought and language. Never, assuredly, was a somewhat inefficient spirit so richly supplied with the outward organs and faculties of maturity and manhood. George Eliot has nothing in common, either in her merits or her defects, with the late Mrs. Browning. The critic is certainly not at his ease with Mrs. Browning until he has admitted, once for all, that she is a born poet. But she is without tact and without taste; her faults of detail are unceasing. George Eliot is not a born poet; but, on the other hand, her intellectual tact is equally delicate and vigorous, her taste is infallible, she is never guilty of errors or excesses. In the whole length of the volume before us we have not observed a single slovenly line, a single sentence unpolished or unfinished. And of strong and beautiful lines what a number; of thoughts deep and clear, of images vivid and complete, of heavily-burdened sentences happily delivered of their meaning, what an endless variety! The whole poem is a tissue of the most elegant, most intelligent rhetoric, from the beautiful exordium descriptive of

> "Broad-breasted Spain, leaning with equal love
>   (A calm earth-goddess, crowned with corn and vines)
>   On the Mid Sea that moans with memories,
>   And on the untravelled Ocean,"

to the majestic pathos of the final scene, in which, contrary to her wont, the author has brought herself fairly to disjoin her young lovers.

But fully to appreciate the writer's skill and the (for the most part) really profound character of her various conceptions, it is needful to acquaint one's mind with the outline of her story. This story, whether invented by the author or borrowed ready-made, is extremely thrilling and touching. It is, of course, a genuine romance, full of color and movement and dramatic opportunities. The scene is laid at the close of the fifteenth century, in the town and castle of Bedmár, in Andalusia. Warriors, inquisitors, astrologers, Moors, gypsies, minstrels—all the consecrated figures of Spanish romance—are effectively represented. "The time was great," as the author says; the Renaissance has just dawned, the Moorish dominion was hard pressed, America lay but just without the circle of the known and soon to be included, Spain had entered into her mighty, short-lived manhood. The hero of the poem—which we must premise is cast in the dramatic form, with occasional narrative interludes—Don Silva, the young Duke of Bedmár, personifies in a very vivid manner all the splendid tendencies and deep aspirations of the scene and the hour. Admirably well, it seems to us, has the author depicted in the mind of this generous nobleman the growth and fusion of a personal and egotistical consciousness into the sense of generic and national honor, governed and directed by his religion, his Christ, his patron saints, his ancestors, and

> "—by the mystery of his Spanish blood
> Charged with the awe and glories of the past."

The young duke's mother, recently deceased, has adopted and educated a girl of unknown parentage and remarkable beauty, by name Fedalma. Don Silva, on reaching manhood, conceives a passionate attachment to this young girl, and determines to make her his wife. The match is bitterly opposed by his uncle, a stern Dominican monk, on the ground that Fedalma is a creature of heretical lineage and sympathies. On the eve of the marriage, the young girl is suddenly claimed as the daughter of a certain Zarca, captain of a band of Zincali, captured by the duke and lodged as prisoners in the dungeons of his castle. The appeal is made to Fedalma by Zarca in person, and the material evidence, besides that of her own filial instincts, is so irresistible that she surrenders herself to her now strange destiny. It is her father's will that she shall cast away her love and her splendor, and espouse only the sorrows and the perpetual exile of her people. She assists Zarca and his followers to escape from Bedmár, and wanders forth into outlawry. Don Silva, distracted, pursues her, secretly, to the camp in which, with the assistance of a neighboring Moorish king, Zarca had fortified himself, and whence he meditates a vengeful attack upon Bedmár; entreats her to return; offers vainly, to ransom her, and finally, in the fervor of his passion, casts off his allegiance to his king and unites himself, for his love's sake, with the beggarly Zincali. Zarca places him under guard, on probation, and proceeds with his Moors to attack Bedmár. The attack is successful and his revenge complete. He slays the dearest comrades of Don Silva and orders the execution of his uncle, the holy

Father Isidor. Meanwhile Silva, hearing of the fate of his town, makes his way back, twice a recreant, inflamed with shame, rage, and grief. He intercedes, vainly, for his uncle, and as the grim old monk is swung into mid air from the shameful gibbet, he rushes upon Zarca and stabs him to the heart. The Gypsy, expiring, transfers his authority to Fedalma, charges her with his hopes of redemption, his visions of increase and empire, and with the burden of conducting her people into Africa, to certain lands granted from the Moors. Of course, with this dark stream of blood flowing between them, Don Silva and his mistress stand severed for ever. Fedalma prepares to embark with her comrades for the African shore and Don Silva determines, purified and absolved by the Papal hands, to consecrate himself, in sad devotion, to the services and glory of his king. The two meet on the shore of the sea in a solemn, supreme farewell. The reader will see that, having brought her hero and heroine to these soaring altitudes of passion, the author had touched a dramatic chord tense almost to breaking, but she raises her hand in time, and the poem ends.

Besides the characters whom we have indicated, there are several subordinate figures, such as George Eliot loves to draw, and such as even in this sombre antique romance she would not willingly dispense with—Lorenzo the innkeeper, Blasco the silversmith, and Roldan the conjurer, to say nothing of Annibal, the conjurer's ape. These persons belong to the delightful race of George Eliot's "worthies"—the simple, subtle, kindly village gossips, all gifted with the same true human accents, the same mild and unctuous humor, whether they be drinking beer beneath the oaks of modern England or quaffing wine beneath the olive trees of mediæval Spain. With these, and yet hardly with these, illumined as he is with a tender poetic glow, we would associate the minstrel Juan—the lounger, talker, singer—

> "Living 'mid harnessed men
> With limbs ungalled by armor, ready so
> To soothe them weary and to cheer them sad.
> Guest at the board, companion in the camp,
> A crystal mirror to the life around,
>
> . . . . . .
> . . . . singing as a listener

To the deep moans, the cries, the wild strong joys
Of universal Nature." . . .

This author has invested this character of Juan with a peculiar and affecting dignity. As a portrait, indeed, it is like those of all its companions, full of the most exquisite intentions, which confess themselves only on a second reading of the work. The chief motive of our interest in Juan is, of course, the contrast offered by his dreamy, sceptical, idle, disinterested mind, with the fervid intensity which burns around him, in war, and traffic, and piety. Let us add, however, that the lyrics which are laid upon his life and his lute, strike us as the least successful passages in the work. They have an unpardonable taint—they are cold, torpid; they are lyrics made, not lyrics born. The other characters, Silva, Zarca, and Fedalma, are all elaborate full-length portraits. The author has not felt it necessary, because she was writing a picturesque romance, to eschew psychology and morals. She has remembered that she was writing a drama, and that she would have written in vain unless each of her leading figures was fully rounded and defined. They are very human, these three props of the tragedy—or the two lovers, at least: they are warm, living and distinct. But we can't help thinking that in making them distinct the author has somehow brought them very much too near to us. We may say, indeed, that here, as in "Romola," morally, she has shifted the action from the past to the present. But this error, if error it be, matters less here; the play goes on, at best, in an ideal world. Zarca, the Zincalo chieftain, is a purely ideal figure, but a figure of so much grandeur and power, that one may declare that if he is not real, so much the worse for reality. His character is conceived in a very large and noble manner, and cast in a massive and imposing shape. Especially well has the author possessed herself of the idea that the absolute obloquy and proscription that weighs upon his race is the basis of his courage and devotion. He moves and acts in a kind of sublime intoxication at the thought of being the all in all of a people alike destitute of a God, a heaven, and a home. "The sanctity of oaths," he says,

"Lies not in lightning that avenges them,
  But in the injury wrought by broken bonds
  And in the garnered good of human trust."

And elsewhere:

"No good is certain but the steadfast mind,
  The undivided will to seek the good:
  'Tis that compels the elements, and wrings
  A human music from the indifferent air.
  The greatest gift the hero leaves his race,
  Is to have been a hero. Say we fail!—
  We feed the high tradition of the world,
  And leave our spirit in Zincalo breasts."

The gypsy captain who utters these great truths with such greatness of diction, certainly views the world from a lofty standpoint. Fedalma, his daughter, is throughout a very lovely and perfect creation, from the moment that we see her dancing on the plaza,

"With gentle wheeling sweep
  Returning like the loveliest of the Hours
  Strayed from her sisters, truant lingering,"

to where she bids farewell to her lover on the strand, and speaks of their ruined love, their "dear young love" having

"Grown upon a larger life
  Which tore its roots asunder."

The author has drawn no purer and more radiant figure than this finely nurtured, deep-souled, double-natured Zincalo maiden; and she has drawn her manners with perfect lightness of touch, with an instrument that never blurs the graceful curve of the outline, or dims the luminous warmth of the coloring. The great success of the work, however, is the figure, Don Silva, with his stormy alternations of passion and reflection, of headlong devotion and intellectual reserve. The finest passages in the book, we think, are the pages descriptive of the restless tumult of his soul during the hours of his confinement, after he has burned his ships and pledged his faith to Zarca. These pages are deeply and nobly imaginative. We have no space to quote: they must be read, re-read, and pondered. But we cannot forego the pleasure of transcribing these few lines, the sweetest in the poem, borne upon Don Silva's lips from the ineffable joy of Fedalma's presence:

> "Speech is but broken light upon the depths
> Of the unspoken: even your loved words
> *Float in the larger meaning of your voice*
> *As something dimmer.*"

Imagine a rich, masculine nature, all refined to the delicate temper of this compliment, and you have an idea of the splendid personality of George Eliot's hero. We may but qualify him by saying that he exhibits the highest reach, the broadest range, of the aristocratic character. This is the real tragedy. Silva is tortured and racked—even if he be finally redeemed—by his deep and exquisite sensibilities. Fedalma, the plebeian, certainly suffers less. If she had been of Silva's blood, she would never have forsworn the beauty of her love to espouse the vast vulgarity of the Zincali.

We had marked many passages for quotation, but we have come to the end of our space. The book itself will be in every one's hands by the time these remarks are printed.

In conclusion, we must express our deep sense of its beauty. One may say, indeed, that it has no faults (except its lyrics). As a composition, it is polished to defiance of all censure. It is, at most, deficient in certain virtues, which the success of the poem, as a whole, would tend to prove non-essential. It is deficient in natural heat; it does not smell of the Spanish soil, but of that of the author's mind. It is neither rapid nor simple. Reflection, not imagination, has presided at the work. Nevertheless it is a most fair achievement, and a valuable contribution to literature. It is the production of a noble intellect, of a moral vision equally broad and deep, and of marvellous ingenuity.

GEORGE ELIOT'S THE LIFTED VEIL;
AND BROTHER JACOB*

In the absence of anything new from George Eliot's hand, the two short tales included in the cheap edition of her works in course of publication by Messrs. Blackwood and now for the first time reprinted, may be accepted as a novelty. They appear at the end of the volume which contains "Silas Marner," and will doubtless procure for this volume an extended circulation. One of them, "The Lifted Veil," was published in *Blackwood's Magazine* in 1859; the other, "Brother Jacob," appeared in the *Cornhill* one year later. They are extremely different, but each is interesting, and the reader who turns to them now will doubtless wonder why the author has not oftener attempted to express herself within the limits of that form of fiction which the French call the *nouvelle*. George Eliot will probably always remain the great novelist who has written fewest short stories. As her genius has unfolded she has departed more and more from the "short story" standard, and become, if not absolutely the longest-winded, at least what may be called the most spacious, of romancers. Of the two tales in question, "Brother Jacob," which is wholly of a humorous cast, is much the better. We say it is of a humorous cast, but it is probable that like everything of George Eliot's it may be credited with something of a philosophic import—offered as it is as an example of the many forms, in the author's own words, "in which the great Nemesis hides herself." The great Nemesis here is the idiot brother of a small criminal, who brings the latter to shame and confusion by an obstinate remembrance of the sweet things he has swallowed. The guilty brother, of whose guilt he has been an accidental witness, has bribed him to secrecy by a present of sugar-plums, and when Mr. David Faux is after the lapse of years flourishing, under an assumed name, upon the indirect fruits of his misdemeanors (a petty robbery) the too appreciative Jacob reappears clamoring for more lozenges, and throwing a fatal light

* George Eliot's The Lifted Veil; and Brother Jacob. (*The Nation*, April 25, 1878).

upon Mr. Faux's past. The story is extremely clever, but it is a little injured, perhaps, by an air of effort, by too visible an attempt to say good things, to bestrew the reader's path with epigrams. As the incident is related wholly in the ironic, satiric manner, the temptation to be pregnantly witty was, of course, particularly strong. But the figure of the diminutively mean and sneaking young man upon whom the great Nemesis descends is a real portrait; it is an admirable picture of unromantic malfeasance. Capital, too, is the fatal Jacob, who, after the manner of idiots, leaves us with a sense of his combined vagueness and obstructiveness. The minor touches are very brilliant, and the story is, generally, excellent reading. "The Lifted Veil," which is more metaphysical, is, we think, less successful. It relates the history of a young man who, growing up in morbid physical conditions, acquires a mysterious intellectual foresight of the things that are to happen to him; together with that of a wicked lady, his wife, whose guilt is brought to light by the experiment of infusing blood into the heart of a person just dead, who revives for an instant and denounces her. The tale is woefully sombre, and there is a want of connection between the clairvoyance of the hero and the incidents we have just related. Each of these things is very wonderful, but in conjunction they are rather violent. "The Lifted Veil," however, is a fine piece of writing; and if they were interesting for nothing else, these two tales would be interesting as the *jeux d'esprit* of a mind that is not often—perhaps not often enough—found at play.

HARDY'S FAR FROM THE MADDING CROWD

Mr. Hardy's novel came into the world under brilliant auspices—such as the declaration by the London *Spectator* that either George Eliot had written it or George Eliot had found her match. One could make out in a manner what the *Spectator* meant. To

---

* 'Far from the Madding Crowd. By Thomas Hardy.' New York: Henry Holt & Co. 1874. (*The Nation*, December 24, 1874).

guess, one has only to open 'Far from the Madding Crowd' at random: "Mr. Jan Coggan, who had passed the cup to Henery, was a crimson man with a spacious countenance and a private glimmer in his eye, whose name had appeared on the marriage register of Weatherbury and neighboring parishes as best-man and chief witness in countless unions of the previous twenty years; he also very frequently filled the post of head godfather in baptisms of the subtly-jovial kind." That is a very fair imitation of George Eliot's humorous manner. Here is a specimen of her serious one: "He fancied he had felt himself in the penumbra of a very deep sadness when touching that slight and fragile creature. But wisdom lies in moderating mere impressions, and Gabriel endeavored to think little of this." But the *Spectator's* theory had an even broader base, and we may profitably quote a passage which perhaps constituted one of its solidest blocks. The author of *Silas Marner* has won no small part of her fame by her remarkable faculty as a reporter of ale-house and kitchen-fire conversations among simple-minded rustics. Mr. Hardy has also made a great effort in this direction, and here is a specimen—a particularly favorable specimen—of his success:

" 'Why, Joseph Poorgrass, you han't had a drop!' said Mr. Coggan to a very shrinking man in the background, thrusting the cup towards him.

" 'Such a shy man as he is,' said Jacob Smallbury. 'Why, ye've hardly had strength of eye enough to look in our young mis'ess's face, so I hear, Joseph?'

"All looked at Joseph Poorgrass with pitying reproach.

" 'No, I've hardly looked at her at all,' faltered Joseph, reducing his body smaller while talking, apparently from a meek sense of undue prominence; 'and when I see'd her, it was nothing but blushes with me!'

" 'Poor fellow,' said Mr. Clark.

" ' 'Tis a curious nature for a man,' said Jan Coggan.

" 'Yes,' continued Joseph Poorgrass, his shyness, which was so painful as a defect, just beginning to fill him with a little complacency, now that it was regarded in the light of an interesting study. ' 'Twere blush, blush, blush with me every minute of the time when she was speaking to me.'

" 'I believe ye, Joseph Poorgrass, for we all know ye to be a very bashful man.'

" ' 'Tis terrible bad for a man, poor soul!' said the malster. 'And how long have ye suffered from it, Joseph?'

" 'Oh, ever since I was a boy. Yes—mother was concerned to her heart about it—yes. But 'twas all naught.'

" 'Did ye ever take anything to try and stop it, Joseph Poorgrass?'

" 'Oh, aye, tried all sorts. They took me to Greenhill Fair, and into a great large jerry-go-nimble show, where there were women-folk riding round standing up on horses, with hardly anything on but their smocks; but it didn't cure me a morsel—no, not a morsel. And then I was put errandman at the Woman's Skittle Alley at the back of the Tailor's Arms in Casterbridge. 'Twas a horrible gross situation, and altogether a very curious place for a good man. I had to stand and look at wicked people in the face from morning till night; but 'twas no use—I was just as bad as ever after all. Blushes have been in the family for generations. There, 'tis a happy providence I be no worse, so to speak it—yes, a happy thing, and I feel my few poor gratitudes.' "

This is extremely clever, and the author has evidently read to good purpose the low-life chapters in George Eliot's novels; he has caught very happily her trick of seeming to humor benignantly her queer people and look down at them from the heights of analytic omniscience. But we have quoted the episode because it seems to us an excellent example of the cleverness which is only cleverness, of the difference between original and imitative talent —the disparity, which it is almost unpardonable not to perceive, between first-rate talent and those inferior grades which range from second-rate downward, and as to which confusion is a more venial offense. Mr. Hardy puts his figures through a variety of comical movements; he fills their mouths with quaint turns of speech; he baptizes them with odd names ("Joseph Poorgrass" for a bashful, easily-snubbed Dissenter is excellent); he pulls the wires, in short, and produces a vast deal of sound and commotion; and his novel, at a cursory glance, has a rather promising air of life and warmth. But by critics who prefer a grain of substance to a pound of shadow it will, we think, be pronounced a decidedly delusive performance; it has a fatal lack of magic. We have found it hard to read, but its shortcomings are easier to summarize than to encounter in order. Mr. Hardy's novel is very long, but his subject is very short and simple, and the work has been distended to its rather formidable dimensions by the infusion of a large amount of conversational and descriptive padding and the use of an ingeniously verbose and redundant style. It is inordinately diffuse, and, as a piece of narrative, singularly inartistic. The author has little sense of proportion, and almost none of composition. We learn about Bathsheba and Gabriel, Farmer Boldwood and Sergeant Troy, what we can rather than what we should; for Mr. Hardy's inexhaustible faculty for spinning smart dialogue makes him forget that dialogue in a story is after all but episode, and that a novelist is after all but a historian, thoroughly possessed of certain facts, and bound in some way or other to impart them. To tell a story almost exclusively by reporting people's talks is the most difficult art in the world, and really leads, logically, to a severe economy in the use of rejoinder and repartee, and not to a lavish expenditure of them. *Far from the Madding Crowd* gives us an uncomfortable sense of being a simple "tale," pulled and stretched to make the conventional three volumes; and the author, in his long-sustained appeal to one's attention, reminds us of a person fishing with an enormous net, of which the meshes should be thrice too wide.

We are happily not subject, in this (as to minor matters) much-emancipated land, to the tyranny of the three volumes; but we confess that we are nevertheless being rapidly urged to a conviction that (since it is in the nature of fashions to revolve and recur) the day has come round again for some of the antique restrictions as to literary form. The three unities, in Aristotle's day, were inexorably imposed on Greek tragedy: why shouldn't we have something of the same sort for English fiction in the day of Mr. Hardy? Almost all novels are greatly too long, and the being too long becomes with each elapsing year a more serious offence. Mr. Hardy begins with a detailed description of his hero's smile, and proceeds thence to give a voluminous account of his large silver watch. Gabriel Oak's smile and his watch were doubtless respectable and important phenomena; but everything is relative, and daily becoming more so; and we confess that, as a hint of the pace at which the author proposed to proceed, his treatment of these facts produced upon us a deterring and depressing effect. If novels were the only books written, novels written on this scale would be all very well; but as they compete, in the esteem of sensible people, with a great many other books, and a great many other objects of interest of all kinds, we are inclined to think that, in the long run, they will be defeated in the struggle for existence unless they lighten their baggage very considerably and do battle in a more scientific equipment. Therefore, we really imagine that a few arbitrary rules—a kind of depleting process—might have a wholesome effect. It might be enjoined, for instance, that no "tale" should exceed fifty pages and no novel two hundred; that a plot should have but such and such a number of ramifications; that no ramification should have more than a certain number of persons; that no person should utter more than a given number of words; and that no description of an inanimate object should consist of more than a fixed number of lines. We should not incline to advocate this oppressive legislation as a comfortable or ideal finality for the romancer's art, but we think it might be excellent as a transitory discipline or drill. Necessity is the mother of invention, and writers with a powerful tendency to expatiation might in this temporary strait-jacket be induced to transfer their attention rather more severely from quantity to quality. The use of the strait-jacket would have cut down Mr. Hardy's novel to half its actual length and, as he is a clever man, have made the abbreviated work very ingeniously pregnant. We should have had a more occasional taste of all the barn-yard worthies—Joseph Poorgrass, Laban Tall, Matthew Moon, and the rest—and the vagaries of Miss Bathsheba would have had a more sensible consistency. Our restrictions would have been generous, however, and we should not have proscribed such a fine passage as this:

"Then there came a third flash. Manœuvres of the most extraordinary kind were going on in the vast firmamental hollows overhead. The lightning now was the color of silver, and gleamed in the heavens like a mailed army. Rumbles became rattles. Gabriel, from his elevated position, could see over the landscape for at least half a dozen miles in front. Every hedge, bush, and tree was distinct as in a line engraving. In a paddock in the same direction was a herd of heifers, and the forms of these were visible at this moment in the act of galloping about in the wildest and maddest confusion, flinging their heels and tails high into the air, their heads to earth. A poplar in the immediate foreground was like an ink-stroke on burnished tin. Then the picture vanished, leaving a darkness so intense that Gabriel worked entirely by feeling with his hands."

Mr. Hardy describes nature with a great deal of felicity, and is evidently very much at home among rural phenomena. The most genuine thing in his book, to our sense, is a certain aroma of the meadows and lanes—a natural relish for harvesting and sheep-washings. He has laid his scene in an agricultural county, and his characters are children of the soil—unsophisticated country-folk. Bathsheba Everdene is a rural heiress, left alone in the world, in possession of a substantial farm. Gabriel Oak is her shepherd, Farmer Boldwood is her neighbor, and Sergeant Troy is a loose young soldier who comes a-courting her. They are all in love with her, and the young lady is a flirt, and encourages them all. Finally she marries the Sergeant, who has just seduced her maid-servant. The maid-servant dies in the work-house, the Sergeant repents, leaves his wife, and is given up for drowned. But he reappears and is shot by Farmer Boldwood, who delivers himself up to justice. Bathsheba then marries Gabriel Oak, who has loved and waited in silence, and is, in our opinion, much too good for her. The chief purpose of the book is, we suppose, to represent Gabriel's dumb, devoted passion, his biding his time, his rendering unsuspected services to the woman who has scorned him, his integrity and simplicity and sturdy patience. In all this the tale is very fairly successful, and Gabriel has a certain vividness of expression. But we cannot say that we either understand or like Bathsheba. She is a young lady of the inconsequential, wilful, mettlesome type which has lately become so much the fashion for heroines, and of which Mr. Charles Reade is in a manner the inventor—the type which aims at giving one a very intimate sense of a young lady's *womanishness*. But Mr. Hardy's embodiment of it seems to us to lack reality; he puts her through the Charles Reade paces, but she remains alternately vague and coarse, and seems always artificial. This is Mr. Hardy's trouble; he rarely gets beyond ambitious artifice—the mechanical simulation of heat and depth and wisdom that are absent. Farmer Boldwood is a shadow, and Sergeant Troy an elaborate stage-figure. Everything human in the book strikes us as factitious and insubstantial; the only things we believe in are the sheep and the dogs. But, as we say, Mr. Hardy has gone astray very cleverly, and his superficial novel is a really curious imitation of something better.

CHARLES KINGSLEY'S LIFE AND LETTERS*

Mrs. Kingsley has given proof, in this voluminous compilation, of no little zeal and industry. It is hardly more than a year and a half since Charles Kingsley died, but she has found time to collect a very large number of letters and other papers, to obtain testimonials of various kinds to the merits of the late Canon of Westminster, to make copious extracts from his sermons, tracts, and other writings, and to connect these things together by a considerable amount of agreeably-written narrative. We may say at the outset that the work seems to us much too long. When the plan is followed of giving not only the letters written by the subject of a memoir, but the letters that he received, and of transferring page upon page of his published works, the writing of biography threatens to assume proportions which may well alarm a very busy age. Mrs. Kingsley has reprinted too many of her husband's sermons—a course which has not enlivened her pages. We may add that they would have gained also by the suppression of a certain number of the letters, consolatory and descriptive, which she received—apparently by invitation—during the progress of her work, and which she has published *in extenso*. A man of Charles Kingsley's value should take his stand with posterity upon

* Charles Kingsley. His Letters and Memories of His Life. Edited by his wife. London: Henry S. King & Co. 1877. (*The Nation*, January 25, 1877).

his own illustrious achievements; it should not be sought to bolster up his reputation by copious proof that this, that, and the other obscure admirer thought very highly of him. This extreme redundancy, however, is the only fault of these volumes, which have evidently been most carefully and laboriously prepared, and which, in spite of their highly appreciative tone, offer no instances of bad taste.

This record of the life of the founder of "Muscular Christianity" will strongly confirm the impression that he produced personally and through his writings, and will be found to contain matter of much pertinence, both for that numerous class of readers who regarded him as something of a prophet and for those others upon whom his effect was less gratefully irritating. It is not in any high degree the record of a literary life; we may almost say that it is hardly the record of an intellectual life. People who have wondered how it was that the author of 'Hypatia' and 'Westward Ho' should not have had in him the writing of more books as good, will, on reading these pages, rather be moved to wonder that even those admirable novels were produced. They were the exceptions; other things, and very different things, were the rule. Charles Kingsley was all his days a hard-working country parson, much devoted to the moral and the practical features of his office; to keeping down gin-shops, establishing "penny-readings," improving sanitary conditions, organizing and regulating charities, and preaching matter-of-fact sermons. In addition to this he was much addicted to harmless sports and to physical science. He was a passionate angler, an ardent botanist, geologist, and marine zoölogist. As regards his own personal "muscularity," we must add, however, Mrs. Kingsley rather tones down the picture. He never went out with a gun, and he could not be called a "fox-hunting parson." His means did not allow him to be brilliantly mounted, and as he preferred not to ride poor horses, he rode rarely. But the inclination was not wanting. He had a great deal of imagination, but he appears in early life to have worked off its fermenting forces, and he had no intellectual needs that did not find comfortable satisfaction within the pale of the English Church. He appears to us as a man of an extremely vigorous temperament and a decidedly simple intellect, with an appreciation of natural things and a power of expressing the pleasures of natural science that amount almost to genius, together with an adoration of all things English and Anglican which almost assimilates him to the typical John Bull of foreign caricature, and a hatred of "Popery" which strongly confirms this resemblance. His strongest quality was his great personal energy, which evidently had an influence of an agreeable and improving sort upon those with whom he came into contact. It seems to the reader, throughout, a striking anomaly that fortune should have forced him into the position of a philosopher or an intellectual teacher. Even literature, with him, was amateurish. His novels, his chief title to reputation, are here disposed of in a few lines, while his parish work receives the tribute of chapters. It is plain that learning and research were more amateurish still. When towards the close of such a career the sympathetic reader finds Mr. Kingsley installed as Professor of History at Cambridge, or engaged in theological controversy with Dr. Newman, he feels as if in offering him these remarkable opportunities for making an unfavorable appearance, fate were playing him a trick which he had not done enough to deserve.

That Mrs. Kingsley is a thorough biographer may be inferred from the fact that she gives us sermons and poems written at the age of four years and of four years and eight months, respectively. For this period of life these compositions are even more remarkable than those which followed them in the author's maturity. Much of his childhood was passed upon that beautiful Devonshire coast which he has commemorated in 'Westward Ho' and 'Two Years Ago,' where his father, who had entered the church late in life, after a somewhat worldly career, was clergyman. He was educated at first at King's College, London, whence he went up to Cambridge. Immediately after graduating he entered the church, and became curate at Eversley, in Hampshire, where, two years later, the living falling vacant, he was promoted to the rectorship, and where the greater part of his life was passed and his greatest activity displayed. His letters during his college years are of a strongly religious cast, though they allude to a period of doubt and temptation from which he had escaped only by hard fighting. This was the time of the famous "Tractarian" movement at Oxford; but Kingsley appears to have stood well out of the current. Mrs. Kingsley prints many letters written to her by her husband during these years, which are those of their engagement. As a correspondence carried on under these circumstances it is very remarkable, and being almost wholly theological and argumentative, does great honor to the elevation of tone of both parties. Though Kingsley was non-Tractarian he could do the Oxford party justice. "So you still like their *tone!* And so do I. There is a solemn and gentlemanlike and gentle earnestness which is most beautiful, and which I wish I may ever attain." That aspiration to a "gentleman-like" attitude in spiritual things is a noticeable symptom of the Kingsley who was to become celebrated. He can do justice, too, to quite another style of error. "Do not reject Wardlaw because he was a Presbyterian. The poor man was born so, you know. It is very different from a man's dissenting personally." In these letters there is a strong expression of that enthusiastic sense of man's physical life and that of the world at large which forms Kingsley's real originality. It is in touching upon these matters and describing them that he always seems to us at his best. There is then something of the magical in his tone. He *saw* admirably, though he thought confusedly.

"To-day it is hotter than yesterday, if possible; so I wandered out into the fields and have been passing the morning in a lonely woodland bath—a little stream that trickles off the moor, with the hum of bees and the sleepy song of birds around me, and the feeling of the density of life in myriads of insects and flowers strong upon me, drinking in all the forms of beauty which lie in the leaves and pebbles and mossy nooks of damp tree-roots, and all the lovely intricacies of nature which no one stoops to see. . . . And over all, as the cool water trickled on, hovered the delicious sense of childhood and simplicity and purity and peace." . . . Elsewhere he says: ". . . The body is the temple of the living God. There has always seemed to me something impious in the neglect of personal health, strength, and beauty. . . . I could wish I were an Apollo for His sake. Strange idea, yet it seems so harmonious to me." This feeling is expressed again in one of his later letters: "Dear man, did you ever ride a lame horse and wish that the earth would open and swallow you, though there was not a soul within miles? Or did you ever sit and look at a handsome or well-made man, and thank God from your heart for having allowed you such a privilege and lesson? Oh! there was a butcher's nephew playing cricket in Bramshill last week whom I would have walked ten miles to see, in spite of the hideous English dress. One looked forward with delight to what he would be in the resurrection."

Of those opinions and sympathies which produced 'Alton Locke,' and which were further expressed in many contributions to three or four of the small socialist periodicals generated by the Chartist agitation of 1848 and the years immediately following, and in various tracts and pamphlets, Mrs. Kingsley gives a full and candid account. This period was the high-water mark of Kingsley's liberalism, and there is something very fine in the completeness of his self-surrender to a cause which, though popular in the literal sense of the word, was fatally unpopular in another, and would have seemed quite of a nature to blight, by contact, the future prospects of a clergyman of the Church of England. Kingsley burnt his ships; he threw himself into the Chartist movement in order to check it and regulate it—in order to get near to the working-classes and make himself heard by them. The impulse was generous and disinterested, but from our present standpoint the whole affair wears the look of a small playing at revolution. The Chartists were not real revolutionists, and Charles Kingsley and his friends were not real radicals. There is something patronizing and dilettantish in Mr. Kingsley's relations with his obscure protégés; it is always the tone of the country parson who lives in an ivied rectory with a pretty lawn. Those who have a sense of the dark, subterraneous forces of English misery will hardly repress a smile at those letters upon "Giovanni Bellini," "The British Museum," "Beauty and Sympathy," and other refined themes, which, under the signature of "Parson Lot," the author of "Alton Locke" addressed to the working-classes. He relates in one of these letters that once, looking at some beautiful stuffed humming-birds in the window of a curiosity shop, and being overcome with their exquisite grace, he turned and made a remark upon the subject to a coal-heaver standing beside him; and he puts forward this anecdote—the story is told, it must be remembered, to a public of possible coal-heavers—as a proof of the democratic passion. Mr.

Kingsley went far, for him, no doubt, and his readers, if they were duly edified, went a good way to meet him. It must be remembered that they were not Parisian Communists, and that the goodwill exhibited on either side was the reasonable British sort, which, if it does not give overmuch, does not ask overmuch either. Mr. Kingsley's momentary radicalism was both kindly and sincere. "I will not be a liar," he writes at this moment to his wife in allusion to certain temporizing counsels. "I will speak in season and out of season. I will not shun to declare the whole counsel of God. I will not take counsel with flesh and blood, and flatter myself into the dream that while every man on earth, from Maurice back to Abel, who ever tried to testify against the world, has been laughed at, misunderstood, slandered, and that, bitterest of all, by the very people he loved best and understood best, I alone am to escape." The amiable and sentimental side of "Christian socialism" is to be spoken of with esteem; but the intellectual side was weak and vague. On the 12th of April, 1848, an address to the workmen of England, written by Charles Kingsley, was posted up in the London streets. It ended with these words, which justify our judgment as to the vagueness: "Workers of England, be wise, and then you *must* be free, for you will be *fit* to be free." The Chartist agitation subsided; but the exact effect of this rather optimistic logic in quelling it history has doubtless not measured.

Mrs. Kingsley says that her husband was for a long time under a cloud, in society and in the church, in consequence of the part he played in these years; and it would perhaps be interesting to trace the process by which he emerged from the shade into the comfortable glow of some of his later preferments—his Professorship at Cambridge (to which he was appointed by selection of the Prince Consort), his Instructorship to the Prince of Wales, his Chaplaincy to the Queen. On the part of both Mr. Kingsley and his biographer a profound admiration for the Prince of Wales is observable—an admiration, as far as Mr. Kingsley is concerned, certainly natural in a thinker who holds, as a passage quoted seems to indicate, that the Prince holds his august position by divine right. Mrs. Kingsley's second volume contains an account of her husband's tour, made shortly before his death, in America, where all his personal impressions appear to have been of the most cordial and genial description. Her work contains, we repeat, much interesting matter, and it explains and characterizes Charles Kingsley even more effectually perhaps than the author intended. He was a man of a great personal—we had almost written of a great physical—force, whose life was mainly practical and extremely useful, and whose activity before the world had several impulsive phases or fits: a fit of Radicalism, a fit of brilliant romance-writing, a fit of ill-starred controversy with Doctor Newman, a fit—the last and longest—of "loyalty" to the throne and the aristocracy.

LOTHAIR BY LORD BEACONSFIELD*

Of the several reviews of "Lothair" which we have read, all have seemed to us to fail of justice in one important particular. Each of the reviewers had evidently read the book in the light of a deep aversion to the author's political character. Not one of them had made an attempt to estimate it on its own merits. It was all savagely negative criticism. The fewer kindly critics, on the other hand, have spoken, we imagine, at the prompting of a stubborn *a priori* enthusiasm and out of the fulness of political sympathy. There is so little profit in criticism of this temper, that we Americans may happily rejoice in the remoteness of the author's political presence and action. It concerns us chiefly that "Lothair" is decidedly amusing. We should call it interesting at once, were it not that we feel this to be in a measure a consecrated, a serious word, and that we cannot bring ourselves to think of "Lothair" as a serious work. It is doubtless not as amusing as it might be, with the same elements and a little firmer handling; but it is pleasant reading for a summer's day. The author has great cleverness, or rather he has a great deal of small cleverness. In great cleverness there must be an element of honest wisdom, we like to imagine, such as "Lothair" is fatally without. Still, he

---

* *Lothair.* By the Right Honorable B. Disraeli. New York: D. Appleton & Co. (*Atlantic Monthly*, August, 1870).

has cleverness enough to elicit repeatedly the reader's applause. A certain cleverness is required for getting into difficulties, for creating them and causing them to bristle around you; and of this peril-seeking faculty Mr. Disraeli possesses an abundant measure. Out of his difficulties he never emerges, so that in the end his talent lies gloriously entombed and enshrined in a vast edifice of accumulated mistakes. The reader persists, however, like a decent chief mourner at a funeral, and patiently waits till the last sod is thrown, till the last block is laid. He puts away the book with an indefinable sense of self-defeated power. Power enough there has been to arouse in his mind the feeling of attention, but not enough to awaken a single genuine impulse of satisfaction. A glance at the character of Mr. Disraeli's "difficulties" will illustrate our meaning. Lothair is a young nobleman (presumably a marquis) of immense wealth, great good looks, great amiability, and a glorious immunity from vulgar family ties. Fate has assigned him two guardians, in the persons of Lord Culloden, a Scotch earl of Presbyterian sympathies, and Cardinal Grandison, an early friend of his father, subsequently promoted to eminence in the Church of Rome. The motive of the romance is not quite what, on the basis of these *data,* it might have been. It is not the contest between opposing agents for the possession of a great prize, a contest rich in dramatic possibilities and in scenes and situations of striking interest. It is simply the attempt of the Cardinal and his accessaries to convert the young nobleman. There is emphatically no struggle and no resistance, and the reader's interest is enfeebled in the direct measure of the author's thoroughly careless and superficial treatment of his material. The grim Scotch Kirk on one side, the cunning Romish Church on the other, the generous young nobleman between, might have furnished the elements of a drama, not remarkable indeed for novelty, but excellent at all events in substance. But here Mr. Disraeli's deplorable levity begins. The whole book is remarkably easy to laugh at, and yet from the first, one may say, the reader's imagination, even the American reader's, is more in earnest than the author's. Imagination obliges; if you are to deal in fine things, it is a grievous pity not to do it with a certain force. The Earl of Culloden evaporates at an early stage of the recital; and as for Lothair, he never attains anything like the needful consistency of a hero. One can hardly say that he is weak, for to be weak you must at least begin by being. Throughout the book Lothair remains but a fine name. Round about him are grouped a number of persons of his distinguished "order," several of whom are to be conceived as bearing directly upon his fortunes. These portraits are of various shades of merit, those of the lighter characters being decidedly the best. A part of the pleasure of reading "Lothair" in London is doubtless to detect the prototypes of the Duke of Brecon and Lord St. Aldegonde, Mr. Phœbus, and Mr. Pinto. We are debarred from this keen satisfaction, but we are free, nevertheless, to apprehend that Lord St. Aldegonde, for instance, has a genuine plausibility of outline.

The author, however, has attempted greater things than this. A hero implies a heroine; in this case we have three, whose various forms of relation to the hero are happily enough conceived. The Church of Rome, in the person of Cardinal Grandison, having marked him for her own, we are invited to see what part the world shall play in contesting or confirming her influence. We have, in the first place, Lady Corisande, the lovely daughter of a mighty duke, a charming girl and a good Protestant; in the second, we have Miss Arundel, equally lovely, and a keen Papist; and lastly, we have the "divine Theodora," an Italian patriot, married, oddly enough, to a "gentleman of the South" of our own country. Corisande appeals to the young nobleman on behalf of his maternal faith and his high responsibilities; Miss Arundel of course operates in subtle sympathy with the Cardinal; and the "divine Theodora" (delicious title!) complicates matters admirably by seducing the young man into the service of Garibaldi. Such a bountiful admeasurement of womankind makes us only regret the more the provoking immateriality of Lothair. He walks through his part, however, to the fall of the curtain. He assists with Theodora at the battle of Mentana, where they are both wounded, the latter mortally. She survives long enough to extract from her young adorer a promise to resist the allurements of Romanism. But being nursed into convalescence by Miss Arundel, and exposed in his debilitated condition to the machinations of purple *monsignori*, he becomes so utterly demoralized, so enfeebled in will and bewildered in intellect, that to recover command of his senses he is obliged to fly secretly from Rome. From this point the interest of the story expires. The hero is conducted to the East, but to no very obvious purpose. We hear no more of the Romish conspirators. Miss Arundel goes into a cloister. Lothair returns to England and goes to stay at the residence of Lady Corisande's ducal parents. He goes with the young lady into her garden and offers her his hand, which she of course accepts; a very pretty episode, with which the book concludes.

If it can be said to have a ruling idea, that idea is of course to reveal the secret encroachments of the Romish Church. With what accuracy and fidelity these are revealed we are not prepared to say; with what eloquence and force the reader may perhaps infer from what we have said. Mr. Disraeli's attempt seems to us wholly to lack conviction, let alone passion and fire. His anti-Romish enthusiasm is thoroughly cold and mechanical. Essentially light and superficial throughout, the author is never more so than when he is serious and profound. He indulges in a large number of religious reflections, but we feel inexorably that it is not on such terms as these that religion stands or falls. His ecclesiastics are lay-figures—his Scarlet Woman is dressed out terribly in the tablecloth, and holds in her hands the drawing-room candlesticks. As a "novel with a purpose," accordingly, we think Lothair a decided failure. It will make no Cardinal's ears tingle, and rekindle no very lively sense of peril in any aristocratic brand snatched from the burning. But as a simple work of entertainment we think many of Mr. Disraeli's critics judge it quite too fiercely, or, what is worse, too ironically. They are rather too hard to please. For ourselves, it has left us much more good-humored than it found us. We are forever complaining, most of us, of the dreary realism, the hard, sordid, pretentious accuracy, of the typical novel of the period, of the manner of Trollope, of that of Wilkie Collins, of that, in our own country, of such writers as the author of "Hedged In," and the author of "Margaret Howth." We cry out for a little romance, a particle of poetry, a ray of the ideal. Here we have a novel abounding in the romantic element, and yet for the most part we do little but laugh at it. " 'And where is Mirabel?' said Lothair. 'It was a green island in the Adriatic,' said the lady, 'which belonged to Colonel Campian. We lost it in the troubles.' " The speaker here is the "divine Theodora." "About sunset Colonel Campian led forth Theodora. She was in female attire, and her long hair, restrained only by a fillet, reached nearly to the ground. Her Olympian brow seemed distended; a phosphoric light glittered in her Hellenic eyes; a deep pink spot burned upon each of those cheeks usually so immaculately fair." This is thoroughly regenerate realism, and we find ourselves able to take all that Mr. Disraeli gives us. Nothing is so delightful, an objector may say, as sincere and genuine romance, and nothing so ignoble as the hollow, glittering compound which Mr. Disraeli gives us as a substitute. But we must take what we can get. We shall endure "Lothair" only so long as Lothair alone puts in a claim for the romantic, for the idea of elegance and opulence and splendor. We find these things neither in the "Vicar of Bullhampton" nor in "Put Yourself in His Place." A great deal of sarcasm has been lavished upon the gorgeous properties and the superfine diction of Mr. Disraeli's drama. The author is like the gentleman who tells his architect that he will not have his house spoiled for a few thousand dollars. Jewels, castles, horses, riches of every kind, are poured into the story without measure, without mercy. But there is a certain method, after all, in the writer's madness. His purpose—his instinct, at least—has been to portray with all possible completeness a purely aristocratic world. He has wished to emphasize the idea, to make a strong statement. He has at least made a striking one. He may not have strictly reproduced a perfect society of "swells," but he has very fairly reflected one. His novel could have emanated only from a mind thoroughly under the dominion of an almost awful sense of the value and glory of dukes and ducal possessions. That his dukes seem to us very stupid, and his duchesses very silly, is of small importance beside the fact that he has expressed with such lavish generosity the ducal side of the question. It is a very curious fact that Mr. Disraeli's age and experience, his sovereign opportunities for disenchantment, as one may suppose, should have left him such an almost infantine joy in being one of the initiated among the dukes. When Lothair is invited to dinner, he assents with the remark, "I suppose a late eight." As the amiable young nobleman utters these apparently simple words, we catch a glimpse over his shoulder of the elegant author looking askance at the inelegant public and repeating them with gentle rapture. Quite the most interesting point with regard to the work is this frequent betrayal of the possible innocence of one who has been supposed to be nothing if not knowing.

TYNDALL'S HOURS OF EXERCISE IN THE ALPS*

PROFESSOR TYNDALL'S volume has not only great merits, but a great and constant charm. Few writers on scientific topics possess in such degree the art of flinging over their stern subject-matter that mellow light of sentiment which conciliates the uninitiated mind without cheapening, as it were, the theme. Science we imagine has few such useful friends in literature: it were much to be wished that literature had a few such friends in science. By which we mean that literary topics would largely gain if writers would wander as far afield in search of a more rigorous method, as Professor Tyndall has travelled hitherward in search of a graceful one. But indeed Professor Tyndall seems to us so admirable a writer chiefly because he is so clear, so educated a thinker. It would be hard to make an unsymmetrical statement of conceptions so definite as those in which he deals. The habit of accurate thought gives a superb neatness to his style. "The mind," he excellently says, in his recent "Fragments of Science," is, as it were, a photographic plate, which is gradually cleansed by the effort to think rightly, and which, when so cleansed, and not before, receives impressions from the light of truth." This sentence may serve at once as an example of the author's admirable way of putting things, and as a text for remark on the highly clarified

---

* *Hours of Exercise in the Alps.* By John Tyndall, L.L.D., F.R.S. New York: D. Appleton & Co. 1871. (*Atlantic Monthly*, November, 1871).

condition of the Professor's own intellect. The reader moves in an atmosphere in which the habit of a sort of heroic attention seems to maintain a glare of electric light. On every side he sees shining facts, grouped and piled like the Alpine ice-masses the author commemorates in the present volume.

When Professor Tyndall starts forth in the early morning to climb an Alpine peak, or when he stands triumphant and still vigilant on the summit, he resolves the mysteries of the atmosphere, the weather, the clouds, the glaciers, into various hard component facts, which, to his eye, deepen rather than diminish the picturesqueness of the scene. In the midst of chaos and confusion the analytic instinct rises supreme. "'As night drew near the fog thickened through a series of intermittances which a mountain-land alone can show. Sudden uprushings of air would often carry the clouds aloft in vertical currents, while horizontal gusts swept them wildly to and fro. Different currents, impinging on each other, sometimes formed whirling cyclones of cloud. The air was tortured in its search of equilibrium." And elsewhere: "Monte Rosa was still in shadow, but . . . . her precipices were all aglow. The purple coloring of the mountains . . . . was indescribable; out of Italy I have never seen anything like it. Oxygen and nitrogen could not produce the effect; some effluences from the earth, some foreign constituent of the atmosphere, developed in those deep valleys by the southern sun, must sift the solar beams, weaken the rays of medium refrangibility, and blend the red and violet of the spectrum to that incomparable hue." These are fair examples of the explanatory gaze, as we may say, at nature, which so richly substantiates the author's perception of the beautiful, making him on all occasions an admirably vivid painter. The source of the reader's satisfaction is his sense of these firm particulars, as it were, close behind the glittering generals of common fine writing. It must be confessed that Professor Tyndall's manner makes our lighter descriptive arts seem somewhat inexpensive. We have had suggested to us, as we read, Mr. Ruskin's strongly contrasted manner of treating the same topics. He is almost equally familiar with mountain scenery, and some of his noblest writing occurs in the Alpine chapters of "Modern Painters." But the difference in tone, in attitude, in method, in result, between the two men, is most striking and interesting. In one we have the pursuit of the picturesque in nature tempered and animated by scientific curiosity; in the other, linked and combined with a sort of passionate sentimentality. Professor Tyndall, to our minds, never rises so high as Mr. Ruskin at certain inspired moments; we doubt if he has ever stood knee-deep in flower-streaked Alpine grasses, and seen, above him, with just that potent longing of vision, "the waves of everlasting green roll silently into their long inlets among the shadows of the pines." But we may say of Professor Tyndall that, on the whole, he gives the mind a higher lift. His pages are pervaded by a cool contagious serenity which reminds one of high mountain air on a still day. He exhales a kind of immense urbanity,—the good-humor of a man who has mastered a multitude of facts. Mr. Ruskin, on the other hand, stands oppressed and querulous among the swarming shapes and misty problems his magnificent imagination and his "theological" sympathies have evoked; as helpless as that half-skilled wizard of the Coliseum, of whom Benvenuto Cellini narrates. He leaves in the mind a bitter deposit of melancholy; whereas Professor Tyndall's recitals have passed through the understanding with the cleansing force of running water. This difference is perhaps owing especially, however, to the fact that in Mr. Ruskin you are fatigued by a perpetual sense of waste exertion; and that half your pleasure in reading Tyndall comes from the admirable economy of his style. He is all concentration. His narrative never ceases to be a closely wrought chain of logically related propositions. No sentence but really fills (and has paid for, so to speak) the space it occupies. If there is no "nonsense" about Professor Tyndall's writing, it is in a deeper sense than through the comparatively vulgar fact that he is a frank materialist, and leaves the whole class of imponderable factors out of his account; in the sense, rather, that his writing is so strictly constructive and positive, leaving in its march no stragglers behind and reaching its goal by the straightest road. He consumes his own smoke. The author of "Modern Painters," on the other hand, though he has written so much (and to such excellent purpose) on "composition" in art, has not practiced it in literature so rigorously as might have been wished. But it would be very absurd to push our comparison too far. It was suggested by the simple fact that, like Mr. Ruskin, Professor Tyndall is a man of powerful imagination.

The volume which has given us a pretext for these remarks is a record of Professor Tyndall's various exploits in the Alps. He has pursued Nature into her highest places and gathered observations at the cost of much personal exertion and exposure. Some of his chapters have already appeared; all of them were substantially written at the time of the adventures they relate, and are full of the immediate freshness, the air of business, of genuine mountaineering. Those who will read at the same time Mr. Leslie Stephen's recent delightful "Playground of Europe" will find here potently recalled their own long summer days in Switzerland. Mr. Stephen, though none the less a mountaineer, is a very happy humorist; and the reader's complaint with Professor Tyndall will be, possibly, that he is too little of one. He is fearfully in earnest; he has an unwavering eye to business; and herewith the reader will scarcely fail to observe, quite ungrudgingly, the author's fine habit of egotism. It is very serene, very robust, and it carries the best conscience in the world. It makes its first appearance when, in the Preface, he erects into peculiarly personal application the very interesting question of the source of the modern interest in fine scenery, and dedicates his book to a friend on the ground, apparently (reversing the common order of obligation), of his being one "whom I taught in his boyhood to handle a theodolite and lay a chain"; it recurs in the various rugged resting-points and rare breathing-spaces of his perilous scrambles, and it rises perhaps to a climax in the last chapter of the volume, where, in an account of a stormy voyage to Algeria, he relates how in the face of danger he "watched with intense interest the workings of his own mind,"—and apparently found them satisfactory. Professor Tyndall indeed gravitates, at all times most naturally, to self-reference. In the "Fragments of Science," before mentioned, having occasion to speak with enthusiasm of Carlyle, he tells us how he "must ever remember with gratitude that, through three long cold German winters, Carlyle placed me in my tub, even when ice was on it's surface, at five o'clock every morning." This seems to us a capital instance of the so-called *naïveté* of genius. But we confess that to ourselves this same *naïveté* is never offensive, and that it

is no mean entertainment to read a powerful mind by flashes of
egotism. The author's self-complacency appears to be but part
and parcel of the fine in good-humor with which he regards things
general. The reader, too, will willingly concede the right of a
genial equanimity to one who has learned it in *action* so thoroughly as Professor Tyndall. His book reveals to us a superb
working organization. That manner of rest from overwork, which
he comes to Switzerland to seek, will seem to many persons a
rather arduous pastime. But once a-trudge on his icy slopes, climbing, noting, straining, buffeting,—with his "solid nutriment for
the day consisting of part of a box of meat-lozenges,"—he feels the
sources of strength renewed. And in case of bad weather he has
other wholesome expedients. During a period of storm on the
Bel-Alp he rolls himself in his plaid, lights his pipe, and masters
"Mozely on Miracles."

We must not enter into the details of our author's various
adventures. They were all as bravely achieved as they are vividly
narrated. Professor Tyndall concedes more than some authori-
ties to the much-discussed perils of mountaineering. Mr. Leslie
Stephen appears to place them at a minimum,—so long, that is,
as vigilance is at its maximum. But Professor Tyndall hints at con-
tingencies in which even the utmost care leaves an all-sufficient
margin for calamity. Such was the occasion in which the guide
Joseph Bennen, here commemorated, found his death; *apropos*
of which one may remark that the author's portraiture of Bennen,
—the *"Garibaldi der Führer,"*—a series of firm touches scattered
here and there through the volume, is one of the best things it
contains. There has recently been much talk in England about
Alpine perils, and an attempt manifested to draw the line between
lawful and wanton self-exposure. The details of this question
need not occupy us here, removed as we are, compared with the
English, from this particular field of enterprise: though indeed
it may well have been raised recently among readers of this magazine by the admirable narratives of a gentleman himself profoundly indifferent to such fine distinctions. Professor Tyndall's
volume, suggestive of so many things, has been so of none more
than of just this point of the vanity of saying to human audacity,
curiosity,—the great motive energy of our Anglo-Saxon race, by

whatever names we call it,—that it shall, in any direction, go thus far and no farther. We shall live to see it go farther than we can yet forecast its course. Mr. Clarence King and his friend, for instance, have been setting fresh examples, in our own Western Alps, for which coming years will surely furnish a sufficient following,—and yet awhile without that "perpetual leather gaiter and ostentation of bath-tub" which they apprehend. What man can attempt, by hook or by crook, he will never consent to abjure on *a priori* grounds even the most elaborately rational. There is no rest for him but after the fact, and in the unfolding of human experiences these defiant yet seductive facts press more and more upon his conscience. Its constant exhibition of the exquisite mettle of the human will gives perhaps its greatest interest to Mr. Tyndall's book. The author himself, indeed, claims that for the wise man there need be nothing vain or wanton in Alpine climbing. It is subjectively as valuable a discipline as it is rich in objective revelations. "Spirit and matter are interfused. The Alps improve us *totally*, and we return from the precipices wiser as well as stronger men." To this, as far as we are able, we heartily subscribe. It seems to us that the perilous ascent of the Matterhorn was amply justified by the inrush of those "musings" the author so eloquently describes, and which were conditioned then and there. After the great efforts of the Alps, the efforts of daily life, pitched chiefly as they are in a lower key, are vanquished with greater ease. Common solitude is more tolerable, after a taste of that palpable loneliness which sits among the upper peaks; the vulgar heats of life seem mild in contrast with the swelter of Swiss hillsides; among our daily fatigues we may recall with profit the resolution which unmeasured itself through the endless phases of a Swiss ascent. The "eloquence of nature," we suppose, is the proper motto of Professor Tyndall's book. It is surely an excellent one. Nature as a teacher, as a friend, as a companion, is, especially among ourselves, decidedly underestimated. But her claims in these respects are, to our mind, to be received with a qualification. We are to remember that nature dwells within us as well as without, and that we have each of us a personal Alp to climb,— some formidable peak of character to dismantle of its frowning mystery and to decorate with the little flag-stick of mastery, before we can roam at our ease through the mysteries of matter. In other words, eternal Nature is less a pure refuge than the poets would have us believe. She is an excellent teacher for those whose education is fairly begun, a most effective comforter for those whom she finds half comforted.

STOPFORD BROOKE'S THEOLOGY IN THE ENGLISH POETS*

UNDER this title, Mr. Stopford Brooke publishes a series of lectures upon Cowper, Coleridge, Wordsworth, and Burns—lectures delivered to his London congregation on Sunday afternoons. The greater part of the volume is devoted to Wordsworth, who is treated of in eight out of the fifteen chapters. Mr. Brooke enjoys much reputation as an eloquent preacher of the extremely liberal school, and these discourses afford evidence both of his eloquence and of his liberality. They strike us as rather too fluent and redundant—the common fault of clerical writing; but they contain a good deal of sensible criticism and of suggestive moral analysis. Mr. Brooke does not always clinch his argument very sharply, but the sentiment of his remarks is usually excellent. His moral perceptions are, indeed, more acute than his literary, and he rather too readily forgives a poor verse on the plea of a fine thought. He gives us a great many passages from Wordsworth—the most prosaic of poets as well as the most poetic—in which the moral flavor has apparently reconciled him to the flatness of the form more effectually than it will do most readers. The author's aim has been to construct the religious belief of the poets from their works; but this aim, as he advances, rather loses itself. His "theology" merges itself in general morality—in any considerations not merely literary. With the exception of Cowper, indeed, we should say that none of the poets we have named had, properly, a theology; their

---

* 'Theology in the English Poets. By the Rev. Stopford A. Brooke, M. A.' New York: D. Appleton & Co. 1875. (*The Nation*, January 21, 1875).

principal dogma was that it is the privilege of poets to be vague. Coleridge, indeed, as a philosopher, "went in," as the phrase is, for the supreme sanctity of the Church of England; but Coleridge as a poet, in so far as he is now read or remembered, had little to say about creeds and churches. In a poet so vast and suggestive as Wordsworth we may find a hint of almost any view of the origin and destiny of mankind that one is disposed to look for; and we think that the author has made the stages and subdivisions of the poet's intellectual history rather too rigid and definite. Of course, Wordsworth was, on the whole, a Deist; but he was a Deist with such far-reaching side-lights into the realms of nature and of human feeling that one fancies that readers of the most adverse spiritual tempers must have often obtained an equal inspiration from him. Burns, as Mr. Brooke admits, was no positive believer at all, and he rests his interest in him on the fact that he was so manly and human—so perfect a subject for redemption and salvation. Of Burns Mr. Brooke writes very well, and probably as few clergymen—apart from certain Scottish divines, whose patriotism has anticipated their morality—have written of him. "He was always—like the Prodigal Son," says the author, "coming to himself and saying, 'I will arise and go to my Father'; but he never got more than half-way in this world."

Mr. Brooke glances first at the theological element in English poetry before Cowper. "The devotional element which belonged to Donne, Herbert, Vaughan, and some of the Puritan poets, died away in the critical school which began with Dryden and ended with Pope. The 'Religio Laici' of Dryden is partly a reproduction of the scholastic theology, partly an attack on the Deists, and it does not contain one single touch of personal feeling towards God." The author recognizes Pope's devoutness of heart; but he illustrates this same absence of the personal accent in his verse. To that of Cowper three things belonged: "Passion, the personal element, and the expression of doctrine." It is puzzling, at first, to be called upon to attribute "passion" to Cowper. Theological he was—terribly, fatally theological—but of how admirably he humanized his theology these lines, quoted by Mr. Brooke, are an example. Mr. Brooke contrasts them, for passion and personal feeling, with one of those familiar fine passages from Pope, in which the rhythm is that of the pendulum, and the philosophy so bent on keeping on terms with the epigram, that one loses half one's faith in its consistency. They seem to us extremely touching:

> "I was a stricken deer that left the herd
> Long since—with many an arrow deep infixed
> My panting side was charged when I withdrew
> To seek a tranquil death in distant shades.
> There was I found by one who had Himself
> Been hurt by the archers. In His side He bore
> And in His hands and feet the cruel scars.
> With gentle force soliciting the darts
> He drew them forth, and healed and bade me live."

Mr. Brooke writes at some length on the poetry of Man and the poetry of Nature as the later poets of the last century handled them, and makes several very good points. They underwent a very similar development—a transition from the abstract to the concrete, from the conventional to the real, the general to the individual; except that Man, at the poet's hands, rather anticipated Nature. What the French would call "intimate" human poetry was fairly established by Goldsmith, with the help, later, of Crabbe; but Nature, as we look at her nowadays, did not really receive anything like her dues until Wordsworth began to set the chords a-murmuring. If the history of that movement toward a passionate scrutiny of Nature, which has culminated in England, in our day, with Tennyson and Browning, could be scientifically written, we imagine it would be found to throw a great deal of light on the processes of the human mind. It has at least drawn into its services an incalculable amount of ingenuity, of imagination, of intellectual force. There are descriptive phrases and touches in Tennyson and Browning which represent, on this subject, an extraordinary accumulation of sentiment, a perfect entanglement of emotion, which give the key, as it were, to a civilization. Mr. Brooke quotes from "The Ancient Mariner" several examples of Coleridge's subtlety of observation of natural phenomena, which are peculiarly striking in a writer of his loosely reflective cast. But, what with Wordsworth and Shelley and Keats, subtlety of observation was then in the air; and Wordsworth himself, moreover, is a proof that observation feeding on Nature, and meditation feeding on itself, are processes which may very well go forward in company. Mr. Brooke gives us as the last word of Coleridge's theology, after many vagaries:

> "Oh! sweeter than the marriage feast,
> 'Tis sweeter far to me
> To walk together to the kirk
> In a goodly company!"

Of Wordsworth, Mr. Brooke writes diffusely—too diffusely, we think, for discretion; for there are reasons in the nature of things why a prolonged commentary on the author of the *Prelude* and the *Excursion* should have an air of superfluity. He is himself so inordinately diffuse that to elaborate his meaning and lead it through further developments is to double the liability to irritation in the reader. He ought to be treated like a vast enclosed section of landscape, into which the reader may be turned to ramble at his pleasure. The critic may give us a few hints—he may hand us the key; but we should advise his making his bow at the gate. In the fine places we wish to be alone for solemnity's sake; and in the dull ones, for mortification's. Mr. Brooke, who is evidently a most zealous and familiar student of the poet, undertakes to relate the complete history of his poetical development on the moral side. It is, of course, an interesting story, though it rather drags at times, and though its conclusion is, as Mr. Brooke admits, anti-climax. The conservatism into which Wordsworth stiffened in the latter half of his career was essentially prosaic, and the "Sonnets to Order" read really like sonnets to order in another sense. But one is thankful for the opportunity of dipping into him again on any terms; for the sake of a few scattered lines of Wordsworth at his best, one would make one's way through a more importunate commentary than Mr. Brooke's. For Wordsworth at his best certainly soars at an altitude which the imagination nowhere else so serenely and naturally reaches. There could surely be no better example of the moral sublime than the lines to Toussaint L'Ouverture:

> "Thou hast left behind
> Powers that will work for thee,—air, earth and skies;
> There's not a breathing of the common wind
> That will forget thee; thou hast great allies:
> Thy friends are exultations, agonies,
> And love, and man's unconquerable mind."

This is very simple, but it is magnificently strong, and the verses, beyond their intrinsic beauty, have for us now the value of carrying an assurance that they have played a part and rendered service—been a stimulus and an inspiration—to many readers. The author has, of course, much to say on Wordsworth's almost fathomless intimacy with Nature, and he quotes these lines in lines in illustration of that imaginative force which had expanded, through years of open-air brooding and musing, to its amplest reach. Wordsworth is speaking of London and its vast human interest, which, to his mind, seemed filled

> "With impregnations like the Wilds
> In which my early feelings had been nursed—
> Bare hills and valleys, full of caverns, rocks,
> And audible seclusions, dashing lakes,
> Echoes and waterfalls and pointed crags.
> That into music touch the passing wind."

The author mentions elsewhere, among Wordsworth's inimitable descriptive touches, his saying of a lonely mountain lake:

> "There sometimes doth a leaping fish
> Send through the tarn a lonely cheer."

That alone seems to us, in trivial parlance, worth the price of the volume. It is fair to Mr. Brooke to transcribe a specimen of his criticism; the following seems to us a favorable one:

> "Our greatest poet since Milton was as religious as Milton, and in both I cannot but think the element of grandeur of style, which belongs so preeminently to them, flowed largely from the solemn simplicity and the strength which a dignified and unbigoted faith in great realities beyond

318

this world gave to the order of their thoughts. Coleridge was flying from one speculation to another all his life. Scott had no vital joy in his belief, and it did not interpenetrate his poetry. Byron believed in fate more than in God. Shelley floated in an ideal world which had not the advantage of being generalized from any realities; and not one of them possesses, though Byron comes near it now and then, the grand style. Wordsworth alone, combining fine artistic powers with profound religion, walks when he chooses, though he limps wretchedly at times, with nearly as stately a step as Milton. He had the two qualities which always go with the grand style in poetry—he lived intensely in the present, and he had the roots of his being fixed in a great centre of power—faith in the eternal love and righteousness of God."

Mr. Brooke intends, apparently, to take up the other poets in turn. Tennyson and Browning, as he says, are full of theology; and in the many-colored transcendental fumes and vapors of Shelley the theological incense mounts with varying density. But with Byron and Keats it will take some shrewdness to discover it. In treating of the theology of Byron, indeed, Mr. Brooke would have a subject worthy of all his ingenuity.

PROFESSOR DAVID MASSON'S "THREE DEVILS: LUTHER'S, MILTON'S, AND GOETHE'S WITH OTHER ESSAYS"

WE always read Professor Masson with interest, but never without a certain feeling of disappointment. He is clear, shrewd, and vigorous, and his style (when it is not Mr. Carlyle's) is quite his own. He attempts to deal with subjects in a first-rate manner, and yet, at the last, he fails to give an impression of first-rate

---

* 'Three Devils: Luther's, Milton's, and Goethe's. With other Essays. By David Masson, M. A., LL.D., etc.' London and New York; Macmillan & Co. 1874. (*The Nation*, February 18, 1875).

power. He is, in a word, in thought and expression the least bit
vulgar. He is fond of rhetoric, which is perfectly legitimate: but
his taste has odd lapses. He writes literary history in the picturesque manner; but it is amusing to have a writer of his apparent sincerity reminding us of Mr. Hepworth Dixon. When
Chatterton, in the author's biography of the young poet, writes
to Horace Walpole, we are told that "whether from the sudden-
ness and naïveté of the attack, or from the stupefying effects of
the warm air in his library of a March evening, Walpole was
completely taken in." Dryden made an attack on Elkanah Settle,
the bad poet. "Settle," says Professor Masson, "replied with some
spirit, with little effect, and was, in fact, 'settled' forever." We
doubt whether Mr. Hepworth Dixon, indeed, would have risked
that. Professor Masson has been republishing some of his early
essays, and one volume of the series was lately noticed in these
pages. They were worth such care as he chose to bestow upon
them; but it is a pity that this should not have included a little
chastening of the style. The first of the volumes before us contains a study of the differences in Luther's, Milton's, and Shakspere's conception of the Devil, a parallel not particularly effective
between Shakspere and Goethe; a sketch—the best thing, perhaps,
in the book—of Milton's youth; an essay on Dryden; a "picturesque" account of Dean Swift; and some reflections, notice-
ably very acute, on "One of the Ways Literature May Illustrate
History." These things are all entertaining, and some of them
interesting. It is particularly interesting, perhaps, to investigate
people's ideas about the Devil, and Professor Masson sets forth
very justly the respective characteristics of Milton's Satan,
Goethe's Mephistopheles, and the Foul Fiend who haunted the
great Reformer. Luther's devil was properly the only real devil of
them all, the only one who carried with him a need of being
believed in. Milton's Satan was an exalted poetic conception, in
which the idea of evil was constantly modified by the beauty of
presentation. Mephistopheles was the exquisite result of Goethe's
elaborate intellectual analysis of evil; but Luther's devil was the
concrete embodiment and compendium of evil, the result of
his intense *feeling* of evil. Luther's devil, indeed, was not an intellectual conception at all, but a huge, oppressive spiritual con-

viction such as only a man of marvellously robust temperament could have had the capacity for. Few men could have afforded to keep, as we may say, such a devil as Luther's—an engine, a machine, which required an inordinate amount of fuel. "Life," says Professor Masson, "must be a much more insipid thing than it was then." Certainly Luther's consciousness was a tolerably exciting affair; the nearest analogy to it that we can imagine is that of a commander-in-chief in the thick of a pitched battle. Suppose this to be chronic and lifelong, and we form an idea of Luther's state of mind. Like a general hard pressed, he had his strategic inspirations. "When he could not drive the devil away by uttering sentences of Holy Writ or by prayers, he used to address him thus: 'Devil, if, as you say, Christ's blood, which was shed for my sins, be not sufficient to ensure my salvation, can't you pray for me yourself, devil?' At this the devil invariably fled, *quia est superbus spiritus et non potest ferre contemptum sui?*"

Professor Masson writes particularly well about Milton, whom he has made an object of devoted study, and draws a very handsome portrait of him as he stood on the threshold of manhood. He was what would be called nowadays a very high-toned young man—what even in some circles would be termed a prig. But Milton's priggishness was in the grand style, and it had a magnificent consistency. It is on the pervading *consistency* of his character that Professor Masson dwells, while he attempts to reconcile his austerity, his rigidity, his self-complacency, his want of humor with his possession of supreme poetic genius. Milton records it as a conviction of his early youth that "he who would not be frustrate of his hope to write well hereafter in laudable things ought himself to be a true poem." "A certain niceness of nature," he elsewhere says, "an honest haughtiness and self-esteem either of what I was or what I might be (which let envy call pride), and, lastly, that modesty whereof, though not in the title-page, yet here I may be excused to make some beseeming profession; all these, uniting the supply of their natural aid together, kept me still above those low descents of mind beneath which he must deject and plunge himself that can agree to salable and unlawful prostitutions." "Fancy," Professor Masson comments upon this, "ye to whom the moral frailty of genius is a consolation, or to whom the association of virtue with youth and Cambridge is a jest—fancy Milton, as this passage from his own pen describes him at the age of twenty-three, returning to his father's house from the university, full of its accomplishments and its honors, an auburn-haired youth, beautiful as the Apollo of a northern clime, and that beautiful body the temple of a soul pure and un-soiled. . . . He had made it a matter of conscientious investigation what kind of moral tone and career would best fit a man to be a poet on the one hand, or would be most likely to frustrate his hopes of writing well on the other, and his conclusion, we see, was dead against the 'wild-oats' theory. . . . The nearest poet to Milton, in this respect, since Milton's time has undoubt-edly been Wordsworth." As Professor Masson indicates, the danger that the extreme "respectability" of each of these great men might operate as a blight upon their poetic faculty was not averted by the interposition of the sense of humor. We know how little of this faculty they possessed. What made them great was what we have called their consistency—the fact that their seriousness, their solemnity, their "respectability" was on so large and unbroken a scale. They were men of a proud imagination—even when Words-worth condescended to the poetry of village idiots and little porringers. In the day of Mark Twain there is no harm in being reminded that the absence of drollery may, at a stretch, be com-pensated by the presence of sublimity. The wild-oats theory, too, may probably be left to take care of itself, and the history of Mil-ton's youthful rigidity be suffered to suggest that there is a fine opening for the next young man of talent who feels within him the spirit to risk something. If, as Milton says, "he would not be frustrate of his hope to write well hereafter in laudable things," he might try the experiment of ignoring trivialities. American readers will probably compare Professor Masson's disquisition on Dryden with that of Professor Lowell, and conclude decidedly in favor of the latter. Professor Masson's essay belongs to a coarser school of criticism, and he points out much less acutely than the American critic's remarkable insight in the poetic mystery enables *him* to do, why it is that in spite of the many accounts against him the balance, on the scroll of fame, has been in Dry-den's favor. The present essay is readable, but Professor Lowell's is suggestive.

One may bestow the praise of suggestiveness, however, on the last paper in the volume—an ingenious plea for the *indirect* testimony of past literatures as to contemporaneous refinement and virtue. The accumulation of science, says Professor Masson, not only adds to the stock of what the mind possesses, but modifies the mind in what it is *per se*. Operating on its new acquisitions, the mental apparatus enlarges its functions and, as a greater quantity of grist is brought to the mill, becomes a more powerful machine. This at least is the common assumption, and this would prove that we of the present day are (besides our character as mere trustees of new discoveries) people of a higher intellectual value than our remote precursors. Professor Masson contests the deduction, in a spirit which most disinterested students of history and literature will probably sympathize with. "Shakspere lived and died, we may say, in the prescientific period; he lived and died in the belief of the fixedness of our earth in space and the diurnal whirling round her of the ten spectacular spheres. Not the less was he Shakspere; and none of us dares to say that there is now in the world, or has recently been, a more expert thinking apparatus of its order than his mind was, a spiritual transparency of larger diameter, or vivid with grander gleamings and pulses. Two hundred and fifty years therefore, chockful though they are of new knowledges and discoveries, have not been a single knife-edge of visible advance in the world's power of producing splendid individuals." And the author continues that, adding two hundred and fifty years many times over to that, and receding to the time of the great Greeks, we are obliged to admit that there has not been a knife-edge of advance in the same process since *that* period. Of course it may be claimed that the increase of science has raised the general level of ability— that the number of clever people is greater than formerly. The discussion of this question Prof. Masson waives; he confines himself to "the assertion that within historic time we find what we are obliged to call an intrinsic coequality of *some* minds at various successive points and at long-repeated intervals, and that consequently, if the human race is gradually acquiring a power of producing individuals more able than their ablest predecessors, the rate of its law in this respect is so slow that

2,500 years have not made the advance appreciable. The assertion is limited; it is reconcilable, I think, with the most absolute and extreme doctrine of evolution; but it seems to me both important and curious, inasmuch as it has not yet been sufficiently attended to in any of the phrasings of that doctrine that have been speculatively put forward." Those who are not ashamed to confess to a sneaking conservatism in their valuation of earlier ages than our own, will agree with Prof. Masson that his assertion is important, and they will do so the more frankly if they happen to be particularly struck with the cleverness of the present age. We ourselves find this very striking; the general level of ability seems to us wonderfully high, and we believe that really candid students of literature must often admit that we allow things nowadays to pass unnoticed which would have made the fortune of earlier writers. We not only beat them in knowledge, but we beat them in wit. And yet who does not know what it is to be divided, half painfully, between his sense of these facts and their brilliant and flattering meaning, and his sense, particularly tender as it often is, of the great movements of the human mind being, or at least seeming, great in virtue of a certain essential and unalterable quality? In some such clinging belief as this your genuine conservative finds a mysterious comfort, which it would take him a long time to explain. It would perhaps be, even to persons of a very discreetly and temperately sentimental turn, one of the most chilling and uncomfortable conquests of the doctrine of evolution, that we should have to reflect that the mind of Shakspere was not only different in degree from our, but different in kind.

MRS. BROWNING'S LETTERS TO
R. H. HORNE*

THE form of this work is a trifle singular, Mr. Horne officiating as editor to Mrs. Browning, and Mr. Mayer rendering the same service to Mr. Horne—though it would not seem that the latter gentleman, who is a literary veteran, stood in need of a sponsor. Mr. Horne, whom the readers of the poetry of forty years ago will remember as the author of a quasi-philosophic epic entitled *Orion,* which enjoyed at that period considerable popularīty, sustained a correspondence with Mrs. Browning during the early years of her celebrity—the years immediately preceding her marriage. These letters he lately published in certain magazines with a slight connecting narrative. They are here republished, supplemented by two or three chapters of literary reminiscence by Mr. Horne, and garnished with an occasional note by Mr. Mayer—the result being a decidedly entertaining book. As nothing in the way of a memoir of the lady who may fairly be spoken of as the first of the world's women-poets had hitherto been published, and as no other letters from her hand had, to our knowledge, ever been given to the world, these two volumes will be held by her admirers to have a biographical value—perhaps even to supply in some degree a sensible want. We may add that they will be read with hardly less pleasure by Mrs. Browning's colder critics.

The letters are very charming and altogether to the author's honor. Mr. Horne's own observations, moreover, are frequently interesting, and characterized by much raciness of style. The correspondents never met face to face, and their topics are almost wholly "intellectual" and literary, Mrs. Browning alluding to no personal affairs except her extreme ill health, to which, moreover, her allusions have the highest degree of cheerfulness and serenity. The letters run from 1839 to 1846, the date of her marriage and her removal to Italy, in pursuit (in some measure

---

* 'Letters of Elizabeth Barrett Browning, addressed to R. H. Horne. With Comments on Contemporaries. Edited by S. R. Townshend Mayer.' London: R. Bentley & Son. 1877. (*The Nation*, February 15, 1877).

successful) of stronger health. During these years Miss Barrett was wholly confined to her sick-room, lying on her sofa "wrapped in Indian shawls" (Mr. Horne begs her on one occasion to "recline for her portrait"), but writing, reading, thinking, and (by letter) talking most copiously, and publishing the poems which laid the foundations of her distinction. She has little to write about except her ideas, her fancies, and her literary impressions, for she sees few people and knows, personally, little of the world's life. Her letters are those of an extremely clever and "highly educated" young lady, of a very fine moral sensibility, who is much interested (as a contributor and otherwise) in the magazines and weekly papers, and whose only form of gossip is literary gossip. She is an inveterate and often an acute critic; Mr. Horne, indeed, informs us that her criticisms in the *Athenæum* "are among the finest ever penned." It may be noted that her admiration for *Orion* and Mr. Horne's other productions was lively and demonstrative; but, as the editor very justly observes, these allusions could not be removed without destroying the coherency of the letters. Miss Barrett's tone is extremely natural and spontaneous, and has often a touch of graceful gayety which the reader of her poetry, usually so anti-jocose, would not have expected. It offers a peculiarly pleasing mixture of the ladylike and the highly-intelligent, and leaves an impression somewhat akin to that of an agreeable woman's voice—soft, substantial, and expressive. Miss Barrett's invalidism evidently only quickened her intellectual activity. "There I had my fits of Pope and Byron and Coleridge," she writes in allusion to the Malvern Hills, "and read Greek as hard under the trees as some of your Oxonians in the Bodleian; gathered visions from Plato and the dramatists, and eat and drank Greek and made my head ache with it." "But as to poetry," she writes of her own contemporaries (about 1841), "they are all sitting (in mistake) just now upon Caucasus for Parnassus—and wondering they don't see the Muses." Whether or no Mrs. Browning herself ever trod the highest peak of Parnassus, she certainly never sat upon Caucasus. An American had sent her a newspaper with a review of Tennyson's poetry, requesting her to forward it to the poet, which she did after some hesitation, the review being "cautious in its admiration." "I was quite ashamed of myself and my newspaper," she writes; "but [Tennyson] was good enough to forgive me for an involuntary forwardness. The people of Yankeeland, I observe, think that we all live in a house together, particularly we who write books. The idea of the absence of forests and savannahs annihilates with them the idea of distance." Mr. Horne had questioned her about Miss Agnes Strickland and her literary claims, and she, answering him tentatively, adds: "But do not trust me an inch; for I feel in a mist and a sort of fear of confounding the maiden didactication of Mrs. Ellis, when she was Sarah Stickney, and this of Miss Strickland's—having been given to confound Stickneys, and Stricklands from the very beginning. . . . Either a Stickney or a Strickland wrote the 'Poetry of Life.'" We quoted just now an allusion to Miss Barrett's copious reading; here is another—the tone of which is singularly just—which should balance against it:

"Mr. Kenyon calls me his 'omnivorous cousin.' I read without principle. I have a sort of unity, indeed, but it amalgamates instead of selecting—do you understand? When I had read the Hebrew Bible from Genesis to Malachi, right through, and was never stopped by the Chaldee"—if Mrs. Browning means this literally, by the way, it is a very considerable achievement for a sick and lonely young girl—"and the Greek poets and Plato right through from end to end, I passed as thoroughly through the flood of all possible and impossible British and foreign novels and romances, with slices of metaphysics laid thick between the sorrows of the multitudinous Celestinas. It is only useful knowledge and the multiplication-table I never tried hard at. And now—what now? Is that matter of exultation? Alas! no. Do I boast of my omnivorousness of reading, even apart from the romances? Certainly, no!—never except in joke. It's against my theories and ratiocinations, which take upon themselves to assert that we *all* generally err by reading too much and out of proportion to what we *think*. I should be wiser, I am persuaded, if I had not read half as much—should have had stronger and better exercised faculties, and should stand higher in my own appreciation. The fact is that the *ne plus ultra* of intellectual indolence is this reading of books. It comes next to what the Americans call 'whittling.' "

Miss Barrett had a particular passion for novels, and one of the most charming passages in these letters, which, in spite of its length, we shall venture to quote, is a eulogy of the reading of fiction. She had a very high opinion of Bulwer, and rendered more liberal justice to George Sand, Victor Hugo, and Balzac than was to have been expected from a quiet young English lady of thirty years ago. She thinks that the French novelists of that period present a much more brilliant front that the English. But here is the passage in question, which sustains what we said above about her "gayety" :

"O that love of story-telling! It may be foolish, to be sure; it leads one into waste of time and strong excitement, to be sure; still, how pleasant it is! How full of enchantment and dream-time gladnesses! What a pleasant accompaniment to one's lonely coffee-cup in the morning or evening to hold a little volume in the left hand and read softly along how Lindoro saw Monimia over the hedge, and what he said to her! After breakfast we have other matters to do, grave business matters—poems to write upon Eden or essays on Carlyle. . . . But everyone must attend to a certain proportion of practical affairs of life, and Lindoro and Monimia bring us ours. And then, if Monimia behaves pretty well, what rational satisfaction we have in settling her at the end of the book! No woman who speculates and practises on her own account has half the satisfaction in securing an establishment that we have with our Monimias—nor *should* have, let it be said boldly. Did we not divine it would end so, albeit ourselves and Monimia were weeping together at the end of the second volume? Even to the middle of the third, when Lindoro was sworn at for a traitor by everybody in the book, may it not be testified gloriously of us that *we* saw through him? . . . What, have you known nothing, Mr. Editor, of these exaltations?"

The only person, in addition to the correspondents, who plays a prominent part in these letters is Miss Mitford, the intimate friend of both parties, and to whom Mr. Horne devotes several pages of recollections. It will be remembered that in the admirable collection of Miss Mitford's own letters published a few years since, and which are certainly among the best in the language, there were a great many addressed to Mrs. Browning. Her friends seem all to have concurred in the opinion that her personal intelligence and brilliancy were much in excess of those to which her writings testify, and certainly her letters have a higher value than her books. Mr. Horne describes and characterizes her with much felicity, though with a certain oddity of phrase. "The expression [of her countenance] was entirely genial, cognoscitive, beneficent. The outline of the face was an oblate round, of no very marked significance beyond that of an apple or other rural 'character.'" And he emphasizes the apple metaphor by saying elsewhere that her countenance had a "fruity hopefulness." But he gives a vivid portrait of Miss Mitford's mellow geniality, her dogged old-English conservatism, and her intimate acquaintance with all rural things. His last pages are occupied with an account of the enterprise known as the "Guild of Literature and Art," which attained some renown upwards of thirty years ago, and of which, as of so many other enterprises, Charles Dickens was the leading spirit. As to the precise design of the "Guild" Mr. Horne is not explicit; it appears to have included the erection of a college for the aspiring, and an asylum for the retiring littérateur and artist. Bulwer, at any rate, offered land on his estates and wrote a comedy for raising money. The comedy was performed by the most distinguished amateurs, with Dickens as stage-manager, at Devonshire House, which its proprietor had lent for the purpose; the Queen came to see it, and sent a hundred guineas for her box, and Mr. Horne was in the cast. His record of the affair is very entertaining, but we may perhaps add without undue harshness that it induces meditation to discover in a writer whom we had accepted as the not unworthy correspondent of an illustrious woman the tip of the ear, as the French say, of that peculiarly British vice of which Thackeray was the immortal historian. Thackeray sometimes did not like to write the word, and we will not do so here. But the reader will perhaps guess it when we say that in relating how Mr. Mark Lemon, one of the actors in Bulwer's comedy, lost his way in the corridors of Devonshire House, Mr. Horne calls our attention to the "delightful urbanity" which the Duke manifested in giving him the necessary indication.

GEORGE BARNETT SMITH'S POETS AND NOVELISTS*

POETS AND NOVELISTS: A Series of Literary Studies. By George Barnett Smith. (New York: Appletons. 1875.)—These essays are marked as having originally appeared in various periodicals—the *Edinburgh, New Quarterly, Fortnightly,* and *Contemporary Reviews,* and the *Cornhill Magazine.* The information is valuable, for we should never have supposed that Mr. Barnett Smith's "literary studies" had been ushered into the world by these illustrious journals. They treat of Thackeray, Mrs. Browning, Peacock the novelist, Hawthorne, the Misses Brontë, Fielding, and Robert Buchanan. Of Thackeray Mr. Smith tells us that "his mode of narrative consists in a series of pictures after the manner of Hogarth." He goes on to say that Pendennis's "love-pasages with Miss Fotheringay are naïvely related," and that the young man's university career "is described with no sparing pen." "The subjectiveness of Thackeray," Mr. Smith pursues, "is another quality which has greatly enhanced the value of his works"; and he adds that, "leading out of his subjectiveness, or, rather, being a broader and grander development of it, we come to his humanity. That is the crown and glory of his work. And yet this man who was sensitive almost beyond parallel, was charged with having no heart! . . . So superficial are the judgments of the world!" The author concludes with a compliment to Thackeray's style. "To the faithfulness with which he spake the English tongue we believe future generations will testify." This last is surely ambiguous. For future generations the English tongue will probably have greatly changed, and we

(*The Nation,* December 30, 1875.)

should say that the testimony of Thackeray's own generation as to the way he "spake" it was the more valuable. But the error is perhaps slighter than to discover that Thackeray's narrative is like a series of pictures by Hogarth, or that the episode of Miss Fotheringay is "naïvely" related. Satirists are not usually remarkable for their naïveté, and if ever a man had little of this virginity of perception we should say it was the world-worn creator of the Pendennises and Costigans. For Mrs. Browning Mr. Smith has a boundless admiration. He devotes some space to considering the question whether it better describes her to say that she is "Tennyson's sister" or "Shakspere's daughter." It is impossible to withhold the suggestion that it might do to try "Wordsworth's niece" or "Swinburne's aunt." There was a chance to say a great many discriminating things about Mrs. Browning, but Mr. Smith has utterly missed it. It would have been interesting to point out the singularly intimate union of her merits and defects, to show how her laxity and impurity of style is constantly vitiating her felicity of thought. Mrs. Browning possessed the real poetic heat in a high degree; but it is not too much to say that her sense of the poetic form was an absolute muddle. Mr. Smith, however, has no eye for the niceties of diction (his own is often decidedly erratic), and he swallows everything whole. "And Burns, with pungent passionings set in his eyes," and "poor, proud Byron, sad as the grave and salt as life"—Mr. Smith thinks those are "excellent touches." In discussing the "Romaunt of Margret" and "Isobel's Child," he might have found something to say about that unwholesome taste, so characteristic of his author, which found a pathos in playing tricks with the spelling of proper names. With regard to another of Mrs. Browning's poems, he remarks that "the poet who loves Lady Geraldine has many excellences, but his vocation has not properly imbued him with the kindly spirit." "The character of the Earl," on the other hand, "is well drawn, his natural dignity being admirably caught in the few lines devoted to his limning." Mrs. Browning's sonnets Mr. Smith thinks "certainly equal to any of Wordsworth's and most of Milton's." Of "Aurora Leigh" he says that "it is a poem which one could imagine Shakspere dropping a tear over for its humanity"; and, again, with his high relish for "intense subjectivity," he remarks that that of the work in question "will exempt its influence on men from decay." Mr. Smith has much to say about Peacock's novels—for instance, that as regards one of them, in which the author has been less successful than in the others, "after the feast of sparkling wines and choice viands which he has again and again placed before us, the palate remains comparatively unexcited and unsatiated with this specimen of intellectual catering." There are many pages upon Hawthorne, from which we cull this allusion to one of the most exquisite of his tales: "The search for the 'Great Carbuncle' has much amusement, notwithstanding it is open to the charge of wild extravagance." To reproach Hawthorne for his "extravagance" is almost as odd as to compliment him on his comicality. From the article on "The Brontës" we learn that the author of 'Jane Eyre' was as "strong and brave as a lion"; that Rochester in that novel was a "Jupiter of rugged strength and passion"; that the situations in the tale are "very vivid: several scenes being depicted which it would be impossible to eradicate from the memory after the most extensive reading of serial literature": and that Emily Brontë "has this distinction, at any rate, that she has written a book which stands as completely alone in the language as does the 'Paradise Lost' or the 'Pilgrim's Progress.' " This is high praise for the crude and morbid story of 'Wuthering Heights,' and Mr. Smith may well say that "this, of itself, setting aside subject and construction, is no mean eminence." He devotes fifty-eight pages of eulogy to Robert Buchanan, in the course of which he makes the somewhat puzzling enquiry—"What would he give, for instance, for the details relative to the *personnel* of Homer and Shakspere, if written by themselves?" What is Mr. Smith's notion of the meaning of the word *personnel*? We have heard of the *personnel* of a hotel, of a theatre, of a fire-company, but never yet of a poet. Mr. Smith says in his preface that he has collected his essays in compliance with the importunities of his friends. He would have done better bravely to make up his mind to seem ill-natured and resist them. He seems to us but scantily furnished with the equipment of a critic.

THACKERAYANA

THACKERAYANA. Notes and Anecdotes. Illustrated by hundreds of sketches. By William Makepeace Thackeray, etc. (New York: Scribner, Welford & Co. 1875.)—This is a very frank piece of bookmaking; but it may be said that if a book was to be made, the subject might have been less happily chosen. The first effect of this bulky and handsome volume is to renew our regret that Thackeray's life should apparently be destined to remain unwritten. Why does not Miss Thackeray attempt a biography of her illustrious father? We should be more grateful for it than for the imaginary memoirs of Angelica Kauffmann. It is certain at least that a most agreeable work might be performed in collecting Mr. Thackeray's letters. These are known to have been delightful, and nobody, surely, ever received one without jealously preserving it. That they were chiefly humorous, and that the humor frequently overflowed in some comical little pen-drawing, are facts of equally general knowledge. A large part of the purpose of this anonymously-edited volume is to reproduce a number of such of Thackeray's sketches as are scattered through early and forgotten publications and over the fly-leaves and margins of old (and otherwise valueless) books, procured at the sale, after his death, of his library. The editor has been a collector of these things, and, so far as knowledge of the subject goes, he appears very competent to perform his task. But it is a question how far this task was worth performing. Thackeray is to our sense very far from being the first-rate caricaturist the editor considers him, and it seems to us a decided mistake to thrust him forward in this light. We cannot agree with the critic in the *North British Review,* whom the editor quotes so commendingly, that the drawing in Thackeray's sketches is always excellent. The drawing seems to us to have almost as little skill as might be; even for an amateur it is exceedingly amateurish. The merit is in a certain frank expressiveness of a broadly comical idea—an expressiveness obvious, but never subtle. It is curious that, while Thackeray's humor in writing was so complex and refined, his

(*The Nation,* December 9, 1875.)

comicality as a draughtsman is always rather bald and primitive. There are few of the rapid scrawls disinterred in the present volume quite worthy of the space they occupy. This reproach would not apply to such sketches as might be incidental to his letters; they would be at one with the comparative laxity of the text.

This volume excites our curiosity for biographical detail without very largely gratifying it. It relates some interesting circumstances about Thackeray's earlier years—such as the history of the establishment of the *Constitutional* newspaper, the luckless enterprise in which he sank the greater part of his patrimony; and it recalls some passages in his career about which most people have vague impressions, such as the very large amount of time which, first and last, he spent in Paris, the very quiet manner in which at first 'Vanity Fair' came into the world, etc.; but it is not apparent that the editor has had access to any recondite sources of information. His strong point is the Thackerayan bibliography. He knows, apparently, everything that Thackeray wrote in his 'prentice years—he knows all the books that he owned, and most of those that he read. Many of these latter seem to be in his hands, and he transfers whole pages of them to the present volume. When we call this a piece of book-making extraordinary, it is to the formidable scale of these interpolations that we allude. The practice of relating a man's life by stringing together whole chapters from books found in his library, and which he may be presumed to have handled, is one which promises to give a formidable extension to the writing of biography. We have here a copious condensation of Walpole's 'Castle of Otranto,' seventeen pages of dreary extracts from Rollin's 'Ancient History,' and a long account of Fielding's 'Joseph Andrews.' The pretext is that Thackeray made some boyish sketches in satirical illustration of these works. Text, therefore, and sketches are given us at formidable length. The reproduction of all might have been spared; the latter have but the minimum of skill. Thus there is a long and minute description, plate by plate, of a certain set of lithographic drawings, entitled "Flore et Zéphire"—a caricature of the ballet of the period, published by Thackeray in his youth. The plates are described as minutely and seriously as if they were drawings by Albert Dürer or Raphael; but even were they more valuable than is to be supposed, the description would be rather ponderous reading. In another part of the book, no less than two hundred and fifty pages are occupied with a series of extracts from Earle's 'Microsmography'; from a certain 'Defence of the Female Sex,' published under William III.; from various works on demonology and magic (including that of Alfred Maury, the familiar French writer); and from the whole collection of the little journals of Queen Anne's time—the Spectators, Tatlers, Worlds, Ramblers, etc. Thackeray wrote 'Esmond' and the 'Humorists' and he had obviously read these publications to good purpose; hence this wholesale transfer of their contents. If its felicity seems questionable, we may at least observe that it has helped to make the volume stout. But surely never was "padding" more ingenuously accumulated. Since the editor has such a taste for extracts, it is a pity that he did not exercise it in performances upon some of Thackeray's own less-known productions—upon those initiatory scribblings, for instance, in the short-lived *National Standard,* of which he has traced out the authorship. This was a weekly exponent of youthful views upon literature and art, published from 1833 to 1834, of which Thackeray was foreign correspondent. We must thank the editor, however, for quoting from the *"Snob" Magazine,* conducted by our author during his residence at Trinity College, Cambridge, the admirable little burlesque poem, with notes, entitled "Timbuctoo"—a parody upon one of the prize-poems of that period:

> "Desolate Afric, thou art lovely yet !
> One heart yet beats which ne'er thee shall forget !
> What though thy maidens are a blackish brown ?
> Does virtue dwell in whiter breasts alone?
> Oh no, oh no, oh no, oh no, oh no !
> It shall not, must not, cannot e'er be so !"

The editor gives also a good deal of miscellaneous gossip about Thackeray's personal and literary career, much of which is welcome, even if not of the newest. There is no writer of whom one bears better being reminded, none from whom any chance quotation, to whom any chance allusion or reference, is more unfailingly delectable. Pick out something at hazard from Thackeray, and ten to one it is a prize. This volume makes us live with him a while, and refreshes our sense of his incomparable humor, and for that we are thankful to it; but we are almost ashamed to express our thanks, lest we should seem to be praising beyond conscience a reprehensible and inartistic style of book. It really strikes us as sad that this is the best that English literature should be able to do for a genius who did so much for it.

REV. FRANCIS HODGSON, A FRIEND OF LORD BYRON*

MR. HODGSON has written his father's life upon a very unusual plan, for which he makes apologies in his preface. The apologies, however, were not strictly necessary, for the book is an interesting one, more so, perhaps, than if it had been composed in the manner usually followed in such cases. The late Archdeacon Hodgson was a genial and accomplished scholar, a man of the world, and an indefatigable versifier; but he was not a brilliant writer, and our loss is not great, in the fact that his letters have for the most part not been preserved. His son and biographer lays before us, in default of any specimens of his own share in his correspondence, a selection from the letters that he received from his friends. These were numerous, for Francis Hodgson had the good fortune to inspire a great deal of affection and confidence. *His chief claim to the attention of posterity resides in the fact that he was an early and much-trusted intimate of Lord Byron.* A good many of Byron's letters to him were printed by Moore, to whom, however, Hodgson surrendered but a portion of this correspondence. His son here publishes a number of new

* Memoir of the Rev. Francis Hodgson, B. D., with Numerous Letters from Lord Byron and Others. By his Son, the Rev. T. P. Hodgson, M. A. London: Macmillan, 1879. (*The North American Review*, April 1879).

letters, together with a great many communications from Mrs. Leigh, the poet's sister, and two or three from Lady Byron. All this portion of these volumes is extremely interesting, and constitutes, indeed, their principal value. It throws a clearer, though by no means a perfectly clear, light upon the much-discussed episode of the separation between Byron and his wife, and upon the character of his devoted sister. The book contains, besides, a series of letters from Hodgson's Eton and Cambridge friends, and in its latter portion a variety of extracts from his correspondence with such people as Lord Denman (Chief Justice of England, who presided at the trial of Queen Caroline, and incurred the bitter animosity of George IV.), James Montgomery, the late Herman Merivale, the late Duke of Devonshire, and the charming Mrs. Robert Arkwright, who figures in the lately published memoirs of Fanny Kemble. The picture of Hodgson's youth and early manhood, with his numerous friendships, his passion for literature, his extraordinary and unparalleled fecundity in the production of poetical epistles, his good spirits, good sense, and great industry, is an extremely pleasant one, and gives an agreeable idea of the tone of serious young Englishmen, sixty or seventy years ago, who were also good fellows. Hodgson's first intention on leaving Cambridge had been to study for the bar; but after some struggles the literary passion carried the day, and he became an ardent "reviewer." He worked a great deal for the critical periodicals of the early years of the century, notably for the "Edinburgh Review," and he produced (besides executing a translation of Juvenal) a large amount of satirical or would-be satirical verse. His biographer gives a great many examples of his poetical powers, which, however, chiefly illustrate his passion for turning couplets à propos of everything and of nothing. The facility of these effusions is more noticeable than their point. In 1815 Hodgson went into the Church, and in 1836, after having spent many years at Bakewell, in Derbyshire, in a living which he held from the Duke of Devonshire, he was appointed Archdeacon of Derby. In 1840 he was made Provost of Eton College, a capacity in which he instituted various salutary reforms (he abolished the old custom of the "Montem," which had become a very demoralizing influence). Archdeacon Hodgson died in 1852.

Mrs. Leigh wrote to him at the time of Byron's marriage, in which she felt great happiness, that her brother had "said that in all the years that he had been acquainted with you he never had a moment's disagreement with you: 'I have quarreled with Hobham, with everybody but Hodgson,' were his own words." Byron's letters and allusions to his friend quite bear out this declaration, and they present his irritable and passionate nature in the most favorable light. He had a great esteem for Hodgson's judgment, both in literature and in life, and he defers to it with a docility which is touching in a spoiled young nobleman who, on occasion, can make a striking display of temper. Mr. Hodgson gives no definite account of the origin of his father's acquaintance with Byron—he simply says that their intimacy, which in 1808 had become complete, had "doubtless been formed previously, during Hodgson's visits to London and Cambridge and to the Drurys at Harrow." In 1808 Hodgson was appointed tutor in moral philosophy at King's College, Cambridge, and in this year "Byron came to Cambridge for the purpose of availing himself of his privilege as a nobleman, and taking his M. A. degree, although he had only matriculated in 1805. . . . From this time until early in 1816 the friends constantly met, and when absent as constantly corresponded." Hodgson was completely under the charm of Byron's richly-endowed nature; but his affection, warm as it was (and its warmth is attested by the numerous copies of verse which he addressed to his noble friend, and which, though they exhibit little poetical inspiration, show great tenderness of feeling), was of that pure kind which leaves the judgment unbribed. Byron's letters have always a great charm, and those quoted by Mr. Hodgson, whether published for the first time, or anticipated by Moore, are full of youthful wit and spontaneity. In 1811, while the second canto of "Childe Harold" (Hodgson was helping to revise it) was going through the press, the poet's affectionate Mentor had, by letter, a religious discussion with him. Hodgson's side of the controversy has disappeared, but Byron's skeptical rejoinders are full of wit, levity, and a cynicism which (like his cynicism through life) was half natural and half affected. "As to your immortality, if people are to live, why die? And any carcasses, which are to rise again, are they worth raising? I hope, if mine is, that I shall have a *better pair of legs* than I have moved on these two-and-twenty years, as I shall be sadly behind in the squeeze into paradise." The letters which throw light upon Byron's unhappy marriage are all, as we have said, of great interest. Hodgson's correspondence with Mrs. Leigh, which became an intimate one, began in 1814 and lasted for forty years. Staying with Byron at Newstead in the autumn of that year, she first writes to him as a substitute for her brother, who, "being very lazy," has begged her to take his pen. It was at this moment that he became engaged to Miss Milbanke, and one of the few extracts from his father's own letters, given by Mr. Hodgson, is a very sympathetic account of a meeting with Byron in Cambridge while the latter was in the glow of just having completed his arrangements for marrying "one of the most divine beings on earth." There are several letters of Mrs. Leigh's during 1815, after the marriage had taken place, going on into the winter of 1816, when they assume a highly dramatic interest. It is interesting, in view of the extraordinary theory which in the later years of her life Lady Byron was known to hold on the subject of the relations between her husband and his sister, and which were given to the world in so regrettable a manner not long after her death, to observe that Mrs. Leigh's letters afford the most striking intrinsic evidence of the purely phantasmal character of the famous accusation, and place the author's character in a highly honorable and touching light. This is the view taken, in the strongest manner, by the editor of these volumes, who regards Mrs. Leigh as the most devoted and disinterested of sisters—as the good genius, the better angel, of the perverse and intractable poet. She appears to have been a very sympathetic and conscientious woman, not very witty or very clever, but addicted to writing rather expansive, confidential, ladylike letters, and much concerned about the moral tone and religious views of her brother, whose genius and poetic fame inspire her with a quite secondary interest. She appeals to Hodgson, as her brother's nearest and most trusted friend, to come up to town and intercede with either party to prevent the separation. Hodgson obeyed her summons, and did his best in the matter, but his efforts were unavailing. His son quotes a remarkable letter which he wrote to Lady Byron, urging her to the exercise of patience and forbearance; and he quotes as well Lady Byron's reply, which on the whole does less credit to her clemency than his appeal had done to his tact and wisdom. There is an element of mystery in the whole matter of her rupture with her husband which these letters still leave unsolved; but, putting this aside, they leave little doubt as to her ladyship's rigidity of nature.

"I believe the nature of Lord B.'s mind to be most benevolent," she says in answer to Hodgson's appeal. "But there may have been circumstances (I would hope the *consequences*, not the *causes* of mental disorder) which would render an original tenderness of conscience the motive of desperation, even of guilt, when self-esteem had been forfeited *too far*." And in reply to Hodgson's request, made on Byron's behalf, that she would specify those acts of his which she holds to have made a reconciliation impossible, she says, "He *does* know, too well, what he affects to inquire." Mrs. Leigh says to Hodgson, in writing of her brother: "If I may give you *mine* [my opinion], it is that *in his own mind* there *were* and *are* recollections fatal to his peace, and which would have prevented his being happy with any woman whose excellence equalled or approached that of Lady B., from the consciousness of being unworthy of it. Nothing," she adds, "could or can remedy this fatal cause but the consolation to be derived from religion, of which, alas! dear Mr. H., our beloved B. is, I fear, destitute." In such allusions as these some people will always read the evidence of some dark and definite wrong-doing on the part of one who delighted in the appearance of criminality, and who, possibly, simply by overacting his part, in the desire to mystify, rather viciously, a woman of literal mind, in whom the sense of humor was not strong, and the imagination was uncorrected by it, succeeded too well and got caught in his own trap.

Even if the inference we speak of were valid, it would be very profitless to inquire further as regards Byron's unforgivable sin; we are convinced that, if it were ascertained, it would be, to ingenuous minds, a great disappointment. The reader of these volumes will readily assent to Mr. Hodgson's declaration that they offer a complete, virtual exoneration of Mrs. Leigh. The simple, touching, pious letters addressed to her brother's friend at the time of Byron's death and of the arrival of his remains in England, strongly contribute to this effect; as does also the tone in which she speaks of Lady Byron's estrangement from her, which took place very suddenly some years after the separation. The tone is that of a person a good deal mystified and even wounded.

MATTHEW ARNOLD*

It seems perhaps hardly fair that while Matthew Arnold is in America and exposed to the extremity of public attention in that country, a native of the United States should take up the tale in an English magazine and let him feel the force of American observation from the rear as well as from the front. But, on the other hand, what better occasion could there be for a transatlantic admirer of the distinguished critic to speak his mind, without considering too much the place or the vehicle, than this interesting moment of Mr. Arnold's visit to the great country of the Philistines? I know nothing, as I write these lines, of the fruits of this excursion; we have heard little, as yet, of Mr. Arnold's impressions of the United States, or of the impression made upon their inhabitants by Mr. Arnold. But I would much rather not wait for information on these points: the elements of the subject are already sufficiently rich, and I prefer to make my few remarks in independence of such knowledge. A personal acquaintance with American life may have offered to the author of *Culture and Anarchy* a confirmation strong of his worst preconceptions; it may, on the other hand, have been attended with all sorts of pleasant surprises. In either event it will have been a satisfaction to one of his American readers (at least) to put on record a sentiment unaffected by the amount of material he may have gathered on transatlantic shores for the most

---

* (*English Illustrated Magazine*, January, 1884.)

successful satirical work of these last years. Nothing could be more delightful than the news that Mr. Arnold has been gratified by what he has seen in the western world; but I am not sure that it would not be even more welcome to know that he has been disappointed—for such disappointments, even in a mind so little irritable as his, are inspiring, and any record he should make of them would have a high value.

Neither of these consequences, however, would alter the fact that to an American in England, and indeed to any stranger, the author of the *Essays in Criticism,* of *Friendship's Garland,* of *Culture and Anarchy,* of the verses on Heine's grave, and of innumerable other delightful pages, speaks more directly than any other contemporary English writer, says more of these things which make him the visitor's intellectual companion, becomes in a singular way nearer and dearer. It is for this reason that it is always in order for such a visitor to join in a commemoration of the charming critic. He discharges an office so valuable, a function so delicate, he interprets, explains, illuminates so many of the obscure problems presented by English life to the gaze of the alien; he woos and wins to comprehension, to sympathy, to admiration, this imperfectly initiated, this often slightly bewildered observer; he meets him half way, he appears to understand his feelings, he conducts him to a point of view as gracefully as a master of ceremonies would conduct him to a chair. It is being met half way that the German, the Frenchman, the American appreciates so highly, when he approaches the great spectacle of English life; it is one of the greatest luxuries the foreign inquirer can enjoy. To such a mind as his, projected from a distance, out of a set of circumstances so different, the striking, the discouraging, I may even say the exasperating thing in this revelation, is the unconsciousness of the people concerned in it, their serenity, their indifference, their tacit assumption that their form of life is the normal one. This may very well be, of course, but the stranger wants a proof of some kind. (The English, in foreign lands, I may say in parenthesis, receive a similar impression; but the English are not irritated—not irritable—like the transplanted foreigner.) This unconsciousness makes a huge blank surface, a mighty national wall, against which the perceptive, the critical effort of the presumptuous stranger wastes itself, until, after a little, he espies in the measureless spaces, a little aperture, a window which is suddenly thrown open, and at which a friendly and intelligent face is presented, the harbinger of a voice of greeting. With this agreeable apparition he communes—the voice is delightful, it has a hundred tones and modulations; and as he stands there the great dead screen seems to vibrate and grow transparent. In other words it is the fact that Mr. Arnold is, of all his countrymen, the most conscious of the national idiosyncrasies that endears him to the soul of the stranger. I may be doing him a poor service among his own people in saying this, I may be sacrificing him too much to my theory of the foreigner and his longing for sympathy. A man may very well not thank you for letting it be known that you have found him detached from the ranks of his compatriots. It would perhaps be discreet on the part of the Frenchman or the American not to say too loudly that to his sense Matthew Arnold is, among the English writers of our day, the least of a matter-of-course Englishman— the pair of eyes to which the English world rounds itself most naturally as a fact among many facts. This, however, is after all unnecessary; for what is so agreeable in his composition is that he is *en fin de compte* (as the foreigner might say) English of the English. Few writers have given such proof of this; few writers have had such opportunity to do so; for few writers have English affairs, the English character, the future, the development, the happiness, of England, been matters of such constant and explicit concern. It is not in the United States that Mr. Arnold will have struck people as not being a devoted child of the mother-country. He has assimilated certain continental ways of looking at things, his style has a kind of European accent, but he is full of English piety and English good-humour (in addition to an urbanity still more personal), and his spirit, in a word, is anchored in the deeps of the English past.

He is both a poet and a critic, but it is perhaps, primarily, because he is a representative of the critical spirit—apart from the accident of his having practised upon the maternal breast, as it were—that the sojourner, the spectator, has a kindness for the author of so many happy formulas, the propagator of so many capital instances. He, too, is necessarily critical, whatever his ultimate conclusion of reconciliation, and he takes courage and confidence from the sight of this brilliant writer, who knowing English life so much better than he can ever hope to do, is yet struck with so many of the same peculiarities, and makes so many of the same reflections. It is not the success of the critical effort at large that is most striking to-day to the attentive outsider; it is not the flexibility of English taste, the sureness of English judgment, the faculty of reproducing in their integrity the impressions made by works of art and literature, that most fixes the attention of those who look to see what the English mind is about. It may appear odd that an American should make this remark, proceeding as he does from a country in which high discernment in such matters has as yet only made a beginning. Superior criticism, in the United States, is at present not written; it is, like a great many superior things, only spoken; therefore I know not why a native of that country should take note of the desuetude of this sort of accomplishment in England, unless it be that in England he naturally expects great things. He is struck with the immense number of reviews that are published, with the number of vehicles for publicity, for discussion. But with the lightness of the English touch in handling literary and artistic questions he is not so much struck, nor with a corresponding interest in the manner, the meaning, the quality, of an artistic effort: corrupted (I should add) as he perhaps may be by communications still more foreign than those he has enjoyed on the other side of the Atlantic, and a good deal more forcible. For I am afraid that what I am coming to in saying that Matthew Arnold, as an English writer, is dear to the soul of the outsider, is the fact, (not equally visible, doubtless, to all judges) that he reminds the particular outsider who writes these lines (and who feels at moments that he has so little claim to the title), just the least bit of the great Sainte-Beuve. Many people do not care for Sainte-Beuve; they hold that his method was unscientific, his temper treacherous, his style tiresome, and that his subjects were too often uninteresting. But those who do care for him care for him deeply, and cultivate the belief, and the hope, that they shall never weary of him; so that as it is obviously only my limited personal sentiment that (with this little play of talk about the outsider in general) I venture to express, I may confess that the measure of my enjoyment of a critic is the degree to which he resembles Sainte-Beuve. This resemblance exists in Matthew Arnold, with many disparities and differences; not only does he always speak of the author of *Causeries* with esteem and admiration, but he strikes the lover of Sainte-Beuve as having really taken lessons from him, as possessing a part of his great quality—closeness of contact to his subject. I do not in the least mean by this that Mr. Arnold is an imitator, that he is a reflection, pale or intense, of another genius. He has a genius, a quality, all his own, and he has in some respects a largeness of horizon which Sainte-Beuve never reached. The horizon of Sainte-Beuve was French, and we know what infinite blue distances the French see there; but that of Matthew Arnold, as I have hinted, is European, more than European, inasmuch as it includes America. It ought to be enough for an American that Sainte-Beuve had no ideas at all about America; whereas Mr. Arnold has a great many, which he is engaged at the moment at which I write, in collating with the reality. Nevertheless, Sainte-Beuve, too, on his side, had his larger movement; he had of course his larger activity, which indeed it will appear to many that Mr. Arnold might have emulated if it had not been for a certain amount of misdirected effort. There is one side on which many readers will never altogether do justice to Matthew Arnold, the side on which we see him as the author of *St. Paul and Protestantism,* and even of many portions of *Literature and Dogma.* They will never cease to regret that he should have spent so much time and ingenuity in discussing the differences—several of which, after all, are so special, so arbitrary—between Dissenters and Anglicans, should not rather have given these earnest hours to the interpretation of literature. There is something dry and dusty in the atmosphere of such discussions, which accords ill with the fresh tone of the man of letters, the artist. It must be added that in Mr. Arnold's case they are connected with something very important, his interest in religious ideas, his constant, characteristic sense of the reality of religion.

The union of this element with the other parts of his mind, his love of literature, of perfect expression, his interest in life at large, constitutes perhaps the originality of his character as a critic, and it certainly (to my sense) gives him that seriousness in which he has occasionally been asserted to be wanting. Nothing can exceed the taste, the temperance, with which he handles religious questions, and at the same time nothing can exceed the impression he gives of really caring for them. To his mind the religious life of humanity is the most important thing in the spectacle humanity offers us, and he holds a due perception of this fact is (in connection with other lights) the measure of the acuteness of a critic, the wisdom of a poet. He says in his essay on Marcus Aurelius an admirable thing—"The paramount virtue of religion is that it has *lighted up* morality;" and such a phrase as that shows the extent to which he feels what he speaks of. To say that this feeling, taken in combination with his love of letters, of beauty, of all liberal things, constitutes an originality is not going too far, for the religious sentiment does not always render the service of opening the mind to human life at large. Ernest Renan, in France, is, as every one knows, the great and brilliant representative of such a union; he has treated religion as he might have treated one of the fine arts. Of him it may even be said, that though he has never spoken of it but as the sovereign thing in life, yet there is in him, as an interpreter of the conscience of man, a certain dandyism, a slight fatuity, of worldly culture, of which Mr. Arnold too has been accused, but from which (with the smaller assurance of an Englishman in such matters) he is much more exempt. Mr. Arnold touches M. Renan on one side, as he touches Sainte-Beuve on the other (I make this double *rapprochement* because he has been spoken of more than once as the most Gallicised of English writers); and if he has gone less into the details of literature than the one, he has gone more than the other into the application of religion to questions of life. He has applied it to the current problems of English society. He has endeavoured to light up with it, to use his own phrase, some of the duskiest and most colourless of these. He has cultivated urbanity almost as successfully as M. Renan, and he has cultivated reality rather more. As I have spoken of the reader who has been a stranger in England feeling that Mr. Arnold meets him half way, and yet of our author being at bottom English of the English, I may add here, in confirmation of this, that his theological pertinacity, as one may call it, his constant implication of the nearness of religion, his use of the Scriptures, his love of biblical phraseology, are all so many deeply English notes. He has all the taste for theology which characterises our race when our race is left to its own devices; he evidently has read an immense number of sermons. He is impregnated with the associations of Protestantism, saturated with the Bible, and though he has little love for the Puritans, no Puritan of them all was ever more ready on all occasions with a text either from the Old Testament or from the New. The appreciative stranger (whom I go on imagining) has to remind himself of the force of these associations of Protestantism in order to explain Mr. Arnold's fondness for certain quotations which doubtless need the fragrance that experience and memory may happen to give them to reveal their full charm. Nothing could be more English, more Anglican, for instance, than our author's enjoyment of sundry phrases of Bishop Wilson—phrases which to the uninitiated eye are often a little pale. This does not take from the fact that Mr. Arnold has a real genius for quotation. His pages are full, not only of his own good things, but of those of every one else. More than any critic of the day he gives, from point to point, an example of what he means. The felicity of his illustrations is extreme; even if he sometimes makes them go a little further than they would and sees in them a little more than is visible to the average reader. Of course, in his frequent reference to the Bible, what is free and happy and personal to himself is the use he makes of it.

If it were the purpose of these few pages to give in the smallest degree a history of Mr. Arnold's literary career, I ought promptly to have spoken of his Poems—I ought to enumerate his works in their order. It was by his Poems that I first knew and admired him, and many such readers—early or late admirers— will have kept them in a very safe corner of memory. As a poet, Matthew Arnold is really singular; he takes his place among the most fortunate writers of our day who have expressed themselves in verse, but his place is somewhat apart. He has an imagination

347

of his own, but he is less complete, less inevitable, as he says in his essay on Wordsworth that that poet said of Goethe, than the others. His form at moments is less rich than it might be, and the Wordsworthian example may perhaps be accused here and there of having sterilized him. But this limited, just a little precarious, character of his inspiration adds to his value for people who like the quality of rareness in their pleasures, like sometimes to perceive just a little the effort of the poet, like to hear him take breath. It reminds them of the awkwardness of line which we see in certain charming painters of early schools (not that Mr. Arnold is early!) and which seems a condition of their grace and a sign of their freshness. Splendour, music, passion, breadth of movement and rhythm we find in him in no great abundance; what we do find is high distinction of feeling (to use his own word), a temperance, a kind of modesty of expression, which is at the same time an artistic resource—the complexion of his work; and a remarkable faculty for touching the chords which connect our feelings with the things that others have done and spoken. In other words, though there is in Mr. Arnold's poems a constant reference to nature, or to Wordsworth, which is almost the same thing, there is even a more implicit reference to civilisation, literature, and the intellectual experience of man. He is the poet of the man of culture, that accomplished being whom he long ago held up for our consideration. Above all he is the poet of his age, of the moment in which we live, of our "modernity," as the new school of criticism in France gives us perhaps license to say. When he speaks of the past, it is with the knowledge which only our own time has of it. With its cultivated simplicity, its aversion to cheap ornament, its slight abuse of meagreness for distinction's sake, his verse has a kind of minor magic and always goes to the point—the particular ache, or regret, or conjecture, to which poetry is supposed to address itself. It rests the mind, after a good deal of the other poetical work of the day—it rests the mind, and I think I may add that it nourishes it.

It was, as every one remembers, in the essay on *The Function of Criticism at the Present Time,* and that on *The Literary Influence of Academies,* that, in 1864, Mr. Arnold first appeared in the character in which since then he has won so much fame, and which he may really be said to have invented; that of the *general* critic, the commentator of English life, the observer and expostulator, the pleader with the Dissenters, the genial satirist. His manner, since this light, sweet prelude, has acquired much amplitude and confidence; but the suggestiveness, the delightful temper were there from the first. Those who have been enjoying Mr. Arnold these twenty years will remember how fresh and desirable his voice sounded at that moment; if since then the freshness has faded a little we must bear in mind that it is through him and through him only that we have grown familiar with certain ideas and terms which now form part of the common stock of allusion. When he began his critical career there were various things that needed immensely to be said and that no one appeared sufficiently detached, sufficiently independent and impartial to say. Mr. Arnold attempted to say them, and succeeded—so far as the saying goes—in a manner that left nothing to be desired. There is, of course, another measure of success in regard to such an attempt— the question of how far the critic has had an influence, produced an effect—how far he has acted upon the life, the feelings, the conduct of his audience. The effect of Mr. Arnold's writings is of course difficult to gauge; but it seems evident that the thoughts and judgments of Englishmen about a good many matters have been quickened and coloured by them. All criticism is better, lighter, more sympathetic, more informed, in consequence of certain things he has said. He has perceived and felt so many shy, disinterested truths that belonged to the office, to the limited specialty, of no one else; he has made them his care, made them his province and responsibility. This flattering unction Mr. Arnold may, I think, lay to his soul—that with all his lightness of form, with a certain jauntiness and irresponsibility of which he has been accused—as if he affected a candour and simplicity almost more than human—he has added to the interest of life, to the charm of knowledge, for a great many of those plain people among whom he so gracefully counts himself. As we know, in the number of the expressive phrases to which he has given circulation, none has had a wider currency than his application of Swift's phrase about sweetness and light. Assuredly it may be said that that note has reverberated, that it has done something—

in the realm of discussion—towards making civility the fashion and facilitating the exchange of ideas. They appear to have become more accessible—they bristle rather less with mutual suspicion. Above all, the atmosphere has gained in clearness in the great middle region in which Philistinism is supposed to abide. Our author has hung it about—the grey confusion—with a multitude of little coloured lanterns, which not only have a charming, a really festive effect, but which also help the earnest explorer to find his way. It was in the volume entitled *Culture and Anarchy,* published in 1869, and perhaps his most ingenious and suggestive production, that he offered his most celebrated definitions, and exposed himself most to the penalties which the general critic is foredoomed to encounter. In some of his later books he has called down the displeasure of the Dissenters, but in the extremely witty volume to which I allude he made it a matter of honour with society at large to retaliate. But it has been Mr. Arnold's good fortune from the first that he has been fed and stimulated by criticism; his antagonist, in the phrase that he is fond of quoting from Burke, has ever been his helper. Rejoinder and refutation have always furnished him with texts and examples and offered a spring-board, as it were, to his polemical agility. He has had the further advantage, that though in his considerate, bantering way a disputant, having constantly to defend himself, as is inevitable for a man who frequently attacks, he has never lost his good humour, never shown a touch of the *odium theologicum,* nor ceased to play fair. This incorrigible fondness for his joke doubtless has had something to do with the reproach sometimes made him that he is not serious, that he does not really care for the causes for which he pleads, that he is a talker, an artist even, a charming humorist, but not a philosopher, nor a reformer, nor a teacher. He has been charged with having no practical advice to offer. To these allegations he would perhaps plead guilty, for he has never pretended to have a body of doctrine nor to approach the public with an infallible nostrum. He has been the plain man that we have alluded to, he has been only a skirmisher and a suggester. It is certain that a good many fallacies and prejudices are limping about with one of his light darts still sticking to them. For myself, when I have heard it remarked that he is not practical, the answer has seemed to be that there is surely nothing more practical than to combine that degree of wit with that degree of good feeling, and that degree of reason with both of them. It is quite enough to the point to be one of the two or three best English prose-writers of one's day. There is nothing more practical, in short, than, if one praises culture and desires to forward it, to speak in the tone and with the spirit and impartiality of culture. The Dissenters, I believe, hold that Mr. Arnold has not been impartial, accuse him of misrepresenting them, of making the absurd proposal that they shall come over to the Church merely because from the church-window, as it were, their chapels and conventicles interfere with the view. I do not pretend to judge this matter, or even to have followed closely enough to give an account of them the windings of that controversial episode, of which the atmosphere, it must be confessed, has at moments been more darkened than brightened with Biblical references and which occupies the middle years of the author's literary career. It is closed, and well closed, and Mr. Arnold has returned to literature and to studies which lie outside the controversial shadow. It is sufficient that, inveterate satirist as he is, it is impossible to read a page of him without feeling that his satire is liberal and human. The much abused name of culture rings rather false in our ears, and the fear of seeming priggish checks it as it rises to our lips. The name matters little, however, for the idea is excellent, and the thing is still better. I shall not go so far as to say of Mr. Arnold that he invented it; but he made it more definite than it had been before—he vivified and lighted it up. We like today to see principles and convictions embodied in persons, represented by a certain literary or political face. There are so many abroad, all appealing to us and pressing towards us, that these salient incarnations help us to discriminate and save us much confusion. It is Mr. Arnold, therefore, that we think of when we figure to ourselves the best knowledge of what is being done in the world, the best appreciation of literature and life. It is in America especially that he will have had the responsibility of appearing as the cultivated man—it is in this capacity that he will have been attentively listened to. The curiosity with regard to culture is extreme in that country; if there is in some quarters a considerable uncertainty as to what it may consist of, there is everywhere a great wish to get hold of it, at least on trial. I will not say that Mr. Arnold's tact has absolutely never failed him. There is a certain want of it, for instance (the instance is small), in his quoting, in *Culture and Anarchy*, M. Renan's opinion on the tone of life in America, in support of his own contention that Philistinism was predominant there. This is a kind of authority that (in such a case) almost discredits the argument— M. Renan being constitutionally, and as it were officially, incapable of figuring to himself the aspect of society in the United States. In like manner Mr. Arnold may now and then have appeared to satisfy himself with a definition not quite perfect, as when he is content to describe poetry by saying that it is a criticism of life. That surely expresses but a portion of what poetry contains—it leaves unsaid much of the essence of the matter. Literature in general is a criticism of life—prose is a criticism of life. But poetry is a criticism of life in conditions so peculiar that they are the sign by which we know poetry. Lastly, I may venture to say that our author strikes me as having, especially in his later writings, pushed to an excess some of the idiosyncrasies of his delightful style—his fondness for repetition, for ringing the changes on his text, his formula—a tendency in consequence of which his expression becomes at moments slightly wordy and fatiguing. This tendency, to give an example, is visible, I think, in the essay which serves as an introduction to Mr. Ward's collection of the English poets, and in that on Wordsworth, contained in the volume of Mr. Arnold's own selections from him. The defect, however, I should add, is nothing but an exaggeration of one of the author's best qualities—his ardent love of clearness, his patient persuasiveness. These are minor blemishes, and I allude to them mainly, I confess, because I fear I may have appeared to praise too grossly. Yet I have wished to praise, to express the high appreciation of all those who in England and America have in any degree attempted to care for literature. They owe Matthew Arnold a debt of gratitude for his admirable example, for having placed the standard of successful expression, of literary feeling and good manners, so high. They never tire of him—they read him again and again. They think the wit and humour of

Friendship's Garland the most delicate possible, the luminosity of *Culture and Anarchy* almost dazzling, the eloquence of such a paper as the article on Lord Falkland in the *Mixed Essays* irresistible. They find him, in a word, more than any one else, the happily-proportioned, the truly distinguished man of letters. When there is a question of his efficacy, his influence, it seems to me enough to ask one's self what we should have done without him, to think how much we should have missed him, and how he has salted and seasoned our public conversation. In his absence the whole tone of discussion would have seemed more stupid, more literal. Without his irony to play over its surface, to clip it here and there of its occasional fustiness, the life of our Anglo-Saxon race would present a much greater appearance of insensibility.

NOTES TO INTRODUCTION

1. I find in my files a copy of a letter I wrote to a publisher dated July 29, 1919 in which I stated, "I have a collection of many essays mainly critical by Henry James, from *The Nation* and elsewhere, uncollected and uncopyrighted." I also find a list of these then made which includes most in the present collection.

Here are extracts from two letters from another publisher dated December 9 and also December 13, 1919.

"Mr. ———— and myself have at last taken time to go through the essays and reviews of Henry James that you left with us . . . . With regard to the essays by James, I will take your suggestion and hope to be able to examine more carefully the material in the *Nation*."

Within two years after I had formed my collection there appeared in 1921 a volume of James's book reviews and literary essays gathered together from periodicals in *Notes and Reviews* for the years 1864-1866, with a Preface by Pierre de la Chaignon la Rose, 1921, through Dunster House. To my dismay it contained eleven articles that I had in my collection, but I weeded them out as my design was to have a volume of articles never gathered before. At least nine of Rose's selections were pet choices of mine, the Epictetus article from the *North American Review*, and I regretted parting with this as well as with the others from *The Nation*. These were *"A French Critic,"* (Edmond Schérer), Eugenie de Guérin's *Journal;* Swinburne's *Chastelard;* Charles Kingley's *Hereward, the Wake;* Hugo's *Toilers of the Sea;* George Eliot's *Felix Holt;* Eugenie de Guérin's *Letters* and Alexander Dumas fils' *Affaire Clemenceau.*

I still have the pages clipped from the periodicals containing these articles.

When this volume was to be issued last year we learned that Mr. Leon Edel was bringing out through Vintage Books, two volumes of James's critical essays. When they appeared I found that they contained both previously collected essays and uncollected essays. Four of the latter which appeared in his volume *The American Essays of Henry James* were in my collection,

an article on William Dean Howells from *The Independent,*
reviews of Francis Parkman's *The Jesuits of America* and Hawthorne's *French and Italian Journals* in *The Nation* and the
article "The Correspondence of Carlyle and Emerson" from the
Century Magazine. I withdrew mine as I was bent on a volume of
uncollected essays and substituted some others.

2. *Gabrielle de Bergerac* appeared in 1918 issued by Boni
& Liveright. It had appeared originally in the *Atlantic Monthly,*
July, August, September, 1889. It bore no introduction or any
notice to indicate the present editor's connection with it. Thomas
Seltzer, then connected with the firm, liked the tale and that is
why it was accepted. It has since been reprinted by Edna Kenton
in her *Eight Uncollected Tales* of Henry James, 1950. The tale
now has a special interest since in a letter Minnie Temple wrote
to James she called it a charming, pretty tale that made her
proud as well as fond of him. Robert C. Le Clair, "Henry James
and Minnie Temple" *American Literature* XXI No. 1 (March
1949 35-48).

I had also offered the other seven tales in Miss Kenton's
collection to publishers, but they rejected them.

3. *Travelling Companions* Boni & Liveright, 1919 Fore-
word by Albert Mordell. It contains seven uncollected tales by
Henry James. Among reviews of it were "The Earliest Henry
James" by Edna Kenton, *The Bookman,* August 1919, pp. 706-
708; "The Resurrection of Henry James" by William Lyon
Phelps, *New York Times Book Review,* April 20, 1919; "Early
Henry James" by W. B. McCormick, New York *Sun,* May 11,
1919; *The New Republic,* July 30, 1919, "Books and Things"
P. L. (Phillip Littell).

4. *A Landscape Painter.* Preface by Albert Mordell. Scott
and Seltzer, 1919. This contained four tales.

Master Eustace. Preface by Albert Mordell. Thomas Seltzer,
1920. This contained five tales.

The stories in the last two volumes had never been collected
by Henry James in America, but in England. They are here
unique in that they were copied directly from the periodicals
wherein they appeared and were not revised like those in the
English editions.

A Landscape Painter was the subject of an article by
Margaret Pickney Allen, in *The Sun Books and the Book
World,* January 18, 1920.

Master Eustace was the subject of an article by Professor Felix Schelling in the *Evening Ledger* (Philadelphia) February 19, 1921 and reprinted in his book *Appraisements and Asperities*, 1922.

The idea and suggestion for reprinting these tales as well as the articles in the present volume came from LeRoy Phillips's *Bibliography of the Writings of Henry James* 1906, probably one of the most valuable and serviceable pieces of James scholarship ever brought out. Phillips himself collected fifteen articles in *Views and Reviews* in 1908. Except in a few cases, Phillips's identification of the anonymous contributions for which of course he had documentary evidence has been later confirmed.

The Phillips *Bibliography* led also to the collection of twenty-five articles and reviews *Notes and Reviews* edited by Pierre de Chaignon la Rose, 1921. The volume contained only those published in James's earliest youth from 1864 to 1866.

It also served as a complete guide to Miss Cornelia Pulsifer Kelley in her thesis *The Early Development of Henry James*, 1930 for her study of the articles and tales of Henry James some of which had not yet been collected.

Phillips in 1930 brought out another edition of the *Bibliography*.

5. It was a review of Nassau W. Senior's *Essay On Fiction* and appeared in the *North American Review,* October 1864 and has been collected by Rose in *Notes and Reviews* under the title "Fiction and Sir Walter Scott."

6. *Notes of a Son and Brother,* 1914, p. 426.

7. *The Nation,* July 15, 1915. The article by James has been reprinted in *The American Essays of Henry James,* 1956, 283-288, by Leon Edel. James's first article in the opening number of the *Nation* was in July 6, 1915, headed "The Noble School of Fiction" and was a review of Henry Kingsley's novel *The Hillyers and the Bartons*. It was headed "noble" because James disapproved of Kingsley's conception of nobility. It was reprinted by Rose.

In the commemorative issue of *The Nation,* one of the early contributors Arthus G. Sedgwick speaks of the solidity of James's literary criticism and of his fullness of knowledge and grasp, as manifested in his first article. Gustav Pollack another early contributor mentions it. Reprinted in *Notes and Reviews.* This also is probably the article which James in a letter to Oliver

Wendell Holmes, Jr., July 14, 1865, says that he is glad Holmes liked "Letters of Henry James to Mr. Justice Holmes." Edited by Mark de Wolfe Howe. *Yale Review,* March 1949, pp. 410-433.

8. Henry James gives his brother's letter in *Notes of a Son and Brother,* p. 450.

The three articles William referred to are on William Morris' *Earthy Paradise* (*The Nation,* July 9, 1868) reprinted by Phillips; the review of George Eliot's *The Spanish Gypsy* (*The Nation* July 2, 1868) and the review of George Sand's *Mademoiselle Merquem, The Nation,* July 16, 1868, both herein reprinted.

9. He reviewed Miss Prescott's novel *Azarian, an Episode* in the *North American Review,* January 1865. It was reprinted by Rose and discussed by Miss Kelley in her *Early Development of Henry James.* He deliberately attacked it,—probably because the *Atlantic Monthly* praised it. (The anonymous review was written by Thomas W. Higginson.)

10. An English translation of *Eugénie Grandet* appeared in London in 1859.

11. These translations were of Alfred de Musset's *Lorenzaccio,* a lengthy drama of a murder by one Medici of another, a tyrant, in the name of liberty, and of three tales by Mérimée, "La Venus d'Ille," "Tamango," and "Matteo Falcone."

12. James himself had a penchant for translations and in his notices of some of the books in French he translated passages. He also translated passages from Taine's eulogy on George Sand, (*The Nation,* July 27, 1876); from the French version of a short poem by Turgenev attacking the indifference of the Disraeli government to the horrible massacre of the Bulgarians by the Turks, since England wanted Turkey as a buffer between her and Russia, for she always feared that Russia was after Constantinople, (*The Nation,* October 5, 1878). He also made a translation of a passage in Renan's letter in *The Revue de deux Mondes* praising the Sicilians for their taste in mental speculation, holding them the heirs of Empedocles; and regarding Sicily as a place where a taste for the beautiful prevails. (*The Nation,* December 30, 1875, p. 419).

(These anonymous notes are attributed to James by his bibliographer.)

As is well known, James in 1890 translated Alphonse Daudet's *Port Tarascon,* though it was for "lucre."

13. *The Nation,* December 28, 1878.

14. *William Wetmore Story and his Friends,* by Henry James. 1903, Vol. 1, p. 205.

15. "In Memory" and "The Hawthorne Aspect" both dealing with James appeared in *The Little Review,* August 1918, pp. 44-53 and were reprinted by Edmund Wilson in *The Shock of Tradition* and by F. W. Dupee in *The Question of Henry James.*

16. "The Art of Fiction" originally appeared in *Longman's Magazine* September 1884, is included in *Partial Portraits,* 1888 and has been reprinted by others.

17. "The Novels of George Eliot," *Atlantic Monthly,* October 1866, collected by Phillips in *Views and Reviews.*

18. *The North American Review,* April 1874. Reprinted in *French Poets and Novelists* (1878).

19. New Orleans *Times-Democrat,* September 10, 1882. *Essays on American Literature.* Edited by Sanki Ichikawa with an Introduction by Albert Mordell, Tokyo, 1929.

20. *American Literature,* November 1951, pp. 315-332. "'The Private Life' and Browning."

21. See *"Criticism in American Periodicals of the Works of Henry James from 1866 to 1916.* A Dissertation by Richard Nicholas Foley, 1944.

When citing the anonymous review of *The Passionate Pilgrim and Other Tales* in *The Nation,* July 24, 1875, Foley is not aware that James Russell Lowell was the author of the review. It is attributed to Lowell by the author's bibliographer George Willis Cooke, and the present writer reprinted it in *The Function of The Poet and Other Essays* (1920) by James Russell Lowell, a volume of hitherto uncollected essays by him.

The same review includes one of *Transatlantic Sketches.* This is interesting in view of the fact that Lowell had also munificently noticed James's literary exploits on the occasion of the appearance of *Gabrielle de Bergerac* in the *Atlantic Monthly.* Robert C. Le Clair reprints a letter dated June 27, 1869 from Henry James, Sr. to Lowell, thanking him for the praise, *Young Henry James,* p. 451, N. 21.

22. *Mammonart,* "The Culture-Class Historian" pp. 316-322.

23. *Papers on Psychoanalysis* by Ernest Jones, 1918.

24. The following are some of the leading psychoanalytical interpretations of Henry James:

a) Edna Kenton: "Henry James to the Ruminant Reader: *The Turn of the Screw*" *The Arts* VI, November 1924, pp. 245-255.

b) Edmund Wilson "The Ambiguity of Henry James" in *The Triple Thinkers,* 1938, 1948. This thesis was first developed by Wilson in *Hound and Horn,* VII. April-May 1934, pp. 385-406.

c) Saul Rosenzweig: "The Ghost of Henry James: A Study in Thematic Apperception." *Character and Personality* XII 79-100, (December 1943). Reprinted in *Partisan Review* Fall 1944, pp. 436-455. This treated largely James's "The Story of the Year", which before Edel's discovery of a predecessor, was then regarded as James's first tale.

d) Robert L. Gale: "Freudian Imagery in James's Fiction" *American Imago* XI, Summer 1954 pp. 181-190.

e) Oscar Cargill: "Henry James as Freudian Pioneer", *Chicago Review,* Summer 1956, pp. 13-29. Professor Cargill thinks that James may have heard of or even read Freud's article, "The Case of Miss Lucy R." in the original German (1893). It is translated in *Selected Papers on Hysteria and Other Psychoneuroses.*"

f) Robert Rogers: "The Beast in Henry James." *American Imago,* Winter 1956 pp. 427-454. This takes up the tale by James, "The Jolly Corner."

g) John Silver: "A Note on the Freudian Reading of 'The Turn of the Screw.'" *American Literature,* May, 1957, pp. 207-211.

h) Harold C. Goddard: A Pre-Freudian Reading of *The Turn of the Screw* (Prefatory Note by Leon Edel), *Nineteenth Century Fiction* Vol. 12, June 1957, No. 1, pp. 1-36. Special Henry James Issue.

Other articles in this issue are opposed to Freudian interpretations of James stories.

One of the best arguments in support of a psychoanalytic interpretation of "The Turn of the Screw" has in my opinion never been resorted to, so far as I know. While a good case may be made out for the governess's frustration in unrequited love, representing James's own, it can be strengthened from what we know of James's obsession on the subject of sufferings by and ill treatment of children. When *David Copperfield* was read to him as a child he burst into tears as he heard of the sufferings of David at the hands of the Murdstones. He of course could not forget that his father had lost a leg at the age of thirteen, and he was always horrified extremely when he heard of the woes of a child. We know he depicted these in some novels and tales. e.g. *What Maisie Knew; "The Pupil."* When he reviewed Hugo's *Toilers of the Sea,* he picked out for special mention an episode dealing with the agonies of a child. He thus came to have the governess imagine that her two cares at the Bly household, Miles and Flora, were marked for persecution, by the ghosts of the former valet and nurse, Quint and Miss Jessel. All this was an unconscious reflex of James's own anger at any one who would injure children. The children were real because the housekeeper Mrs. Grose was cognizant of their existence, but she was not of that of Quint and Miss Jessel in their ghostly garments and deeds. I think that there can be no doubt that the two ghosts were products of the governess's brain and symbolized James's obsession on the subject of the treatment of children, extending even probably to cases where they were not in danger.

25. Mr. Edel has also made use of the theory of projection as applied to literary criticism without using the word. In his first book in English, *The Prefaces of Henry James* (Paris, 1931) he says that when James in the Preface to the *The Portrait of a Lady* in the New York edition quoted from Turgenev's conversation setting forth his theory what a novel should be, James was merely adding weight of authority to what he already had expressed in his essay on fiction.

Edel again turned virtually to the idea of projection in his essay "Hugh Walpole and Henry James: The Fantasy and the Slain" *American Imago,* December 1951, pp. 351-369, where he said that Walpole was imitating "The Turn of the Screw" in the novel which he dedicated to James after the latter's death, that Walpole was really finding justification for the kind of novel he had just written by falling back upon and accepting features from James's tale. This is really projection.

I am glad that I discovered these two items by Edel in time enough to record them here in my notes.

26. The undated letter is among the manuscripts in the Historical Society of Pennsylvania. Another letter is there also to Osgood, his publisher, dated Venice April 15, 1881, in connection with the change he had made to the publishers for *The Portrait of a Lady*.

27. *The Nation*, February 2, 1867, p. 168.

28. *Gail Hamilton's Life in Letters*. Edited by H. Augusta Dodd. 2 Vol. Boston Lee and Shepard, 1901. Vol. I, pp. 588-591.

It is singular that of the four writers who have written books about the elder James alone or in connection with his distinguished sons, none has referred to the friendship of Gail Hamilton with him. There are printed in the book about ten letters from her to him, most of them long, five or six pages, and one or two others discussing him. There are no letters in ms. in the James collection at the Houghton Library from Gail Hamilton to either James, and none from them to her, I am so informed by Carolyn E. Jakeman.

29. *A History of English Literature*. In a Series of Lectures by Lafcadio Hearn. The Hokuseido Press, Kanda, Tokyo, Japan, 1927, 2 vol. Vol II p. 911.

30. "London Notes", January 1897. *Notes on Novelists with Some Other Notes*, pp. 426-427, 1914.

In transcribing the names of books, I have followed James. Undoubtedly his copy was made to conform to the custom of the various periodicals for which he wrote, and that is the reason why such names appear at times italicized, in quotes, or neither. It was, therefore, no inconsistency on my part in having the proper names of books, as they thus appear in his articles. As is well-known, the usual practice today is to have such names italicized.

NOTES TO ARTICLES

NOTE TO THE REMINISCENCES OF RENAN

1. As Thomas Sergeant Perry informs us, he and Henry James first heard of Ernest Renan from William James in the late fifties. Henry in his essay on Emerson (1887) noted that Renan could not imagine why people should write works of fiction. Some unkind critics might respond that Renan wrote considerable fiction in his many volumes of the history of Christianity and particularly in his history of the Hebrew people.

James in his second essay on Turgenev (1884) refers to a beautiful speech Renan made at Turgenev's funeral.

In his second article on Matthew Arnold, (herein reprinted), James, in defending him for his religious preoccupations, avails himself of Renan as a worthy example, stating that he had treated religion as he might have treated of one of the fine arts, that is, using his imagination, though James did not state to what excessive extent Renan had used it.

James also refers to Renan's urbanity.

NOTE TO TAINE'S ENGLISH LITERATURE

2. In connection with the article by James on Taine's *English Literature* in the *Atlantic Monthly* for April 1872, one should read his comment on this book in a letter dated August 14, 1912 to Hugh Walpole who had been reading the work. James who had once been an extremely subjective literary critic, praises Taine for his objective writing.

In a letter to Thomas Sergeant Perry, September 23, 1867, he said that he had found Taine's philosophy of things superficial.

NOTE TO SAINTE-BEUVE'S ENGLISH PORTRAITS

3. As a *finale* to the reviews of books by Sainte-Beuve, James concluded with the magnificent article on him in reviewing his correspondence of 1822-1869 in the *North American Review* for January 1880. He revised it for inclusion in an

anthology, *American Literary Criticism,* edited by William Morton Payne, 1904.

In the early form of the article, on which I am dwelling, James set forth his ideals of criticism and identified those of Sainte-Beuve with his own. He concluded by stating that Sainte-Beuve was the very genius of observation, discretion, and taste. He found the personal and grave parts of the correspondence the most interesting, and he marked the autobiographical touches. He said that Sainte-Beuve's wonderful mind made his personal accent acquire a superior savor and that he imported into literature the largest element of life. "No scholar," James added, "was ever so much of an observer, of a moralist, of a psychologist, and no observer surely was ever so much of a scholar. He valued life and literature equally for the light they throw upon each other; to his mind one implied the other, he was unable to conceive of them apart."

If one reads between the lines, one may recognize James's appraisal of himself as a critic and detect the principles which guided him in his own literary criticism.

When he wrote his review of James Elliot Cabot's life of Emerson, in 1887, (reprinted in *Partial Portraits*), he criticised Cabot for not doing as Sainte-Beuve used to do, who gave a picture of the surrounding society to enable one more perfectly to understand the literary protagonists that flourished in it.

I would have reprinted the unrevised Sainte-Beuve essay, but have not done so because it had been collected, though revised, previously.

NOTE TO GAUTIER'S POSTHUMOUS WORKS

4. Interest attaches to the articles in connection with Théophile Gautier not only because two of these relate to books of travel of which James was to review many, but because the earliest article in literary criticism that he reprinted was one on Gautier, from the *North American Review,* April 1873 (*French Poets and Novelists*). His brother William had found this article admirable and delightful; in fact as good as anything Gautier himself had written, as he told Henry in a letter. He suggested the writing of other articles on French literature and collecting them in book form. James had already written on

French literature. Henry followed his brother's advice and the book mentioned above was the result.

James's great admiration for Gautier is a little surprising in view of the fact that the latter was a romanticist and above all an out-and-out advocate of the theory of art for art's sake, a theory which James veritably riddled in a famous passage in his article on Baudelaire.

Another enthusiast of Gautier, Lafcadio Hearn, was then working on a newspaper in Cincinnati and soon was translating a number of stories by him which later began appearing in New Orleans newspapers with which he became connected and for which he eventually found a publisher in book form, *One of Cleopatra's Nights* (1882). Both American writers were delighted with the same tales and poems by Gautier. One reviewer attacked Hearn's book for the lust displayed and said it reeked of the miasma of the brothel.

A translation of a book by Gautier in English had appeared as early as 1853 in England, *"Wanderings in Syria."*

James wrote a review of another book by Gautier which I have not reprinted because nearly one half of it is made up of quotations translated from the French. The book was *Tableux de Siege,* and the review appeared in *The Nation,* January 25, 1872. He expatiates on Gautier's magical descriptive powers, saying his pen is almost a brush. But he notes that Gautier is so absorbed by what he is describing that he shows little concern about the French disasters.

The passage is worth quoting:

"Just as his visual perception and his verbal instinct have grown strong, his power of thought has declined. It is a strange spectacle to see exquisite genius conditioned, as it were, upon such moral aridity."

NOTE TO SCHERER'S LITERARY STUDIES

5. It is interesting to compare the Edmond Schérer article herein reprinted from *The Nation* of April 6, 1876 with the one entitled "A French Critic" in a review of Schérer's *Nouvelles Etudes sur la Litterature Contemporaine* in *The Nation,* October 12, 1865 and reprinted by Rose in *Notes and Reviews.* In the early article James's enthusiasm was without bounds, he, not of course realizing that he would make a *volte face.* He admits

that Sainte-Beuve may be called the first of living critics, but says that he is a small critic when compared with a great critic like Goethe, because the latter dealt with pure philosophy while Sainte-Beuve was concerned only with pure literary criticism.

James admired in his first article Schérer's eclecticism and moral consistency, his liberalism, his mind which showed itself acquisitive of truth and knowledge, and he found in him a solid embodiment of Matthew Arnold's ideal critic, since his moral sense and religious convictions animated his literary views. He was ready to set Schérer above Taine as a critic, except for the fact that Taine was more analytic.

Yet James's early view that Schérer was a great critic is sound. Though his fame has been somewhat dimmed, he was important enough for Arnold to devote two articles to him, to his essays on Goethe and Milton (*Mixed Essays*). Schérer's courage is attested by the fact that he attacked *Paradise Lost* because of its subject matter and theology, finding its value depended on its grand style. Arnold endorsed this view. Strangely enough the attacks upon Milton in the last generation have been just because of his style.

George Saintsbury was a great admirer of Schérer and translated a volume of his essays.

Note to George Sand's Mademoiselle Merquem

6. James returned to the novel *Mademoiselle Merquem* in the last article he wrote about George Sand, reprinted in *Notes on Novelists and Some Other Notes* (1914). It was written a couple of years after the appearance of the third volume of George Sand's *Vie et ses Oeuvres* (1838-1848) by Wladimir Karénine. James refers to the fact that *Mademoiselle Merquem* was based on the author's relation with a displeasing daughter and had been written while the latter was still living. He says that the novel strikes one as "the last word of superiority to blighted association." I suspect that some of his own stories were written, in the same mood showing himself above being too much affected by a painful event in the past, with a similar detachment.

In a letter to Bruce L. Richmond of the London *Times*, December 19, 1913, James asked for permission to withdraw this long article he had given them as he wished to use it in a book. He promised instead an article entitled "The New Novel." He did not think his George Sand article appropriate for the Spring Fiction Number, holding that it had no current significance, since he regarded her as superannuated and rococo as a novelist. Thus had evaporated his enthusiasm for a novelist about whom he had written on a number of occasions, whom he once placed above Balzac and considered in some respects superior to George Eliot. The article was withdrawn and appeared in the *Quarterly Review* for April 1914. The article "The New Novel" did appear in the London *Times Literary Supplement* March 19 and April 2, 1914 under the title "The Younger Generation," and caused quite a flutter in the dovecotes of contemporary English fiction. This article was also reprinted by him.

NOTE TO GEORGE SAND (TRIBUNE ARTICLE)

7. There appeared in *The Nation* for July 27, 1876 an anonymous note by James quoting extensively from a recent eulogy on George Sand by Taine, on the occasion of her death June 8. James wrote: "Mr. Taine says (justly to our mind) that if George Sand's novels have not the solid realism of Balzac, their species is a higher one." Still James differed with him in the view that the ideas, the morals thesis, and other abstractions would obtain for her a permanent and sympathetic attention.

In a letter to his brother William he asked him to inform him whether his article on George Sand written for the *Tribune* had yet appeared there. This is the article herein reprinted, and it was already in print, but Henry had not yet seen it. At the same time he told William that all desire was dead within him to produce something on George Sand, though he added that he would write an article upon her mercenarily and mechanically, only if forced He finally did write a lengthy article for the *Galaxy*, July 1877, and he reprinted it in his *French Poets and Novelists*. Here the Puritan in him disappears in his treatment of her novels of passion.

In his 1902 article on Flaubert, James called her loose, liquid, and irridescent, and he said that there was too little for the critical mind to rest upon. Once he had been attracted by her passionate earnestness and flood of feelings. However, little more need be said to show James's variations in critical appraisal with respect to George Sand than to read his 1868 article on her *Mademoiselle Merquem* and contrast the eulogies there with his later apathy.

It may be stated here that it is not impossible that James have been led to write Prefaces to the collected edition of his works because George Sand had done so to one of her own. Walter Scott had engaged upon a similar procedure. Of course we are all thankful that James did so.

NOTE TO HUGO'S NINETY-THREE

8. James reviewed in *The Nation* of April 12, 1866 Hugo's *Toilers of the Sea,* collected by Rose.

The review of *Ninety-Three* is most certainly adverse and where it is approving it is annoyingly patronizing. But James justifies the writing of the book largely because of an account of three chubby children who face death but are rescued. This is the episode selected out of a work giving a sympathetic account of an event in the French Revolution and some of its staunch active fighters in its behalf. Clearly James is prejudiced against the novel not so much because it is badly constructed or deals with scenes of violence, and other surface matters such as catalogues and many names, but because it offends his conservative mind. Nor is he set against it mainly because of its anticlerical cast, a motive that has incited a number of books in French and English against Hugo. It is amazing to find him deploring the attention that has been paid in literature to the French Revolution, and stating that it would enure to France's intellectual improvement if she forgot the Revolution for fifty years. Of course he could never dream that a time would come when she would abandon its principles under Petain, and drop its motto, but only temporarily—with vast injury to herself materially and spiritually.

James laughs in the face of Swinburne for his adulation of Hugo's poetry, and ventures to say that sometimes he wonders whether Hugo is even a small poet. And he picks out in his article on the volume in the series of the *Légende de Siècles* a story of a child for special approbation.

LITERARY REVIEWS and ESSAYS by HENRY JAMES

James never afterwards wrote an article about Hugo; indeed he rarely mentions him. Dumas, Jr. gets a separate essay collected in book form. But Hugo is antipathetic to James. After all he was a romantic. He dealt in scenes of violence. It made no difference that his favorite Gautier worshipped Hugo, that Hugo showed courage in defying Napoleon III and lived in exile because he had championed democracy; Hugo had committed the great sin in art; he was a propagandist for radicalism and besides he did not construct a novel according to Turgenevian and Jamesian standards. But great novels have been written by writers who mixed up in one book several novels, who rambled, and introduced irrelevant matters—the importance of the subject was paramount. Judged by James's standards neither *Don Quixote* nor the tragedies of violence by the Greek dramatists or Shakespeare would be great art.

James overlooks the great sense of justice which Hugo shows. In short James had a blind spot, when it came to Hugo. He condemned his later novels. He gave him advice even as a poet when speaking of Mérimée. He said that Hugo would have been none the worse for Mérimée's sobriety.

Mr. Edel has wondered that James never wrote about Herman Melville. Could he be expected to care for a novel like *Pierre*? And how many canons against artistic novel writing were violated in *Moby Dick*? He disliked sprawling novels and would no doubt have found these two vulgar if he had read them. Anyhow he never mentioned these great novels.

He knew of the close relations between Melville and Hawthorne even though his own book on Hawthorne appeared before the Julian Hawthorne's biography which dwells on them. Yet James never mentions Melville in his book on Hawthorne in spite of the tributes Hawthorne paid him in *The English Note Books* and elsewhere.

The review of the *Toilers of the Sea* in *The Nation* of April 12, 1866 was based on the French edition and was entitled "Victor Hugo's Last Novel." James says that Hugo embarks upon a different spirit from Captain Marryat. The review is written, as he says, with levity because Hugo writes here from the head and not the heart. Nature, James says, which is supposed to be here is not, but Hugo is everywhere. In short it is a work of decline. He summarised the novel and does not take seriously its most powerful scenes.

The tone of this youth of 23 to the most distinguished man of letters alive in that day is certainly not very reverent.

How differently did Pater speak of *Les Miserables* when he classed it as a great work of world art because it was motivated by a sense of justice! How different was Tolstoy when he puts the novel in his first of two classes of the highest art, as flowing from the love of God and man!

James does not even mention the novel except to quote Hugo's own reference to it.

He knew that it was a favorite book among the soldiers of the Civil War.

To return to *Ninety Three,* an authority on the French novel Benjamin W. Wells in his *Century of French Fiction* considers it Hugo's best novel.

NOTE TO FLAUBERT'S TEMPTATION OF ST. ANTHONY

9. James conceived a dislike for Flaubert's *Temptation of St. Anthony* and gave his reasons therefor in his review. He again went into them in his later articles on Flaubert. I need not quote his critical remarks against it in the 1902 essay collected in *Notes on Novelists with Some Other Notes,* but they had their genesis in the *Nation* review. He did not like to find it compared with *Madame Bovary.* His calling it queer and strange irritated Rebecca West in her little book about James.

On the contrary, Lafcadio Hearn greatly admired the book and already was translating it in Cincinnati about the time or shortly therefter when James was attacking it. It was the first translation into English and appeared posthumously, but D. F. Hannigan's translation appeared before it in 1895.

James wrote three articles about Flaubert besides the review, in 1876, 1893, and 1902, duly collected in his books. His views changed and while he admired him, he here and there carped.

It was however one of the pleasures of his life to become acquainted with him personally, meeting him through Turgenev. One wonders whether he ever told Flaubert about the hostile review he had written of his novel, or if Flaubert ever found out.

Georg Brandes in his magnificent essay on Flaubert is more generous to the *Temptation of St. Anthony*. He summarizes it at length, and says it displayed a modern stamp, depicted humanity as having waded up to its ankles in blood, and pointed to science as the sole salvation. He adds, however, that Flaubert did not possess that native harmony of spirit which reconciles the profound antitheses of the world of ideas; the book was crushed by its materials; it was not a poetic work; Flaubert had passed into abstract erudition and abstract style. (*Eminent Authors of the Nineteenth Century.*)

George Saintsbury considered it the best example of dream literature that he knew of and said it was his own favorite among Flaubert's novels. (*Essays on French Novelists.*)

NOTE TO HENRY BEYLE

10.   James's review of the biography of Stendhal, (misspelled in the original article, "Stendhal" or a variation), (Beyle), by Andrew A. Paton, was one of the most savage he wrote, although he might have given him some credit for being the first man to write a book on him in English, before any of his novels had as yet been translated. Though James was an admirer of Stendhal, and considered the *Chartreuse de Parme* one of the finest of a dozen novels that we possess, he showed his lack of critical acumen, and his moral prejudice in berating *The Red and The Black,* which he found unreadable and having an air of unredeemed corruption amounting to positive blight and dreariness. He thought it was a special ill fortune for Stendhal that his relations with women and his views on love should be presented for judgment at an English tribunal unaccustomed to dealing with such temperament and with such opinions. In view of the fact that Stendhal's greatness has been attributed to his doing this very thing, parading his love affairs and showing himself a keen student of the love emotion, James was mistaken. And many of these affairs were published for the world more fully after the date of this biography. The British tribunal has become quite accustomed to temperaments and opinions akin to those of Stendhal.

As a matter of fact James's method as a novelist followed largely that of Stendhal. Professor Matthiessen has said that

James's whole artistic production might be considered an illustration of Stendhal's view of a novel as "a mirror dawdling down a road." Stefan Zweig, who has written one of the best essays on Stendhal, has described the novelist's art in words that might well apply to James's. He dwelt on the French writer's attitude towards his characters in that he expatiated on their self-observation, the throbbings of their own personality, on their self-consciousness, and on their psychological insight. All this James has done. In one respect he differs vastly from James. As Zweig says, Stendhal's characters are free from moral prejudices. Joseph Conrad has pointed out that James was notable in analyzing a fine conscience, and that this manifested itself in showing his characters emerging from their struggles, triumphant through renunciation. The idea of self-sacrifice however unless in a great cause has no longer since Ibsen the aureole it used to have. But it is undoubtedly a virtue on the right occasion. James never pardons vice, Stendhal almost boasts of his characters' indulgence in it; yet he also often does so in a manner that shows he is averse to it. We do not think of his approving of Julien Sorel's hypocrisy, although he seems to do so. We find references to Stendhal long before James published his book *French Poets and Novelists,* and one wonders why he did not include in it an article on him. In the tale "Travelling Companions" (1870) he recalls that a gallery similar to one he was visiting was described in the palace of the Duchess of San Severino in the *Chartreuse de Parme.* In another tale "At Isella" (1873) an Italian woman he meets reminds him of Lucrezia Borgia, of Bianca Capello, and the heroines of Stendhal (both tales collected in *Traveling Companions* [1919]). In "The Pension Beurepas" (1879), (included in the volume *The Siege of London*) the narrator, an admirer of the *Chartreuse de Parme,* quotes from a letter by Stendhal to his sister to the effect that he had a passionate desire to know human nature, and had a great mind to live in a boarding-house, where people cannot conceal their characters. The narrator decided to follow in the footsteps of Stendhal and do likewise—at the same time not forgetting Balzac's description and account of the boarding-house kept by Madame Vauquer in *Père Goriot.*

In his book *A Little Journey in France* (1884) James quoted Stendhal on a number of occasions, and said that every traveler in France should carry in his portmanteau the two volumes of

Memoirs d'un Touriste. He also devotes some pages to Stendhal's excellent art criticism (pp. 163-164). He quotes him again later in the book. "It is a pleasure to me to reflect," James says, "that five and forty years ago (i.e. 1837 before 1882) he [Stendhal] had alighted in that city (Nantes) at the very inn at which I spent a night." He however thought that Stendhal missed the charm of landscape scenes.

Two books of Stendhal were translated in England in the early part of the Nineteenth Century. *Rome, Naples and Florence* (1817) by Count de Stendhal (sic), and *The Lives of Haydn, and Mozart with Observations on Metastasio* (1818) by L. A. C. Bombet (one of Stendhal's pseudonyms).

Several Americans have made solid contributions to Stendhal literature: Norman Hapgood, Benjamin W. Wells, James Huneker, and Harry Levin in articles, and Matthew Josephson in his biography of him. There have been four or five other contributions.

NOTE TO MINOR FRENCH NOVELISTS: THE GONCOURTS, ETC.

11. An unusual interest attaches to this article dealing mainly with the Goncourt brothers, since it was the third part of an essay of which the first two sections dealt with Charles de Bernard and Gustave Flaubert, but which he did not reprint in *French Poets and Novelists,* as he did these two sections. The inclusion of it in the present volume fills a gap.

The article is interesting as showing a good opinion of the Goncourts and because of its summary of their novel *Renée Mauperin* and the translation of a passage from it. It is even more valuable as an emphatic statement of James's objection to literature dealing with low life. He was decidedly opposed to an art that "begins to overhaul the baser forms of suffering and the meaner forms of vice, to turn over and to turn again the thousand indecencies and impurities of life."

He deals in a few words with some "minor French novelists," Gustave Droz and Victor Cherbuliez. He said more about them when he reviewed Cherbuliez's *Meta Holdenis* in the *North American Review*, October, 1873, and *Miss Rovel* in *The Nation*

June 3, 1875, and when he reviewed Droz's *Autour une Source* in the *Atlantic Monthly,* August, 1871.

He called the Goncourts minor novelists, which is hardly true; he even says that the names of Cherbuliez and Droz suggest the idea of genius, while the Goncourts were not geniuses.

The conclusion of the article shows how he then worshipped George Sand.

Though he merely mentions Octave Feuillet, as a brilliant talent, he wrote reviews, herein reprinted, of two of his novels.

NOTE TO EDMOND DE GONCOURT'S LA FILLE ELISA

12. The attack on Edmond Goncourt's novel *La fille Elisa* is unusually severe. He came back to the Goncourts when he considered their Journal in the *Fortnightly Review,* October 1880, reprinted in *Essays in London and Elsewhere* (1893). Here he was favorable to them in spite of his deep-seated aversion to the revealing of events from private life to the public. He had not changed his mind about the inferiority of the novels written by Edmond since the death of his brother Jules. He had something much better to say about the novels written in collaboration, like *Germinie Lacerteux* and *Manette Salomon,* stating that they showed in an unmistakable way the act of presenting and expressing a sense of life that some readers (meaning himself) did not find interesting. He added that still the authors had a point in holding, as Edmond maintained, that *Germinie Lacerteux* could not have been written if they had been afraid of being called coarse. To this James replies that there arises a reality in the danger of *feeling* coarse, that the epithet represents also a subjective condition.

On February 3, 1876 James wrote to Howells that he heard a talk between Flaubert and Edmond Goncourt in which the latter said that he was coming to the episode which greatly interested him, and into which he was going far, and that it was "a whore-house *de province.*" One may imagine how shocked James was. What would he have said had he lived to read the translation of Alexander Kuprin's novel *Yama, The Pit?*

Yet later on he told Howells that he had been seeing Goncourt and the other French realists, and that in spite of their ferocious pessimism and handling of unclean things, they were serious and honest.

George Moore, however, in a later edition of *Confessions of a Young Man* says that *La Fille Elisa* enchanted him in his lonely lodging.

NOTE TO MERIMEE, LAST TALES

13. Mérimée fascinated James all his life. M. Augustin Filon's book about him gave James an opportunity to return to him in an article in *Literature*, July 9, 1898, still uncollected. James says here that in his early years he was curious as to how Mérimée "was put together." He says he "fluttered deliciously" one summer day with his sensitive spirit at the touch of the story "La Venus d'Ille." Elsewhere, he has told us that John La Farge introduced the story to him, that he translated it, and sent it to a magazine which ignored it. In his *Literature* article he speaks of two other stories by Mérimée he translated, "Tamango" and "Matteo Falcone," which also suffered rejection as previously mentioned.

From Mérimée he learned conciseness, compression, and economy, and he speaks as if these qualities in Mérimée had been his own discovery and choice. He apparently forgot that he had once blamed his brother William for teaching him condensation through Mérimée as an example, and thus making him ruin *Washington Square* which he himself thought should have been more expanded. William had written to him àpropos this novel commending its conciseness, as against the diffusiveness of *The Portrait of a Lady*. Henry replied that the latter novel was, because of its very spaciousness, inevitably more human and more sociable.

James struggled with the problem of conciseness and expansiveness throughout his literary career, varying between resorting to each. He would sometimes set out with the purpose of writing a tale, and under his hands it expanded into a novel. He wrote several two-volume novels; he wrote some tales which were novels in a nut-shell. Lincoln once said a man's legs should be long enough to reach the ground. Likewise a novel should be long enough to finish the story whether it takes two volumes or more, or five chapters like the novelette *Ruth*.

NOTE TO FEUILLET'S LES AMOURS DE PHILIPPE

14. It is notable that James should devote so long an article to Octave Feuillet's *Camors*. For one, he gives as usual a masterly and comprehensive analysis and summary of the novel. He bestows honors upon the author because in the case of this novel and *Les Amours de Philippe* he can tell a tale. Of course he does not approve of the immoralistic features of the novelist but on the whole he has a good opinion of Feuillet. In this he agrees with Saintsbury, who later devoted a lengthy article to Feuillet in his *Essays on French Novelists,* and Walter Pater who devoted a lengthy essay to a novel by Feuillet—*La Morte*—in his *Appreciations*. A rather derogatory—and probably more correct—attitude towards Feuillet was taken by Benjamin W. Wells in *A Century of French Fiction*.

It is not necessary to go into controversy about the merits or demerits of the author of these novels or the more widely read novel in America, *The Romance of a Young Man*.

What is strange is that James should speak sympathetically of a writer so different from himself; and that he could even see the side of an immoral situation from the point of view of the character involved in it, without becoming indignant about his conduct, though of course deprecating it; and that he could say a good word for a romance in which episodes were recounted that he thought artificial.

NOTE TO ALPHONSE DAUDET

15. James tells us that the idea of his *The Bostonians* (1885) came to him from Alphonse Daudet's *Évangéliste*. He had been obsessed with the idea that the invasion of privacy by newspapers was an obnoxious crime, a subject to which he returns in *The Reverberator*. Matthiessen doubts the importance of the influence of Daudet upon James's novel, in helping him to draw a woman character; and he quotes James's own criticism in an article on Daudet for getting up his material from the outside; in fact James had found Madame Autheman in *Évangéliste* quite automatic and blank. (This article appeared in the *Century Magazine,* August 1883 and was collected in *Partial Portraits*.)

James on the occasion of his translating *Port Tarascon* also wrote a preface for it.

Subsequent to the author's death he wrote an article on him for *Literature,* December 25, 1897, still uncollected. His early admiration for Daudet had disappeared. He stated that in the light of Anatole France and Maurice Barrés, Daudet had grown virtually antique and ancestral. He, however, praised him for being personal and using all his experiences to the last drop for his fiction. He still liked him best of all those novelists who had not the greater imagination of the moralist. He found that Daudet's vision was "of the brighter and weaker things, weaker natures, about us, the people, the passions, the complications that we either commiserate or laugh at." He apparently, as opposed to Daudet, holds that one should sit over the lesson even though it is cruel or in bad taste. What a change again from some of his early concepts! Daudet like George Sand had become a casualty.

On the day the article in *Literature* appeared James wrote to Grace Norton that he did not care to go to the funeral of Daudet and find privacy invaded and hear him compared to Christ once more. He had not seen Daudet for two years.

He noted in him an absence of the greater mind, as it were—the greater feeling. *Letters of Henry James,* Vol. I p. 269.

NOTE TO IVAN TURGENEV'S VIRGIN SOIL

16.   James the critic wrote best when he was in full sympathy with his author and hence we have the splendid 1877 article on *Virgin Soil.* The novel had not yet been published at the time James wrote his 1874 article on Turgenev gathered together in *French Poets and Novelists.* When he wrote the 1884 article on Turgenev that was reprinted in *Partial Portraits,* which was quite personal and written after the novelist's death, all that he said about this novel was that it was a good story. Here in the review we learn why he thought so and we get James's presentation of Turgenev's principles of fiction.

When Thomas Wentworth Higginson, writing on James in 1879, complained that James said nothing in his essay on Turgenev in *French Poets and Novelists* about his masterpiece *Terres Vierges,* he was not aware that the essay had been originally written before the novel had been published but gathered into the book (1878) afterwards, nor further was he aware that James had published a lengthy review of the novel in *The Nation* April 26, 1877.

Henry James read Turgenev very early, before he went to Europe in 1869, for we find his brother William writing to him in that year that he himself was reading a new volume by "your old friend Turgenev." Edel says that Thomas Sergeant Perry through his admiration for Turgenev influenced Henry James in his theory of the novel.

Since James read Turgenev before he went to Europe to live, George Moore's famous remark that appears in *Confessions of a Young Man*, "Henry James went to France and read Turgenev. W. D. Howells stayed at home and read Henry James," is untrue and without point. It has often been quoted.

Howells did not stay at home; he had been in Europe in the sixties before James began his career as a story writer. Howells was not an imitator of James, as Moore implied. Still, again as Howells tells us, in the middle seventies he was a devout reader of Turgenev, reading most of his books many times over. And in that period James had written only one novel which Howells accepted for the *Atlantic Monthly*, and he himself had published several novels before *Roderick Hudson*.

Commenting on this remark by Moore, Howells wrote to the present writer, May 2, 1916: "He (Moore) had so long been a brilliant expatriate in Paris that he felt obliged to prove his familiarity with continental literature by insulting our own." (Quoted with permission of Professor William W. Howells, grandson of William Dean Howells, and representing the Howells estate.)

Moore conceived a high regard for James as a literary critic. They met in the eighties, and in his *Avowals*, he said he was struck with some incisive remarks that James made about Pater's *Marius the Epicurean*, a book that Moore worshipped. James had said that Pater gave over the first volume to praise of Pagan civilization and a large part of the second to an equal admiration of Christianity, and that we cannot admire opposites equally. Moore thought James reasoned well and believed that literature had lost in him an excellent critic, an extraordinarily able one. He even felt that James was too analytic for creation. Yes, James had detected an insincere note in Pater when he said that the latter wanted to hunt with the Pagan hounds and run with the

Christian hare. Moore was highly impressed with this shrewdness (although he soon qualified his praise in another matter).

To come back to *Virgin Soil,* James soon changed or modified his laudatory opinion of that novel. It will be noticed that he concluded *The Nation* article on the novel that Turgenev's omnipresent subtle intentions "throw into relief the author's great quality—the union of the deepest reality of substance, of *fonds* as the French say, with the most imaginative, most poetic touches."

When he wrote his article in connection with Turgenev and Tolstoy for the *World's Best Literature* (1897), he said that it was not incontestable that *Virgin Soil,* has, although full of beauty, a minor perfection. (Reprinted by Morton Dauwen Zabel in *The Portable Henry James* and Leon Edel in *The Future of the Novel*.)

An author undoubtedly has a right in the course of twenty years to alter a literary opinion. But it is a question whether the view expressed in the earlier article is not sounder.

Two other opinions on *Virgin Soil* are hereby given to contrast or harmonize with both James's earlier and later views of the book. Georg Brandes thinks it inferior to the other novels because he had become an expatriate, but still holds that it is "the richest and most complete expression of Turgenev's humanity and wordly wisdom, and of his love of freedom and truth." (*Impressions of Russia,* p. 296.)

Count Kropotkin does not judge the book so much as a work of art but as to whether it fully caught the spirit of a new movement in Russia in the seventies, and he says it referred only to the earlier phases of the movement. He admits that Turgenev by intuition caught some of the most striking features of the movement. Kropotkin read the novel in proof. (*Russian Literature,* p. 108.)

Note to Howells's Italian Journeys

17. In James's article on Howells's *Italian Journeys* printed in the *North American Review* for January 1868, he speaks of his keenness of observation and vivacity of sympathy, compares him in his perfection as a descriptive writer to Hawthorne, and refers to his taste, culture, and imagination. Yet in a letter to Charles Eliot Norton in January, 1871, he writes àpropos Howells's

Suburban Sketches that he can write solely of what his fleshly eyes have seen, and says that he lacks a master's *really* grasping situation to write about American scenes. *The Letters of Henry James,* Vol. I pp. 30-31. There seems here to be a retraction of what James had written three years previously.

Howells and James had met in 1866. "Poor Richard" had been accepted by Howells for the *Atlantic Monthly* where it appeared serially during the summer of 1867. Howells undoubtedly was pained when he read this comment. But still he came to the defence of James for going to live abroad, and he criticized the editor of the letters, Percy Lubbock, for not realizing that sickness played a part in James's decision to live abroad, and he also mentioned the rudeness and harshness of American rejection of his work, which also incited him to go to Europe to live.

James in his public letter to Howells in 1912, on the occasion of the celebration of his 75th birthday, admitted not only that Howells had made his reputation, but beginning in 1866 had given him the confidence that required help and sympathy. He said that otherwise he might have strayed and stumbled about a long time without acquiring such confidence.

Note to Howells's A Foregone Conclusion
(second article)

18. Howells's novel *A Foregone Conclusion* was not the only book that James reviewed in two different periodicals. He wrote in 1868 two reviews of George Eliot's *The Spanish Gypsy,* one for *The Nation,* July 2, 1868, herein reprinted, and one for the *North American Review,* October 1868 (reprinted by Phillips) and he wrote two reviews of William Morris's *The Earthly Paradise,* one for *The Nation,* July 9, 1868, also reprinted by Phillips, and another for the *North American Review,* July 1868, not hitherto collected.

One of the objections to anonymous book reviewing has been that the reviewer could help a friend or hurt an enemy by writing more than one review and misleading the reader into thinking that the reviews came from different hands.

It is obvious that in the Howells case James wanted to reciprocate for favors done, while in the others he may have been prompted by the need for an extra dollar.

NOTE TO HOWELLS'S POEMS

19. The review of the poems of Howells by James in the *Independent,* January 8, 1874, was especially pleasing to him; it must be remembered that he really began his literary career with poetry. He knew the review was soon to appear, for James's mother had permitted him to read the manuscript, and he wrote to James that he had done so with consolation and thankfulness. He appreciated the gracious kindness with which James had treated his "poor little book."

And was it not proper that James should perform this little service for a man who had accepted for periodical publication in his capacity as editor quite a number of stories and a novelette by James?

But we have this fortuitous coincidence that in the month when Howells began serializing James's first important novel *Roderick Hudson* in the *Atlantic Monthly*—January 1875, James published the two anonymous reviews of Howells's novel, *A Foregone Conclusion*, herein reprinted, in two different periodicals.

Howells returned James's kindness in the fullest measure. He was writing reviews of James's books for the rest of his life, beginning with one on James's first book *A Passionate Pilgrim and Other Tales* in the *Atlantic Monthly*. No man had a better friend in court than James had in Howells who became connected with Harper's *Monthly Magazine* and Harper's *Weekly,* and still had access to the *Atlantic* and also the *North American Review*. So for several decades articles and reviews came forth. Among the novels and collections of tales that Howells reviewed were *The Princess Casamassima, The Reverberator, A London Life, The Tragic Muse, Terminations,* and *The Soft Side,* and he also reviewed critical works like the biography of Hawthorne and *French Poets and Novelists*.

Howells had published also in the *North American Review* an article on James's later work, January 1903, reprinted by F. W. Dupee. And there were articles by him in the *Century Magazine,* November 1882, and in *Harper's Bazar,* January 1912 dealing with James's "masterpiece," *Daisy Miller*.

On the other hand, James wrote beside the four articles about Howells herein reprinted, the one in *Harper's Weekly,* July 19, 1886, which has been reprinted by Edmund Wilson and Leon Edel, and an article about Howells's novel *The Story of a Play*, in *Literature*, July 9, 1898; and then there was the tribute by James to Howells on the occasion of the dinner on his seventy-fifth birthday, which was published in the *North American Review*, April, 1912, and reprinted by Matthiessen.

This might be called log-rolling carried to excess. It happens that James particularly needed help to awaken an apathetic public to the merits of his work.

James had in the beginning of his career another great ally and this was his friend James Russell Lowell, who had publicly praised one of his early tales. But the real benediction came in the anonymous review in *The Nation* by Lowell in one article of both the *Passionate Pilgrim* and *Transatlantic Sketches* previously referred to. The authorship of *The Nation* article has remained unknown to several James scholars.

It must be said that Howells was singularly noble in that he betrayed no literary jealousy of his friend, though he read appraisals of James that placed him higher than himself as a literary personage. In fact he agreed with them.

"In literary handling," Howells wrote, "no one who has written fiction in our language can approach him, and his work has shown an ever-deepening insight." (*My Literary Passions* [1895] p. 224.)

Note to Francis Parkman: The Jesuits in North America

20. Many readers will be surprised to learn that James was assigned reviews of histories where special knowledge was required, but he did well with the two Francis Parkman reviews, written no doubt at the special instance of Edwin L. Godkin, the editor of *The Nation*, a close friend of Parkman. I had intended reprinting both reviews, but since Edel reprinted the review of *The Old Régime in Canada*, I contented myself with retaining the earlier review of *The Jesuits in North America*.

Parkman was twenty years older than James. He was a devout reader of *The Nation* and contributed to it. Undoubtedly Godkin told him who was the author of these two reviews.

NOTE TO THE PROPHET: A TRAGEDY. BY BAYARD TAYLOR

21.   James's article on *The Prophet,* the play by Bayard
Taylor (1825-1878) is one of the most analytic pieces of dramatic criticism that he ever wrote. It is of special interest because he too later wrote plays. He does not regard the play as
dull as anything that Taylor ever wrote as is the opinion of
the latter's latest biographer, Richmond Croom Beatty, *Bayard Taylor, Laureate of the Gilded Age (1936)*. Taylor devoted about eight years to the play and his letters are full of
comments upon it; he considered it "the most steady, con-
scientiously elaborated, and uninterruptedly carried out work
of my life" *(Life and Letters of Bayard Taylor* Edited by
Marie Hansen-Taylor and Horace E. Scudder, 1884. Vol. II
p. 664). Taylor resented the misunderstandings to which he
was subjected by his portrayal of the protagonist David Starr,
of whom the Rev. Edward Irving was the prototype. He
regarded the play as "a two-edged sword, cutting the fossil-
ized Orthodox to the heart no less than the Mormons"
(ibid. p. 635). Albert H. Smyth in his biography in 1896 selects for approbation David Starr's vision in the wilderness
beginning with the lines "Came languid peace, then awe
and shuddering Without a cause", and he states that it is
the recollection of an actual experience that Taylor had
near the foothills of the Sierra Nevada in 1849 (Page 251).
The play however, is seldom read. It is one of the many
instances where an author had put his sincerest thoughts
into his work and labored over it assiduously to find that
it has been ignored.

NOTE TO NERO: AN HISTORICAL PLAY BY W. W. STORY

22.   The restrained remarks by James upon William
Wetmore Story's historical play *Nero* are of interest, since 28
years later he returned to the subject in his two volume
work *William Wetmore Story and his Friends* (1903). He
tells us there that he had been privileged around the early
seventies to hear in the company of three or four others,
among whom was Frances Anne Kemble, Story read the
play. Apparently there had been no doubts in his mind as to
his right to speak his mind freely anonymously about the

work to which he had been introduced under these circumstances. At that time he could not have foreseen that he would one day write the biography of the great man (1819-1895).

In his comments on the play in the book, James repeats the criticisms he made upon it in his *Nation* article, never mentioning he had written one! He adds that he finds the epistolary dedication to Miss Kemble its most attaching page. He says the play is not open to the charge of want of amplification, that it is but a scenic chronicle and that it represents the author's interest in the Roman horrid past.

Note to Saxon Studies By Julian Hawthorne

23.   As will be noticed Henry James reviewed two of the novels of Julian Hawthorne (1846-1934) rather patronizingly, though perhaps justly, while he condemned Hawthorne's *Saxon Studies*. This latter attack in *The Nation* probably was in the mind of Julian Hawthorne when he referred to this periodical as " a rather poisonous one" (*Shapes That Pass*, p. 157, 1928). However in view of the fact that Hawthorne unreservedly lauded James in the highest terms, and spoke with pride of the few occasions on which he met him in later days since their acquaintance in youth, it is likely that he never knew that James had written those anonymous reviews. It is well known that anonymous criticism in periodicals has carried with it the possibilities of a writer's going out to dinner with another, whom he had not spared in an adverse review. It is not likely that Hawthorne would in his book *The Memoirs of Julian Hawthorne,* published by his wife Edith Garrigues Hawthorne posthumously (1938), have written so glowingly and affectionately of James had he known he had been the subject of three unfavorable articles by him. In his biography, he boasts even that he had introduced him to the Pacific Ocean, calls him modest, states that he was devoted to true art and had never written a careless or shallow line. In spite of the fact that James's book on Nathaniel Hawthorne, the father of Julian, had been in 1879 violently attacked by American reviewers, Julian calls it an honest and painful performance that will endure (pp. 123-128).

The only reservations Hawthorne makes are in his comment upon the novelist's puritanism that he was shocked by reading a pornographic work or two unknowingly in Lord Houghton's library (*Shapes That Pass*, pp. 53-54) and in his account of how young James even before he had published a book audaciously told Louisa M. Alcott that she was not a genius, in spite of her success with *Little Women* (ibid. p. 157).

NOTE TO CHARLES NORDHOFF'S COMMUNISTIC SOCIETIES

24. Had Phillips's bibliography not assigned the article on Nordhoff's *Communistic Societies* to James, no one would ever have thought of attributing it to him. It contains the most daring statements that he ever perpetrated. I select these from the body of the article. "There is a kind of wholesome Conservatism in the Shaker philosophy, as Mr. Nordhoff depicts it, which we confess rather takes our fancy." "We regret to hear that their (the Shakers's) number is decidedly not increasing." "Mr. Nordhoff's volume seems to establish fairly that, under certain conditions and with strictly rational hopes, communism in America may be a paying experiment." Needless to add, this communism was not of the Soviet species, being merely a peaceful Utopia in the heart of America, the principles of the government of which were not discarded. The most amazing statement is àpropos a stanza embodying the principle of the Oneida Perfectionists ending with the lines," "And we have all one home, and one family relation." James underscores this last line and says that he "has outlined it in the *charming* stanza for its *delightful* naiveté, shadowing forth as it does the fact that these ladies and gentlemen are all indifferently and interchangeably each other's husbands and wives." (Italics supplied) The point here is not that James of course does not approve of such a course, but that he records the matter without any shock.

Whether the fact that Hawthorne's interest, though not approval, of the Shakers whom he visited, had something to do with James's kind words about them we do not know. We do know that he did not treat the Brook Farm experimentalists with scorn in his book on Hawthorne.

Yet the writer who drew as unpleasant characters women with a penchant for reform as in *The Bostonians* and the *Princess Casamassima,* is here not altogether averse to reformers.

Nordhoff was more famous two and three generations ago, not so much for his book on Communistic societies as for three of the most entertaining sea stories based on personal experience and issued in the fifties. His *Man-of-War Life, The Merchant Vessel,* and *Whaling and Fishing,* were once read by boys along with the sea tales of Cooper, Marryat, Melville, and Dana. Although Nordhoff never achieved the literary distinction that these authors had, the present writer recalls the delight with which he read over and over these three books. Something of this interest and ability to write of adventure at sea must have been transmitted to his late grandson and namesake Charles B. Nordhoff who collaborated in *Mutiny in the Bounty.*

NOTE TO CARLYLE'S TRANSLATION OF WILHELM MEISTER

25. Miss Cornelia Pulsifer Kelley states that Goethe influenced James more than any other writer, giving his fiction its introspective psychological nature. She says that *Wilhelm Meister* sent him to studying the human mind and that this brought philosophy and psychology into his novels. There is some truth in what she says, but she was probably led to overstate her case because she had discovered from the General Index of the *North American Review* that he wrote an article on *Wilhelm Meister* and that it had inadvertently not been cited in the Phillips bibliography, and hence had not been included by Rose in his book containing the articles James had written from 1864 to 1865.

In noticing the Goethe novel, James observed that it had no plot, no life-like characters, no detailed descriptions, all of which he thought essential for a novel. Yet here was a great novel in spite of these deficiencies. Though perplexed he began to realize that it was important for a novelist to be a philosopher besides a historian. Goethe was too sublime for rules. Miss Kelley speculates that it is possible that the bewilderment that James felt, started him in a search for the means that would help him to become a novelist.

Certainly Goethe had nothing to teach James about technique. Intellectual influence there may have been but Miss Kelley, being aware that the same issue of the periodical contained James's mature essay reviewing Matthew Arnold's *Essays in Criticism,* might have modified her view as to the extent of the Goethe influence. What was important was the unbounded enthusiasm; the New Englander was not shocked in the manner a very great writer and critic, Thomas De Quincey was, who years before had poured out the most unmitigated abuse upon it in his *Encyclopedia Britannica* article on Goethe, and especially in a lengthy essay where he analyzed the various characters to Goethe's disparagement. In the former he referred to the novel as something repulsive, lacking in moral purity and dignity of nature. In the latter article he finds even the much admired Mignon episode evidence "of depraved taste and defective sensibility." And we all know that Wordsworth's opinion of the book was no higher than the one he had of Voltaire's *Candide.*

Now James was more puritanical than De Quincey, who had an affair with Ann, the prostitute, and who lived with his wife before marriage. It is amazing that James showed such critical genius in his regard for the book.

Twelve years later he came to the rescue of Goethe from the attack by Alexander Dumas, Jr., in the Preface to a French translation of *Faust.* In a review in *The Nation* (herein reprinted) he pointed out Dumas's Gallic prejudice and said that Goethe had an immense respect for reality, and that the multifarious use he made of the facts he collected was an extension of his poetic faculty.

James always remained an admirer of Goethe, but probably not as a disciple ready to follow him in his pagan and pantheistic views. He spoke highly of him on a number of occasions; in the *American Scene* in 1907 he referred to the sense of moving in large intellectual spaces he had when reading Goethe, and said that he reads *Dichtung und Wahrheit* for a gush here and there of poetry.

One therefore may let Miss Kelley entertain her thesis that there was a great influence.

NOTE TO HISTORICAL NOVELS BY THE AUTHOR
OF MARY POWELL

26.   The name of the author of *Mary Powell,* as she signed herself to the two novels that gave James an opportunity to present his views in "Historical Novels" was Anne Manning (1809-1879). The novels were *The Household of Thomas More* and *Jacques Bonneval; or The Days of the Dragonnades.* She was a very popular English writer and was related to a number of prominent English jurists. When James wrote his article she was already the author of about forty books. She was especially adept in writing about the sixteenth century and she knew several languages. The full title of her most famous novel, often reprinted, which first appeared in *Sharpe's Magazine* in 1849 was *The Married Life of Mistress Powell, Afterwards Mistress Milton.*

In the review James soon leaves the authoress and gives us an essay on the art of fiction. He extols *Henry Esmond* and the *Cloister on the Hearth* by Charles Reade, but calls *Romola* beautiful, but worthless as a picture of life in the fifteenth century.

NOTE TO GEORGE ELIOT'S THE LIFTED VEIL;
AND BROTHER JACOB

27.   In connection with the two articles by James reprinted here, on *"The Spanish Gypsy"* (*The Nation* July 2, 1868) and *The Lifted Veil* and *Brother Jacob* (*The Nation,* April 25, 1878), something should be said about his other writings about her. He himself collected two articles of which she is the subject in his *Partial Portraits,* "Daniel Deronda: A Conversation" (1876) and a review of her biography by her husband J. W. Cross (1885). Phillips collected the *Atlantic Monthly* article of October 1866, "The Novels of George Eliot," written by James before *Middlemarch* and *Daniel Deronda* had appeared; he also collected James's reviews of two of her books of poetry, the other review he wrote of *The Spanish Gypsy* from the *North American Review* of October 1868 besides the one mentioned above which I have collected herein, and he collected a review of *The Legend of Jubal,* also from the *North American Review* of October 1874.

James's first review of a book by her was of the novel, *Felix Holt,* a review which appeared in *The Nation* August 16, 1866, and which has been collected by Rose.

Edel identified through manuscript letters an unsigned review of *Middlemarch* in the *Galaxy* of March 1873. He reprinted it in *The Future of the Novel.*

Edel states that James wrote five essays and reviews of George Eliot between 1866 and 1878. As we see from the above he wrote eight reviews during this period, and, counting the 1885 article about the Cross biography, nine altogether.

George Eliot figures also in some other early James reviews, in his correspondence, his autobiographies, and his Notebooks.

O. F. Matthiessen quotes from an unpublished letter James wrote to his father in the spring of 1869, where he says he fell in love with this "great horse-faced blue stocking." He mentions this visit briefly in *Notes of a Son and Brother,* saying that it was at North Bank on a Sunday afternoon, no other person being present except Miss Caroline Norton who introduced him, and that the visit had peculiarly thrilling accompaniments. In a letter to his brother William on May 1, 1878 he mentions a visit to her when George H. Lewes also introduced him to Herbert Spencer, and in November of the same year he refers to another visit to her. He goes into details about some of these visits in his unfinished autobiography *The Middle Years.*

He saw her alone, only once, before her death in 1880.

Speaking in this book of his first visit to her in 1869, he states that he had read *Felix Holt* on a sick bed getting up to write a review of "the delightful thing," but he refused to name the periodical in which it appeared being ashamed of the review. This was of course the review in *The Nation* for August 16, 1866. James praised the quality of her mind in *The Nation* review, but he seemed to forget, when in his *Middle Years* he referred to the "delightful thing," that in his review, he said that he had found her plot artificial, the conduct of her story slow, and her style diffuse.

He further says in his *Middle Years* that he rejoiced without reserve in *Felix Holt.* The book was a feast of fine rich natural tone. Still unforgettable to him was the art and truth with which this note was struck. He also then seemed to forget that in his comment on *Felix Holt* in his 1866 *Atlantic Monthly* article, he said that the book was without character as a composition, that the radicalism was utterly choked amidst a mass of subordinate details, and that no representation was attempted by the author of the growth of Felix Holt's opinions, or of their action upon his character. The general outline, he also had said, was timid and undecided and that there was no person attained to triumphant vitality. He, of course, also did point out merits.

Thus he says in his autobiography here is a great novel, and he was under the impression that he always thought so, or he would not have called it a "delightful thing." If he was ashamed of *The Nation* review, which apparently he did not reread, it may have been that unconsciously he wanted to disown what at present he considered a great novel but which he had written up (twice at that) as a very poor one. In short the memory of what he once had written played him false and he contradicted himself.

With our knowledge of his hostility toward the novel in the early days, we become amused at the enthusiastic reference to it in his Notebooks of March 1905, at Coronado Beach, when he was recalling his first reading of *Felix Holt* and said that he had read it in a thrilled state and here he named *The Nation* for which he wrote the review, still thinking the review was favorable. The whole time lived for him again, as he recalled reading the opening pages of the novel. He becomes poetic: "Oh, strange little intensities of history, of ineffability." It was undoubtedly on these treacherous notes written nearly forty years after the review that he relied when he wrote *The Middle Years*.

However, in his later years he was an admirer of George Eliot. He was consistent about *Daniel Deronda* which he praised, when it was appearing serially. In a note in *The Nation*, February 24, 1876 when he was reading the opening chapters, he said that he had high expectations of it. He was impressed with the intellectual luxury in the early instalments; he added that her writing was charged fully with reflection and intellectual experience; he spoke of her multitudinous world—"a world ideal only in the soft clear light under which it lies, and most real in its close appeal to our curiosity." He found in her work, to quote her own phrase, "the sense of the universal."

Percy Lubbock tells us that James, on one occasion having watched Turgenev and Flaubert seriously discussing Daudet's *Jack,* probably in 1876 when that book and *Daniel Deronda* appeared, reflected that none of the three had read or knew enough English to read *Daniel Deronda*. Yet only two years before in his 1874 article on Turgenev he spoke of her rounded plots, her mechanical episodes, and the evaporation of her moral unity.

His final words on her in *The Middle Years* are of adulation. He defended her and deplored the thin prevalent criticism which saw no rich thought in her philosophy or which stated that she had no right to thrust her philosophy through to the "confounding of the picture." He boasted of the fact that he had been and remained a "Derondist of Derondists" for his own wanton joy.

And no finer tribute has been paid to the novel than in *Daniel Deronda*, written in 1876, where two of the characters outdo each other in extolling the book, Constantius who appears to be James himself and Theodora who in greater outbursts of lavishing praise also speaks for James, against Pulcheria the disparager of the book. James remained loyal to the book although it was criticised, but which has today much more importance than ever, since the subject with which it is partly concerned, the founding of a Jewish state, became a reality.

Note to Thomas Hardy's Far From the Madding Crowd

28. James's attack upon Hardy's novel *Far from the Madding Crowd* was partly due to its having been attributed to George Eliot. It is not likely that Hardy did not see so long an article about one of his early novels in so important a periodical in America as *The Nation*.

The passage quoted on pages 292 and 293 is from the eighth chapter. It was revised when Hardy later reprinted the novel.

One is amused by the complaint by James about the length of the Hardy novel and the suggestion that a censorship should be imposed upon novelists and none be permitted to allow a novel to run over two hundred pages. His own *Roderick Hudson* was soon to exceed that number while *The Portrait of a Lady*, in 520 closely printed pages, was to be longer than any novel that Hardy ever wrote. We need not refer to the two volume novels that James wrote later.

Incidentally, it was not uncommon for James to castigate an author for doing something that he himself did later in his own novels, as when he complained of the bringing in of titled people in a novel by Feuillet or Lord Beaconsfield.

The opinions of Hardy and James of each other's work were not such as to lead to a close friendship. A few of these have been gathered together by Simon Howell-Smith in *The Legend of the Master* (1948). We have a number of James's remarks about Hardy, notably in a letter to Stevenson, which was published while Hardy was still living, in which James calls *Tess of the d'Urbervilles* "vile." "The presence of sexuality is only equalled by the absence of it, and the abomination of the language by the author's reputation for style." Yet James also wrote to Stevenson that the novel in spite of its faults had a singular beauty and charm.

James admired Howells more than he did Hardy, though undoubtedly the latter is the greater novelist. On the other hand Howells was a constant and devoted reader of Hardy's novels and though at the time he paid his tribute to them in his *My Literary Passions* he had not yet read *Tess* since the book was still new, he said he did not even balk at Hardy's paganism and thought that he gave a rich and sweet sense of the unity of nature with human nature.

Of course James, like George Moore, was entitled to a derogatory opinion of Hardy; and Andrew Lang's two articles attacking *Tess* were the sensation of the day. (The latter of these has been reprinted by the present author from *Longman's Magazine, November* 1892 in *Notorious Literary Attacks,* 1926.)

Arthur C. Benson describes an encounter between Hardy and James in 1904 at the Athenaeum where Hardy discoursed about Cardinal Newman, and Hardy spoke about Flaubert.

We can get some light on the relations of Hardy and James in their contacts and opinions of each other from Mrs. Hardy's life of her husband and from James's letters. They met at affairs a number of times. Hardy saw James in January 1884 in London to which the Wessex novelist had come for a visit. They both were at a dinner given by the publisher G. M. Smith at the Continental Hotel where Matthew Arnold was also present. In the following summer they met at Alma-Tadema, the painter's, and Hardy recorded in his Diary, James's "nebulous gaze." In May, 1886 Hardy met James when the latter was a guest of the

Rabelais Club, and he recorded his impression. "James has a ponderously warm manner of saying nothing in infinite sentences." In July of the following year we have Hardy's criticism of James's novel *The Reverberator,* and it was to the effect that James was concerned with the minutiae of manners, which subject Hardy believed would be of little concern to the great novels of the future; when there was nothing larger to think of, Hardy said, one might be interested in James's subjects. Hardy concluded that one feels now one may be careless of details. James was led to write the novel by an incident he records in his Notebooks. He became indignant because some woman had written to the *New York World* about the personal lives of some people in Venice; this made him lose his temper in his diatribe about our bad American manners of invading privacy. James may have been right but a tirade against yellow journalism was hardly a worthy theme for a novel. And *The Reverberators* is not considered one of his best.

Hardy again met James at a masked ball in 1896, and again in 1909 at a memorial service to George Meredith. Half a dozen years later after reading a review of James, he paid him a tribute by writing: "It is remarkable a writer who has no grain of poetry or humor or sponteneity in his productions can yet be a good novelist." He said that he could read James, though he was no poet, but that he could not read Meredith who was a poet.

Perhaps Hardy was mistaken in saying that James was no poet. Certainly the author of the many passages of poetic prose in *Italian Hours* was a poet. There surely are passages in the three autobiographical works he wrote that have veins of poetry.

Edmund Wilson has designated some of James's later fiction poetic. He calls *The Bench of Desolation* a sort of poem of loneliness and poverty among some nondescript people of an English seaside resort and he says that *The Ivory Tower* is not only comic, human, and brilliantly observed, but that it is poetic in the highest sense, like all these later novels.

Professor Morris Roberts says that James's later prose has "the intensity, the deep intimations and the finality of poetry." "Henry James and the Art of Foreshortening," *The Review of English Studies,* July 1946, p. 208.

The relations of Hardy and James closed on a strange note, formal and yet revealing a somewhat changed attitude by Hardy. On the 10th of January, 1916, as President of The Incorporated

Society of Authors, Playwrights & Composers he wrote to James who was then ill, and had just been awarded the Order of Merit, congratulating him at the request of the Committee of Management. He also took advantage of the situation by at the same time welcoming him as a new British citizen which James had become about five months previous. Every one of the twenty-five hundred members of which James was one, Hardy said, felt that he was honored in Henry James. Hardy closed with a wish of all in the society for the re-establishment of his health. Seven weeks later James was dead. It will be noticed, however, that Hardy expressed no opinion here about the literary merits of James's fiction.

(I am indebted for a photostatic copy of this letter in the Houghton Library of Harvard University to the kindness of Professor William A. Jackson and Carolyn E. Jakeman.)

NOTE TO CHARLES KINGSLEY'S LIFE AND LETTERS

29. James displays in his review of *Charles Kingsley* a faculty at which he was proficient, in summarizing and passing judgment on literary biographies. He showed his hand more than once in this, both in youth and age. Kingsley seems not to have influenced him much, but James was an admirer of his historical novels. He had reviewed *Hereward, the Last of the English,* for *The Nation,* January 25, 1866 (collected by Rose) enthusiastically, finding the author a heaven-commissioned *raconteur.* He sets forth his own creed about the essential feature of a novel which was to tell a story. He had little regard for Kingsley's sermons or his philosophy of history, and did not appear too much in sympathy either with the muscular Christianity wrongly attributed to him as Mrs. Pope-Hennessy says or mild attempts at reform. But it is interesting to know that James was an admirer of two novels by Kingsley, a writer who was so different from him, *Westward Ho,* and *Two Years Ago.* The review of the biography is no amateurish work; it is one of the best and last reviews he did for *The Nation,* after he himself had achieved the dignity of being the author of a volume of tales and of a novel. To illustrate the maturity of James, one, not knowing what were the dates when the reviews of the novel of 1866 and of the biography appeared, would be hard

put in deciding whether that by the 23 year old youth or the arrived novelist of 34 had appeared first.

Incidentally in both reviews James deplores Kingsley's intellectual pretensions.

The summary in the review of the biography illustrates James's own gift in biographical writing. Though he produced only one biography of length, that of William Wetmore Story (I am not at present thinking of autobiography), quite a few of his so-called critical essays are biographical sketches as in the case of those he collected of Turgenev and Daudet.

NOTE TO LOTHAIR BY LORD BEACONSFIELD

30. The anonymous review of *Lothair* by Lord Beaconsfield is of interest for the light it sheds on James's own personality. He was subjective in this review in a large degree. He poured contempt upon an experienced statesman and novelist, treating a work that had been written in a white heat as if it were a light, insincere product done for self-amusement and entertainment of the reader.

The once best selling novel issued early in 1870 was prompted by the conversion of the youthful Earl of Bute, John Patrick Crichton Stuart, to Catholicism in 1868. The struggle of the Catholics to have the Protestant Irish Church dis-established was opposed by Beaconsfield, while he was Prime Minister. Gladstone defeated him and dis-established the Church. Yet Beaconsfield had many English people with him. He had not opposed free political rights for the Catholics but he was haunted by the specter of a Catholic menace and he had no sympathy with their religion. When the novel appeared it was seen that he was almost a Freethinker and an exponent of either Protestantism or secularism, in spite of the fact that he was opposed to the theory of evolution, and was on the side of the angels instead of the apes. However, he was in dead earnest in drawing the heroine Theodora Campian, wife of an American, who was anti-Catholic and was interested in the cause of Italian independence. She influenced the hero, Lothair, who was about to become a Catholic under one of his guardians. When she was on her death-bed she besought him never to do so. She was killed in the battle of Mentana and Lothian himself wounded. The Catholics were again resolved to convert him and he almost succumbed until he recalled her dying words never to become a Catholic.

Beaconsfield also drew an artist, a Mr. Phoebus, with theories of Aryanism and hatred for Semiticism, a foreshadowing of a Nazi. However, Phoebus forgot his theories when he got a commission from the Czar to paint scenes in Palestine—a piece of delicious irony on the author's part.

Beaconsfield, the Tory, wrote a radical novel defending a woman in her anti-Catholic views and her fight for the freedom of Italy. He was however in a Protestant country free to air his views on Catholicism.

The book was attacked by many critics for various reasons, that of poor taste, improper assault on a religion, and for his fight against the abolishment of the Irish Church.

James almost after half a year from the date of publication takes up the book and starts off with saying it shows a cleverness, a small one actually, on the part of the author. James apparently is not averse to the purpose of the novel but thinks it a failure as such. He finds the author light and superficial, more so when he seeks to be profound. As a matter of fact Beaconsfield presents both sides, the Catholic side almost more forcefully than the anti-Catholic. He is familiar with all the Catholic arguments. He has read much literature in defense of the Church, even giving a seemingly plausible argument in favor of the Inquisition. James regards the novel as a romance and will endure it as long only as it puts in a claim for the romantic.

James is unfair. He passes by descriptions of the magnificent army scenes, social events, and portrayals of characters, faithfully drawn from members of the nobility whom Lord Beaconsfield had met and prominent characters of the day, such as Wilberforce (the Bishop), Msgr. Capel (Catesby) and Cardinal Manning (Grandison). In short, we begin to feel that there is something almost impudent about James. He will not take this veteran novelist and statesman seriously. He derides him and says that his anti-Catholicism is cold and mechanical. He finds Lothair a weakling because he did not struggle, though he was young and sick, and did become a hero on the battlefield, and his love for Theodora was inevitable. Beaconsfield lived to see the political ideals for which Theodora stood realized in the independence of Italy. His feelings as a Protestant however soon were outraged in the promulgation of the dogma of the infallibility of the Pope by the Vatican Council.

Brandes himself, a Freethinker, in his life of Beaconsfield says that the author loses sight in this novel of the more profound or exalted way of looking at life, uniting all embracing nature; Beaconsfield just gives us opposing doctrines.

James regarded this novel one of entertainment which left him good humored and at times laughing at it. He said it would make no Cardinal's ears tingle. He added that the author lacked conviction, passion, and fire. One suspects that James approved of the attack, complaining only because of its weakness. He uses the reprehensible word "papist" describing one of the girls who is in the plot to convert Lothair.

The novel is a battle for the church to capture a soul, and as James puts it, the ruling idea is to reveal the secret encroachments of the "Romish" Church, another reprehensible word. But he does not think the task is done with eloquence or force.

A year later James contributed a novel to the *Atlantic Monthly, Watch and Ward,* which he revised and published in book form in 1878, wherein he set forth through one of the characters his reaction to the novels of the day. This character, a clergyman, named Hubert Lawrence, although engaged to a girl, still sought to wean away from his cousin, Roger Lawrence, Nora Lambert for himself. It does not matter that the words about novels are put in the mouth of a person James disapproves, they are clearly James's own conception. Hubert finds Nora reading a novel wherein a clergyman in love with a Catholic comes near being converted but instead converts her and marries her. Hubert says that the clergyman should have first married his "Romish" sweetheart and converted her afterwards, for a clergyman is after all, before all, a man.

Curiously enough over 20 years later in his play *Guy Domville,* James drew a man who put religion before love altogether.

"Nothing irritates me so as to the flatness of people's imagination," says Hubert. "Common life—I don't say it's a vision of bliss, but it's better than that. Their stories are like the underside of a carpet,—nothing but the stringy grain of the tissue,—a muddle of figures without shape and flowers without color. When I read a novel my imagination starts off at a gallop and leaves the narrator hidden in a cloud of dust; I have to come jogging twenty miles back to the dénouement." (Chapter VII).

Of the two American novels referred to in the text, *Hedged In,* was by Elizabeth Stuart Phelps, then recently published; and *Margaret Howth* was by Rebecca Harding Davis. It had run serially in the *Atlantic Monthly* Oct. 1861—March 1862, under the title *A Story of To-Day.*

NOTE TO STOPFORD BROOKE'S THEOLOGY
IN THE ENGLISH POETS

31. The chief interest in the review of Stopford A. Brooke's *Theology in the English Poets* is that it shows the great esteem that James had for Wordsworth of whom Brooke writes and quotes from at length. James after declaring that the poet as well as his critic is diffuse, and deploring Wordsworth's later conservatism, says that the poet at his best soars at an altitude where the imagination nowhere else reaches. He quotes some lines from the poem to Toussaint L'Ouverture, and also a passage from Brooke calling the poet the greatest next to Milton in English literature and drawing attention to his faith in the eternal love and righteousness of God.

William James was early an admirer of the poet and Henry paid him a tribute in his essay on Emerson where he says that both Goethe and Wordsworth found their form, more so than Emerson, in expatiating on character as a real and supreme thing.

It will also be recalled that in *Mme. Mauves* the unfaithful husband of Euphemia complains to Longmore, that his wife is an admirer of Wordsworth and suggests to him that he talk to her about Alfred de Musset.

A real service that Brooke performed for James was nearly twenty years later when, as James records in his Notebooks, Brooke suggested to him two ideas, which James half a dozen years later made the nucleus of his novel *The Sacred Font.*

Brooke became more liberal than ever after he had published his book, and published some critical works on Anglo-Saxon literature, Tennyson, Browning, and Shakespeare. His comprehensive little book on English literature is the subject of an article by Matthew Arnold, whose suggestions for revision he largely took. He is one of the finest representatives of Victorian literary criticism.

NOTE TO GEORGE BARNETT SMITH'S POETS AND NOVELISTS

32. George Barnett Smith (1841-1899) was not so well known, when James castigated him, as he later became. He wrote an article on Elizabeth Browning for the ninth edition of the *Encyclopedia Britannica* and he was a friend of her husband. He was connected at different times as an editorial writer with newspapers, and contributed to the London *Times* and the leading periodicals, from which some of the essays in his book were collected. Beginning with a life of Shelley in 1877, he wrote other biographies, among them of Gladstone and Hugo. His chief work was a *History of the English Parliament*. He also contributed to the *Dictionary of National Biography* and published several volumes of poetry, under the pseudonym Guy Roslyn. He became an invalid in 1889 and received a Civil Pension.

James is captious because he differs with Smith in some literary opinions in which James is wrong, as when he called *Wuthering Heights* a "crude" story, or refuses to believe that Thackeray's subjectivity had enhanced the value of his stories. This is rather strange in view of the fact that James's own subjectivity has been declared to give an air of reality to quite a number of his novels and tales. Lionel Trilling has sponsored the view that the personal element had entered into the novel (where it might not have been expected)—*The Princess Casamassima* and even to some extent in *The Bostonians*.

It might be thought that the present editor has dwelt too much on the autobiographical phases in James's fiction. As a matter of fact James himself furnished the key to unlock his heart, in his autobiographies, in stating that a personal angle had influenced several of his early tales. His revelations about his friendship with Minnie Temple and the publication of his letters have added force to this admission. No one can ever write of *The Portrait of a Lady* or *The Wings of the Dove* without referring to her. We also know that in several of his tales relating to artists and writers and to American sojourners in Europe, he was consciously or unconsciously writing about himself. What has given added value to the studies of some of James's tales by Edel is that he has not hesitated to link them up with a personal experience or a frustration. James concentrated throughout his life on personality and personal relations, as Matthiessen says.

The present writer in an article "The Early Lucid Henry James" in the April 1916 issue of the *Book News Monthly* (Philadelphia), shortly after James's death, commented on his employment of fictitious writers and artists as pathways of self-revelation. In the Preface to *Master Eustace* (1920), he especially singled out the tale "Benvolio" as to some extent autobiographical, and he was happy to learn that Edel had also done so in one of the James books he edited.

NOTE TO REV. FRANCIS HODGSON, A FRIEND OF LORD BYRON

33. It surely is worth reprinting Byron's article on the *Memoirs of the Rev. Francis Hodgson, B.D., with Numerous Letters from Lord Byron and Others,* by his son the Rev. T. P. Hodgson, for James's adverse view of Harriet Beecher Stowe's revelations ten years previous in the *Atlantic Monthly* about the sexual relations of Byron with his half-sister Augusta Leigh. When James expressed his opinion he was 36 years old and not prone to give a hasty judgment. The issuance of this volume with letters of Byron to the pious friend of his youth convinced James. Thomas Moore printed ten letters from Byron to Hodgson, the first one in 1809 and the last in 1814. Some of these were sent to Hodgson when Byron was on his travels and one of them contains an amusing doggerel poem on his embarking on the Lisbon packet. He took Hodgson into his confidence and wrote about his forthcoming publication *Childe Harold.* Walter E. Henley in his *The Works of Lord Byron* (1897) (alas, uncompleted) reprinted 27 letters to Hodgson.

To-day the so-called controversy about Byron's relations with his sister has been regarded as settled, and even some Byron scholars who before had not accepted the theory that there were criminal relations, have yielded to what they consider unshakable evidence. Only recently a voice or two has arisen in dissent. A correspondence between Hodgson and Byron's half-sister lasted for many years after Byron's death. "Mrs. Leigh's letters," says

James, "afford the most striking intrinsic evidence of the purely phantasmal character of the famous accusation, and place the author's character in a highly honorable and touching light." Hodgson's son did not believe in the charge either.

James admits that there was some mystery involved, and Mrs. Leigh herself says to Hodgson who had tried to bring about a reconciliation between Byron and his wife, that her brother had certain recollections fatal to his peace which would have made him think himself unworthy of any woman. Would she have written thus if she herself was the cause of this guilty feeling on his part? Byron himself asked Hodgson what the grievance was that Lady Byron had against him for refusing the reconciliation. She told Hodgson that "he does know too well what he affects to inquire." James believed that Mrs. Leigh is completely exonerated by this volume, that whatever did disturb Byron's mind it was a tendency to dramatise himself, and he suggested that even if the reason were known for Byron's so-called unforgivable sin, it would bring the expectant reader looking for a hideous crime, disappointment.

We gather that James himself was an admirer of Byron and his poetry. He even seems to quote half with approbation Byron's light dismissal cynically of his belief in immortality of the soul, when he said he hoped he would have a better pair of legs than he has had if he ever gets into paradise, and he gave the argument to Hodgson, that if people are to live, why should they die? It is singular that out of the many passages to be quoted James selects this one, since late in life he wrote an article of his own belief in immortality of the soul, based however on intuition, desire, and his artistic nature.

After Lord Lovelace published *Astarte* in 1905 seeking to show that the relation between Byron and his sister was criminal, he convinced two of Byron's leading biographers, Ethel C. Mayne and André Maurois.

Curiously enough James's father, like Dr. Oliver Wendell Holmes, was convinced by Mrs. Stowe's article that Byron was guilty of incest.

NOTE TO MATTHEW ARNOLD

34. In his essay on Arnold, James reveals himself as a passionate champion of culture, a crusader for an intellectual

outlook, in quest of the literary relation to life and in demand of a broadness of spirit. He admires Arnold because he approaches Sainte-Beuve in quality of ideas and critical method, and finds little in him to criticise seriously. He loves everything that Arnold ever wrote, having started as an admirer of his poems. He even courageously defends Arnold's entry into the theological arena (which many had deprecated) on the ground that his literary ideas are properly linked with his liberal religious attitude. He will speak his mind favorably of Arnold, he says, even if he may be writing a book criticising America, which he had recently visited.

James's enthusiam for Arnold was permanent. He first read the critical essays when James T. Field who was about to publish an American edition of *Essays in Criticism*, allowed him to read the compositor's besmirched copy. As late as 1915, the year before his death, he told of the thrill with which he read the essays while lying on a sofa after an accident. This was in an article "Mr. and Mrs. Field" which appeared in the *Atlantic Monthly*, July 1915 and which Edel has reprinted in *The American Essays*. He did not want the part that relates to Arnold under any circumstances omitted from his article.

The difference in attitude towards Arnold as shown in his first article on Arnold in the *North American Review*, July 1865, (reprinted by Phillips) and the essay herein reprinted is not great. Yet whereas in the first article James saw in Arnold an objective critic using an intellectual yard-stick, in the later essay he made allowance for and defended his personal mannerisms and subjective treatment.

Incidentally the American edition of *Essays in Criticism* which James reviewed contained Arnold's earlier essays, "A French Eton" and his two articles on the translating of Homer. Arnold was especially impressed with the essays on Poetry and Literary Academies. He thought the weakest, the one on Maurice Guérin as he has told us in his own article on Maurice Guérin, herein reprinted.

There is here a maturity of style, a confidence, nay cock-sureness that in fact impress one. How pleased James would have been had he known that the subject of his article was writing to his sister Miss Arnold (in November 1865) that he liked an article about him in the *North American Review* as well as any thing he had seen. And incidentally, because Arnold took the author of the article as representative of the best products of our country, he entered into a eulogy of America. How surprised he would have been to learn that the author was a youth of 22! Arnold's compliment meant that he thought that this review was superior to the many reviews written by veteran authors about his book. Probably when Arnold's letter appeared in his published correspondence in 1895, *Letters of Matthew Arnold*, Vol. I p. 359, James read the tribute.

Rarely did James differ with Arnold, one of the few cases being when he resented Arnold's view in *Discourses in America* that Emerson had not complete right to the title of a man of letters.

As Matthiessen says, James set out to prove in his novels the value of the farthest reaches of curiosity. This was probably motivated by a remark of Arnold that "curiosity" in French had a good sense, but in English only a bad one. James bestirred himself to show that curiosity may be turned to good usage in the creation of English literature.

POSTSCRIPT

There has been little appraisal of James's early critical work. There were the introductions by Phillips and Rose to their volumes of a limited number of James articles collected by them. Rose's volume was the occasion for several reviews by notable critics, Brander Matthews in the New York *Times Book Review*, June 12, 1921, "Henry James, Book Reviewer"; William Lyon Phelps, "Henry James, The Reviewer" in *Literary Review*, June 4, 1921 and Van Wyck Brooks in *The Freeman*, August 24, 1921, "A Reviewer's Note Book, (reprinted in *"Sketches in Criticism,"* 1932). Brooks commented rightly on James's maturity as a youth but believed that he merely rewrote Arnold's *Essays in Criticism* and Sainte-Beuve's *Causeries du Lundi* in a slightly personal idiom.

Morris Roberts, however, was the pioneer in treating some of James's uncollected reviews in his book *Henry James's Criticism*, 1929. Miss Cornelia Pulsifer Kelley objects that Roberts in the first chapter of a thin volume considers James's criticism independent of its relation to his early tales which he certainly was entitled to do; but Professor Robert E. Spiller in his article on James in *Eight American Authors* 1956, p. 390 holds that Roberts deals fairly with the limitations and paradoxes of James's personality and art. As a matter of fact, this is noticeable in Morris's comment on James's article in *The Atlantic Monthly*, August, 1871, Droz's *Autour une Source*. Morris concluded that James held that the artist must be free and that his choice of subject was his own affair. The subject was the supreme test of the artist's value, because it was the test of the reach of his perception and so of his moral quality. Intelligent realism in art carries its own morality. He said that James, however, thought it was more important in those days to be an artist than to have a wide experience in life. Attention to form was paramount; the artist must surmount technical difficulties. As a matter of fact such remained his views although he came to attach great importance to experience.

Miss Kelley's book *The Early Development of Henry James* is really the fullest study of the early reviews and criticism by Henry James just as it is the fullest study of his first period of fiction. She has connected the early criticism by James with his fiction and even dealt at length with the uncollected tales. She gave suggestive criticism on the early novels. Her book is fuller in exposition and criticism than the books by Edel and Le Clair dealing with the same period but they were writing biographies with the advantage of having before them the Note Books, letters and manuscript material. Her studies, however, of the fiction are often weak because with several exceptions, as in the case of *Roderick Hudson,* she neglected the personal angle and resorted to seeking to discover "influences."* She is academic with regard to the tale "Poor Richard." She sees only the influence of George Sand in even the love emotions described, and she holds that the characters are French people transferred to America. Compare Edel's treatment of the same story which he traces back to an episode that took place, and shows how James's own frustration entered into the tale and that he drew on several real persons, on Minnie Temple for the female character and for the male characters on young Oliver Wendell Holmes, John Chapman Gray and himself. The story was the result of modified personal experience. Le Clair takes a middle attitude but inclines towards the Kelley interpretation.

The most enthusiastic but all too brief article on the reviews is that by Laurence Barrett in *American Literature* January, 1949, pp. 385-400, "Young Henry James," but he had to be confined to a limited number of early reviews. He is right in maintaining the importance of these because they expressed the theories which produced James's later narrative technique.

I am not so unbalanced a partisan for my cause that James's early criticism is always of high quality as not to deny that some articles herein reprinted are included for the light they thrown on his personality, for the sake of continuity in the matter of James's career as a critic, and to round out the process. Certainly some of his judgments are faulty, as in the

---

* Thus Gautier's travel books influenced *Transatlantic Sketches;* for "The Last of the Valerii," hints were taken from Mérimée; *The American* is a hybrid of Turgenev and George Sand; Roderick Hudson's character was patterned upon Dimitri Rudin; Lavretsky was the prototype for Christopher Newman; *Washington Square* was modeled upon *Eugénie Grandet;* Gwendolen Harleth in *Middlemarch* was the prototype of Isabel Archer in the *Portrait of a Lady.*

At least nine tales are listed where the influence of George Sand is said to have entered.

cases of *Wuthering Heights* and *The Red and the Black* or his rejection of Hugo. And it is likely that he had altered some of the views he entertained in essays which he did not reprint himself for this very reason. But a critic does not lose stature because he advances a preference or a condemnation for a writer in which posterity has differed with him, as in the cases respectively of Hazlitt with regard to Ossian, or Arnold with Shelley. Sainte-Beuve himself disparaged Balzac. James Russell Lowell disavowed Whitman, yet it will be noticed that even in the articles where we think that James erred he pointed out faults in books, where we can agree with him, as in Hardy's *Far From the Madding Crowd* and even in the Hugo article on *Ninety Three*.

There is no doubt that some readers will think a few essays in this volume did not deserve reprinting, and they will probably be right. But we should remember that the worst review that James wrote, that on Whitman has been reprinted by at least five of the best James scholars in their anthologies and James collections, by Phillips, Richardson, Matthiessen, Zabel, and Edel; and this in spite of the fact that James repudiated the review of which he was ashamed. But it has willy-nilly become part of his critical equipage. It is like the case of Robert Southey who fought in vain in the courts to suppress a piratical publication of his play *Wat Tyler* containing republican sentiments which he later discarded. And he finally took the foundling into the collected edition of his poetical works with all its sins upon its head—with ample apologies that he need not be ashamed of a frailty of his youth in which he then was really right.

Yet James had a serious defect as a literary critic, the same as manifested itself in some of his fiction, an aversion to advanced and liberal ideas. In the earlier essays he was broader in outlook, however, than in many of the later ones. I have referred to the fact that he never wrote about or mentioned in print Georg Brandes,—probably because the latter went too far in the other direction, appraising his subject with a liberal tape-measure. Yet, except for this difference as to what constitutes liberalism, there was something in common between them—both disciples of Sainte-Beuve and Taine. As a matter of fact when James gave himself a wide berth, he was oblivious of his Puritan heritage, as in his essay on George Sand in the French *Poets and*

Novelists where his attitude towards her was not much different from that of Brandes in his *The Romantic School in France*. Of course James knew of Brandes. In the January 1875 *Atlantic Monthly* where his *Roderick Hudson* began appearing serially there was an anonymous sympathetic article on the German translation from the Danish by Adolf Strodtmann of *Emigrant Literature,* the first volume of the *Main Currents of Nineteenth Century Literature,* the earliest article possibly on Brandes in America. Its author was Thomas Sergeant Perry, James's friend. Perry noted that Brandes had been designated in his own country, "freethinker," "corrupter of morals," and "upsetter of society." Possibly these very designations made James turn away from Brandes.

James did not sympathetically portray characters who were rebellious against economic conditions, and where they did battle against social conditions, his dealing with the situation was that of a lukewarm reformer. As a matter of fact he disliked reformers, and especially women reformers.

While there is a general consensus that James's later novels represent his best work, we cannot dismiss the cogent objections to it by Van Wyck Brooks in his *New England: Indian Summer,* and in his book on James. I register a few rash opinions against it. "After his early period his novels become interesting only as museum pieces," Percy H. Boynton: *Literature and American Life,* p. 733. Walt Whitman said that James was only "feathers" to him, doubted whether the novels had future significance, and compared them to a butterfly skimming daintily in fragile literary vessels, *With Walt Whitman in Camden* (March 28-July 14, 1888) [Vol. I] Horace Traubel. A representative view of Harold Laski among very hostile ones scattered throughout his letters to Justice Holmes, edited by Mark A. De Wolfe Howe, is the following: "A second-class mind dealing with fundamentally third-rate material." The magnificent letters of Henry James made him vomit!

APPENDIX

While the treatment of James's tales is not within the province of this work, I cannot forbear from giving a psychoanalytic interpretation of a tale of his because it reveals his personality and seems to disclose a hidden chapter in his life. The tale lends itself readily to treatment because it contains a dream that is clearly authentic; it reveals something of the author's own struggle with temptation, and while showing his restraint, disclòses him as yielding to it in his unconscious. I refer to the excellent story "Mme. de Mauves," written abroad in the summer of 1873 and published the next year. It was one of the few of his early tales that he included in the New York Edition of his novels and tales. My references, however, are to the unrevised tale as collected in *The Passionate Pilgrim and Other Tales.*

James states in the preface to the later edition that he cannot in the least trace the origin of the tale and has no knowledge of what put it into his head. He does say however that Euphemia—which was the first name of his heroine—visited him in a dreary inn at Bad Homburg in the Taunus Hills and gave him her confidences but left twenty questions unanswered. These confidences no doubt constituted the plot of the tale wherein Longmore—the "hero"—sought to console James's informant when her husband was unfaithful to her,—a plot which tells also how a love arose between Longmore and her, Madame Mauves, till she dismissed him because her husband's sister told Longmore to make advances to her.

When he came to writing the tale, James, the listener, became a split personality and then identified himself with the protagonist Longmore struggling with temptation. No wonder James forgot. Longmore after being urged by Mme. Mauves's sister-in-law into having an affair ostensibly to justify her brother for his illicit relationship, began finding some dangerous ideas intruding into his mind. In theological terms, that old serpent the Devil was tempting him; in Freudian language his unconscious hitherto dormant was beginning to stir itself. At first, of course, Longmore is shocked by the proposal. And the husband it is clear wants his wife to be unfaithful to him because he has been unfaithful to her. So Longmore is soon indulging in reflections about the wisdom of living fully and wholly and defying conventional morality, such reflections as were developed in James's later novel *The Ambassador*. Longmore now balks in rebellion against the principle of asceticism in his composition, "To renounce—to renounce again—to renounce forever—was this all that youth and longing and resolve—were meant for?" he questions. James was giving us something of his own mind. He was drawing his portrait when he added, "Was a man to sit and deliberately condemn his future to be the blank memory of a regret, rather than the long reverberation of a joy? Sacrifice? The word was a trap for minds muddled by fear, and ignoble refuge of weakness." So, did James come to feel that he had remained virtuous out of fear and weakness?

Longmore was really in love with Euphemia and she with him. Of course Longmore, we know in advance, is never going to succumb because first we know Henry James, and also because we must take into consideration the fact that sin triumphant was not permitted in American literature in James's day. Longmore is really in his initial mood prepared to go after what he wanted and let convention be damned. The notion becomes strong when he accidentally runs across her husband entertaining his unlawful flame in a cafe and when he has even been seen by him. So he is going to seek Mme. Mauves out. Well, the upshot is that he finds that she knows of the proposal that had been made to him—and she bids him farewell. The interference of the sister-in-law had spoiled the affair as far as she was concerned. Longmore's design to consummate his love was nipped in the bud. His problem had been solved for him by the dismissal—the dismissal coming about because her husband wanted this affair consummated.

We know, however, the state of Longmore's mind before the dismissal when he was facing temptation from a dream that is recorded. How did James know of the dream, or at least how could he present it so authentically? It was his own dream. The dream was strange and vivid. Longmore saw a woman on the opposite side of a deep stream who looked at him pityingly and he made up his mind to plunge into it and reach her. But he did not have to plunge; by good fortune an oarsman appeared in a boat and transported him across. But the dreamer already had fears that when he reached the other side, Mme. Mauves—for now he gives her name and identifies her—would disappear.

And this is exactly what happened; she was now on the side of
the stream he had left. She walked up the stream, the boatman
continued on his course, looked back, and saw that the couple
had not met. Longmore recognized in the boatman Mme. Mauves's husband whom he had recently seen in the cafe with a
woman and who had also noticed him.

It will be seen how the dream arose out of what was happen-
ing in the daytime. It does not take a profound knowledge of
Freud's theory of dreams to tie up this dream with the tale, and
both with some possible event in the author's life that he wanted
unconsciously to forget. He was telling the truth when he said
in his Preface that he did not know how the idea came to him.
He had forgotten an unpleasant episode in his life. James must
have been interested in a real Mme. Mauves. The dream hints
that at one time James (like Longmore) may have been in love
with an unattainable woman and in his unconscious, faced temptation. The stream dividing Longmore and Euphemia was
James's conscience; he refused to listen to it and was ready to
plunge into it. As often in dreams when he thought he was about
to attain the prey, it escaped. When the boatman, her husband,
brought him across the stream, Longmore was symbolically re-
hearsing the accomplishment of the suggestion made by Euphemia's sister-in-law with the consent of the husband. The dream
was a fulfilment wish to have that woman; the inability to attain
her was the anxiety part of the dream.

It does not matter that whatever actually happened to James
himself was not in full accordance with the events in the tale.
His mind and emotions went through the experience recorded
there. How often had he said that fiction should be based on
experience and transformed by the author! What is of particular
interest is that James, like Stevenson after him, correctly employed and applied the Freudian technique of dreams long before he had ever heard of Freud.

Selected Grove Press Paperbacks

E417	BIRCH, CYRIL and KEENE, DONALD, eds. / Anthology of Chinese Literature, Vol. I: From Early Times to the 14th Century / $5.95
E584	BIRCH, CYRIL, ed. / Anthology of Chinese Literature, Vol. II: From the 14th Century to the Present / $4.95
E368	BORGES, JORGE LUIS / Ficciones / $2.95
E472	BORGES, JORGE LUIS / A Personal Anthology / $3.95
E478	BRAUTIGAN, RICHARD / A Confederate General from Big Sur / $1.95
B60	BRECHT, BERTOLT / Baal, A Man's A Man, The Elephant Calf / $1.95
B312	BRECHT, BERTOLT / The Caucasian Chalk Circle / $1.95
B414	BRECHT, BERTOLT / The Mother / $2.95
B108	BRECHT, BERTOLT / Mother Courage and Her Children / $1.95
E580	BRETON, ANDRE / Nadja / $3.95
B193	BULGAKOV, MIKHAIL / The Heart of a Dog / $2.95
B147	BULGAKOV, MIKHAIL / The Master and Margarita / $3.95
B115	BURROUGHS, WILLIAM / Naked Lunch / $2.95
B147	BURROUGHS, WILLIAM / The Ticket That Exploded / $1.75
E717	CLURMAN, HAROLD, ed. / Seven Plays of the Modern Theater (Waiting for Godot by Samuel Beckett, The Quare Fellow by Brendan Behan, A Taste of Honey by Shelagh Delaney, The Connection by Jack Gelber, The Balcony by Jean Genet, Rhinoceros by Eugene Ionesco, The Birthday Party by Harold Pinter) / $6.95
B405	CRAFTS, KATHY and HAUTHER, BRENDA / The Student's Guide to Good Grades / $2.45
E713	CROCKETT, JIM, ed. / The Guitar Player Book / $9.95
E190	CUMMINGS, E.E. / 100 Selected Poems / $1.95
E159	DELANEY, SHELAGH / A Taste of Honey / $2.95
B412	DOYLE, RODGER and REDDING, JAMES / The Complete Food Handbook. Revised and Updated ed. / $2.95
B75	DURAS, MARGUERITE / Four Novels (The Afternoon of Mr. Andesmas, 10:30 On a Summer Night, Moderato Cantabile, The Square) / $3.95
E284	DURAS, MARGUERITE / Hiroshima Mon Amour. Text for the Film by Alain Resnais. Illus. / $3.95
E380	DURRENMATT, FRIEDRICH / The Physicists / $2.95
E344	DURRENMATT, FRIEDRICH / The Visit / $2.95
GP4038	EXNER, JUDITH / My Story / $2.25
B179	FANON, FRANTZ / Black Skin, White Masks / $2.95

GROVE PRESS, INC., 196 West Houston St., New York, N.Y. 10014